CROSSED

VOLUME 17

CHRISTOS GAGE story
FERNANDO HEINZ chapters 1-4 art
EMILIANO URDINOLA chapters 5-8 art

JAYMES REED letters
DIGIKORE STUDIOS color

chapter breaks & gallery
**CHRISTIAN ZANIER, FACUNDO PERCIO,
GERMAN NOBILE, DANIEL GETE**

CHRISTIAN ZANIER softcover art
RAULO CACERES hardcover art

COLLECTING CROSSED: BADLANDS #93-100

WILLIAM CHRISTENSEN editor-in-chief
MARK SEIFERT creative director
JIM KUHORIC managing editor
ARIANA OSBORNE production assistant

CROSSED CREATED BY GARTH ENNIS

www.crossedcomic.com   www.avatarpress.com   www.twitter.com/avatarpress

CROSSED Volume 17. October 2016. Published by Avatar Press, Inc., 515 N. Century Blvd. Rantoul, IL 61866. ©2016 Avatar Press, Inc. Crossed and all related properties TM & ©2016 Garth Ennis. All characters as depicted in this story are over the age of 18. The stories, characters, and institutions mentioned in this magazine are entirely fictional. Printed in Canada.

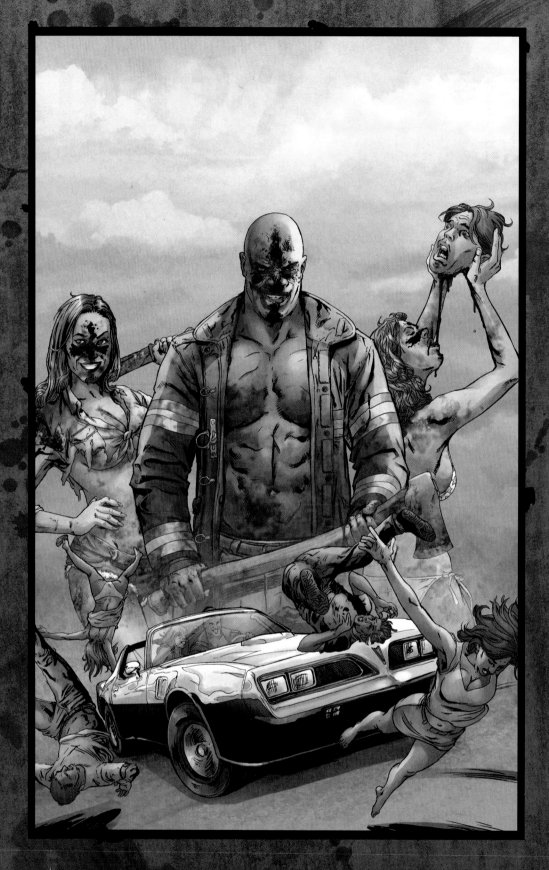

PART 1

THERE'S AN ACRONYM YOU'D SEE A LOT ON PREPPER MESSAGE BOARDS: "SHTF."

THAT'S "PREPPER" AS IN "PREPARER." *SURVIVALIST.* SOMEONE MAKING PLANS FOR THE APOCALYPSE.

BUT THERE'S A LOT OF DIFFERENT KINDS OF APOCALYPSES. NATURAL DISASTER. NUCLEAR EXCHANGE. SUPER-PLAGUE. AND THE CATCH-ALL: SHTF.

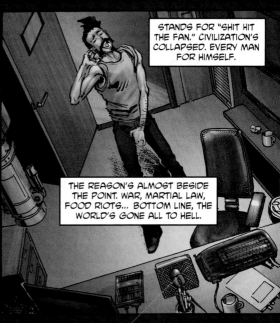

STANDS FOR "SHIT HIT THE FAN." CIVILIZATION'S COLLAPSED. EVERY MAN FOR HIMSELF.

THE REASON'S ALMOST BESIDE THE POINT. WAR, MARTIAL LAW, FOOD RIOTS... BOTTOM LINE, THE WORLD'S GONE ALL TO HELL.

SOME PREPPERS LIKED TO ARGUE ABOUT WHAT WAS MOST LIKELY TO SET IT OFF. ME, I NEVER MUCH THOUGHT THE "WHY" OF IT MATTERED.

BECAUSE, AT THE END OF THE DAY, ALL THAT REALLY COUNTS...

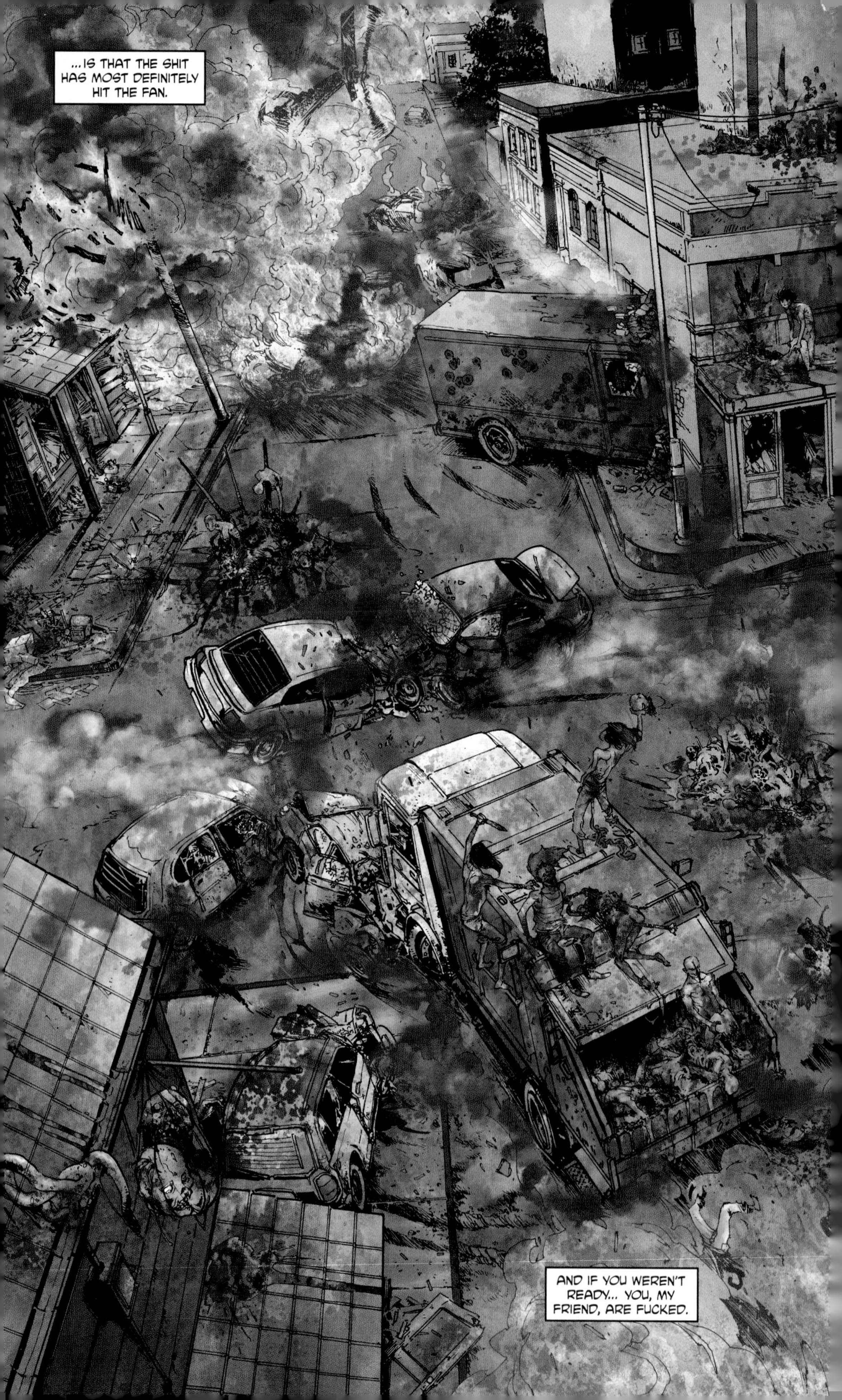
...IS THAT THE SHIT HAS MOST DEFINITELY HIT THE FAN.
AND IF YOU WEREN'T READY... YOU, MY FRIEND, ARE FUCKED.

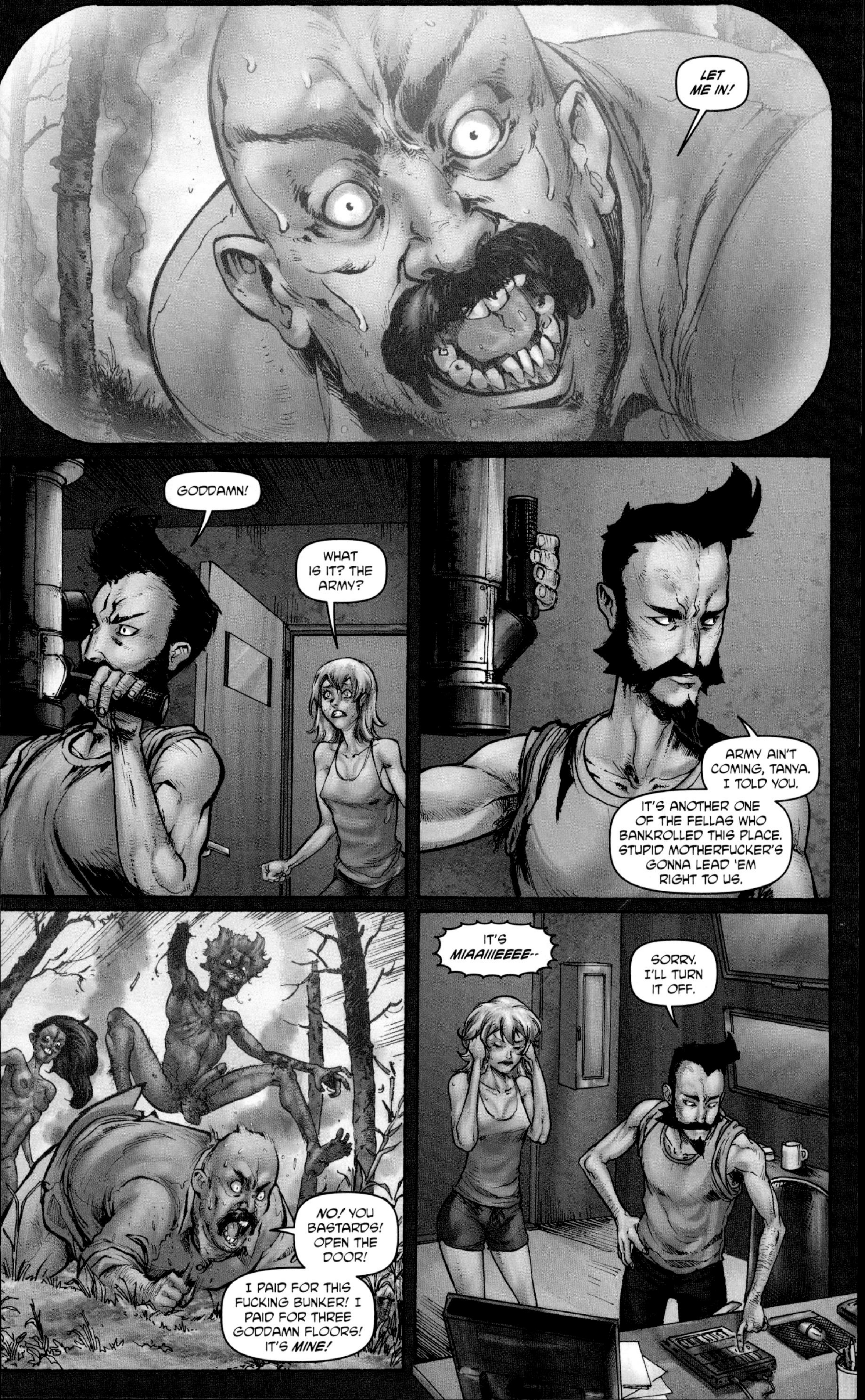
LET ME IN!
GODDAMN!
WHAT IS IT? THE ARMY?
ARMY AIN'T COMING, TANYA. I TOLD YOU.
IT'S ANOTHER ONE OF THE FELLAS WHO BANKROLLED THIS PLACE. STUPID MOTHERFUCKER'S GONNA LEAD 'EM RIGHT TO US.
NO! YOU BASTARDS! OPEN THE DOOR!
I PAID FOR THIS FUCKING BUNKER! I PAID FOR THREE GODDAMN FLOORS! IT'S MINE!
IT'S MIAAIIIEEEE--
SORRY. I'LL TURN IT OFF.

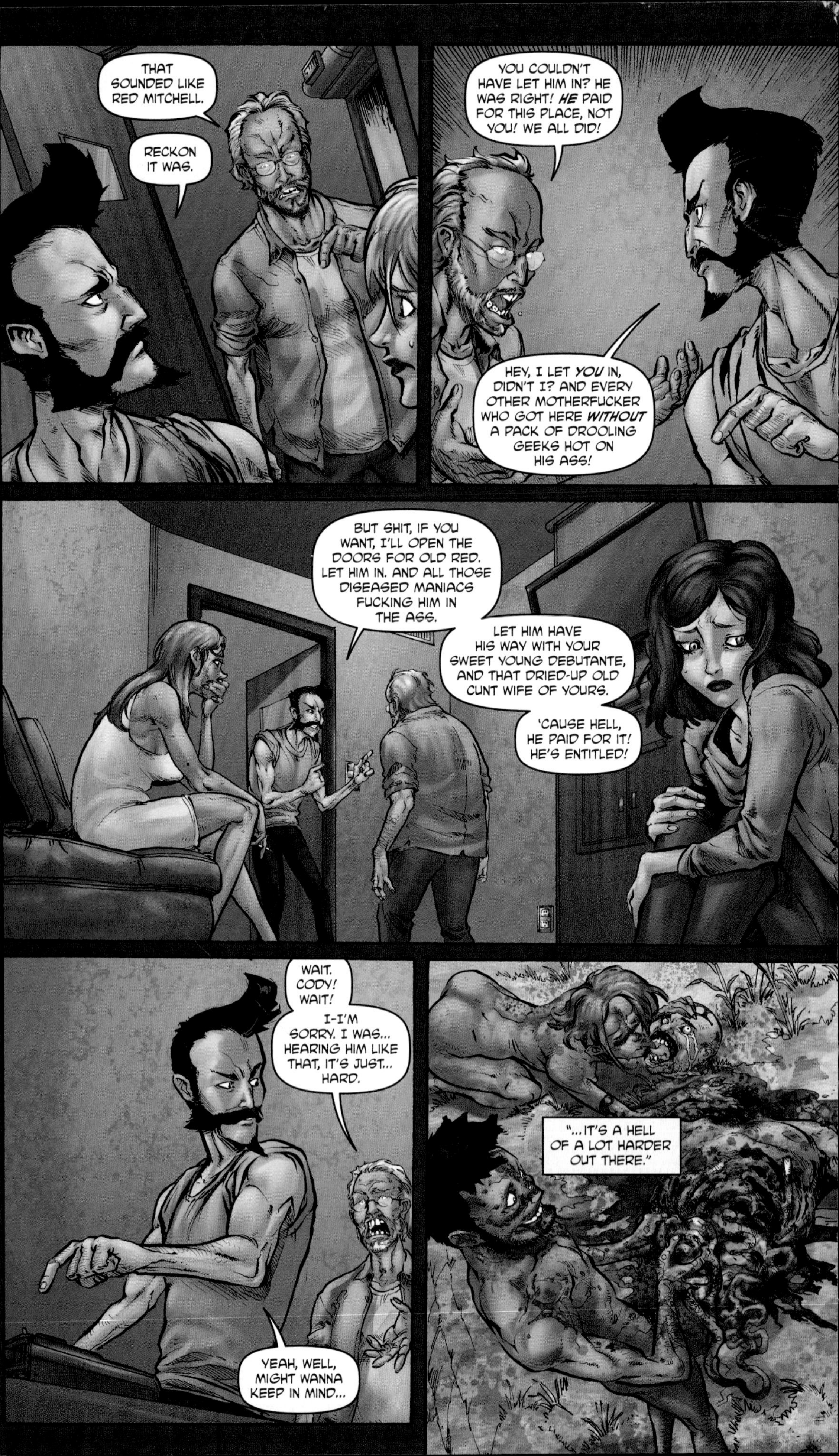

THAT SOUNDED LIKE RED MITCHELL.
RECKON IT WAS.
YOU COULDN'T HAVE LET HIM IN? HE WAS RIGHT! HE PAID FOR THIS PLACE, NOT YOU! WE ALL DID!
HEY, I LET YOU IN, DIDN'T I? AND EVERY OTHER MOTHERFUCKER WHO GOT HERE WITHOUT A PACK OF DROOLING GEEKS HOT ON HIS ASS!
BUT SHIT, IF YOU WANT, I'LL OPEN THE DOORS FOR OLD RED. LET HIM IN. AND ALL THOSE DISEASED MANIACS FUCKING HIM IN THE ASS.
LET HIM HAVE HIS WAY WITH YOUR SWEET YOUNG DEBUTANTE, AND THAT DRIED-UP OLD CUNT WIFE OF YOURS.
'CAUSE HELL, HE PAID FOR IT! HE'S ENTITLED!
WAIT. CODY! WAIT!
I-I'M SORRY. I WAS... HEARING HIM LIKE THAT, IT'S JUST... HARD.
YEAH, WELL, MIGHT WANNA KEEP IN MIND...
"...IT'S A HELL OF A LOT HARDER OUT THERE."

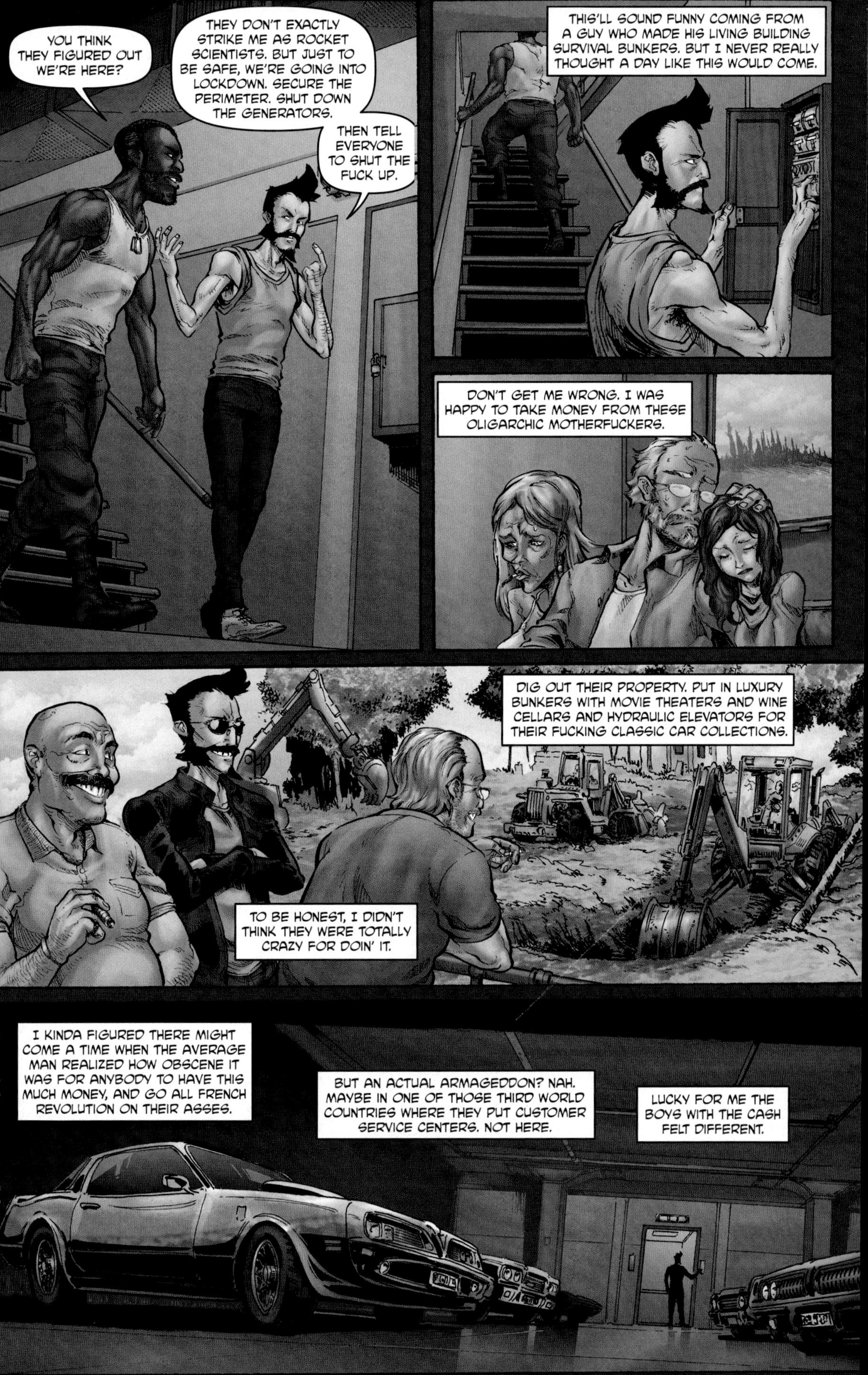

YOU THINK THEY FIGURED OUT WE'RE HERE?
THEY DON'T EXACTLY STRIKE ME AS ROCKET SCIENTISTS. BUT JUST TO BE SAFE, WE'RE GOING INTO LOCKDOWN. SECURE THE PERIMETER. SHUT DOWN THE GENERATORS.
THEN TELL EVERYONE TO SHUT THE FUCK UP.
THIS'LL SOUND FUNNY COMING FROM A GUY WHO MADE HIS LIVING BUILDING SURVIVAL BUNKERS. BUT I NEVER REALLY THOUGHT A DAY LIKE THIS WOULD COME.
DON'T GET ME WRONG. I WAS HAPPY TO TAKE MONEY FROM THESE OLIGARCHIC MOTHERFUCKERS.
DIG OUT THEIR PROPERTY. PUT IN LUXURY BUNKERS WITH MOVIE THEATERS AND WINE CELLARS AND HYDRAULIC ELEVATORS FOR THEIR FUCKING CLASSIC CAR COLLECTIONS.
TO BE HONEST, I DIDN'T THINK THEY WERE TOTALLY CRAZY FOR DOIN' IT.
I KINDA FIGURED THERE MIGHT COME A TIME WHEN THE AVERAGE MAN REALIZED HOW OBSCENE IT WAS FOR ANYBODY TO HAVE THIS MUCH MONEY, AND GO ALL FRENCH REVOLUTION ON THEIR ASSES.
BUT AN ACTUAL ARMAGEDDON? NAH. MAYBE IN ONE OF THOSE THIRD WORLD COUNTRIES WHERE THEY PUT CUSTOMER SERVICE CENTERS. NOT HERE.
LUCKY FOR ME THE BOYS WITH THE CASH FELT DIFFERENT.

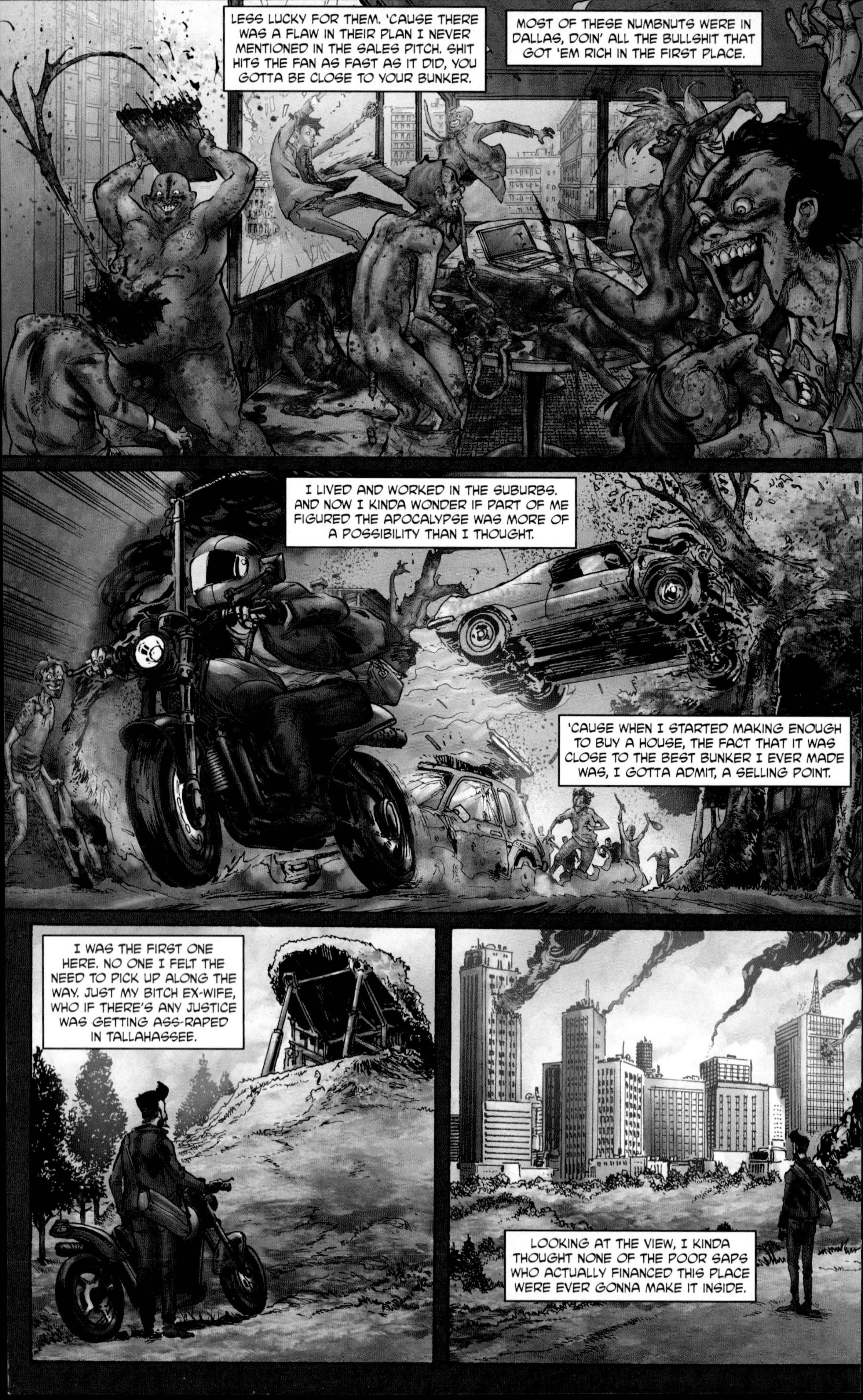
LESS LUCKY FOR THEM. 'CAUSE THERE WAS A FLAW IN THEIR PLAN I NEVER MENTIONED IN THE SALES PITCH. SHIT HITS THE FAN AS FAST AS IT DID, YOU GOTTA BE CLOSE TO YOUR BUNKER.
MOST OF THESE NUMBNUTS WERE IN DALLAS, DOIN' ALL THE BULLSHIT THAT GOT 'EM RICH IN THE FIRST PLACE.
I LIVED AND WORKED IN THE SUBURBS. AND NOW I KINDA WONDER IF PART OF ME FIGURED THE APOCALYPSE WAS MORE OF A POSSIBILITY THAN I THOUGHT.
'CAUSE WHEN I STARTED MAKING ENOUGH TO BUY A HOUSE, THE FACT THAT IT WAS CLOSE TO THE BEST BUNKER I EVER MADE WAS, I GOTTA ADMIT, A SELLING POINT.
I WAS THE FIRST ONE HERE. NO ONE I FELT THE NEED TO PICK UP ALONG THE WAY. JUST MY BITCH EX-WIFE, WHO IF THERE'S ANY JUSTICE WAS GETTING ASS-RAPED IN TALLAHASSEE.
LOOKING AT THE VIEW, I KINDA THOUGHT NONE OF THE POOR SAPS WHO ACTUALLY FINANCED THIS PLACE WERE EVER GONNA MAKE IT INSIDE.

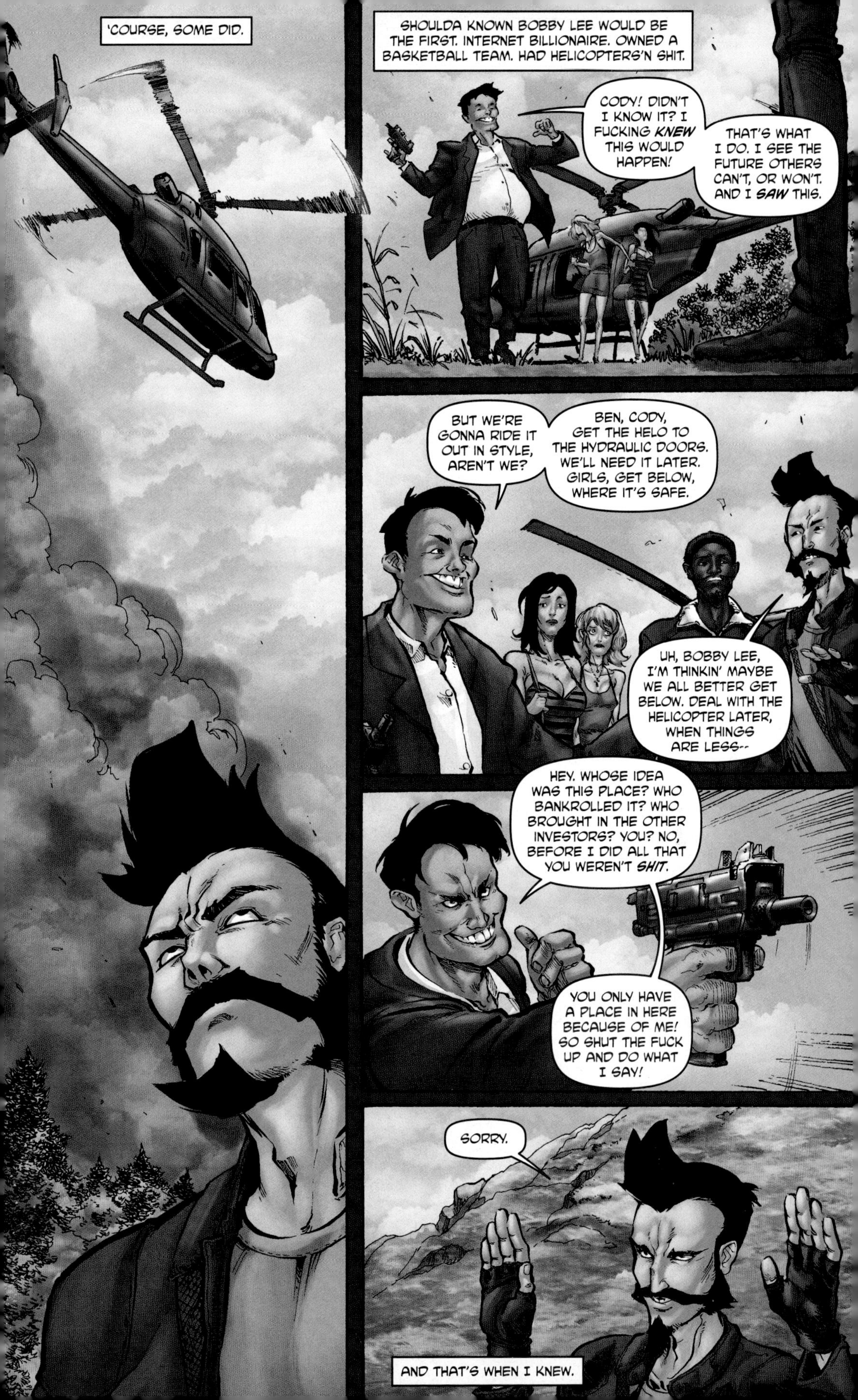
'COURSE, SOME DID.
SHOULDA KNOWN BOBBY LEE WOULD BE THE FIRST. INTERNET BILLIONAIRE. OWNED A BASKETBALL TEAM. HAD HELICOPTERS'N SHIT.
CODY! DIDN'T I KNOW IT? I FUCKING *KNEW* THIS WOULD HAPPEN!
THAT'S WHAT I DO. I SEE THE FUTURE OTHERS CAN'T, OR WON'T. AND I *SAW* THIS.
BUT WE'RE GONNA RIDE IT OUT IN STYLE, AREN'T WE?
BEN, CODY, GET THE HELO TO THE HYDRAULIC DOORS. WE'LL NEED IT LATER. GIRLS, GET BELOW, WHERE IT'S SAFE.
UH, BOBBY LEE, I'M THINKIN' MAYBE WE ALL BETTER GET BELOW. DEAL WITH THE HELICOPTER LATER, WHEN THINGS ARE LESS--
HEY. WHOSE IDEA WAS THIS PLACE? WHO BANKROLLED IT? WHO BROUGHT IN THE OTHER INVESTORS? YOU? NO, BEFORE I DID ALL THAT YOU WEREN'T *SHIT*.
YOU ONLY HAVE A PLACE IN HERE BECAUSE OF ME! SO SHUT THE FUCK UP AND DO WHAT I SAY!
SORRY.
AND THAT'S WHEN I KNEW.

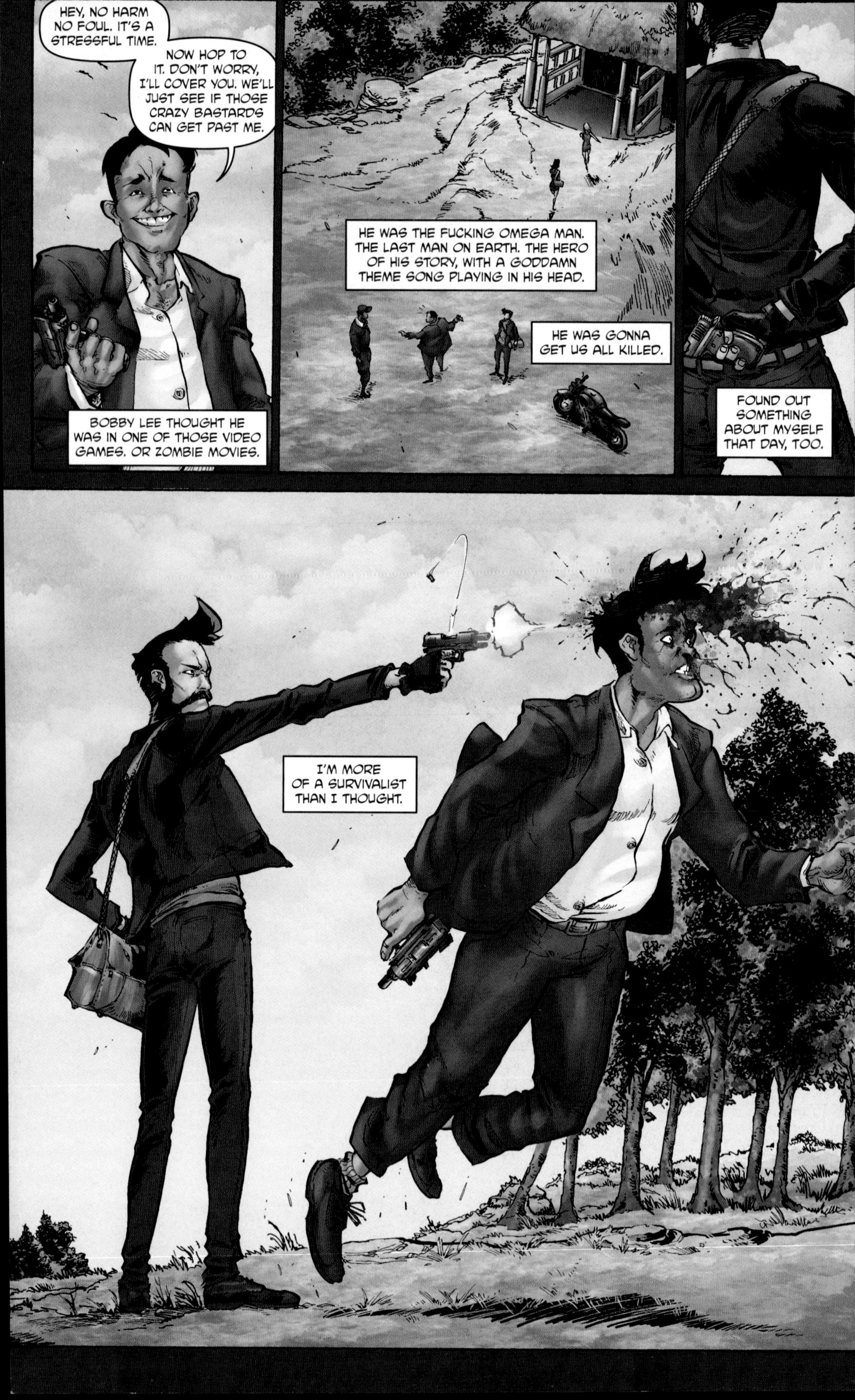
HEY, NO HARM NO FOUL. IT'S A STRESSFUL TIME.
NOW HOP TO IT. DON'T WORRY, I'LL COVER YOU. WE'LL JUST SEE IF THOSE CRAZY BASTARDS CAN GET PAST ME.
BOBBY LEE THOUGHT HE WAS IN ONE OF THOSE VIDEO GAMES. OR ZOMBIE MOVIES.
HE WAS THE FUCKING OMEGA MAN. THE LAST MAN ON EARTH. THE HERO OF HIS STORY, WITH A GODDAMN THEME SONG PLAYING IN HIS HEAD.
HE WAS GONNA GET US ALL KILLED.
FOUND OUT SOMETHING ABOUT MYSELF THAT DAY, TOO.
I'M MORE OF A SURVIVALIST THAN I THOUGHT.

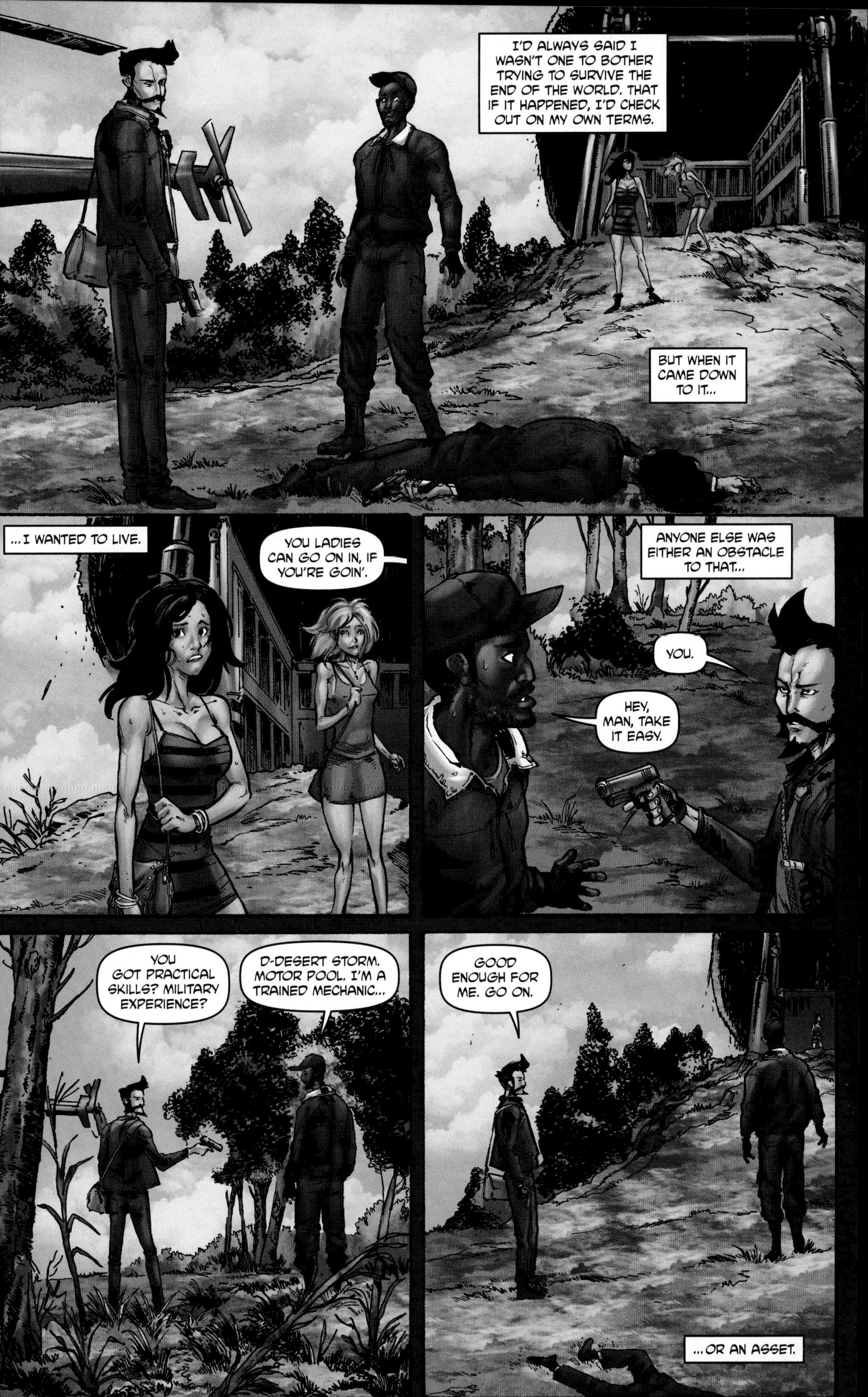

I'D ALWAYS SAID I WASN'T ONE TO BOTHER TRYING TO SURVIVE THE END OF THE WORLD. THAT IF IT HAPPENED, I'D CHECK OUT ON MY OWN TERMS.
BUT WHEN IT CAME DOWN TO IT...
...I WANTED TO LIVE.
YOU LADIES CAN GO ON IN, IF YOU'RE GOIN'.
ANYONE ELSE WAS EITHER AN OBSTACLE TO THAT...
YOU.
HEY, MAN, TAKE IT EASY.
YOU GOT PRACTICAL SKILLS? MILITARY EXPERIENCE?
D-DESERT STORM. MOTOR POOL. I'M A TRAINED MECHANIC...
GOOD ENOUGH FOR ME. GO ON.
...OR AN ASSET.

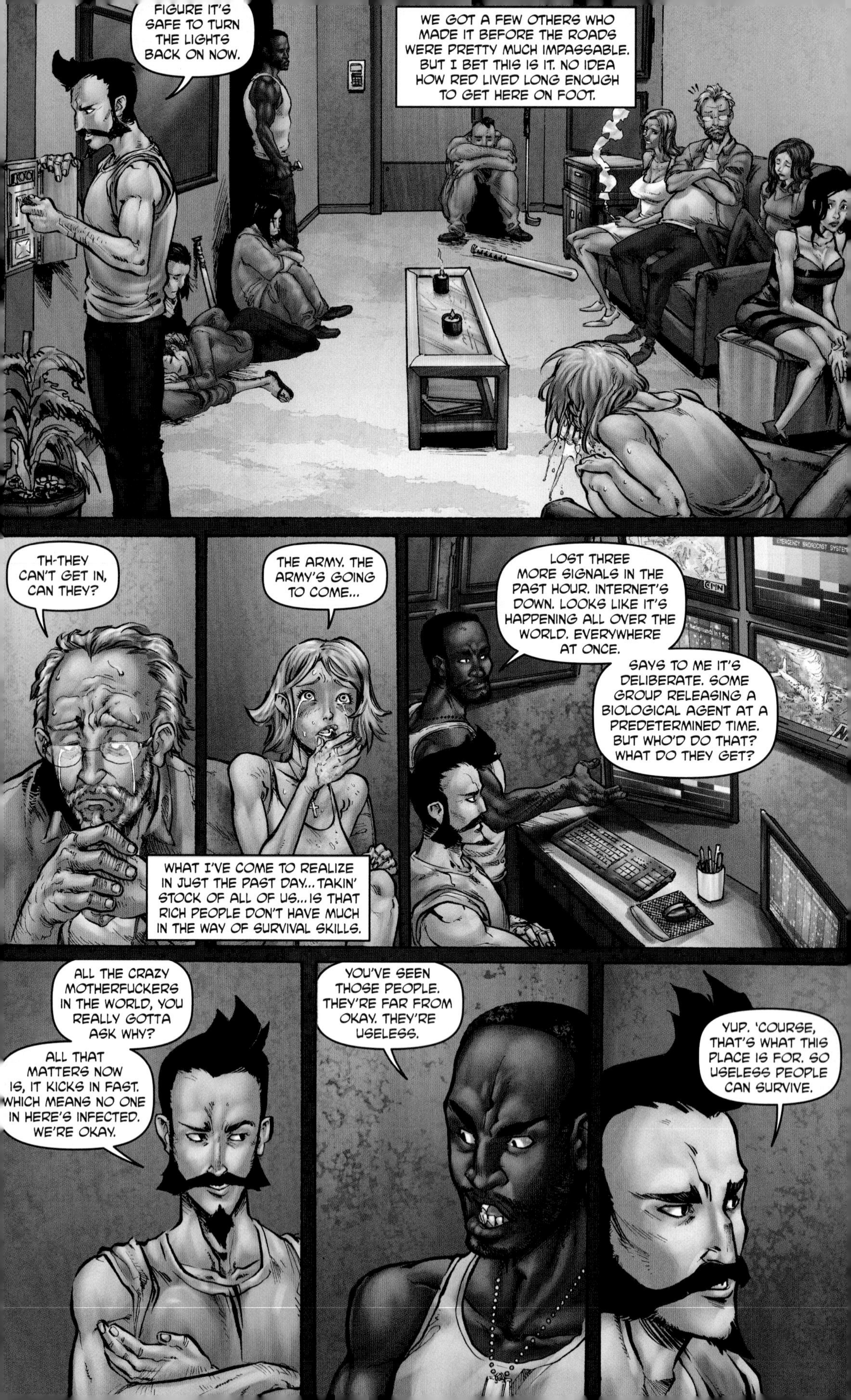
FIGURE IT'S SAFE TO TURN THE LIGHTS BACK ON NOW.
WE GOT A FEW OTHERS WHO MADE IT BEFORE THE ROADS WERE PRETTY MUCH IMPASSABLE. BUT I BET THIS IS IT. NO IDEA HOW RED LIVED LONG ENOUGH TO GET HERE ON FOOT.
TH-THEY CAN'T GET IN, CAN THEY?
THE ARMY. THE ARMY'S GOING TO COME...
WHAT I'VE COME TO REALIZE IN JUST THE PAST DAY... TAKIN' STOCK OF ALL OF US... IS THAT RICH PEOPLE DON'T HAVE MUCH IN THE WAY OF SURVIVAL SKILLS.
LOST THREE MORE SIGNALS IN THE PAST HOUR. INTERNET'S DOWN. LOOKS LIKE IT'S HAPPENING ALL OVER THE WORLD. EVERYWHERE AT ONCE.
SAYS TO ME IT'S DELIBERATE. SOME GROUP RELEASING A BIOLOGICAL AGENT AT A PREDETERMINED TIME. BUT WHO'D DO THAT? WHAT DO THEY GET?
ALL THE CRAZY MOTHERFUCKERS IN THE WORLD, YOU REALLY GOTTA ASK WHY?
ALL THAT MATTERS NOW IS, IT KICKS IN FAST. WHICH MEANS NO ONE IN HERE'S INFECTED. WE'RE OKAY.
YOU'VE SEEN THOSE PEOPLE. THEY'RE FAR FROM OKAY. THEY'RE USELESS.
YUP. 'COURSE, THAT'S WHAT THIS PLACE IS FOR. SO USELESS PEOPLE CAN SURVIVE.

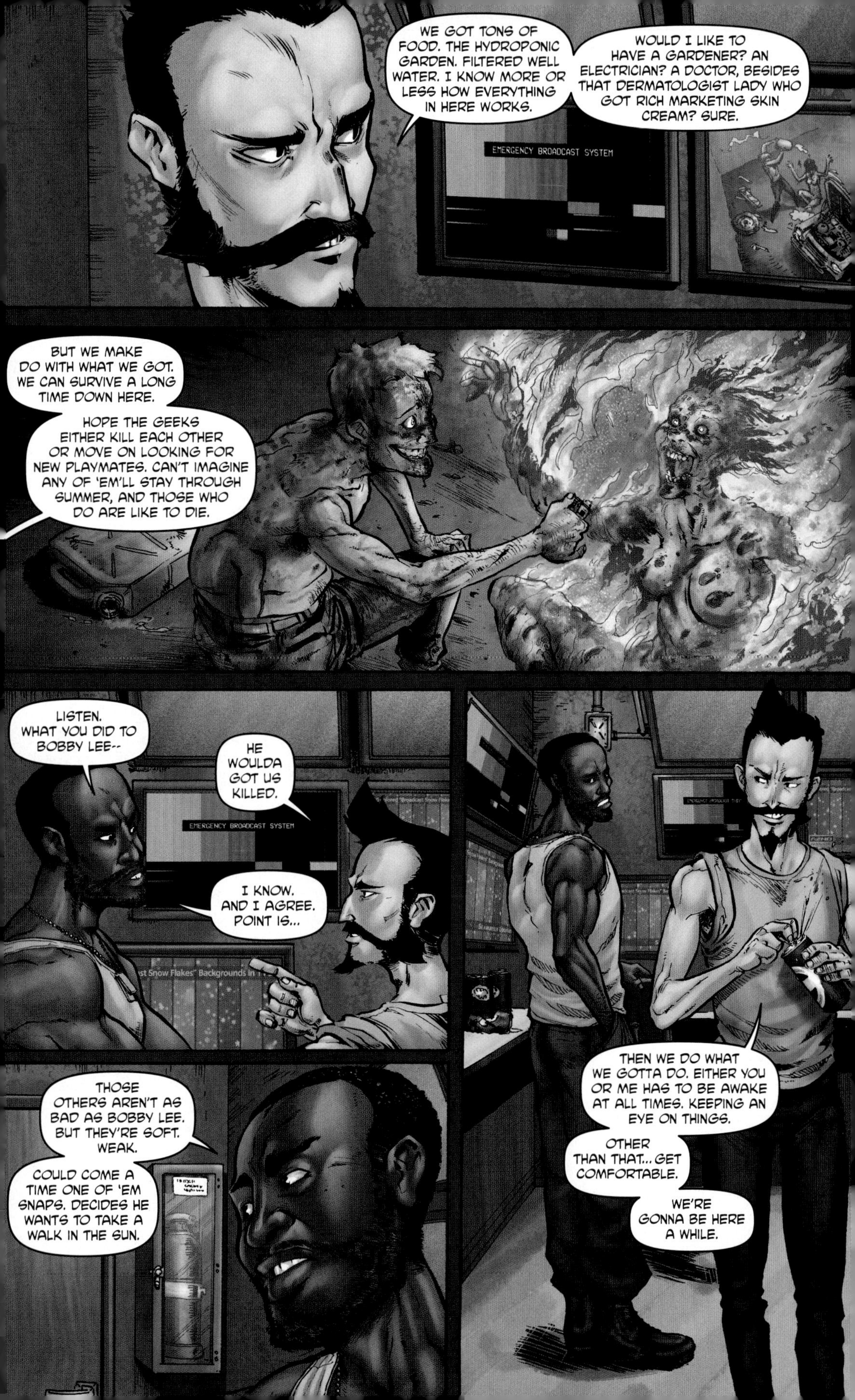
WE GOT TONS OF FOOD. THE HYDROPONIC GARDEN. FILTERED WELL WATER. I KNOW MORE OR LESS HOW EVERYTHING IN HERE WORKS.
WOULD I LIKE TO HAVE A GARDENER? AN ELECTRICIAN? A DOCTOR, BESIDES THAT DERMATOLOGIST LADY WHO GOT RICH MARKETING SKIN CREAM? SURE.
EMERGENCY BROADCAST SYSTEM
BUT WE MAKE DO WITH WHAT WE GOT. WE CAN SURVIVE A LONG TIME DOWN HERE.
HOPE THE GEEKS EITHER KILL EACH OTHER OR MOVE ON LOOKING FOR NEW PLAYMATES. CAN'T IMAGINE ANY OF 'EM'LL STAY THROUGH SUMMER, AND THOSE WHO DO ARE LIKE TO DIE.
LISTEN. WHAT YOU DID TO BOBBY LEE--
HE WOULDA GOT US KILLED.
EMERGENCY BROADCAST SYSTEM
I KNOW. AND I AGREE. POINT IS...
THOSE OTHERS AREN'T AS BAD AS BOBBY LEE. BUT THEY'RE SOFT. WEAK.
COULD COME A TIME ONE OF 'EM SNAPS. DECIDES HE WANTS TO TAKE A WALK IN THE SUN.
THEN WE DO WHAT WE GOTTA DO. EITHER YOU OR ME HAS TO BE AWAKE AT ALL TIMES. KEEPING AN EYE ON THINGS.
OTHER THAN THAT... GET COMFORTABLE.
WE'RE GONNA BE HERE A WHILE.

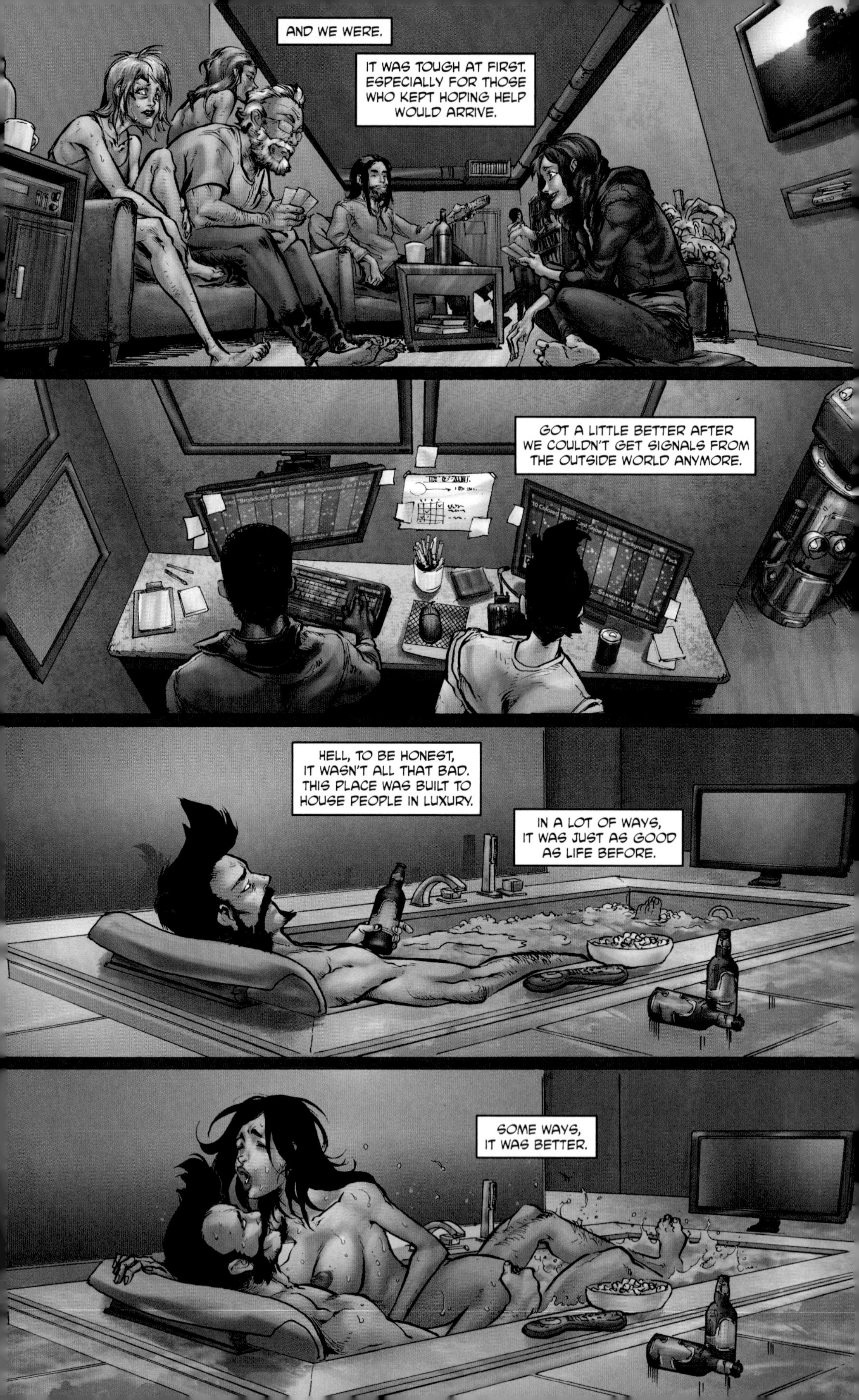
AND WE WERE.
IT WAS TOUGH AT FIRST. ESPECIALLY FOR THOSE WHO KEPT HOPING HELP WOULD ARRIVE.
GOT A LITTLE BETTER AFTER WE COULDN'T GET SIGNALS FROM THE OUTSIDE WORLD ANYMORE.
HELL, TO BE HONEST, IT WASN'T ALL THAT BAD. THIS PLACE WAS BUILT TO HOUSE PEOPLE IN LUXURY.
IN A LOT OF WAYS, IT WAS JUST AS GOOD AS LIFE BEFORE.
SOME WAYS, IT WAS BETTER.

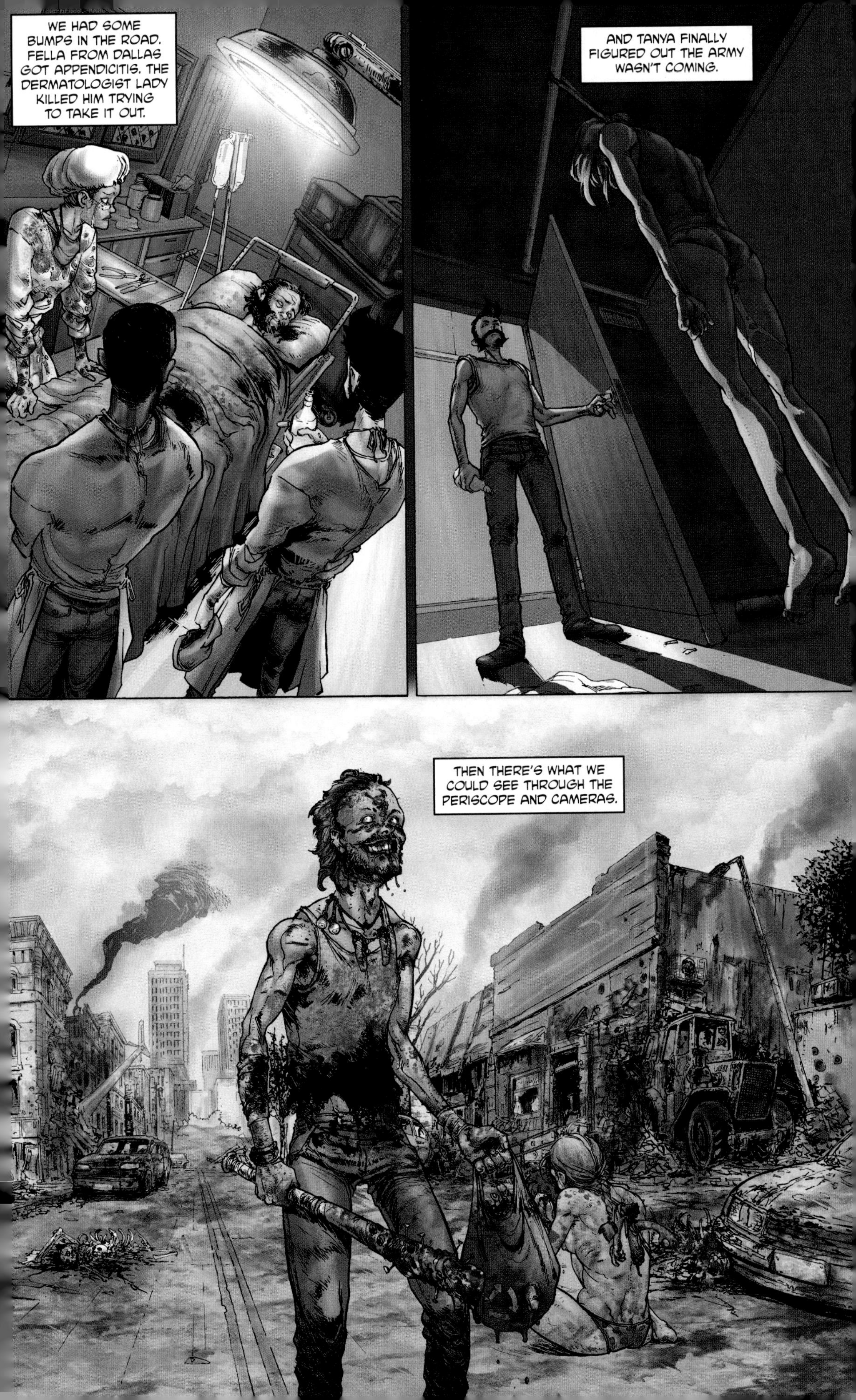
WE HAD SOME BUMPS IN THE ROAD. FELLA FROM DALLAS GOT APPENDICITIS. THE DERMATOLOGIST LADY KILLED HIM TRYING TO TAKE IT OUT.
AND TANYA FINALLY FIGURED OUT THE ARMY WASN'T COMING.
THEN THERE'S WHAT WE COULD SEE THROUGH THE PERISCOPE AND CAMERAS.

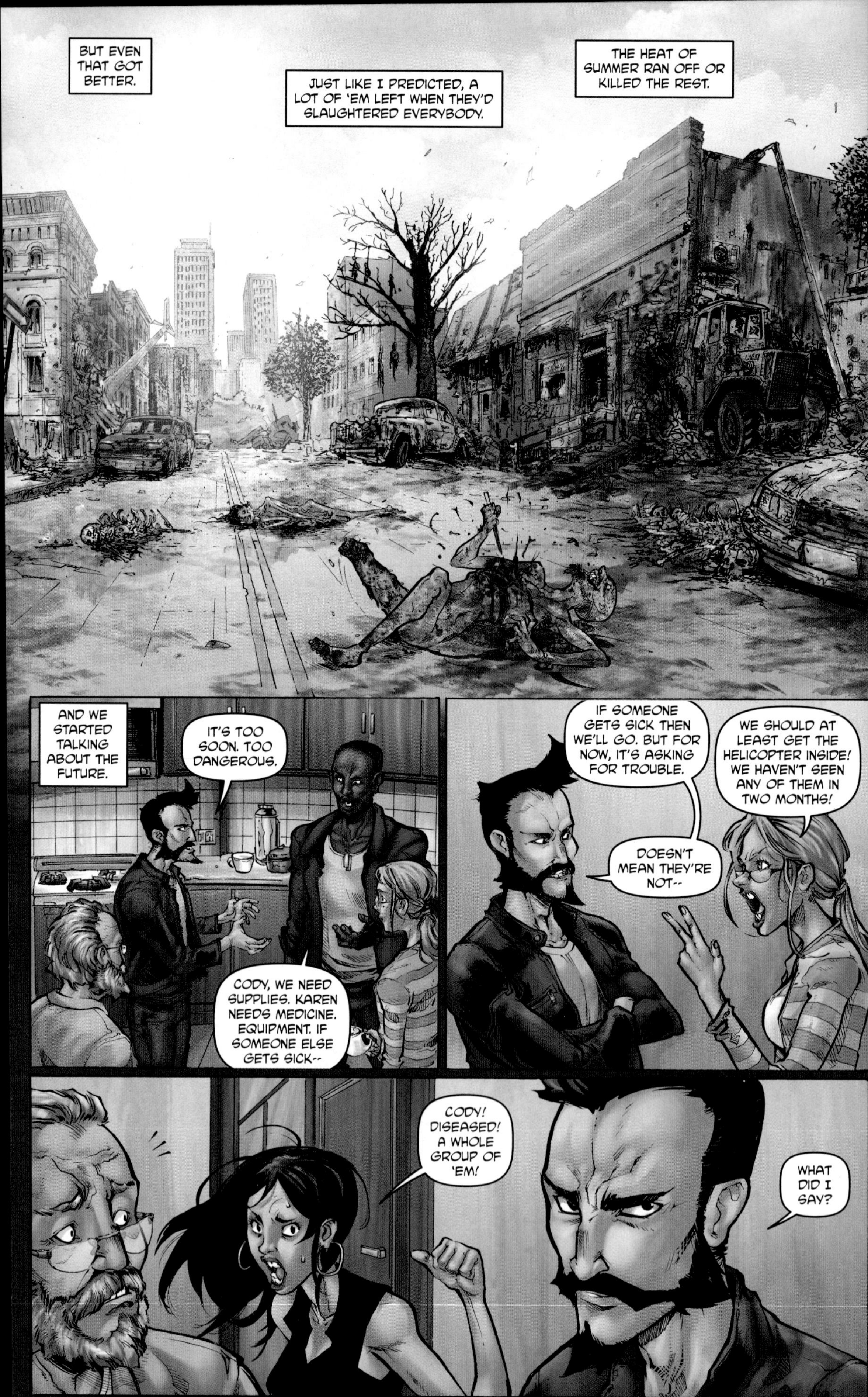
BUT EVEN THAT GOT BETTER.
JUST LIKE I PREDICTED, A LOT OF 'EM LEFT WHEN THEY'D SLAUGHTERED EVERYBODY.
THE HEAT OF SUMMER RAN OFF OR KILLED THE REST.
AND WE STARTED TALKING ABOUT THE FUTURE.
IT'S TOO SOON. TOO DANGEROUS.
CODY, WE NEED SUPPLIES. KAREN NEEDS MEDICINE. EQUIPMENT. IF SOMEONE ELSE GETS SICK--
IF SOMEONE GETS SICK THEN WE'LL GO. BUT FOR NOW, IT'S ASKING FOR TROUBLE.
WE SHOULD AT LEAST GET THE HELICOPTER INSIDE! WE HAVEN'T SEEN ANY OF THEM IN TWO MONTHS!
DOESN'T MEAN THEY'RE NOT--
CODY! DISEASED! A WHOLE GROUP OF 'EM!
WHAT DID I SAY?

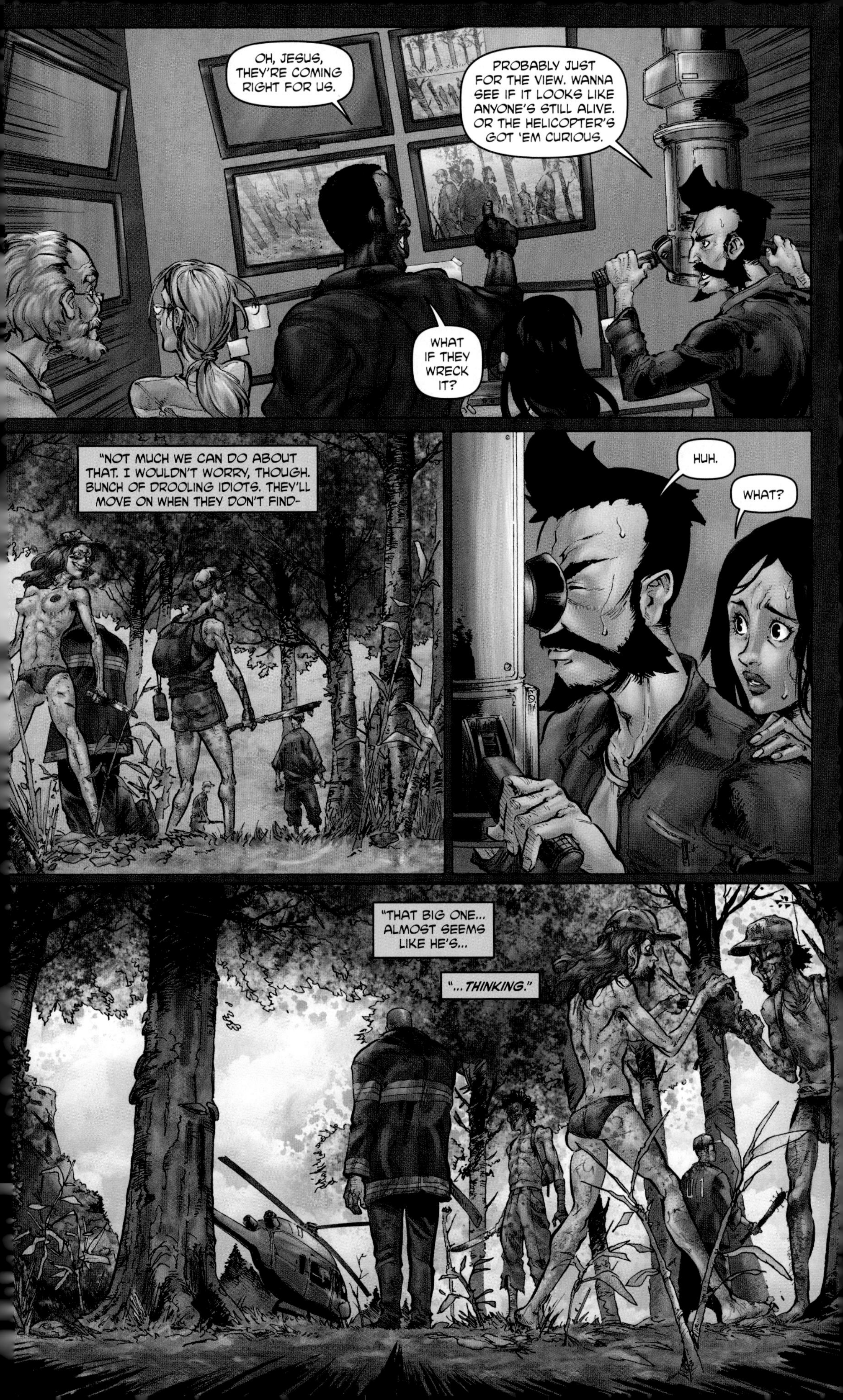
OH, JESUS, THEY'RE COMING RIGHT FOR US.
PROBABLY JUST FOR THE VIEW. WANNA SEE IF IT LOOKS LIKE ANYONE'S STILL ALIVE. OR THE HELICOPTER'S GOT 'EM CURIOUS.
WHAT IF THEY WRECK IT?
"NOT MUCH WE CAN DO ABOUT THAT. I WOULDN'T WORRY, THOUGH. BUNCH OF DROOLING IDIOTS. THEY'LL MOVE ON WHEN THEY DON'T FIND-
HUH.
WHAT?
"THAT BIG ONE... ALMOST SEEMS LIKE HE'S...
"...THINKING."

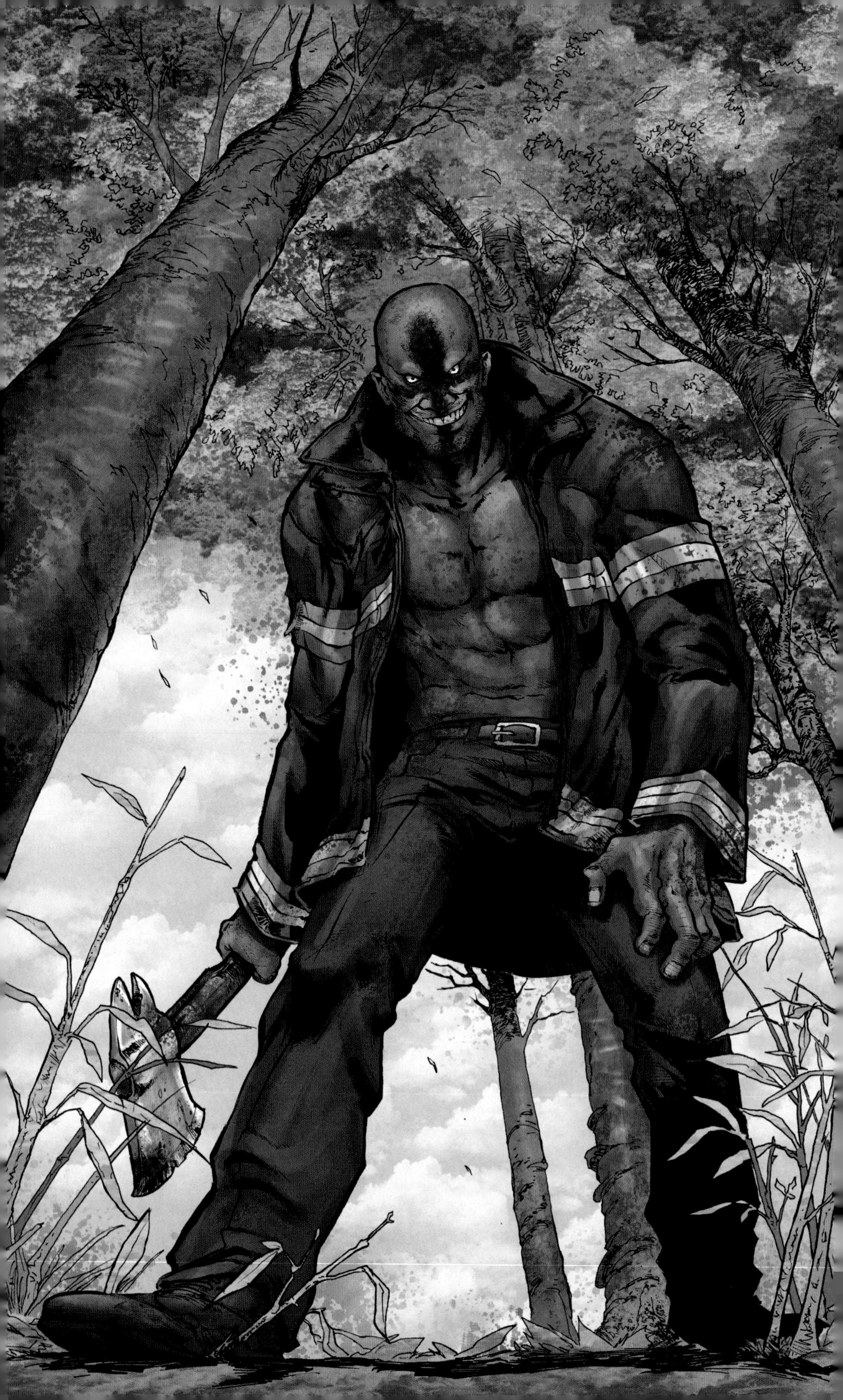

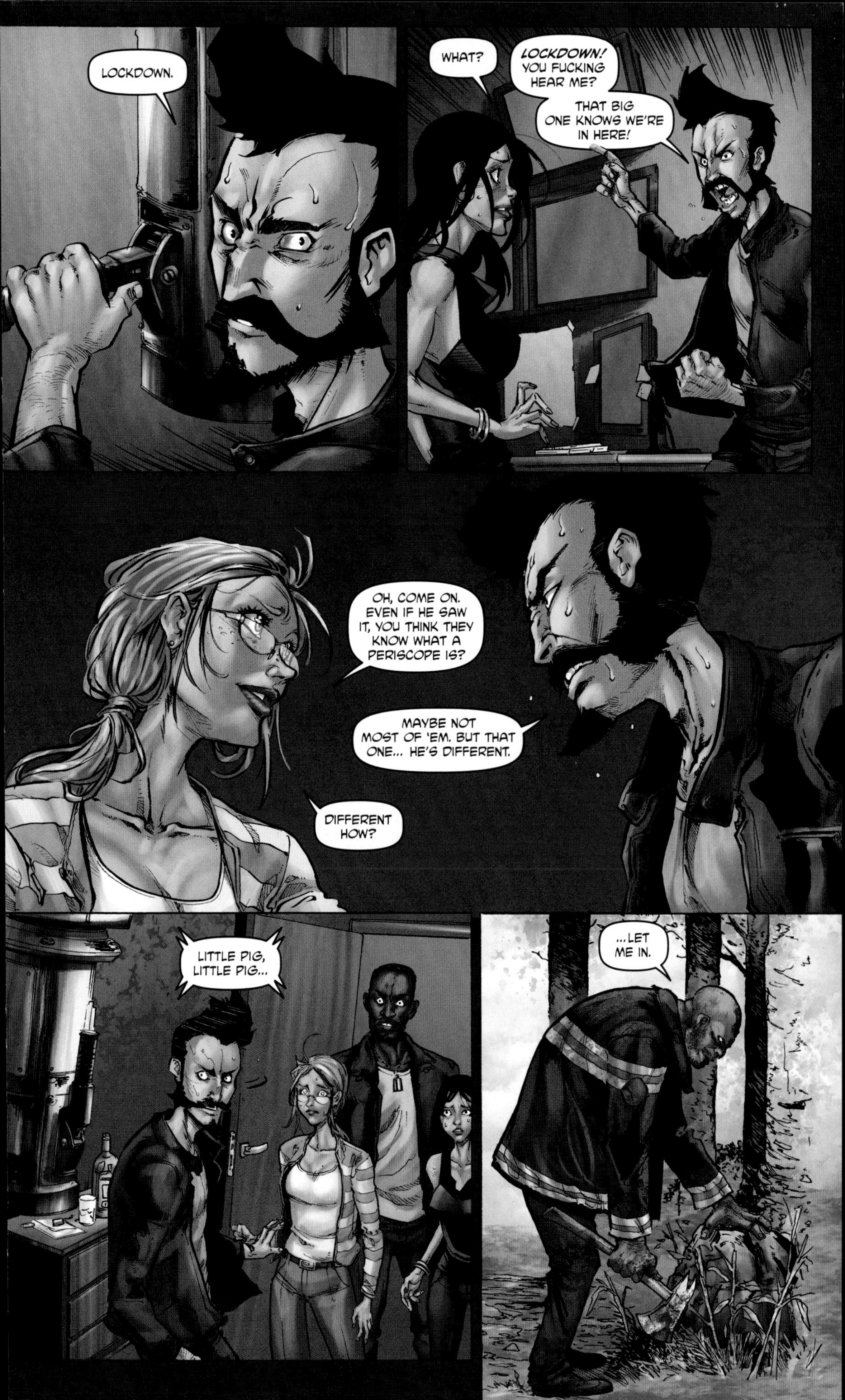
LOCKDOWN.
WHAT?
LOCKDOWN! YOU FUCKING HEAR ME?
THAT BIG ONE KNOWS WE'RE IN HERE!
OH, COME ON. EVEN IF HE SAW IT, YOU THINK THEY KNOW WHAT A PERISCOPE IS?
MAYBE NOT MOST OF 'EM. BUT THAT ONE... HE'S DIFFERENT.
DIFFERENT HOW?
LITTLE PIG, LITTLE PIG...
...LET ME IN.

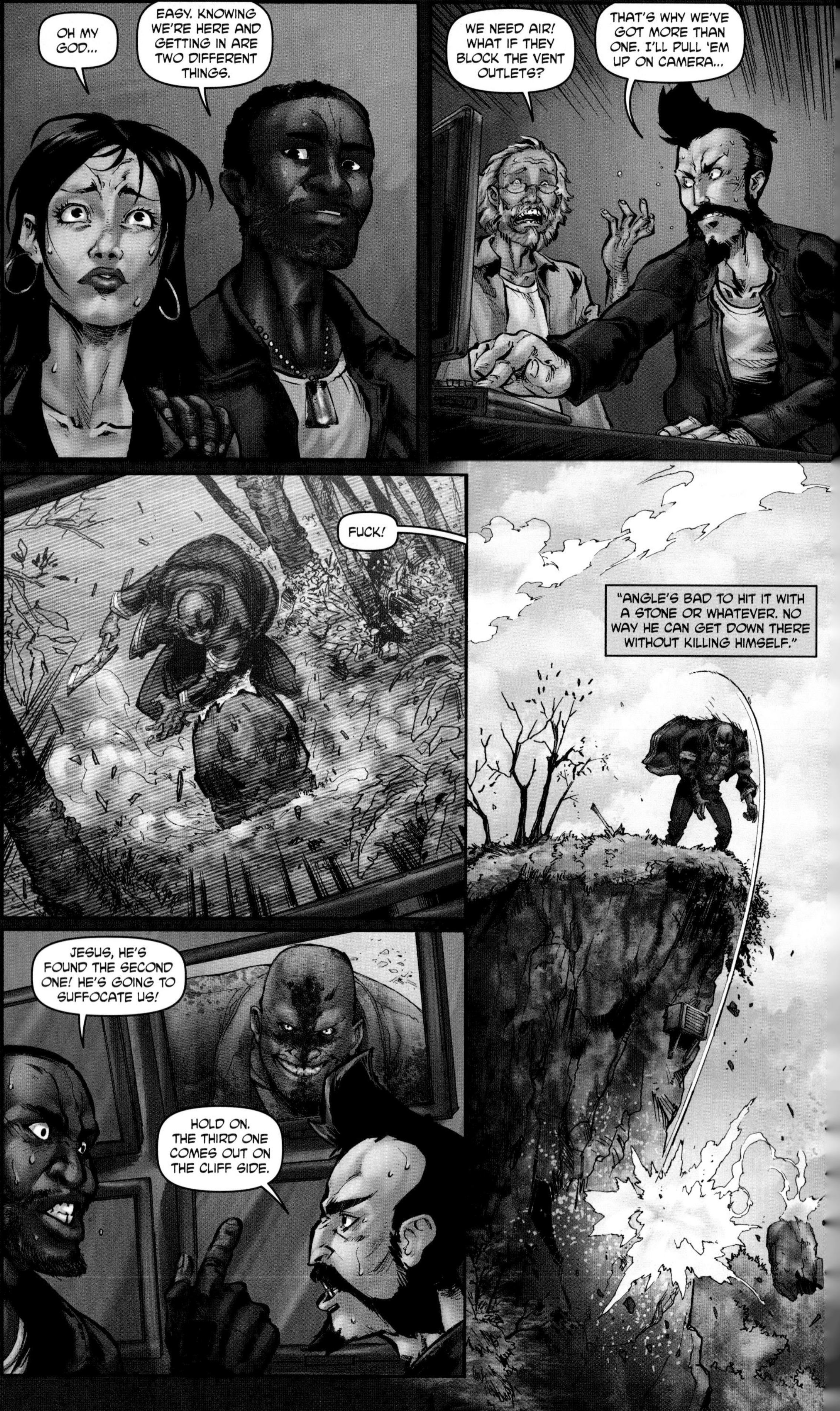
OH MY GOD...
EASY. KNOWING WE'RE HERE AND GETTING IN ARE TWO DIFFERENT THINGS.
WE NEED AIR! WHAT IF THEY BLOCK THE VENT OUTLETS?
THAT'S WHY WE'VE GOT MORE THAN ONE. I'LL PULL 'EM UP ON CAMERA...
FUCK!
"ANGLE'S BAD TO HIT IT WITH A STONE OR WHATEVER. NO WAY HE CAN GET DOWN THERE WITHOUT KILLING HIMSELF."
JESUS, HE'S FOUND THE SECOND ONE! HE'S GOING TO SUFFOCATE US!
HOLD ON. THE THIRD ONE COMES OUT ON THE CLIFF SIDE.

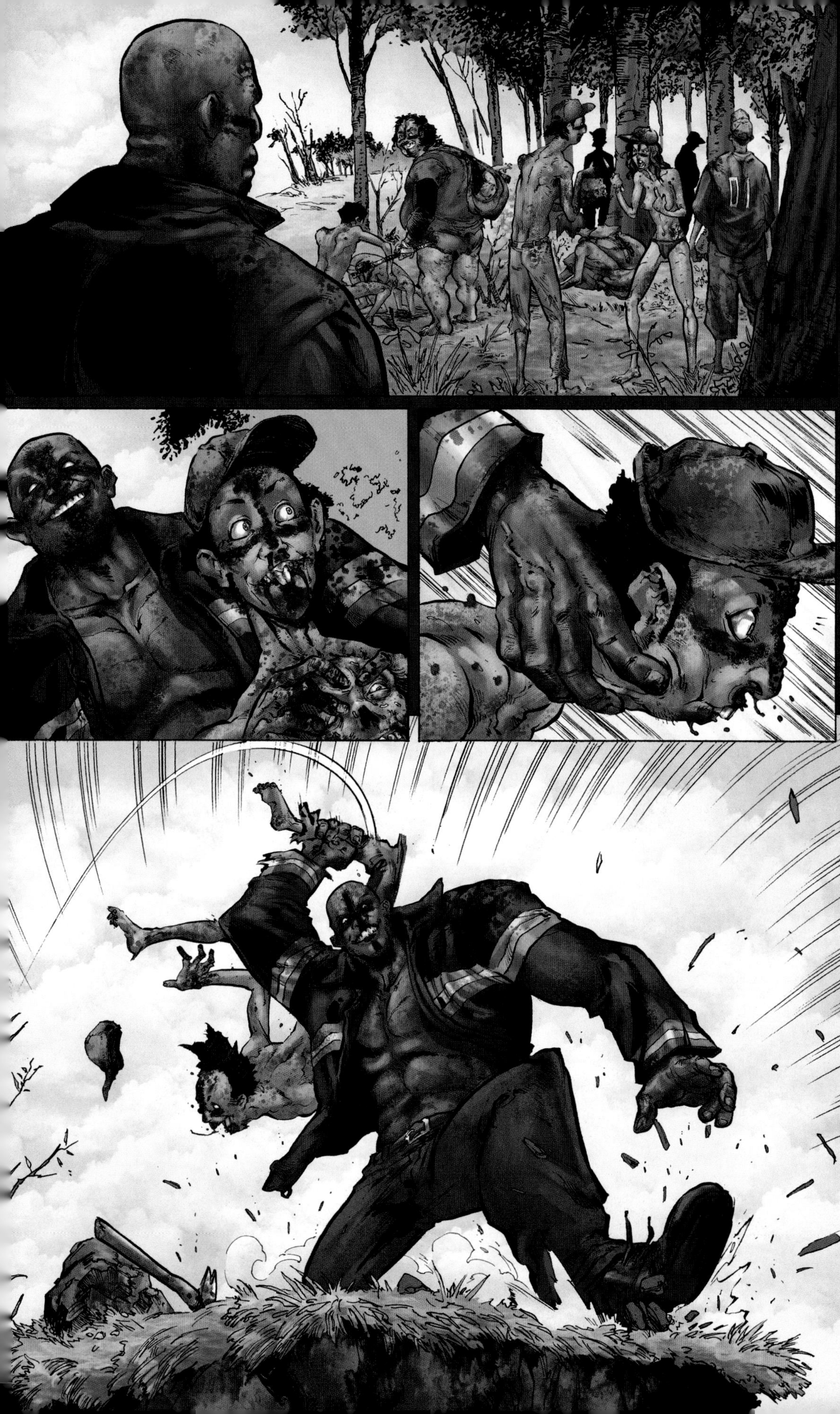

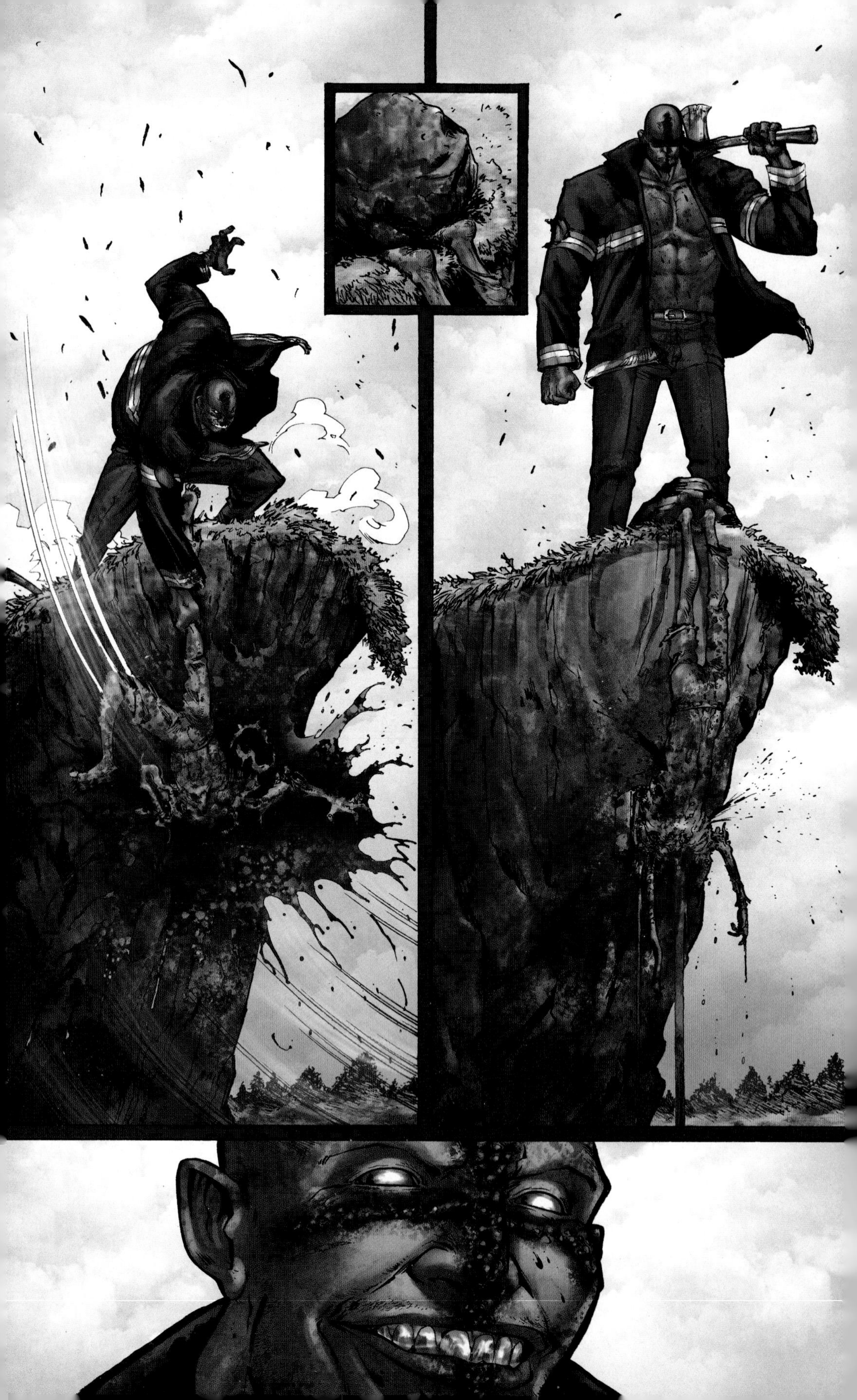

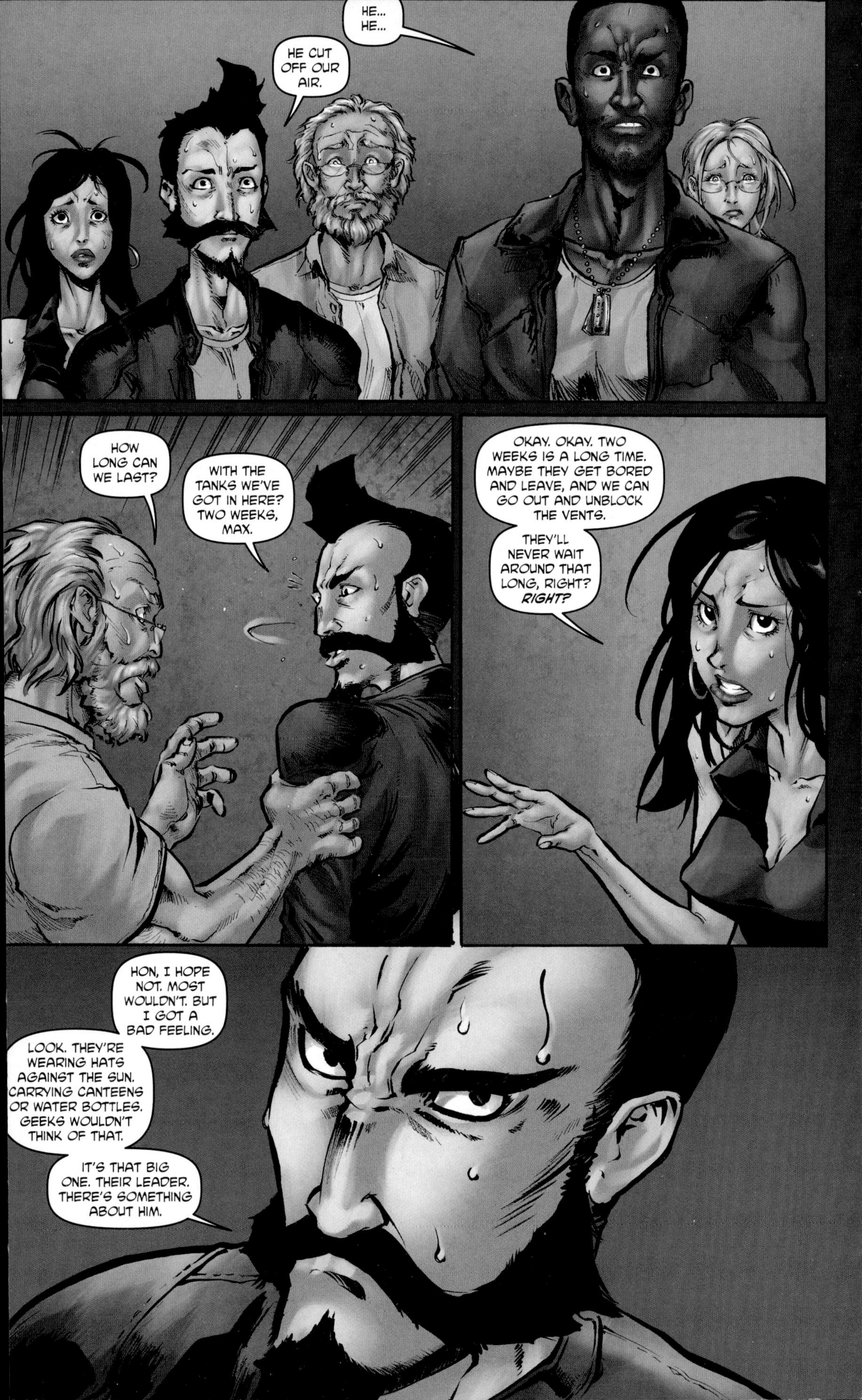
HE... HE...
HE CUT OFF OUR AIR.
HOW LONG CAN WE LAST?
WITH THE TANKS WE'VE GOT IN HERE? TWO WEEKS, MAX.
OKAY. OKAY. TWO WEEKS IS A LONG TIME. MAYBE THEY GET BORED AND LEAVE, AND WE CAN GO OUT AND UNBLOCK THE VENTS.
THEY'LL NEVER WAIT AROUND THAT LONG, RIGHT? *RIGHT?*
HON, I HOPE NOT. MOST WOULDN'T. BUT I GOT A BAD FEELING.
LOOK. THEY'RE WEARING HATS AGAINST THE SUN. CARRYING CANTEENS OR WATER BOTTLES. GEEKS WOULDN'T THINK OF THAT.
IT'S THAT BIG ONE. THEIR LEADER. THERE'S SOMETHING ABOUT HIM.

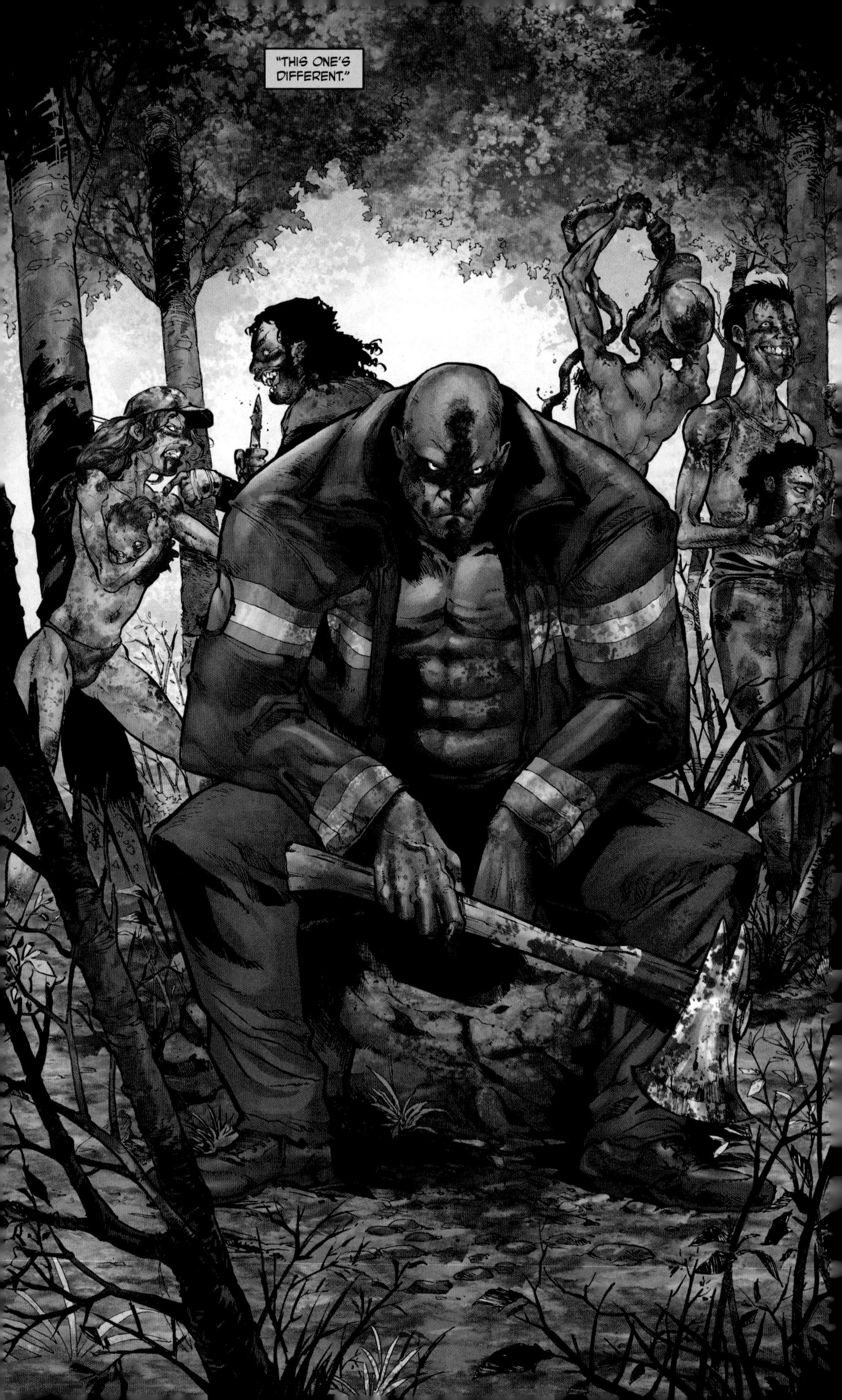
"THIS ONE'S DIFFERENT."

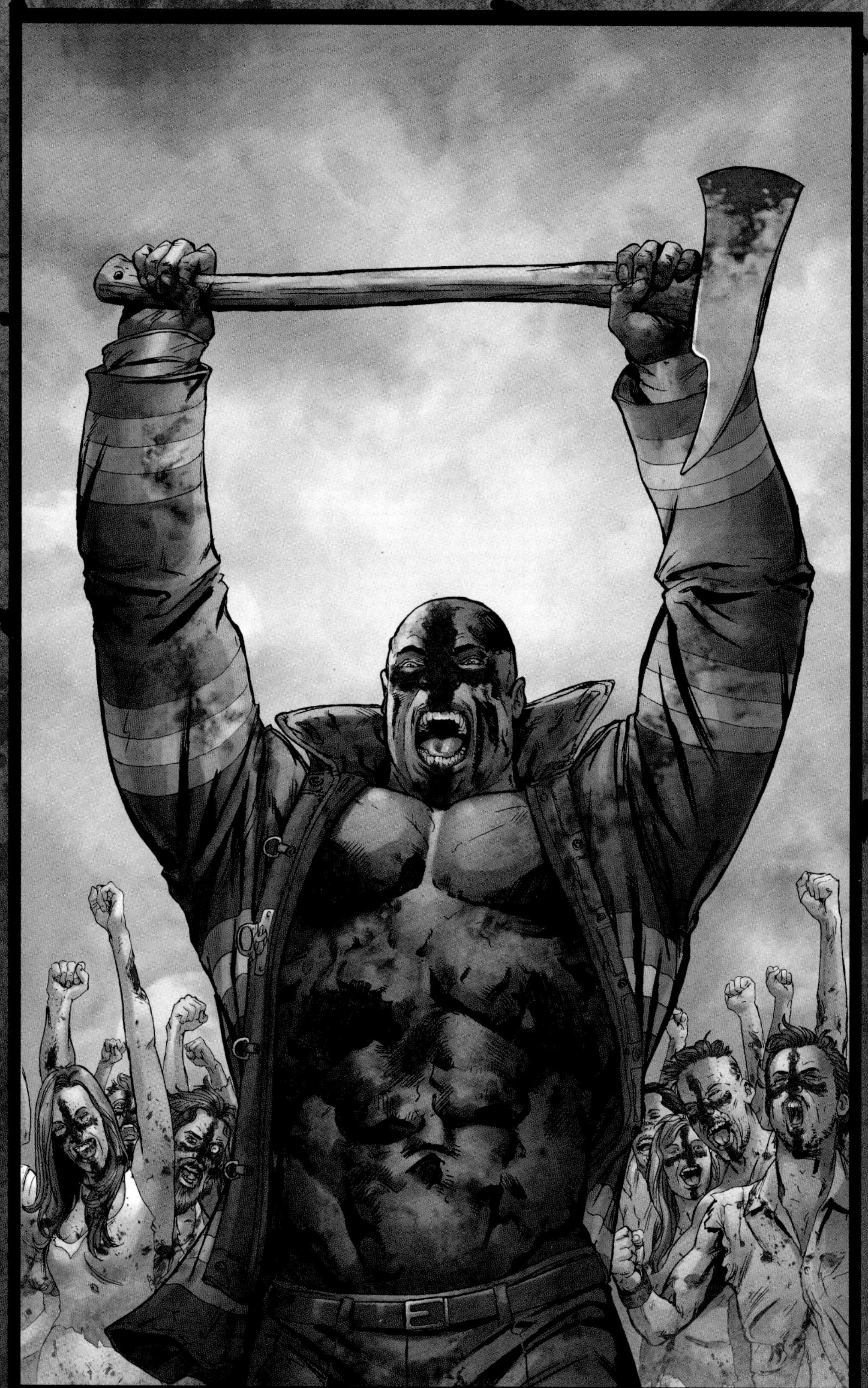

PART 2

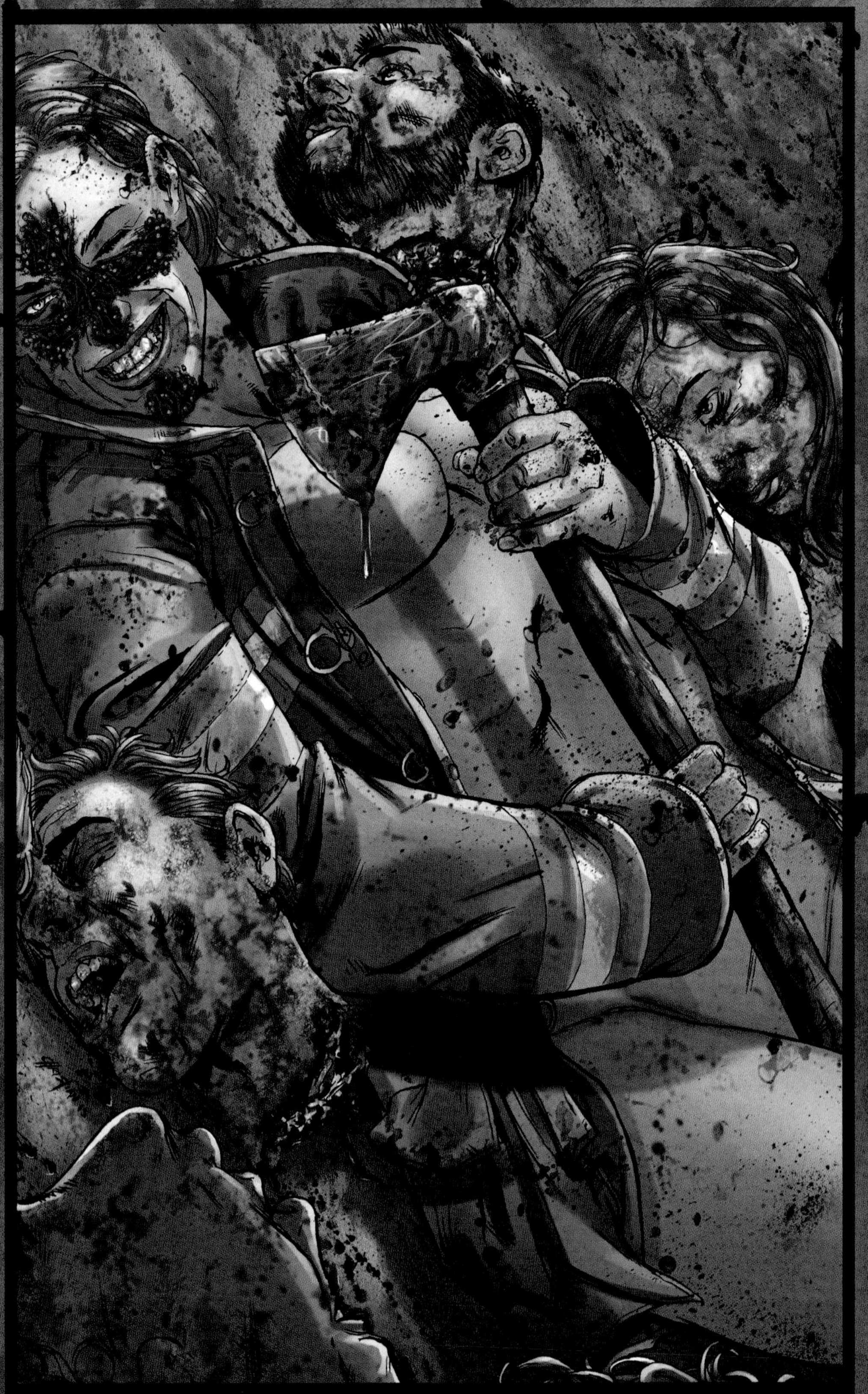

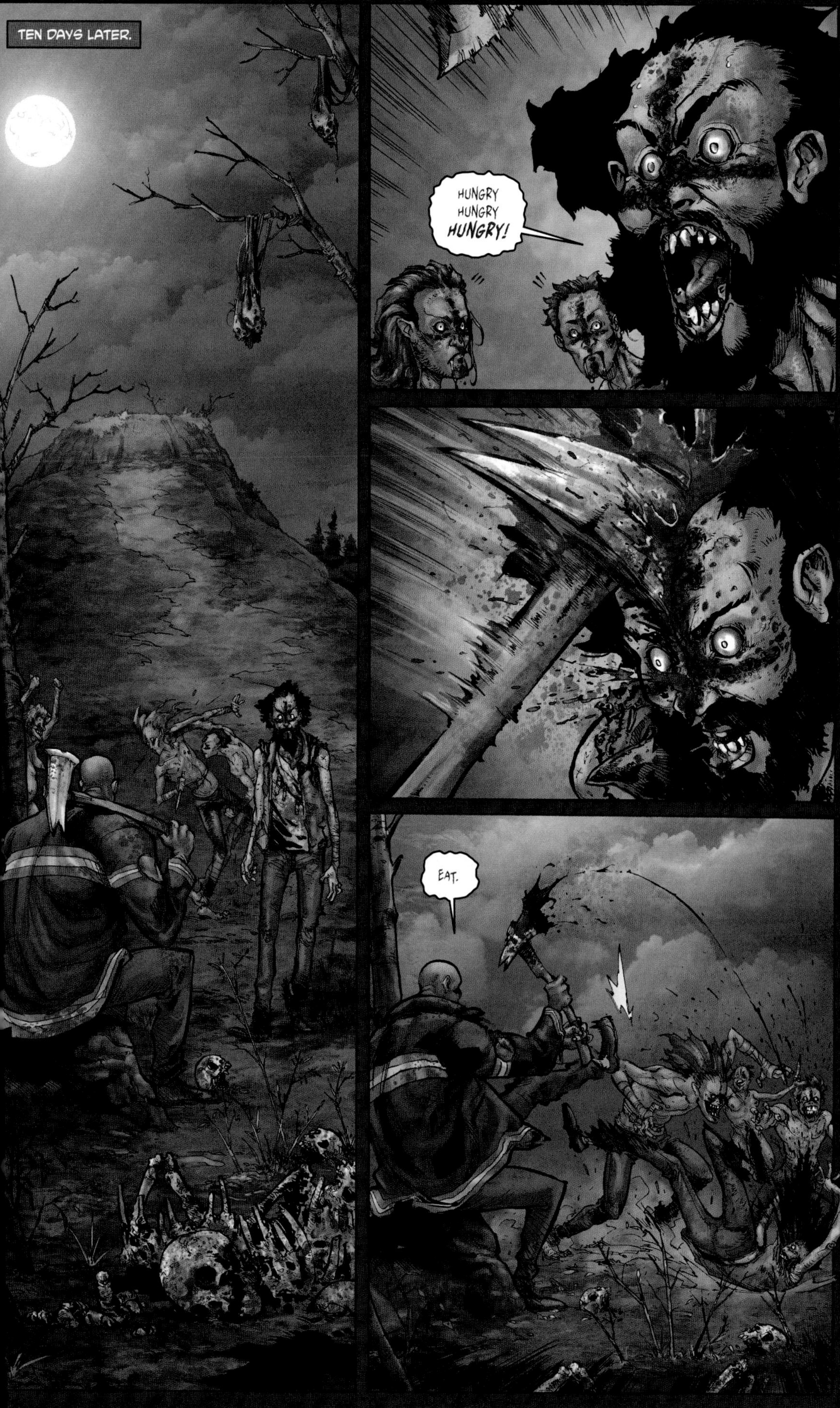
TEN DAYS LATER.
HUNGRY HUNGRY HUNGRY!
EAT.

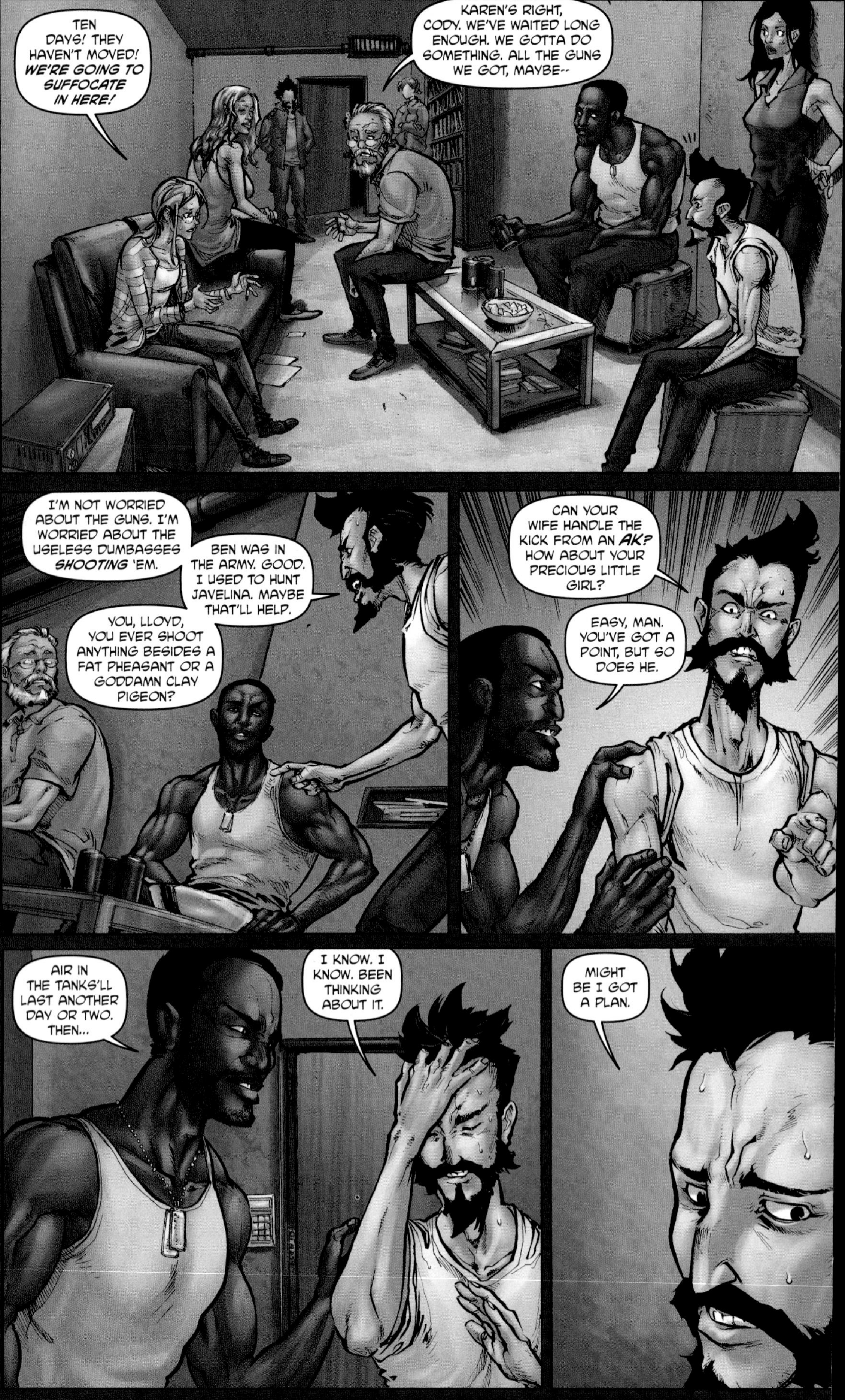
TEN DAYS! THEY HAVEN'T MOVED! WE'RE GOING TO SUFFOCATE IN HERE!
KAREN'S RIGHT, CODY. WE'VE WAITED LONG ENOUGH. WE GOTTA DO SOMETHING. ALL THE GUNS WE GOT, MAYBE--
I'M NOT WORRIED ABOUT THE GUNS. I'M WORRIED ABOUT THE USELESS DUMBASSES SHOOTING 'EM.
BEN WAS IN THE ARMY. GOOD. I USED TO HUNT JAVELINA. MAYBE THAT'LL HELP.
YOU, LLOYD, YOU EVER SHOOT ANYTHING BESIDES A FAT PHEASANT OR A GODDAMN CLAY PIGEON?
CAN YOUR WIFE HANDLE THE KICK FROM AN AK? HOW ABOUT YOUR PRECIOUS LITTLE GIRL?
EASY, MAN. YOU'VE GOT A POINT, BUT SO DOES HE.
AIR IN THE TANKS'LL LAST ANOTHER DAY OR TWO. THEN...
I KNOW. I KNOW. BEEN THINKING ABOUT IT.
MIGHT BE I GOT A PLAN.

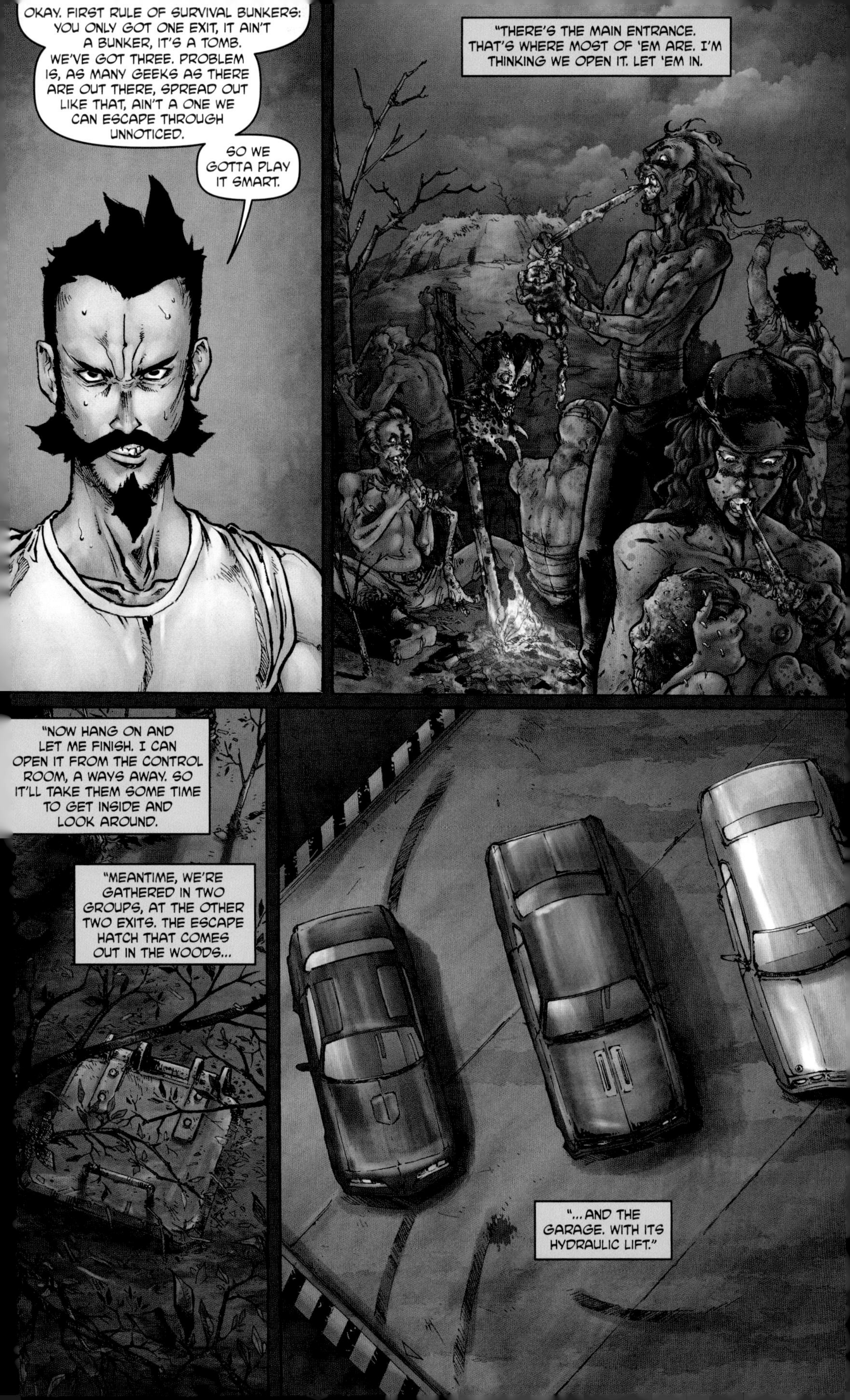
OKAY. FIRST RULE OF SURVIVAL BUNKERS: YOU ONLY GOT ONE EXIT, IT AIN'T A BUNKER, IT'S A TOMB. WE'VE GOT THREE. PROBLEM IS, AS MANY GEEKS AS THERE ARE OUT THERE, SPREAD OUT LIKE THAT, AIN'T A ONE WE CAN ESCAPE THROUGH UNNOTICED.
SO WE GOTTA PLAY IT SMART.
"THERE'S THE MAIN ENTRANCE. THAT'S WHERE MOST OF 'EM ARE. I'M THINKING WE OPEN IT. LET 'EM IN.
"NOW HANG ON AND LET ME FINISH. I CAN OPEN IT FROM THE CONTROL ROOM, A WAYS AWAY. SO IT'LL TAKE THEM SOME TIME TO GET INSIDE AND LOOK AROUND.
"MEANTIME, WE'RE GATHERED IN TWO GROUPS, AT THE OTHER TWO EXITS. THE ESCAPE HATCH THAT COMES OUT IN THE WOODS...
"...AND THE GARAGE. WITH ITS HYDRAULIC LIFT."

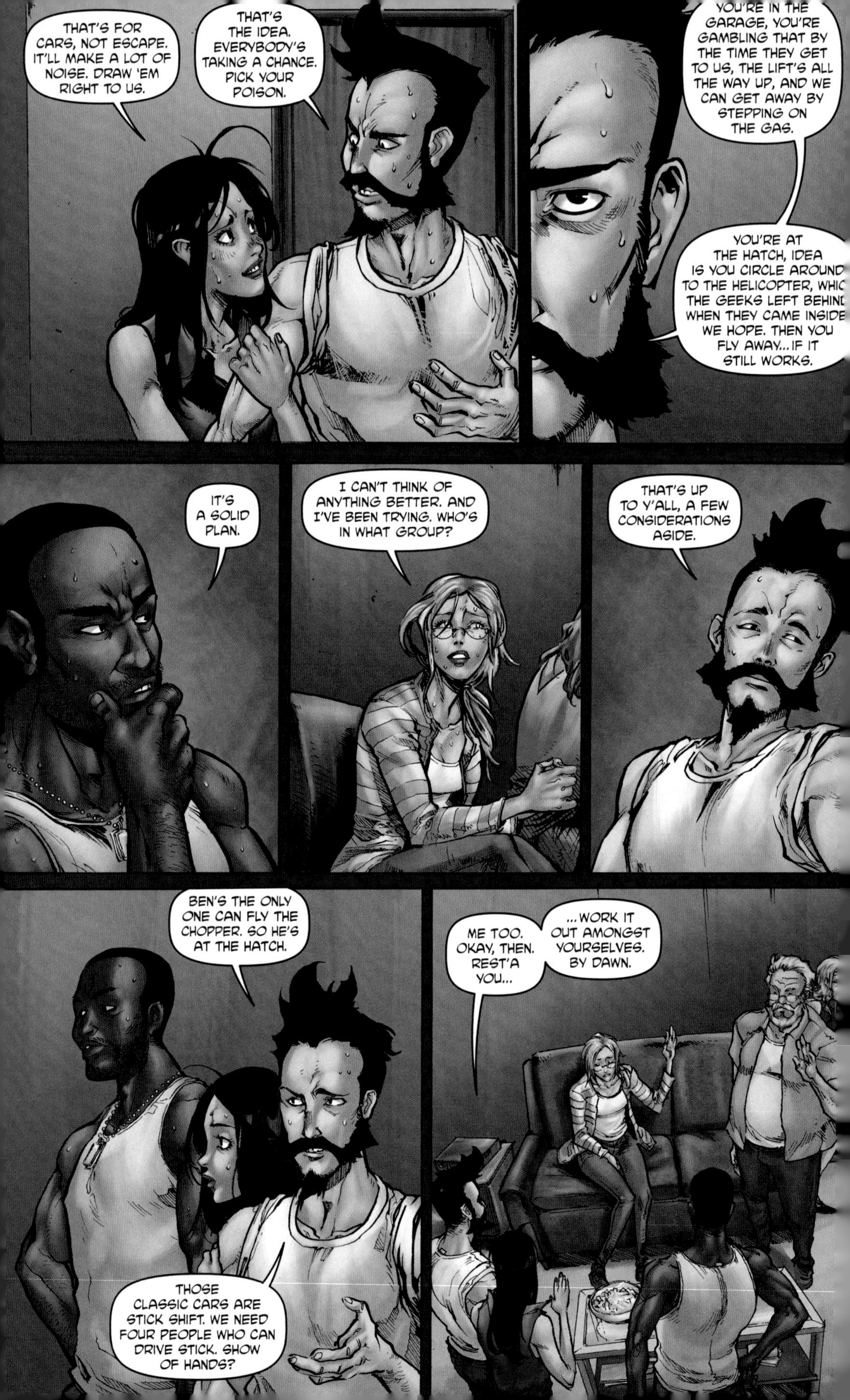
THAT'S FOR CARS, NOT ESCAPE. IT'LL MAKE A LOT OF NOISE. DRAW 'EM RIGHT TO US.
THAT'S THE IDEA. EVERYBODY'S TAKING A CHANCE. PICK YOUR POISON.
YOU'RE IN THE GARAGE, YOU'RE GAMBLING THAT BY THE TIME THEY GET TO US, THE LIFT'S ALL THE WAY UP, AND WE CAN GET AWAY BY STEPPING ON THE GAS.
YOU'RE AT THE HATCH, IDEA IS YOU CIRCLE AROUND TO THE HELICOPTER, WHIC THE GEEKS LEFT BEHIND WHEN THEY CAME INSIDE WE HOPE. THEN YOU FLY AWAY... IF IT STILL WORKS.
IT'S A SOLID PLAN.
I CAN'T THINK OF ANYTHING BETTER. AND I'VE BEEN TRYING. WHO'S IN WHAT GROUP?
THAT'S UP TO Y'ALL, A FEW CONSIDERATIONS ASIDE.
BEN'S THE ONLY ONE CAN FLY THE CHOPPER. SO HE'S AT THE HATCH.
THOSE CLASSIC CARS ARE STICK SHIFT. WE NEED FOUR PEOPLE WHO CAN DRIVE STICK. SHOW OF HANDS?
ME TOO. OKAY, THEN. REST'A YOU...
...WORK IT OUT AMONGST YOURSELVES. BY DAWN.

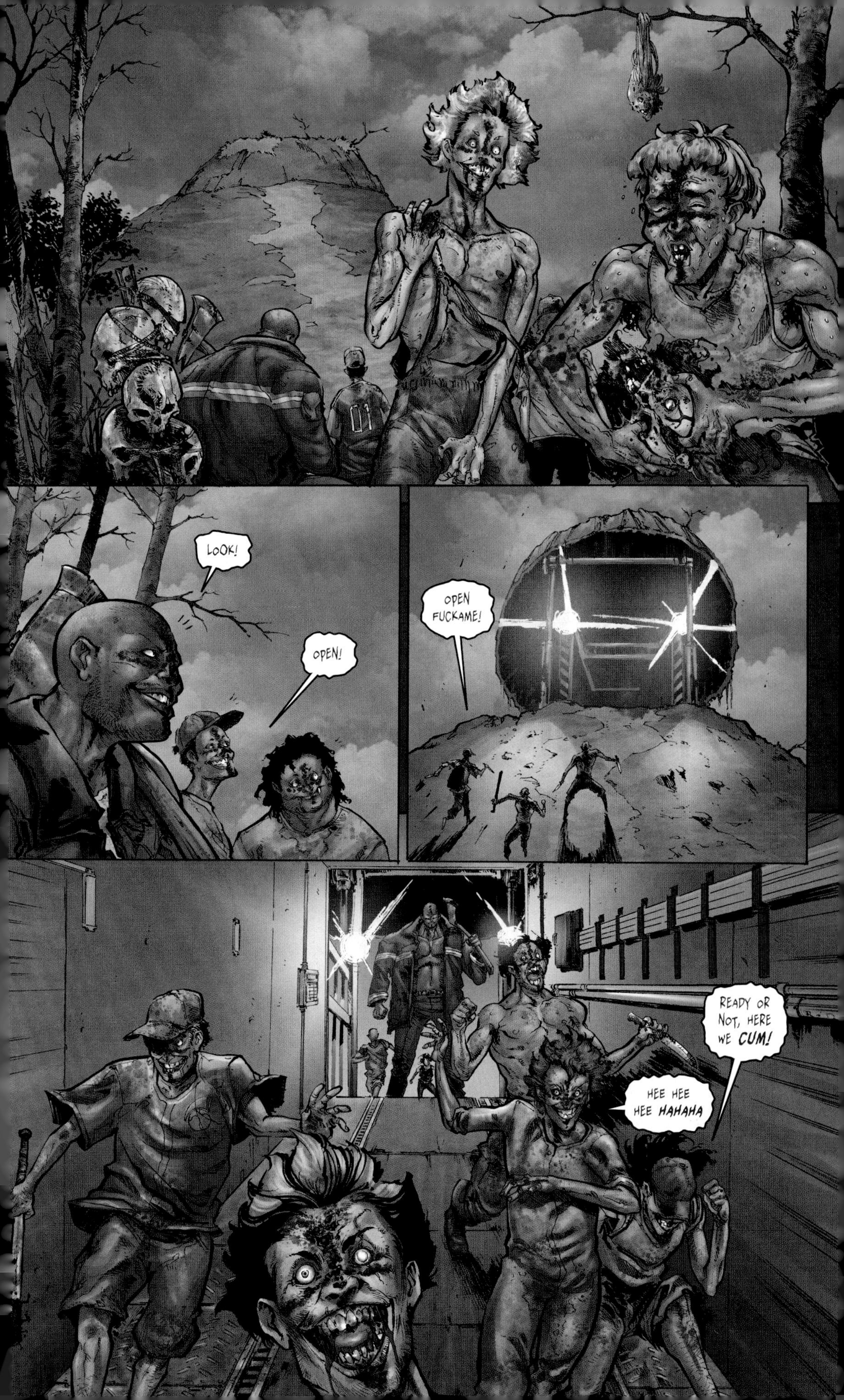
LOOK!
OPEN!
OPEN FUCKAME!
READY OR NOT, HERE WE CUM!
HEE HEE HEE HAHAHA

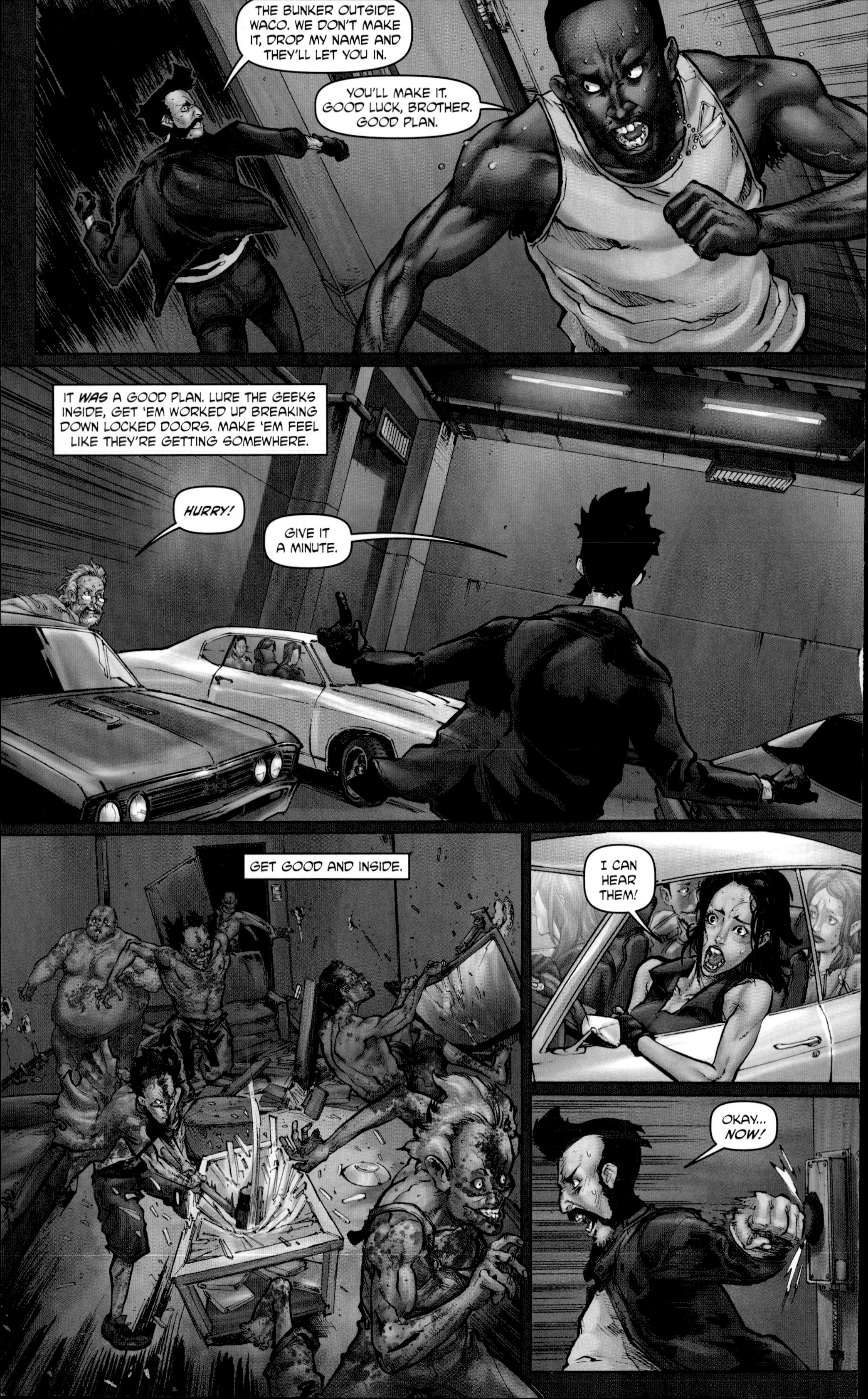
THE BUNKER OUTSIDE WACO. WE DON'T MAKE IT, DROP MY NAME AND THEY'LL LET YOU IN.
YOU'LL MAKE IT. GOOD LUCK, BROTHER. GOOD PLAN.
IT *WAS* A GOOD PLAN. LURE THE GEEKS INSIDE, GET 'EM WORKED UP BREAKING DOWN LOCKED DOORS. MAKE 'EM FEEL LIKE THEY'RE GETTING SOMEWHERE.
HURRY!
GIVE IT A MINUTE.
GET GOOD AND INSIDE.
I CAN HEAR THEM!
OKAY... *NOW!*

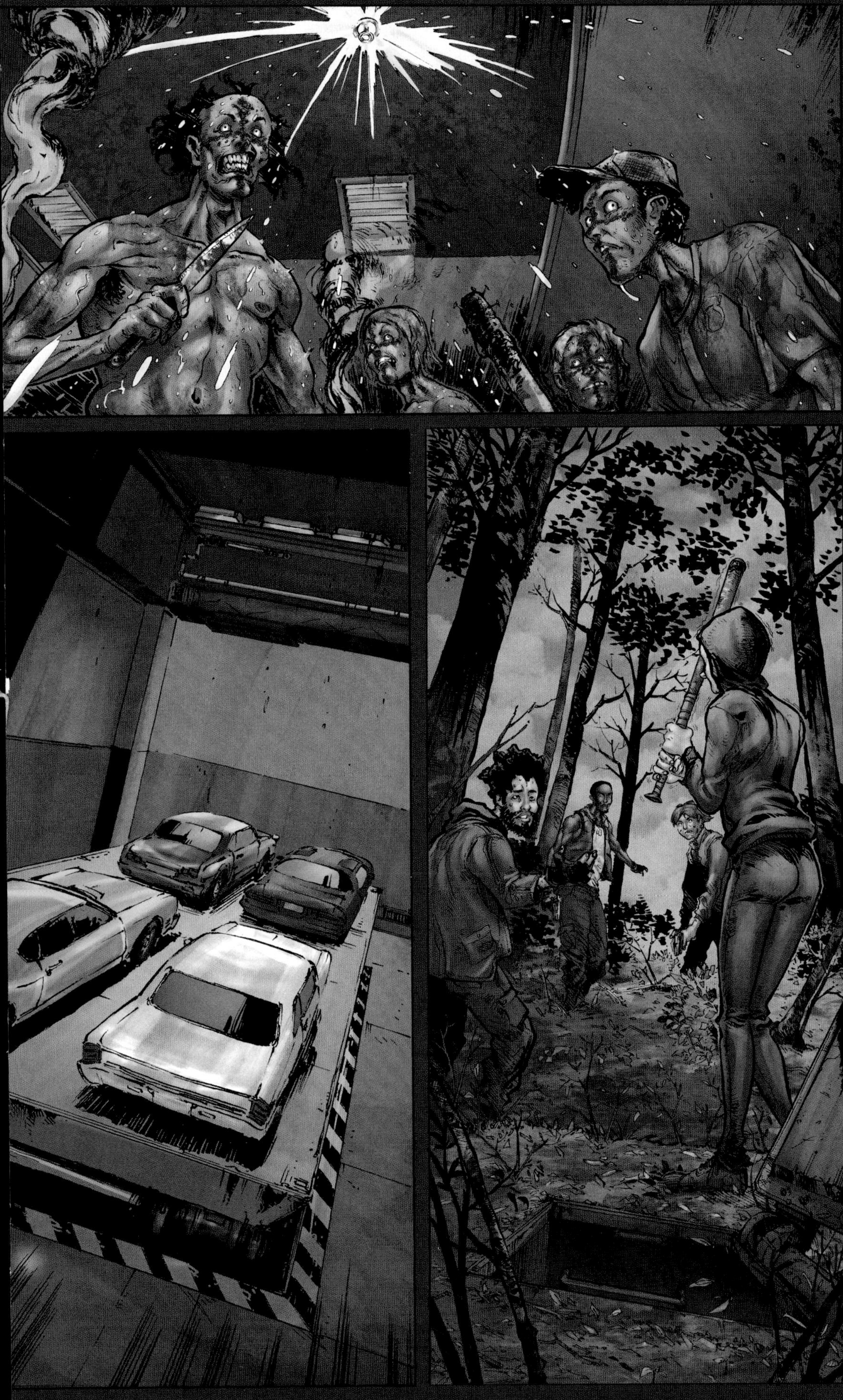

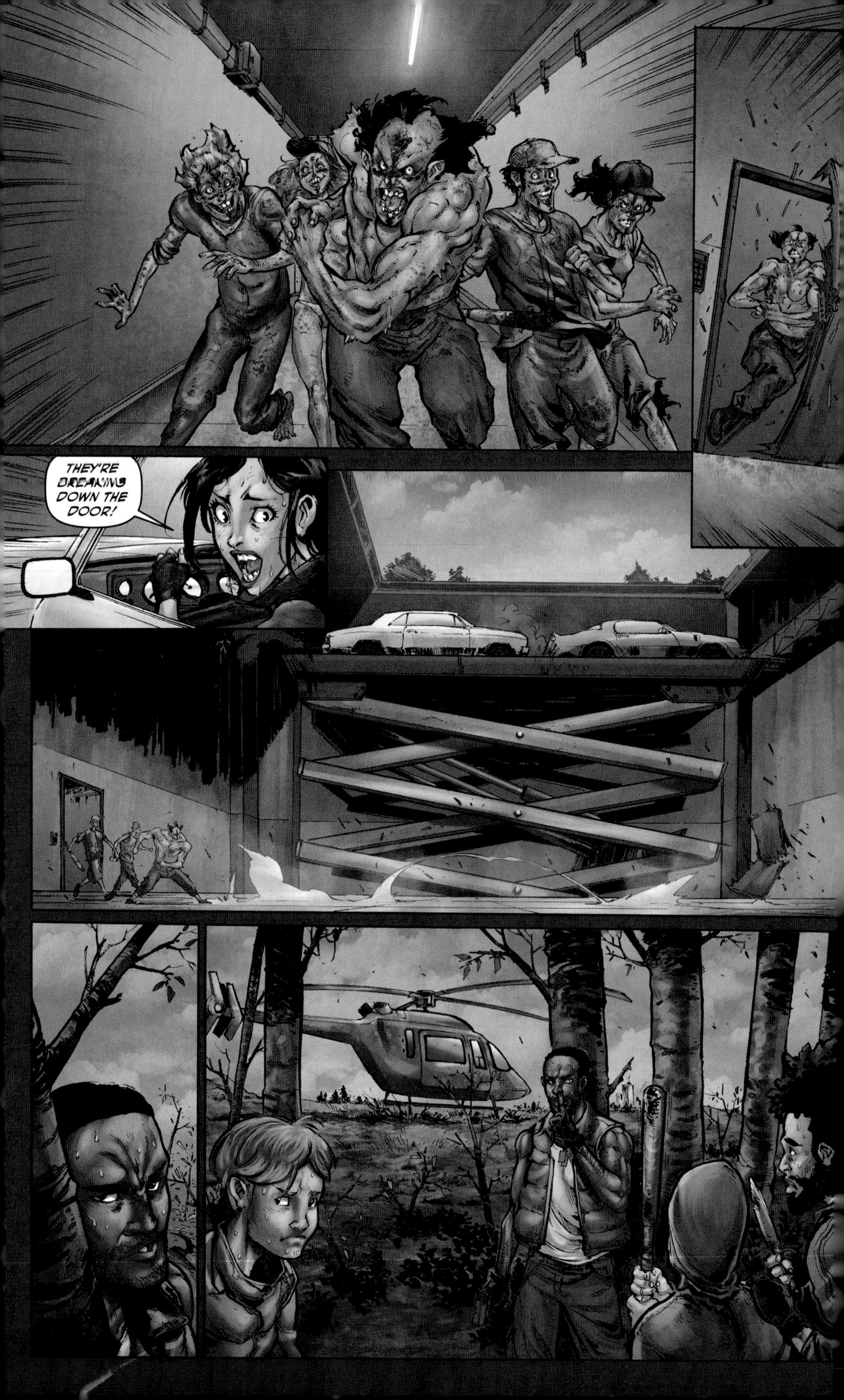
THEY'RE BREAKING DOWN THE DOOR!

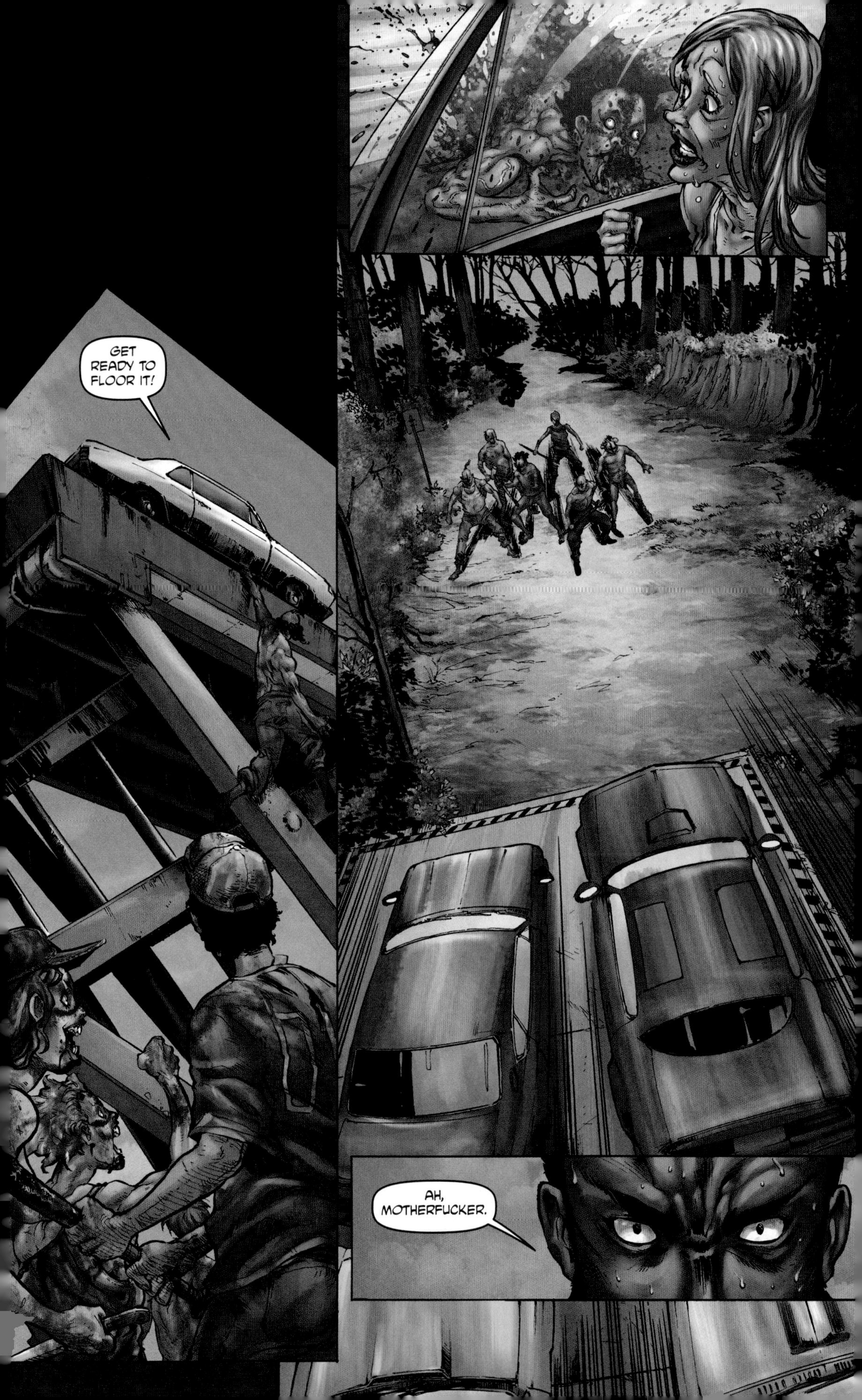
GET READY TO FLOOR IT!
AH, MOTHERFUCKER.

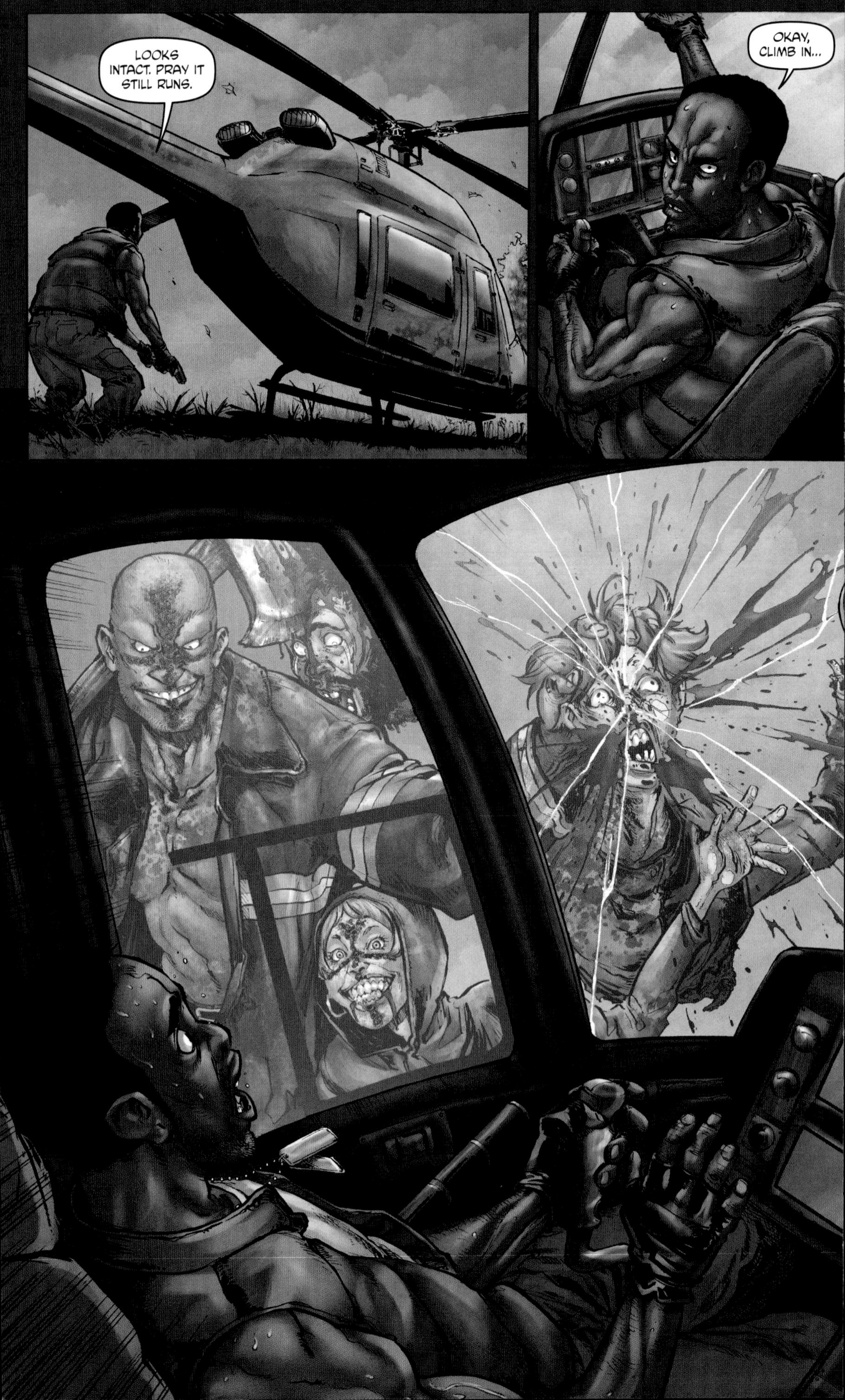
LOOKS INTACT. PRAY IT STILL RUNS.
OKAY, CLIMB IN...

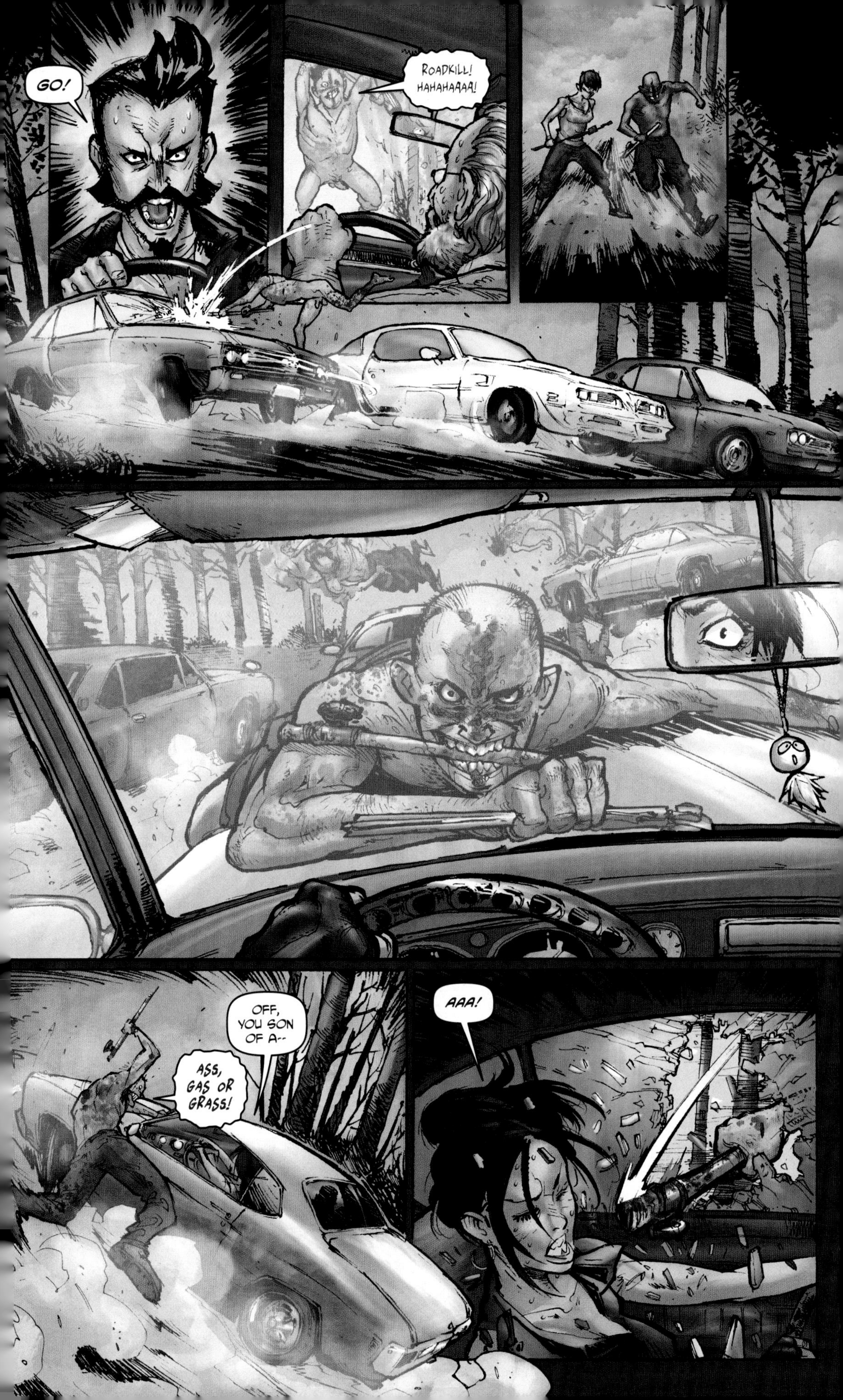
GO!
ROADKILL! HAHAHAAAA!
OFF, YOU SON OF A--
ASS, GAS OR GRASS!
AAA!

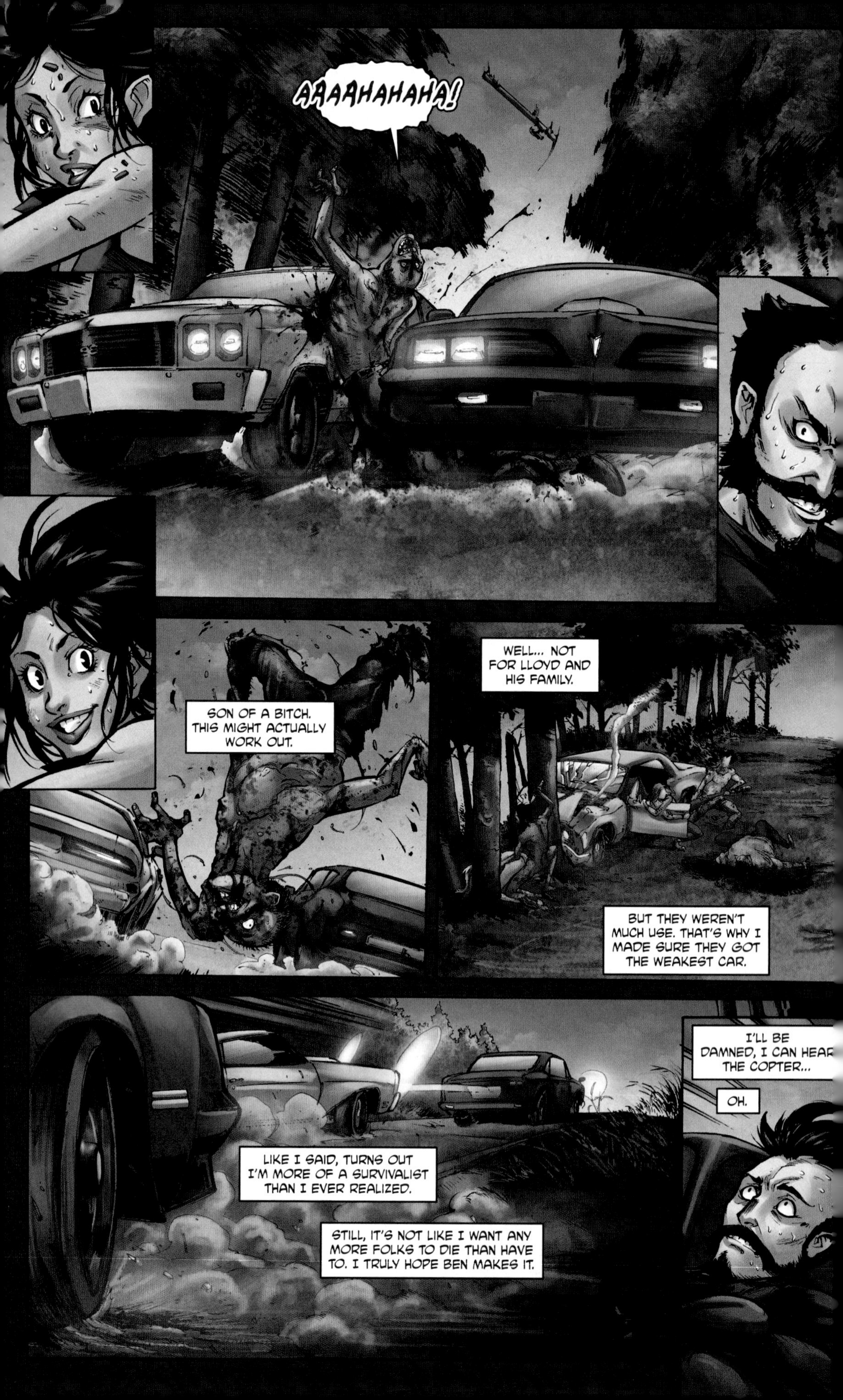
AAAAHAHAHA!
SON OF A BITCH. THIS MIGHT ACTUALLY WORK OUT.
WELL... NOT FOR LLOYD AND HIS FAMILY.
BUT THEY WEREN'T MUCH USE. THAT'S WHY I MADE SURE THEY GOT THE WEAKEST CAR.
LIKE I SAID, TURNS OUT I'M MORE OF A SURVIVALIST THAN I EVER REALIZED.
STILL, IT'S NOT LIKE I WANT ANY MORE FOLKS TO DIE THAN HAVE TO. I TRULY HOPE BEN MAKES IT.
I'LL BE DAMNED, I CAN HEAR THE COPTER...
OH.

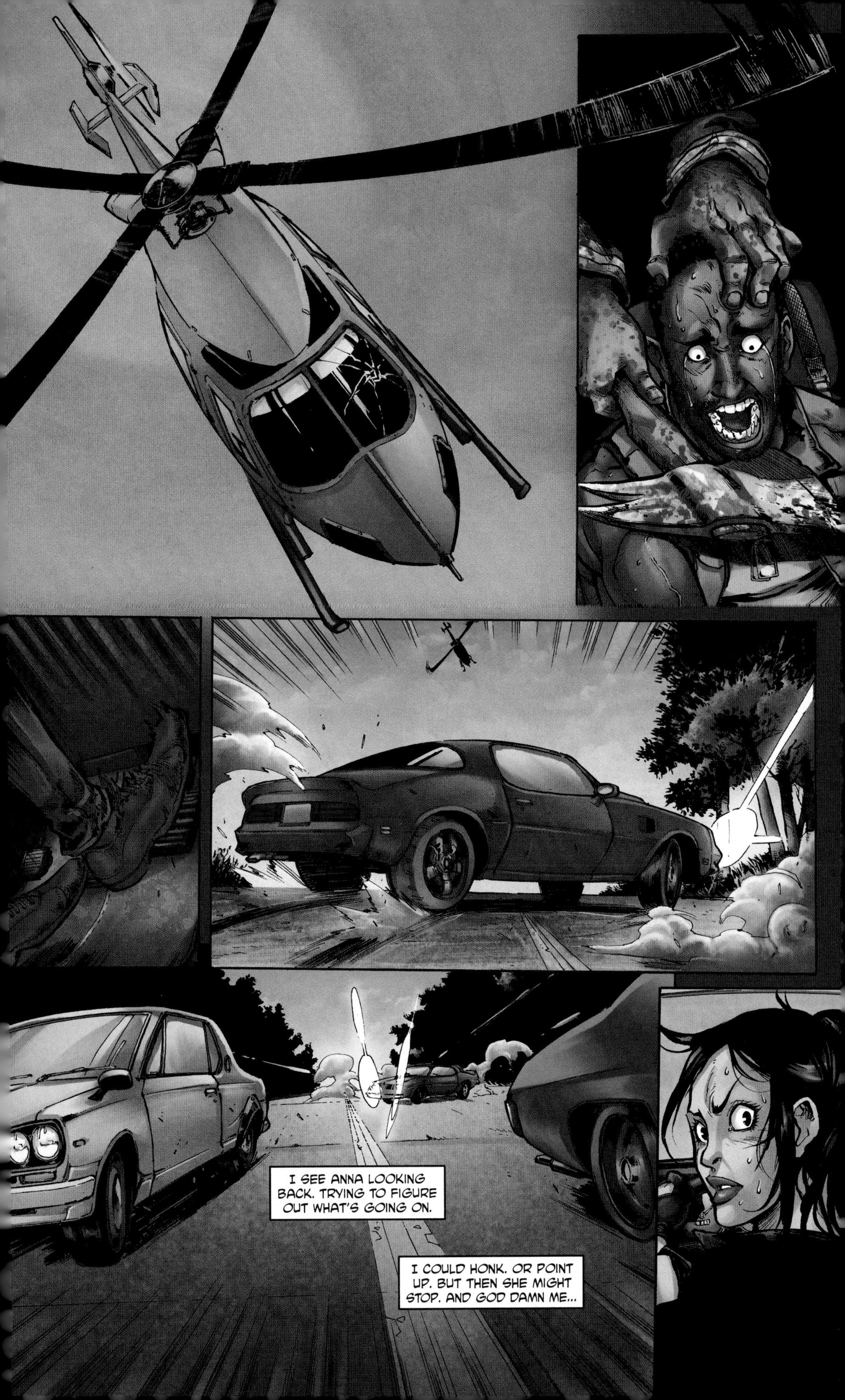
I SEE ANNA LOOKING BACK. TRYING TO FIGURE OUT WHAT'S GOING ON.
I COULD HONK. OR POINT UP. BUT THEN SHE MIGHT STOP. AND GOD DAMN ME...

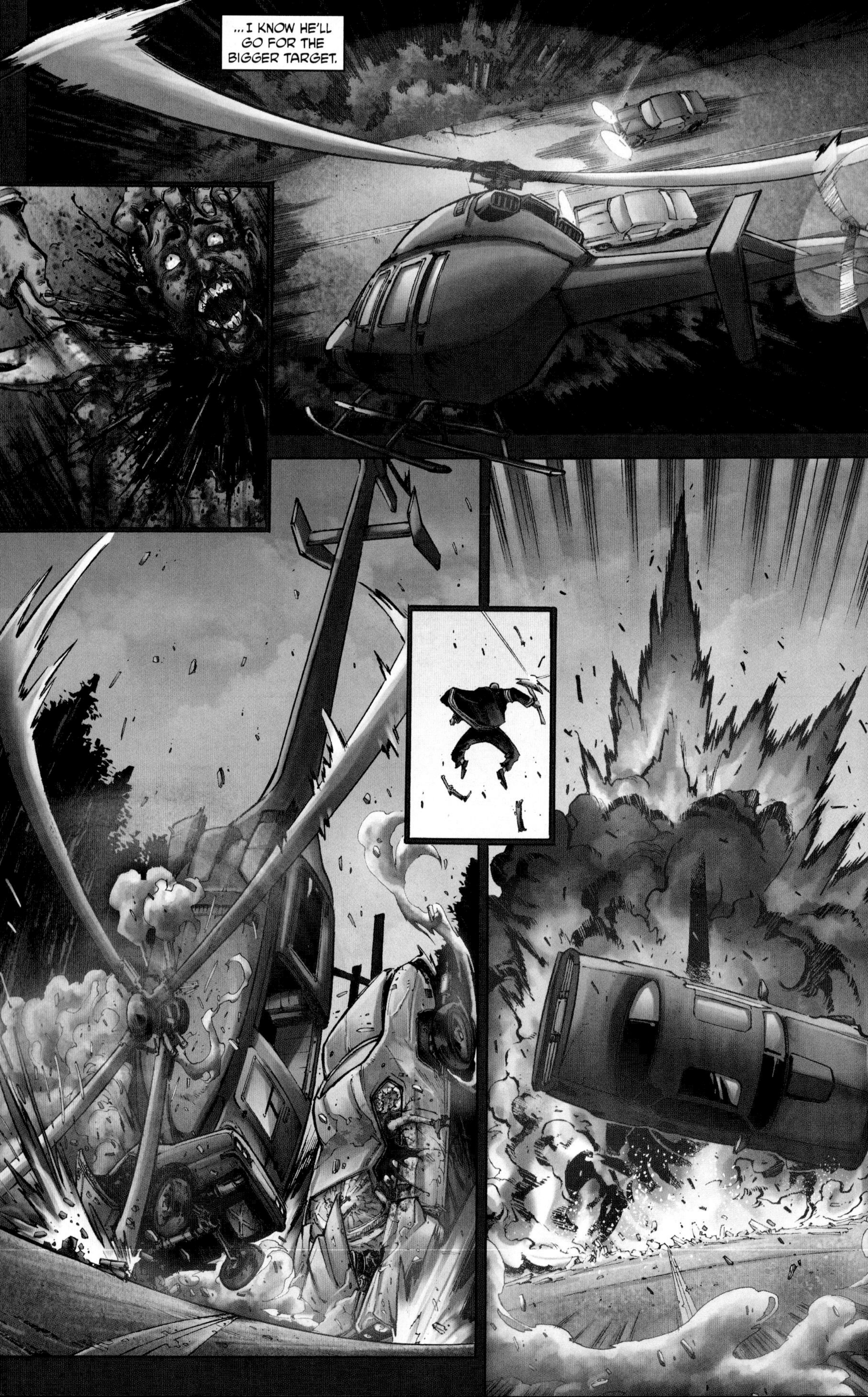
...I KNOW HE'LL GO FOR THE BIGGER TARGET.

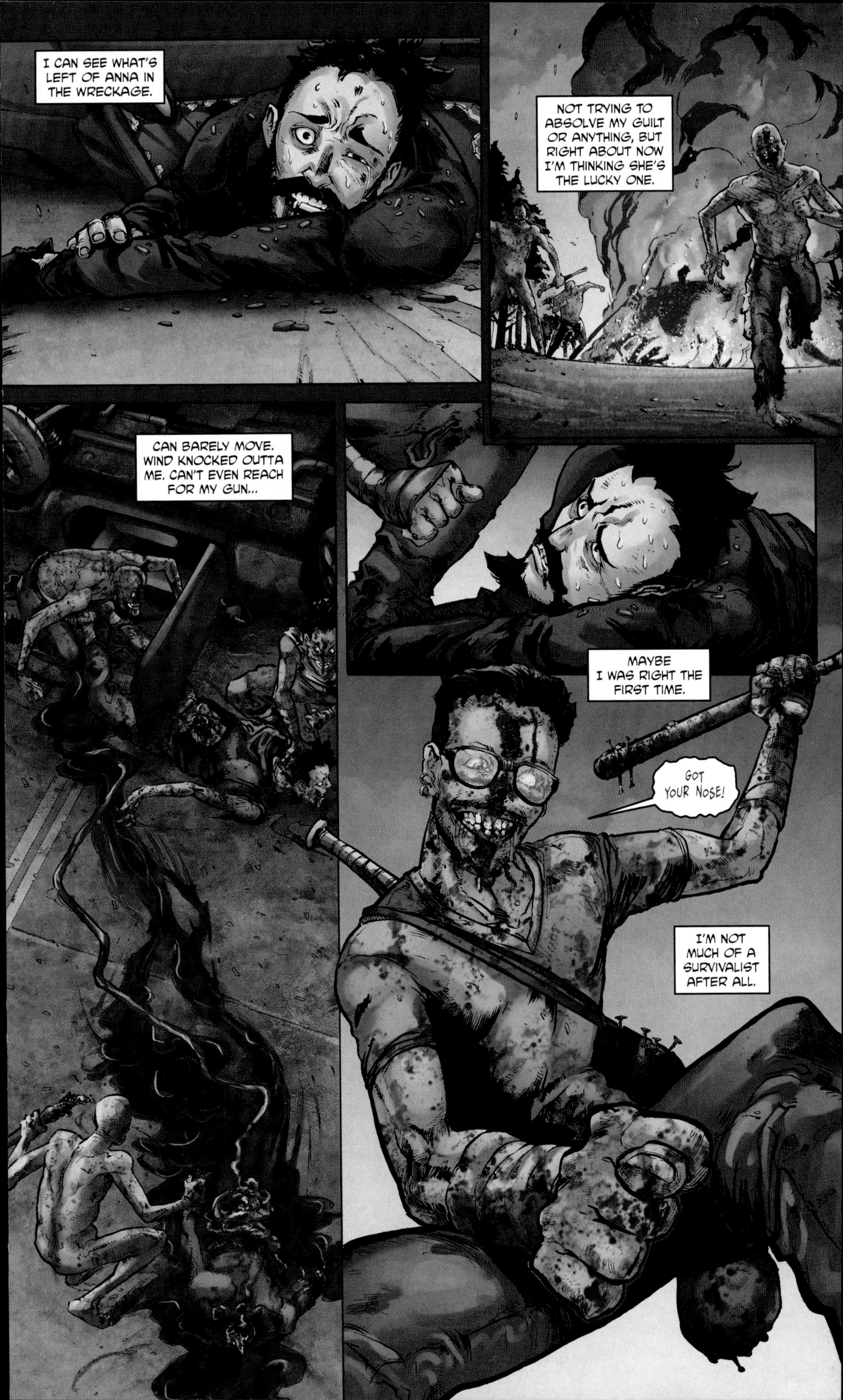
I CAN SEE WHAT'S LEFT OF ANNA IN THE WRECKAGE.
NOT TRYING TO ABSOLVE MY GUILT OR ANYTHING, BUT RIGHT ABOUT NOW I'M THINKING SHE'S THE LUCKY ONE.
CAN BARELY MOVE. WIND KNOCKED OUTTA ME. CAN'T EVEN REACH FOR MY GUN...
MAYBE I WAS RIGHT THE FIRST TIME.
GOT YOUR NOSE!
I'M NOT MUCH OF A SURVIVALIST AFTER ALL.

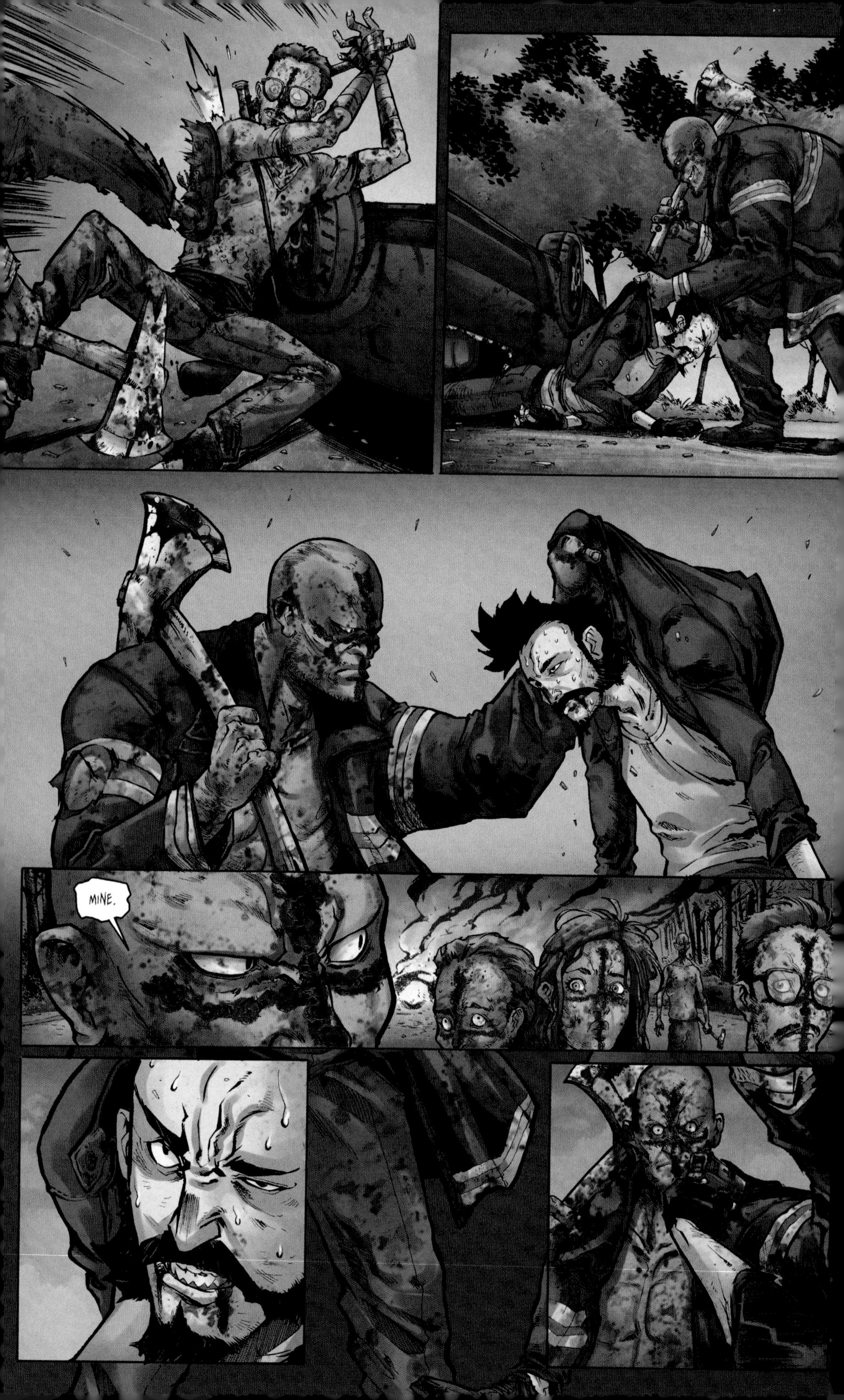
MINE.

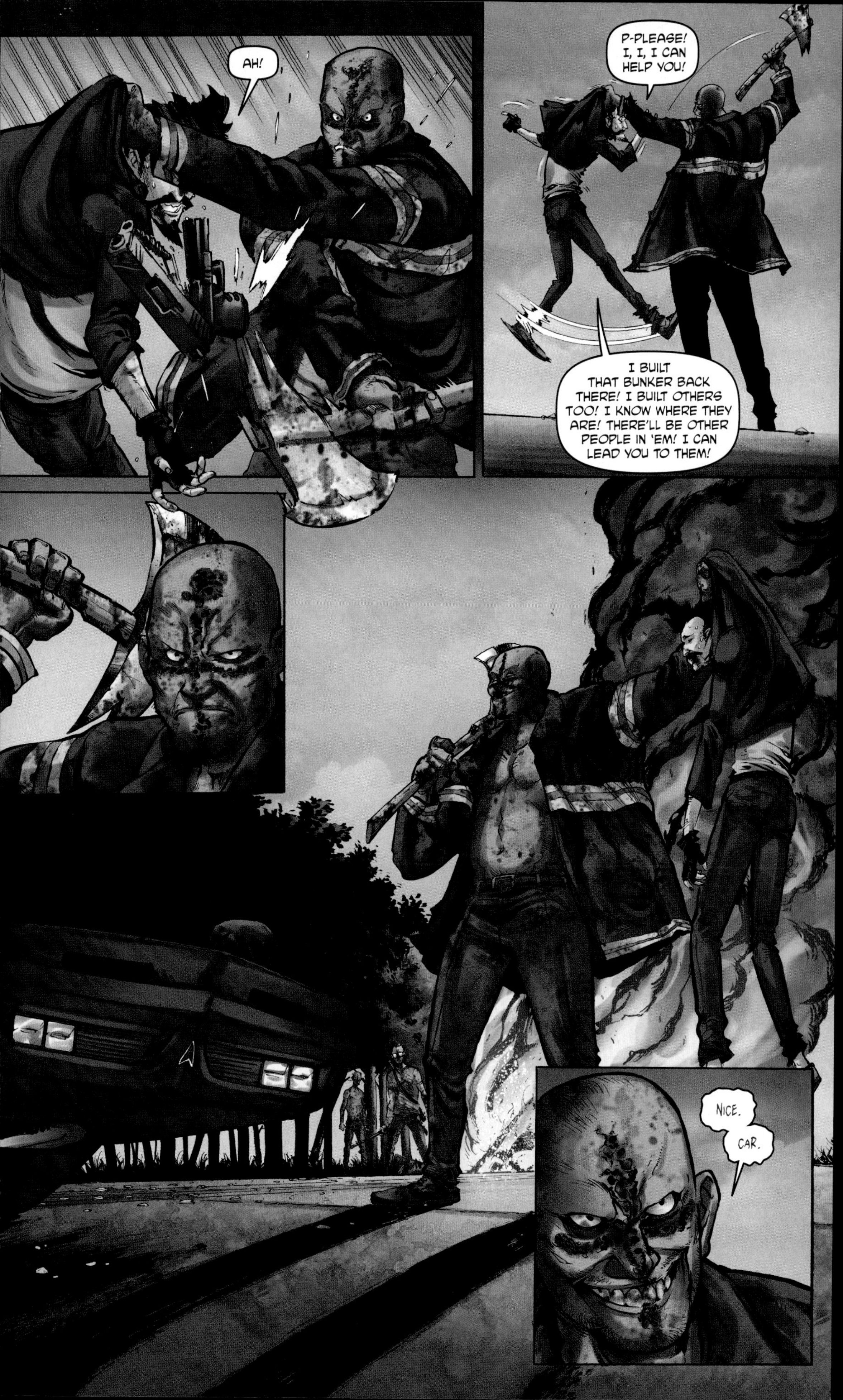
AH!
P-PLEASE! I, I, I CAN HELP YOU!
I BUILT THAT BUNKER BACK THERE! I BUILT OTHERS TOO! I KNOW WHERE THEY ARE! THERE'LL BE OTHER PEOPLE IN 'EM! I CAN LEAD YOU TO THEM!
NICE.
CAR.

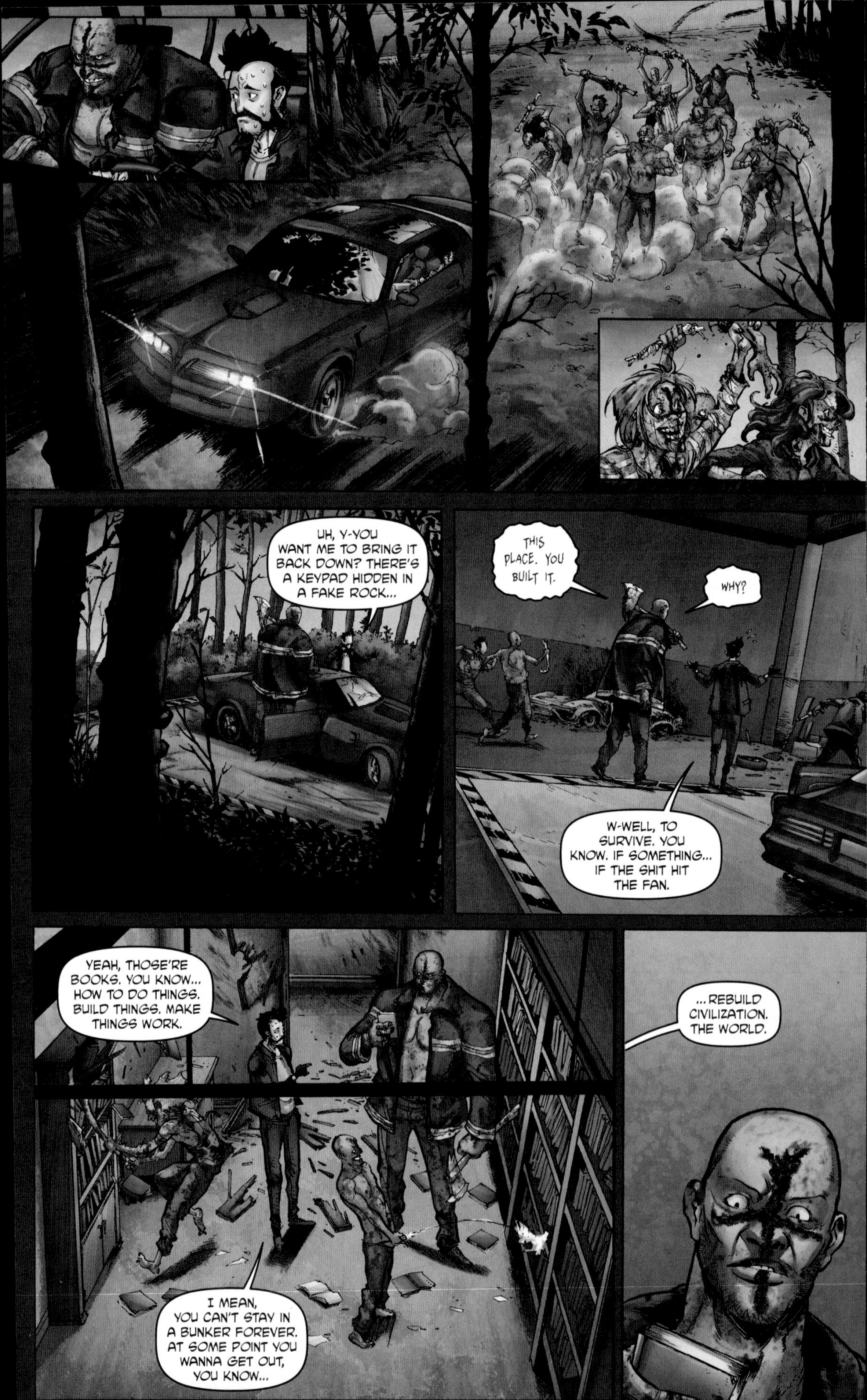
UH, Y-YOU WANT ME TO BRING IT BACK DOWN? THERE'S A KEYPAD HIDDEN IN A FAKE ROCK...
THIS PLACE. YOU BUILT IT.
WHY?
W-WELL, TO SURVIVE. YOU KNOW. IF SOMETHING... IF THE SHIT HIT THE FAN.
YEAH, THOSE'RE BOOKS. YOU KNOW... HOW TO DO THINGS. BUILD THINGS. MAKE THINGS WORK.
I MEAN, YOU CAN'T STAY IN A BUNKER FOREVER. AT SOME POINT YOU WANNA GET OUT, YOU KNOW...
...REBUILD CIVILIZATION. THE WORLD.

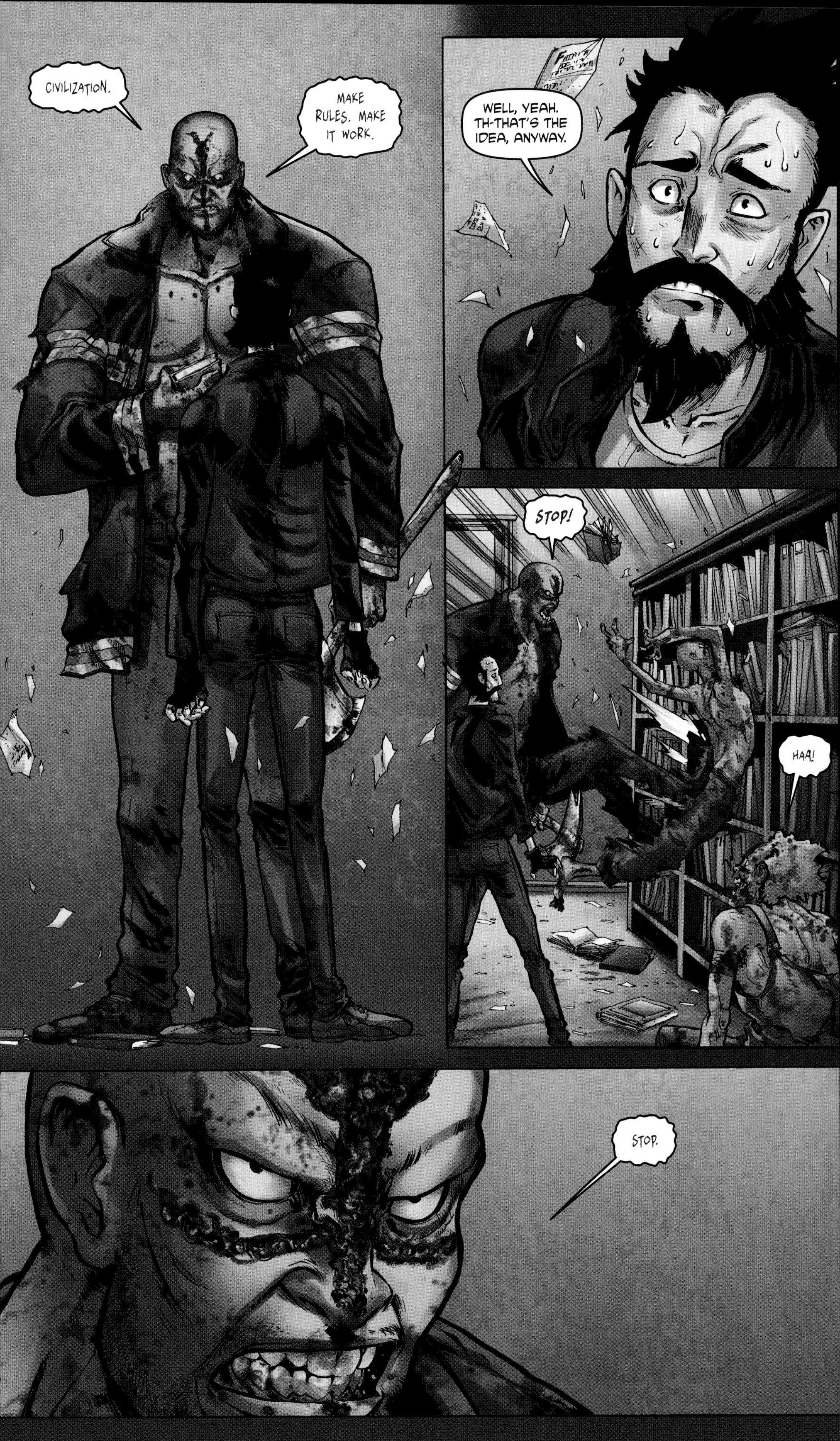
CIVILIZATION.
MAKE RULES. MAKE IT WORK.
WELL, YEAH. TH-THAT'S THE IDEA, ANYWAY.
STOP!
HAA!
STOP.

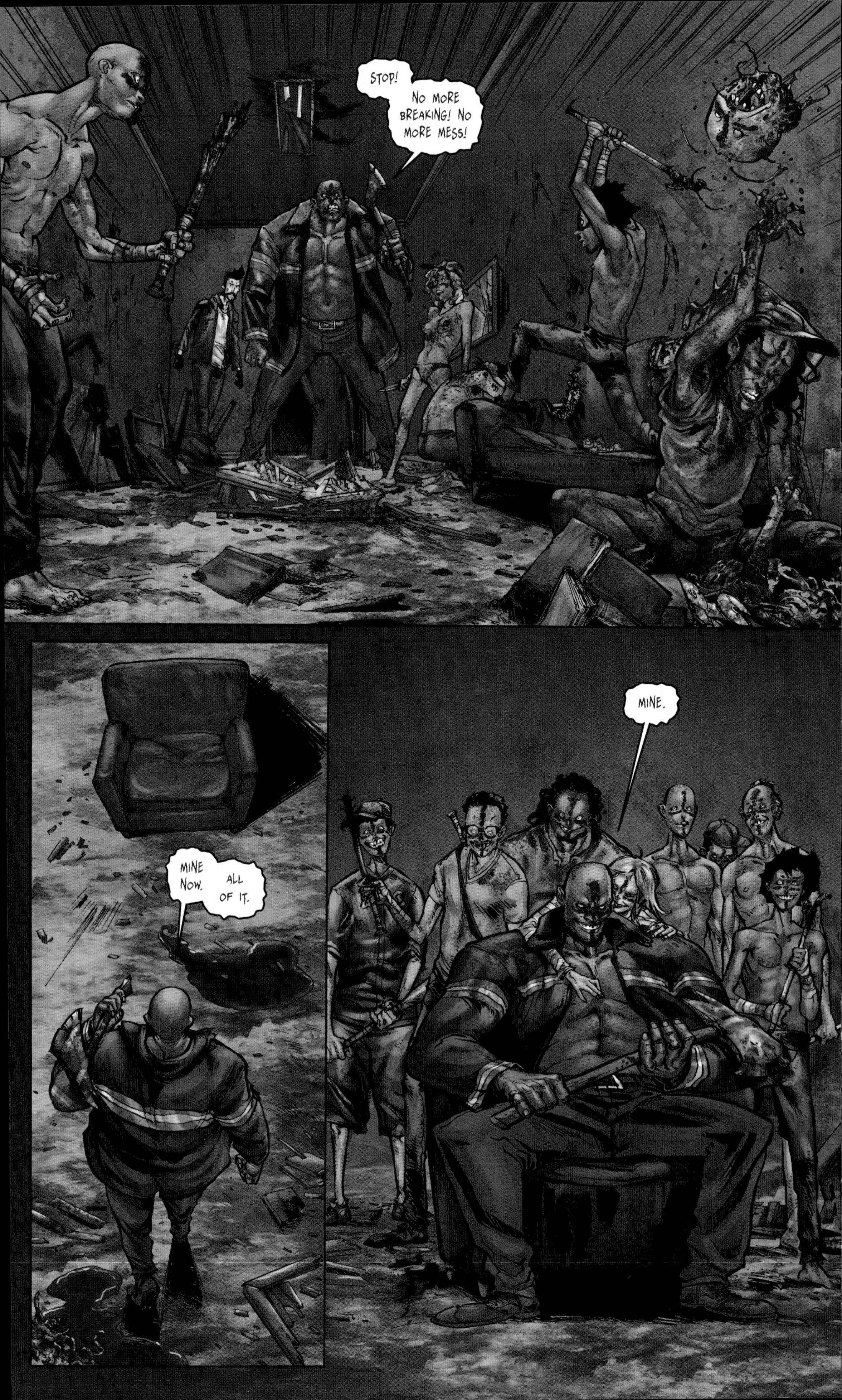
STOP!
NO MORE BREAKING! NO MORE MESS!
MINE NOW.
ALL OF IT.
MINE.

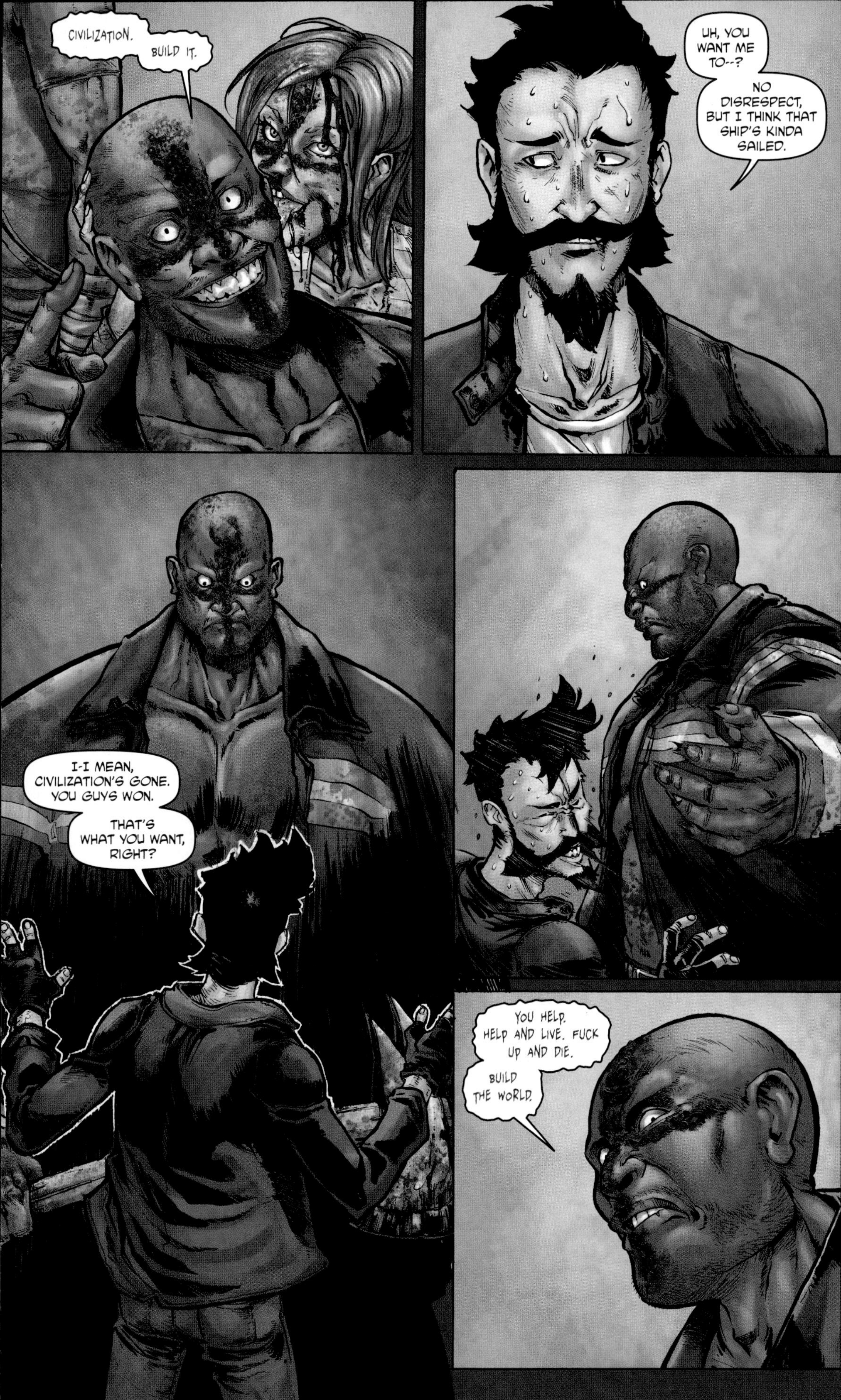
CIVILIZATION.
BUILD IT.
UH, YOU WANT ME TO--?
NO DISRESPECT, BUT I THINK THAT SHIP'S KINDA SAILED.
I-I MEAN, CIVILIZATION'S GONE. YOU GUYS WON.
THAT'S WHAT YOU WANT, RIGHT?
YOU HELP. HELP AND LIVE. FUCK UP AND DIE.
BUILD THE WORLD.

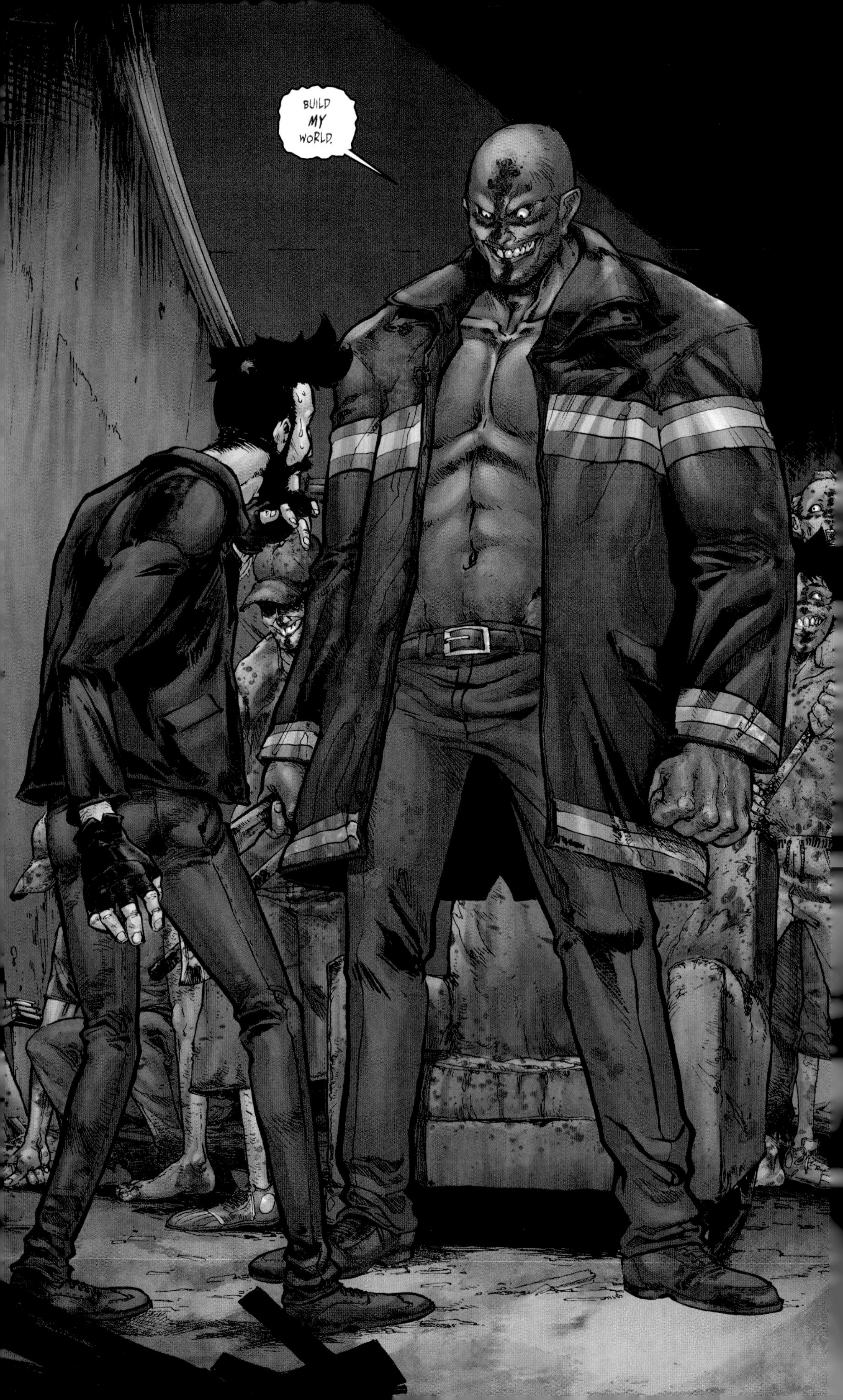
BUILD MY WORLD.

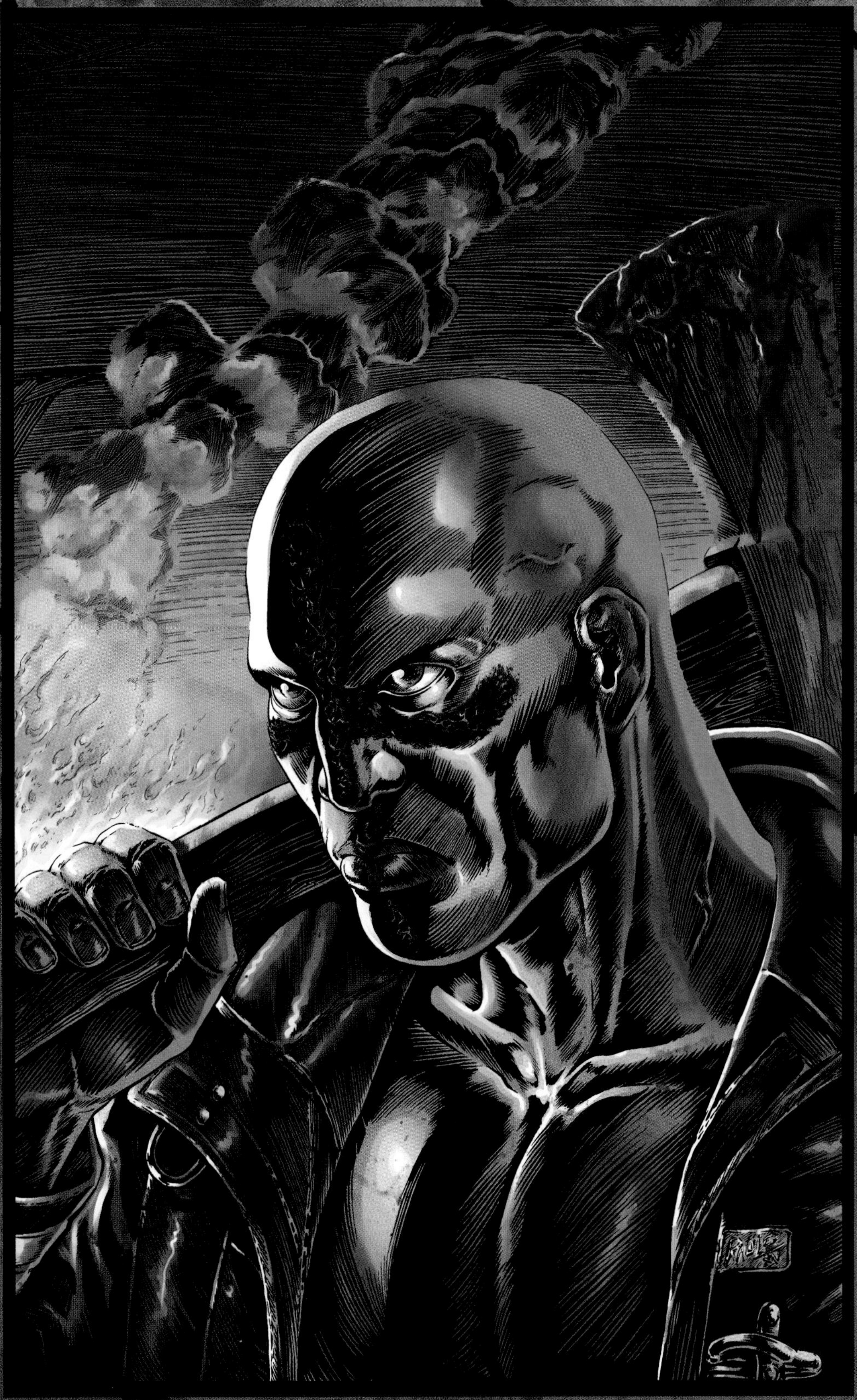

PART 3

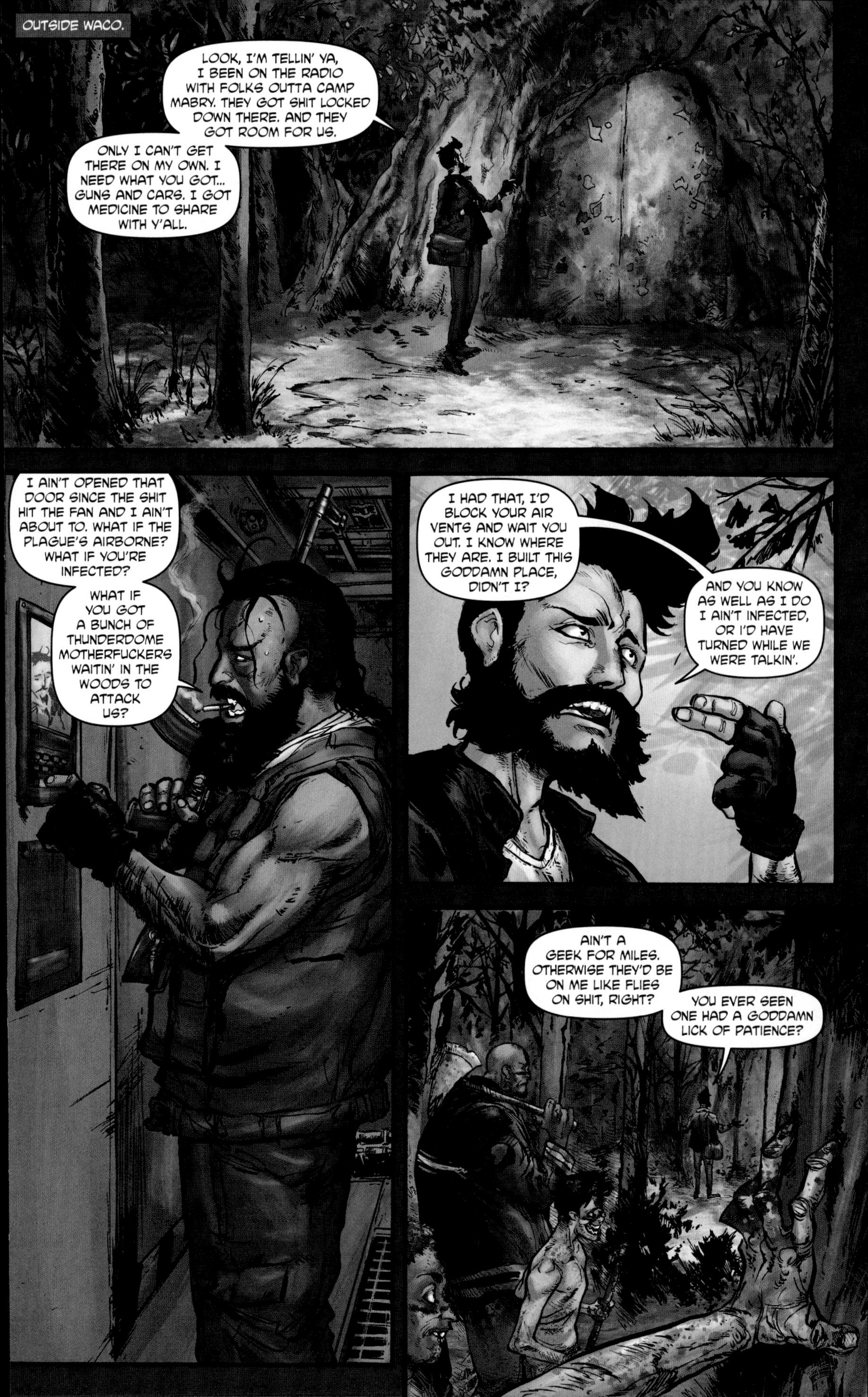
OUTSIDE WACO.
LOOK, I'M TELLIN' YA, I BEEN ON THE RADIO WITH FOLKS OUTTA CAMP MABRY. THEY GOT SHIT LOCKED DOWN THERE. AND THEY GOT ROOM FOR US.
ONLY I CAN'T GET THERE ON MY OWN. I NEED WHAT YOU GOT... GUNS AND CARS. I GOT MEDICINE TO SHARE WITH Y'ALL.
I AIN'T OPENED THAT DOOR SINCE THE SHIT HIT THE FAN AND I AIN'T ABOUT TO. WHAT IF THE PLAGUE'S AIRBORNE? WHAT IF YOU'RE INFECTED?
WHAT IF YOU GOT A BUNCH OF THUNDERDOME MOTHERFUCKERS WAITIN' IN THE WOODS TO ATTACK US?
I HAD THAT, I'D BLOCK YOUR AIR VENTS AND WAIT YOU OUT. I KNOW WHERE THEY ARE. I BUILT THIS GODDAMN PLACE, DIDN'T I?
AND YOU KNOW AS WELL AS I DO I AIN'T INFECTED, OR I'D HAVE TURNED WHILE WE WERE TALKIN'.
AIN'T A GEEK FOR MILES. OTHERWISE THEY'D BE ON ME LIKE FLIES ON SHIT, RIGHT?
YOU EVER SEEN ONE HAD A GODDAMN LICK OF PATIENCE?

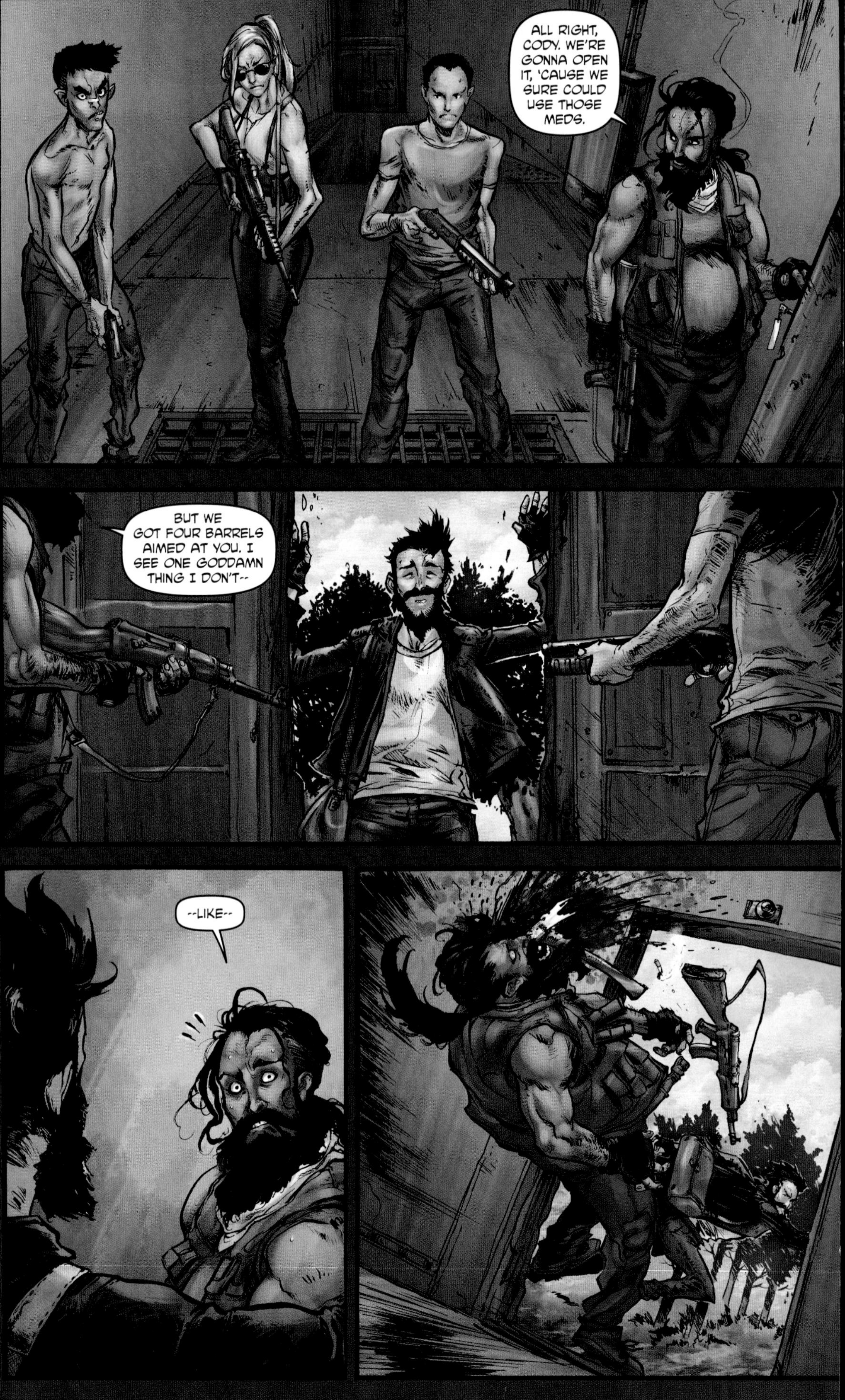
ALL RIGHT, CODY. WE'RE GONNA OPEN IT, 'CAUSE WE SURE COULD USE THOSE MEDS.
BUT WE GOT FOUR BARRELS AIMED AT YOU. I SEE ONE GODDAMN THING I DON'T--
--LIKE--

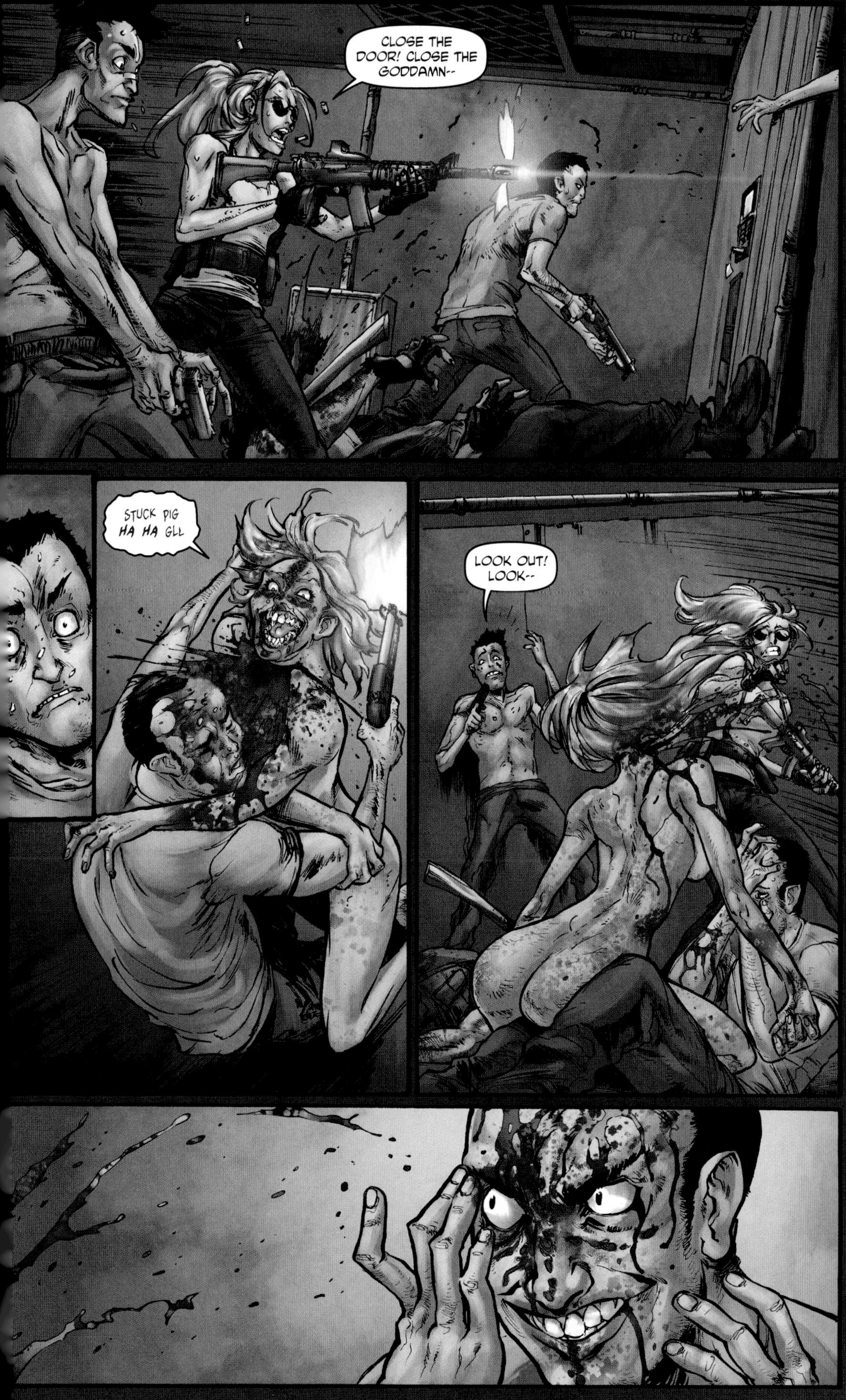
CLOSE THE DOOR! CLOSE THE GODDAMN--
STUCK PIG HA HA GLL
LOOK OUT! LOOK--

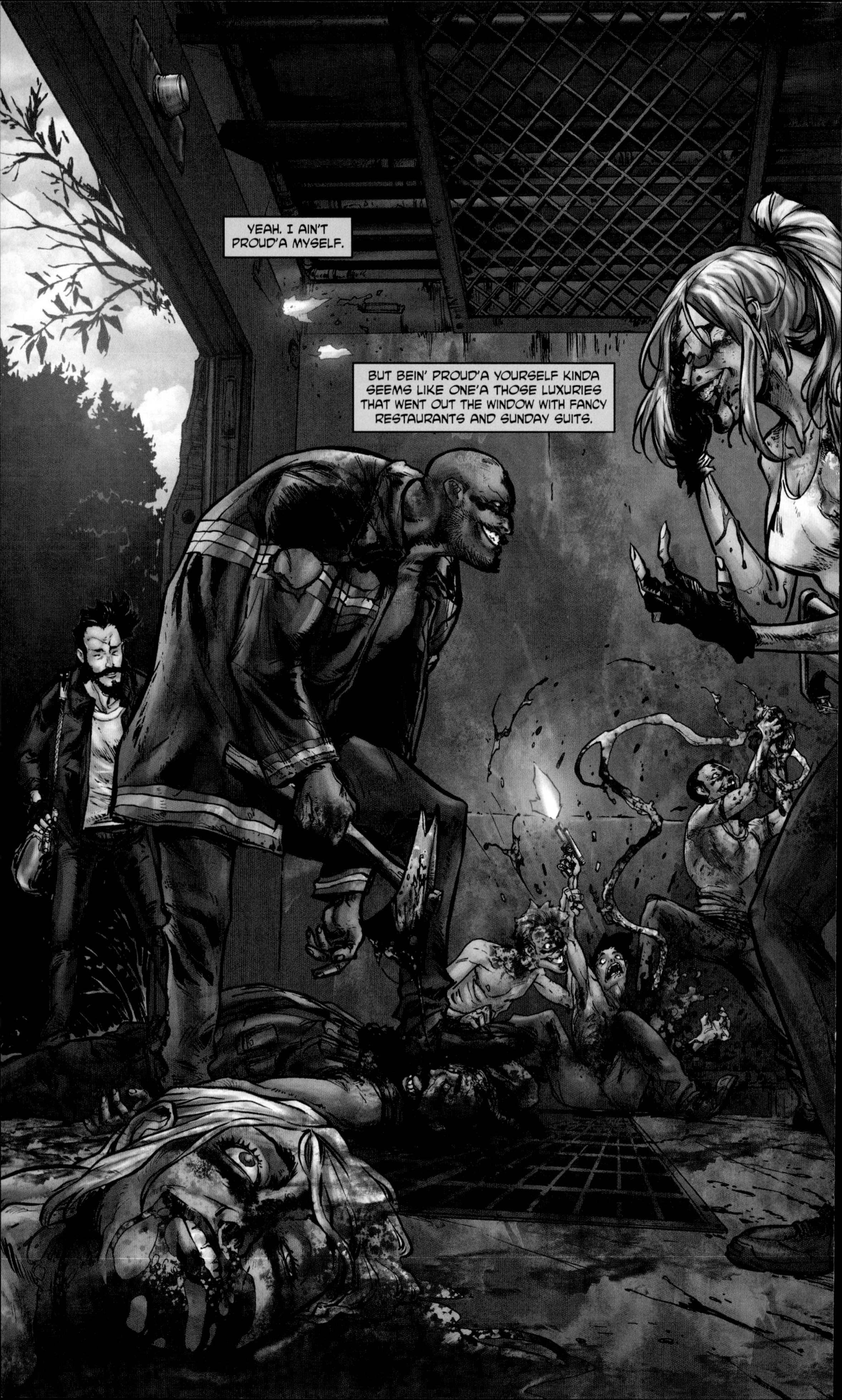
YEAH. I AIN'T PROUD'A MYSELF.
BUT BEIN' PROUD'A YOURSELF KINDA SEEMS LIKE ONE'A THOSE LUXURIES THAT WENT OUT THE WINDOW WITH FANCY RESTAURANTS AND SUNDAY SUITS.

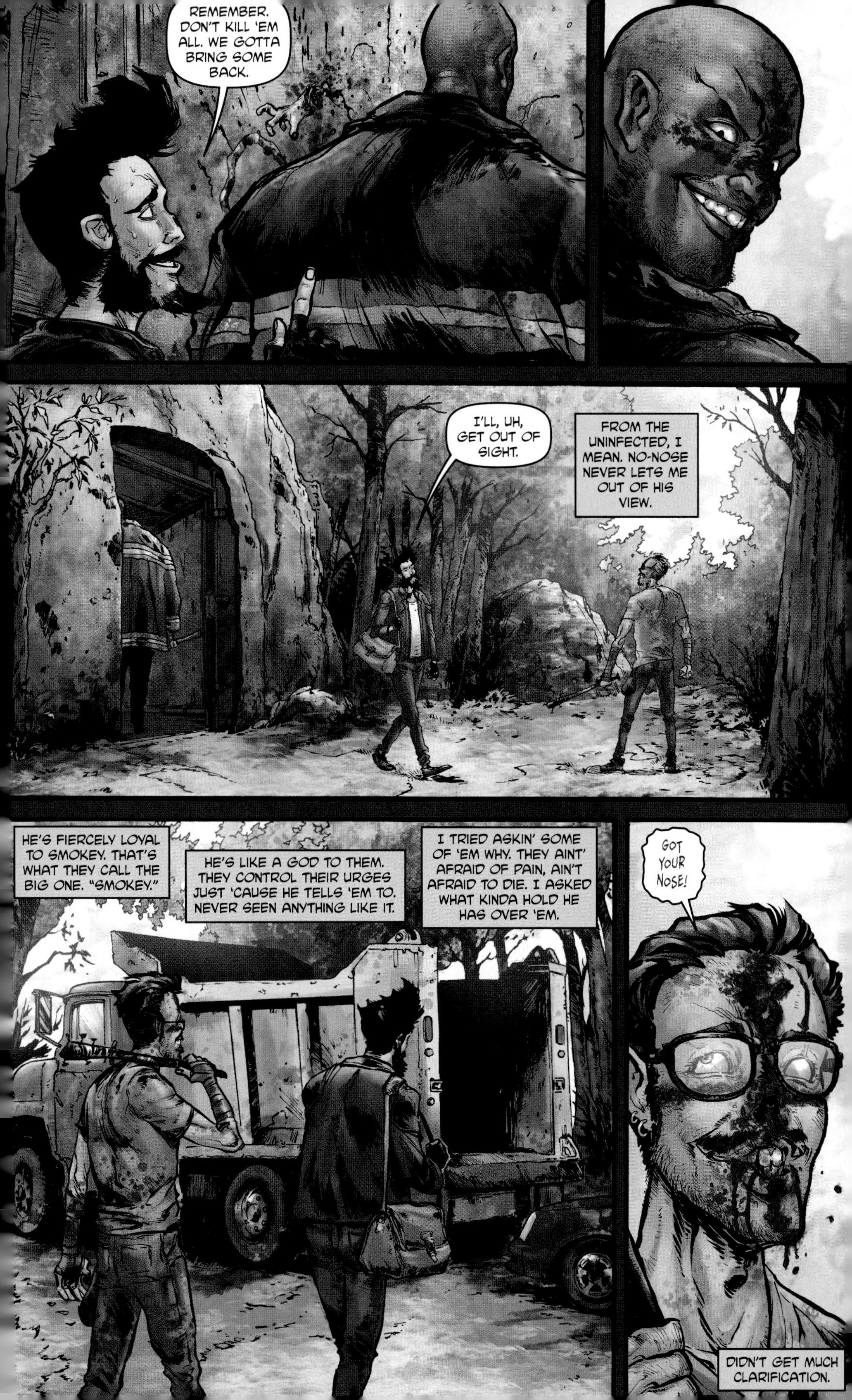
REMEMBER. DON'T KILL 'EM ALL. WE GOTTA BRING SOME BACK.
I'LL, UH, GET OUT OF SIGHT.
FROM THE UNINFECTED, I MEAN. NO-NOSE NEVER LETS ME OUT OF HIS VIEW.
HE'S FIERCELY LOYAL TO SMOKEY. THAT'S WHAT THEY CALL THE BIG ONE. "SMOKEY."
HE'S LIKE A GOD TO THEM. THEY CONTROL THEIR URGES JUST 'CAUSE HE TELLS 'EM TO. NEVER SEEN ANYTHING LIKE IT.
I TRIED ASKIN' SOME OF 'EM WHY. THEY AINT' AFRAID OF PAIN, AIN'T AFRAID TO DIE. I ASKED WHAT KINDA HOLD HE HAS OVER 'EM.
GOT YOUR NOSE!
DIDN'T GET MUCH CLARIFICATION.

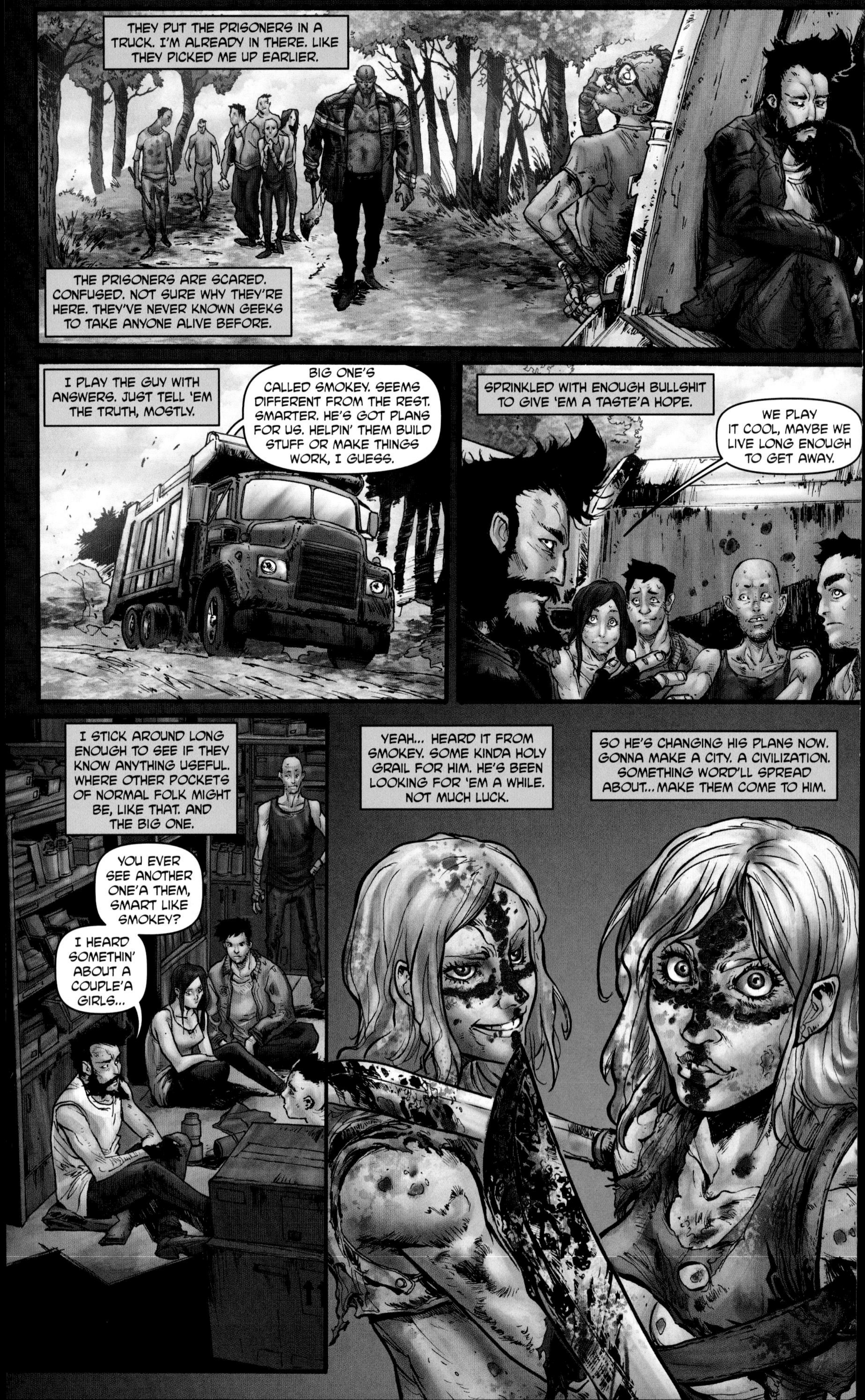
THEY PUT THE PRISONERS IN A TRUCK. I'M ALREADY IN THERE. LIKE THEY PICKED ME UP EARLIER.
THE PRISONERS ARE SCARED. CONFUSED. NOT SURE WHY THEY'RE HERE. THEY'VE NEVER KNOWN GEEKS TO TAKE ANYONE ALIVE BEFORE.
I PLAY THE GUY WITH ANSWERS. JUST TELL 'EM THE TRUTH, MOSTLY.
BIG ONE'S CALLED SMOKEY. SEEMS DIFFERENT FROM THE REST. SMARTER. HE'S GOT PLANS FOR US. HELPIN' THEM BUILD STUFF OR MAKE THINGS WORK, I GUESS.
SPRINKLED WITH ENOUGH BULLSHIT TO GIVE 'EM A TASTE'A HOPE.
WE PLAY IT COOL, MAYBE WE LIVE LONG ENOUGH TO GET AWAY.
I STICK AROUND LONG ENOUGH TO SEE IF THEY KNOW ANYTHING USEFUL. WHERE OTHER POCKETS OF NORMAL FOLK MIGHT BE, LIKE THAT. AND THE BIG ONE.
YOU EVER SEE ANOTHER ONE'A THEM, SMART LIKE SMOKEY?
I HEARD SOMETHIN' ABOUT A COUPLE'A GIRLS...
YEAH... HEARD IT FROM SMOKEY. SOME KINDA HOLY GRAIL FOR HIM. HE'S BEEN LOOKING FOR 'EM A WHILE. NOT MUCH LUCK.
SO HE'S CHANGING HIS PLANS NOW. GONNA MAKE A CITY. A CIVILIZATION. SOMETHING WORD'LL SPREAD ABOUT... MAKE THEM COME TO HIM.

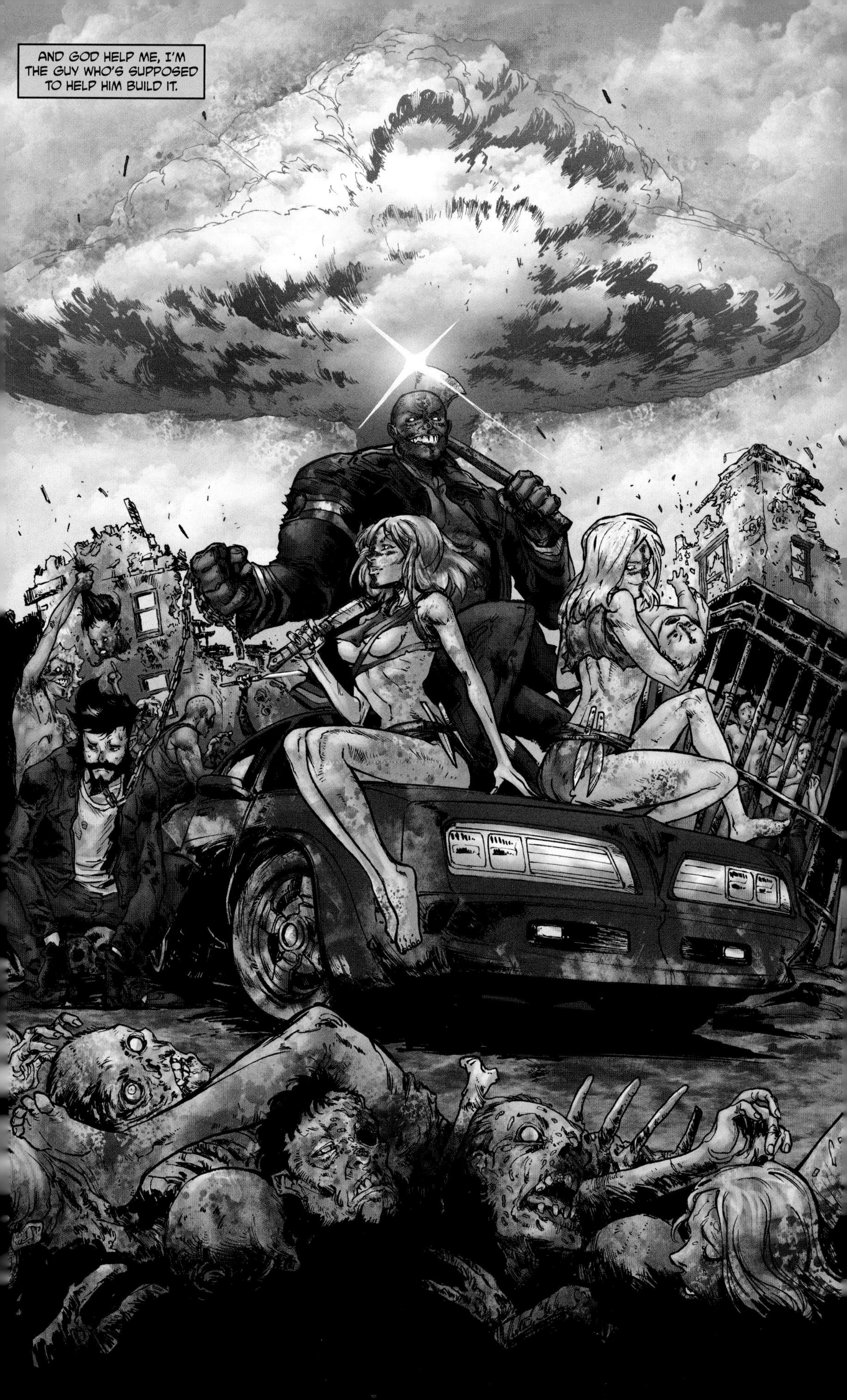
AND GOD HELP ME, I'M THE GUY WHO'S SUPPOSED TO HELP HIM BUILD IT.

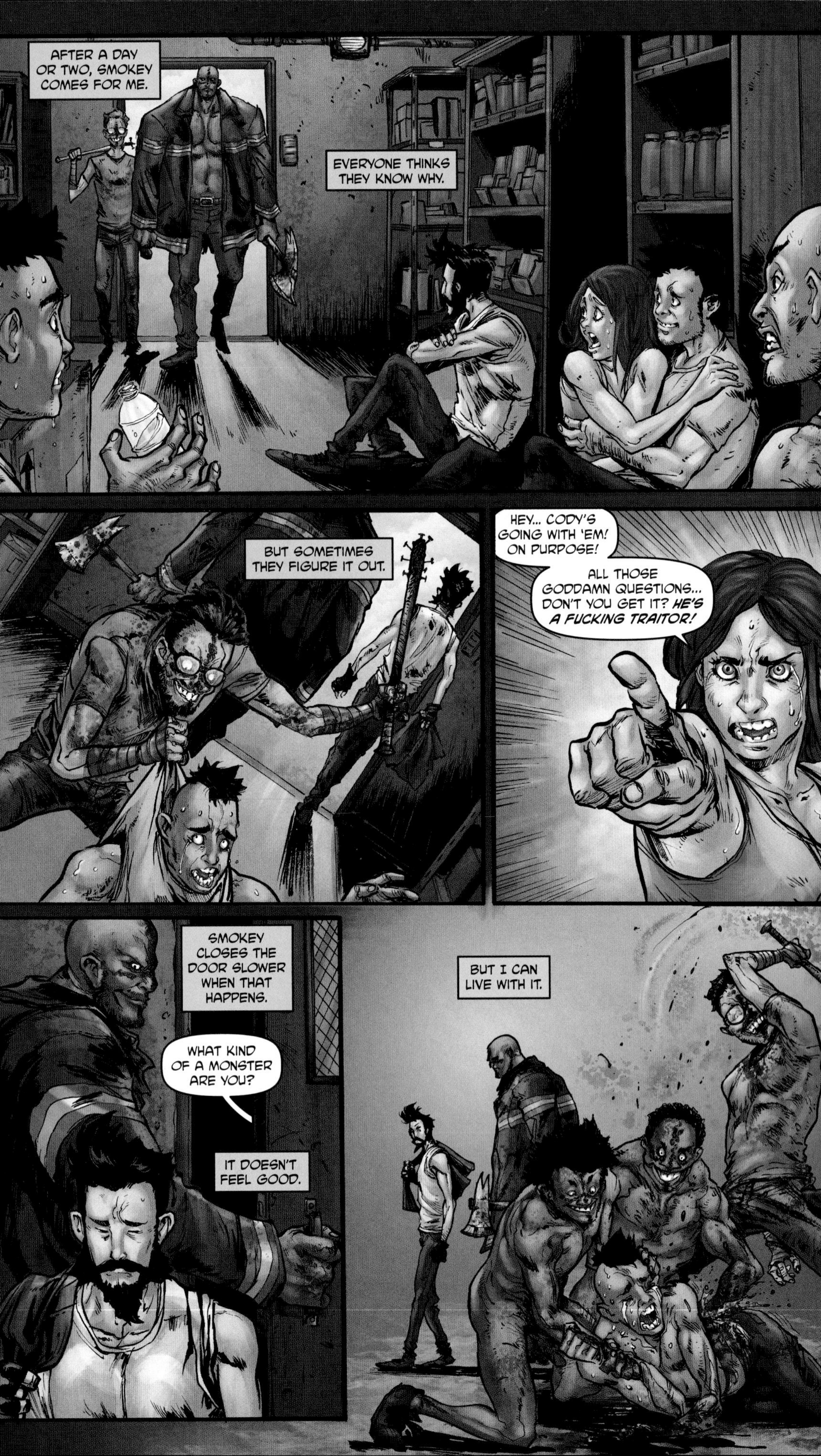
AFTER A DAY OR TWO, SMOKEY COMES FOR ME.
EVERYONE THINKS THEY KNOW WHY.
BUT SOMETIMES THEY FIGURE IT OUT.
HEY... CODY'S GOING WITH 'EM! ON PURPOSE!
ALL THOSE GODDAMN QUESTIONS... DON'T YOU GET IT? HE'S A FUCKING TRAITOR!
SMOKEY CLOSES THE DOOR SLOWER WHEN THAT HAPPENS.
WHAT KIND OF A MONSTER ARE YOU?
IT DOESN'T FEEL GOOD.
BUT I CAN LIVE WITH IT.

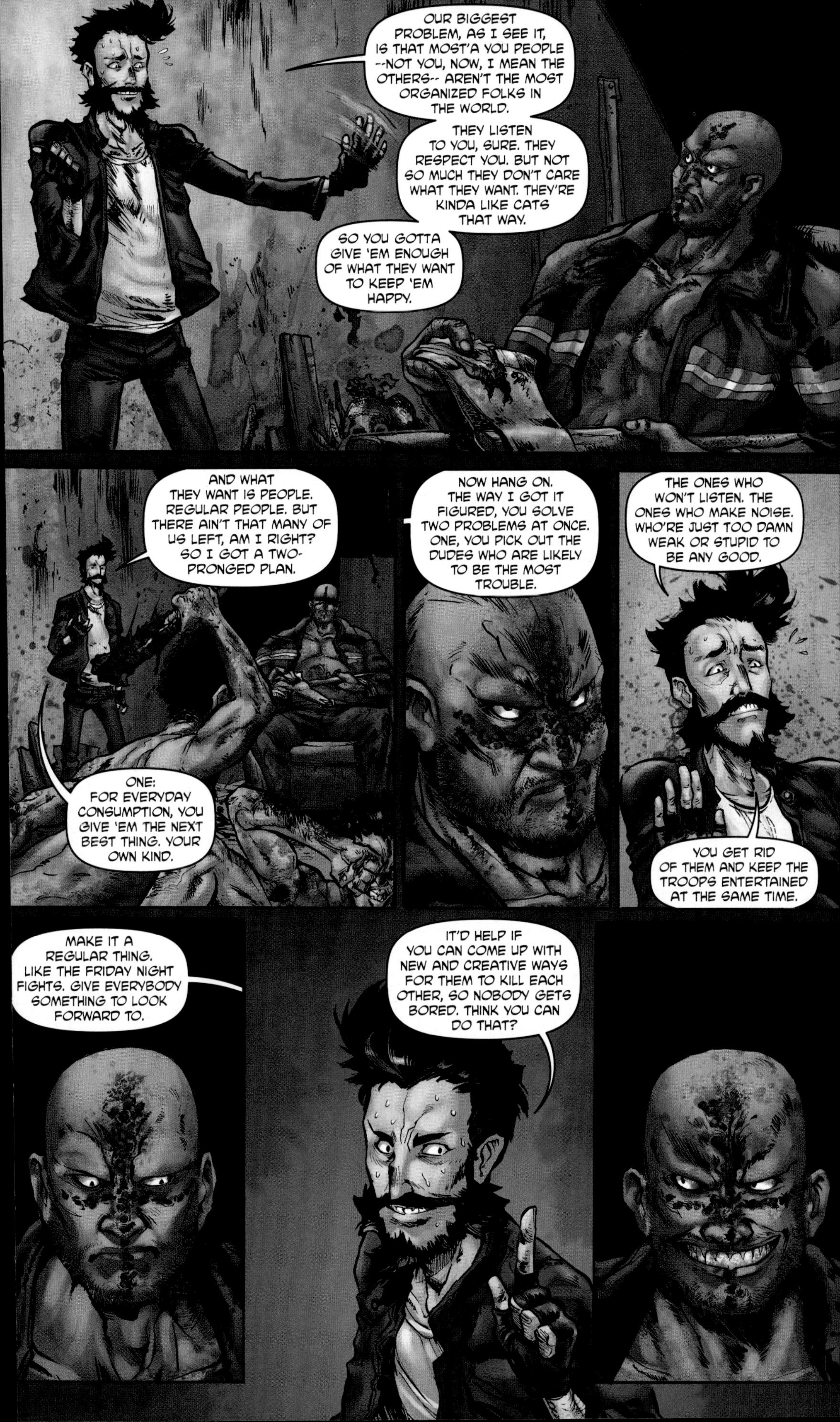
OUR BIGGEST PROBLEM, AS I SEE IT, IS THAT MOST'A YOU PEOPLE --NOT YOU, NOW, I MEAN THE OTHERS-- AREN'T THE MOST ORGANIZED FOLKS IN THE WORLD.
THEY LISTEN TO YOU, SURE. THEY RESPECT YOU. BUT NOT SO MUCH THEY DON'T CARE WHAT THEY WANT. THEY'RE KINDA LIKE CATS THAT WAY.
SO YOU GOTTA GIVE 'EM ENOUGH OF WHAT THEY WANT TO KEEP 'EM HAPPY.
AND WHAT THEY WANT IS PEOPLE. REGULAR PEOPLE. BUT THERE AIN'T THAT MANY OF US LEFT, AM I RIGHT? SO I GOT A TWO-PRONGED PLAN.
ONE: FOR EVERYDAY CONSUMPTION, YOU GIVE 'EM THE NEXT BEST THING. YOUR OWN KIND.
NOW HANG ON. THE WAY I GOT IT FIGURED, YOU SOLVE TWO PROBLEMS AT ONCE. ONE, YOU PICK OUT THE DUDES WHO ARE LIKELY TO BE THE MOST TROUBLE.
THE ONES WHO WON'T LISTEN. THE ONES WHO MAKE NOISE. WHO'RE JUST TOO DAMN WEAK OR STUPID TO BE ANY GOOD.
YOU GET RID OF THEM AND KEEP THE TROOPS ENTERTAINED AT THE SAME TIME.
MAKE IT A REGULAR THING. LIKE THE FRIDAY NIGHT FIGHTS. GIVE EVERYBODY SOMETHING TO LOOK FORWARD TO.
IT'D HELP IF YOU CAN COME UP WITH NEW AND CREATIVE WAYS FOR THEM TO KILL EACH OTHER, SO NOBODY GETS BORED. THINK YOU CAN DO THAT?

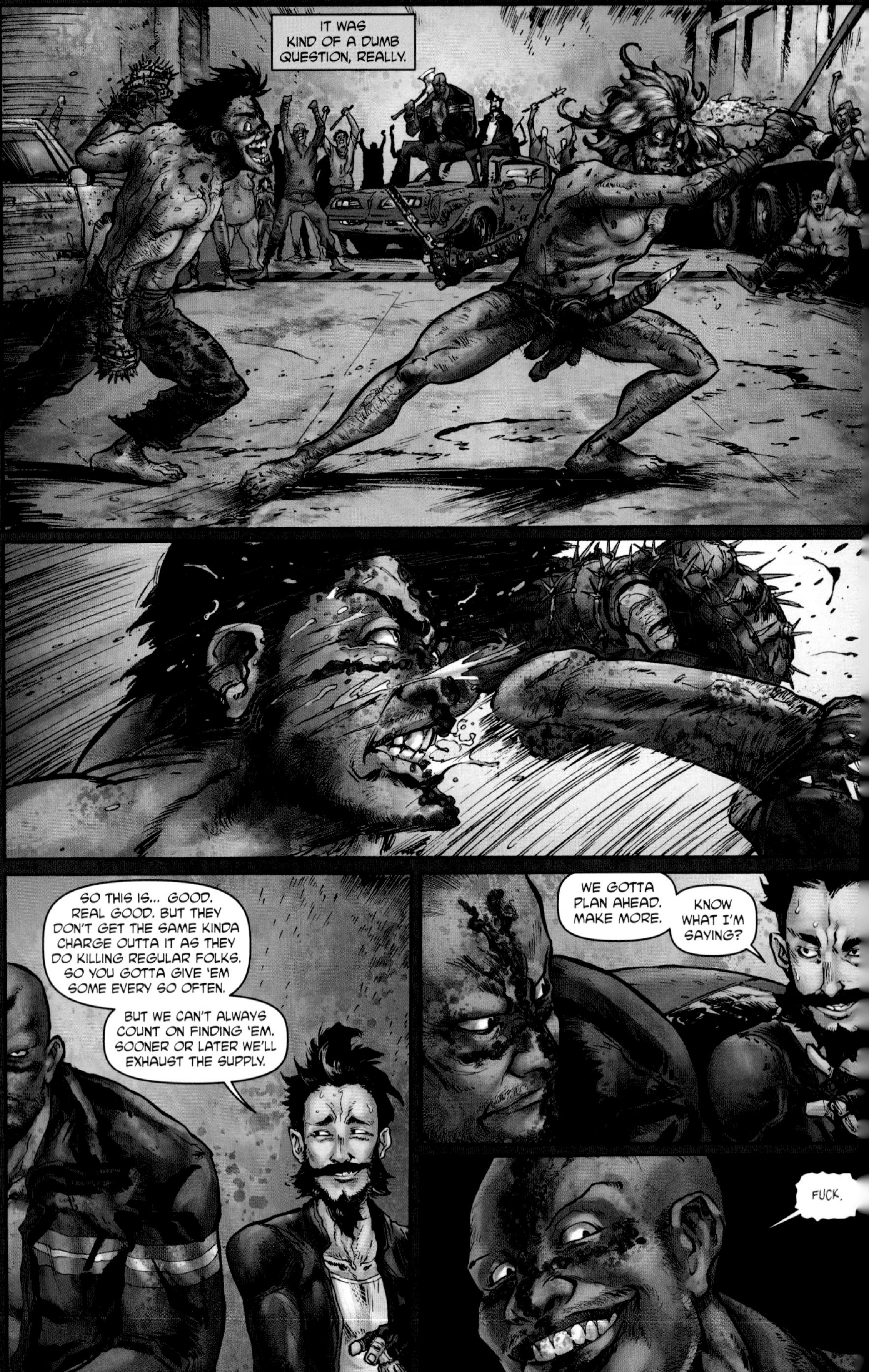
IT WAS KIND OF A DUMB QUESTION, REALLY.
SO THIS IS... GOOD. REAL GOOD. BUT THEY DON'T GET THE SAME KINDA CHARGE OUTTA IT AS THEY DO KILLING REGULAR FOLKS. SO YOU GOTTA GIVE 'EM SOME EVERY SO OFTEN.
BUT WE CAN'T ALWAYS COUNT ON FINDING 'EM. SOONER OR LATER WE'LL EXHAUST THE SUPPLY.
WE GOTTA PLAN AHEAD. MAKE MORE.
KNOW WHAT I'M SAYING?
FUCK.

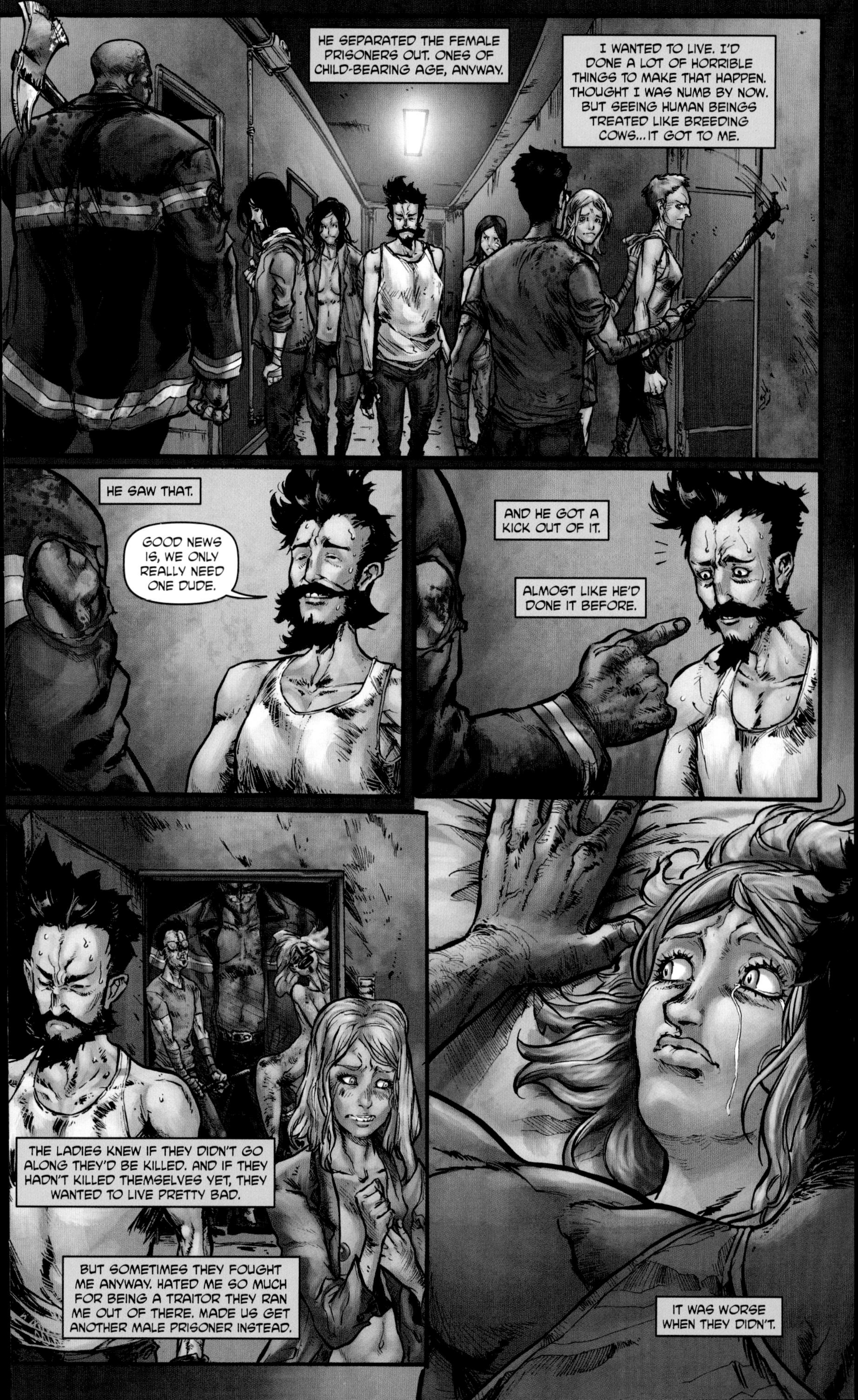
HE SEPARATED THE FEMALE PRISONERS OUT. ONES OF CHILD-BEARING AGE, ANYWAY.
I WANTED TO LIVE. I'D DONE A LOT OF HORRIBLE THINGS TO MAKE THAT HAPPEN. THOUGHT I WAS NUMB BY NOW. BUT SEEING HUMAN BEINGS TREATED LIKE BREEDING COWS... IT GOT TO ME.
HE SAW THAT.
GOOD NEWS IS, WE ONLY REALLY NEED ONE DUDE.
AND HE GOT A KICK OUT OF IT.
ALMOST LIKE HE'D DONE IT BEFORE.
THE LADIES KNEW IF THEY DIDN'T GO ALONG THEY'D BE KILLED. AND IF THEY HADN'T KILLED THEMSELVES YET, THEY WANTED TO LIVE PRETTY BAD.
BUT SOMETIMES THEY FOUGHT ME ANYWAY. HATED ME SO MUCH FOR BEING A TRAITOR THEY RAN ME OUT OF THERE. MADE US GET ANOTHER MALE PRISONER INSTEAD.
IT WAS WORSE WHEN THEY DIDN'T.

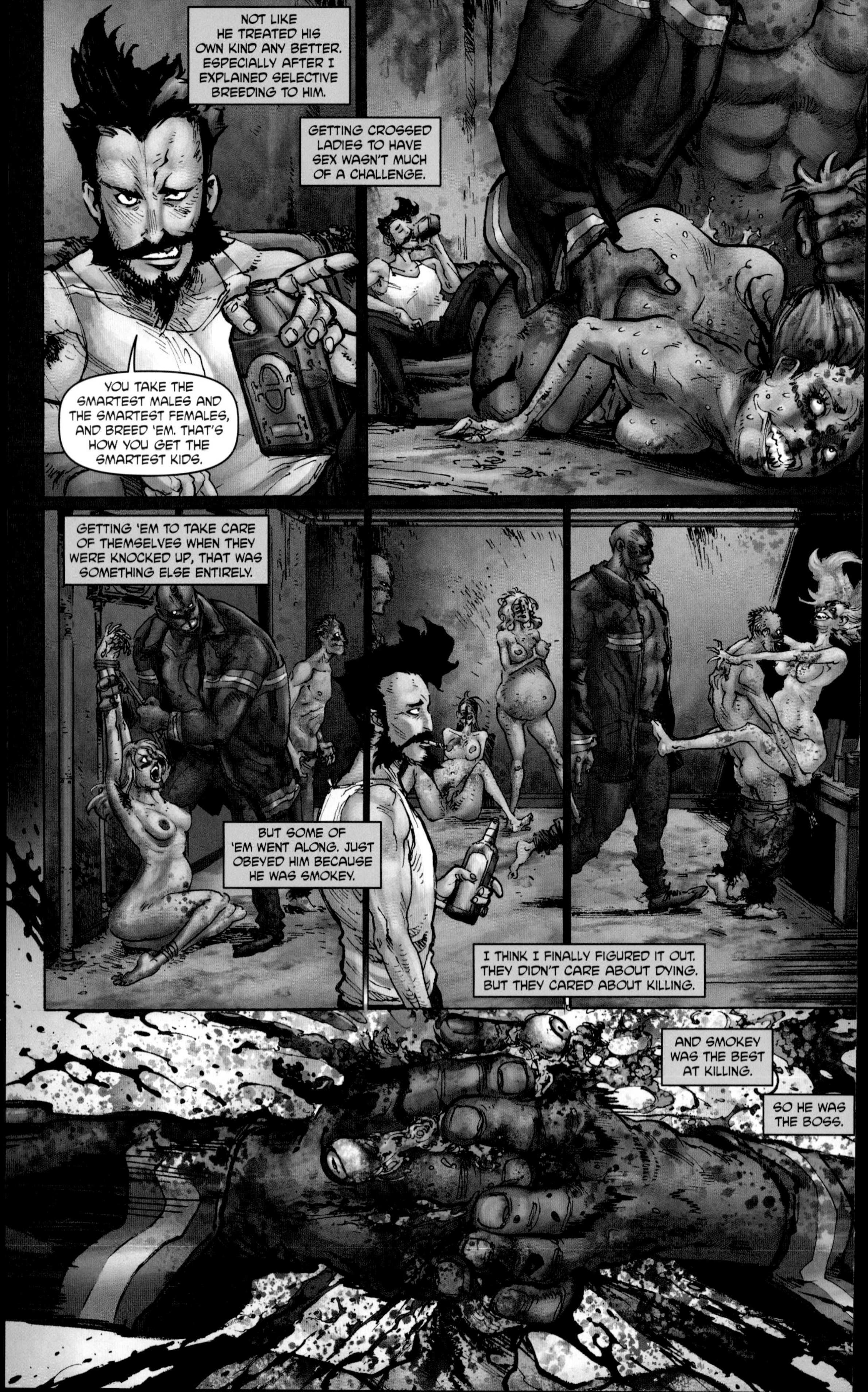
NOT LIKE HE TREATED HIS OWN KIND ANY BETTER. ESPECIALLY AFTER I EXPLAINED SELECTIVE BREEDING TO HIM.
YOU TAKE THE SMARTEST MALES AND THE SMARTEST FEMALES, AND BREED 'EM. THAT'S HOW YOU GET THE SMARTEST KIDS.
GETTING CROSSED LADIES TO HAVE SEX WASN'T MUCH OF A CHALLENGE.
GETTING 'EM TO TAKE CARE OF THEMSELVES WHEN THEY WERE KNOCKED UP, THAT WAS SOMETHING ELSE ENTIRELY.
BUT SOME OF 'EM WENT ALONG. JUST OBEYED HIM BECAUSE HE WAS SMOKEY.
I THINK I FINALLY FIGURED IT OUT. THEY DIDN'T CARE ABOUT DYING. BUT THEY CARED ABOUT KILLING.
AND SMOKEY WAS THE BEST AT KILLING.
SO HE WAS THE BOSS.

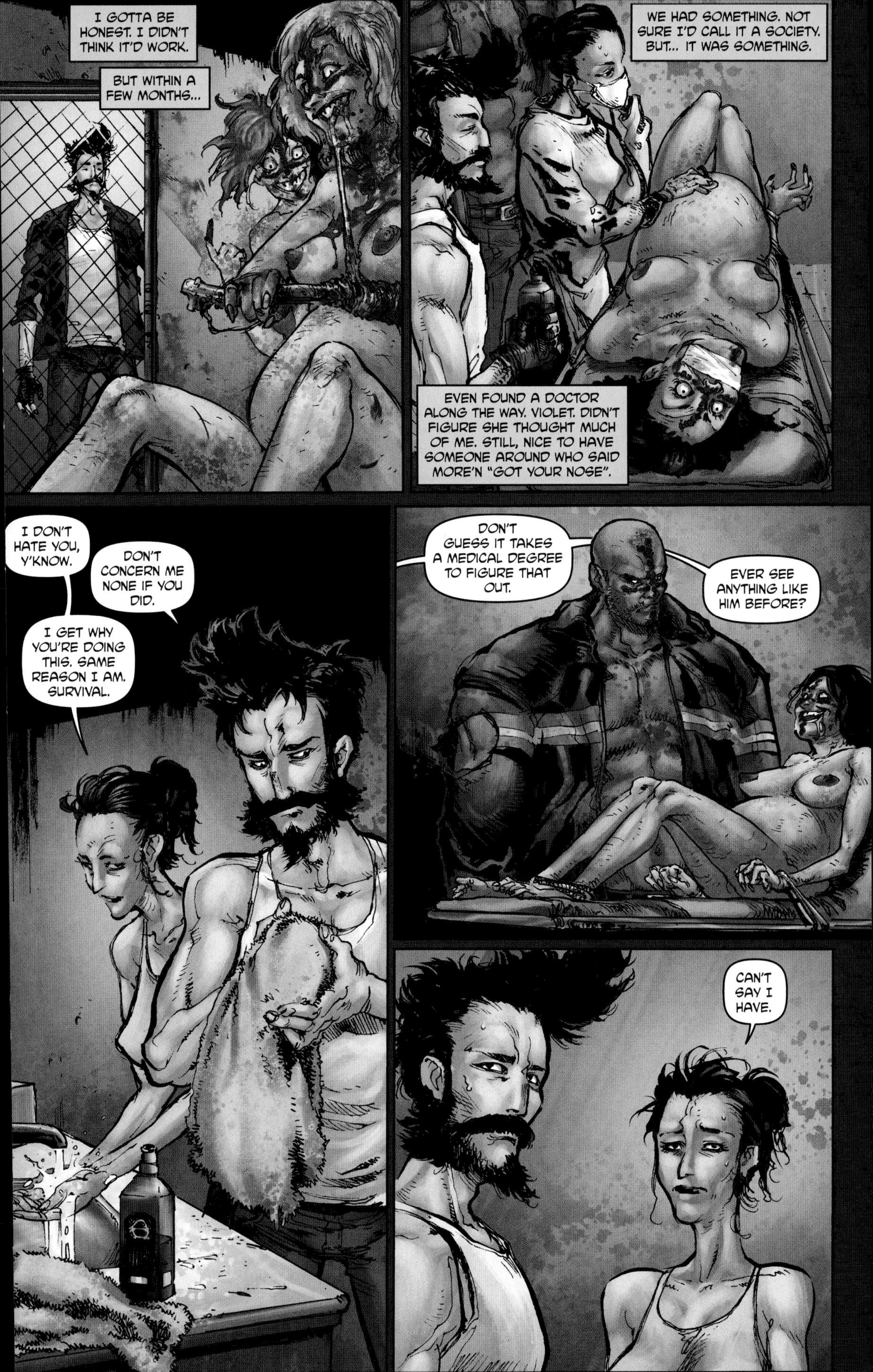

I GOTTA BE HONEST. I DIDN'T THINK IT'D WORK.
BUT WITHIN A FEW MONTHS...
WE HAD SOMETHING. NOT SURE I'D CALL IT A SOCIETY. BUT... IT WAS SOMETHING.
EVEN FOUND A DOCTOR ALONG THE WAY. VIOLET. DIDN'T FIGURE SHE THOUGHT MUCH OF ME. STILL, NICE TO HAVE SOMEONE AROUND WHO SAID MORE'N "GOT YOUR NOSE".
I DON'T HATE YOU, Y'KNOW.
DON'T CONCERN ME NONE IF YOU DID.
I GET WHY YOU'RE DOING THIS. SAME REASON I AM. SURVIVAL.
DON'T GUESS IT TAKES A MEDICAL DEGREE TO FIGURE THAT OUT.
EVER SEE ANYTHING LIKE HIM BEFORE?
CAN'T SAY I HAVE.

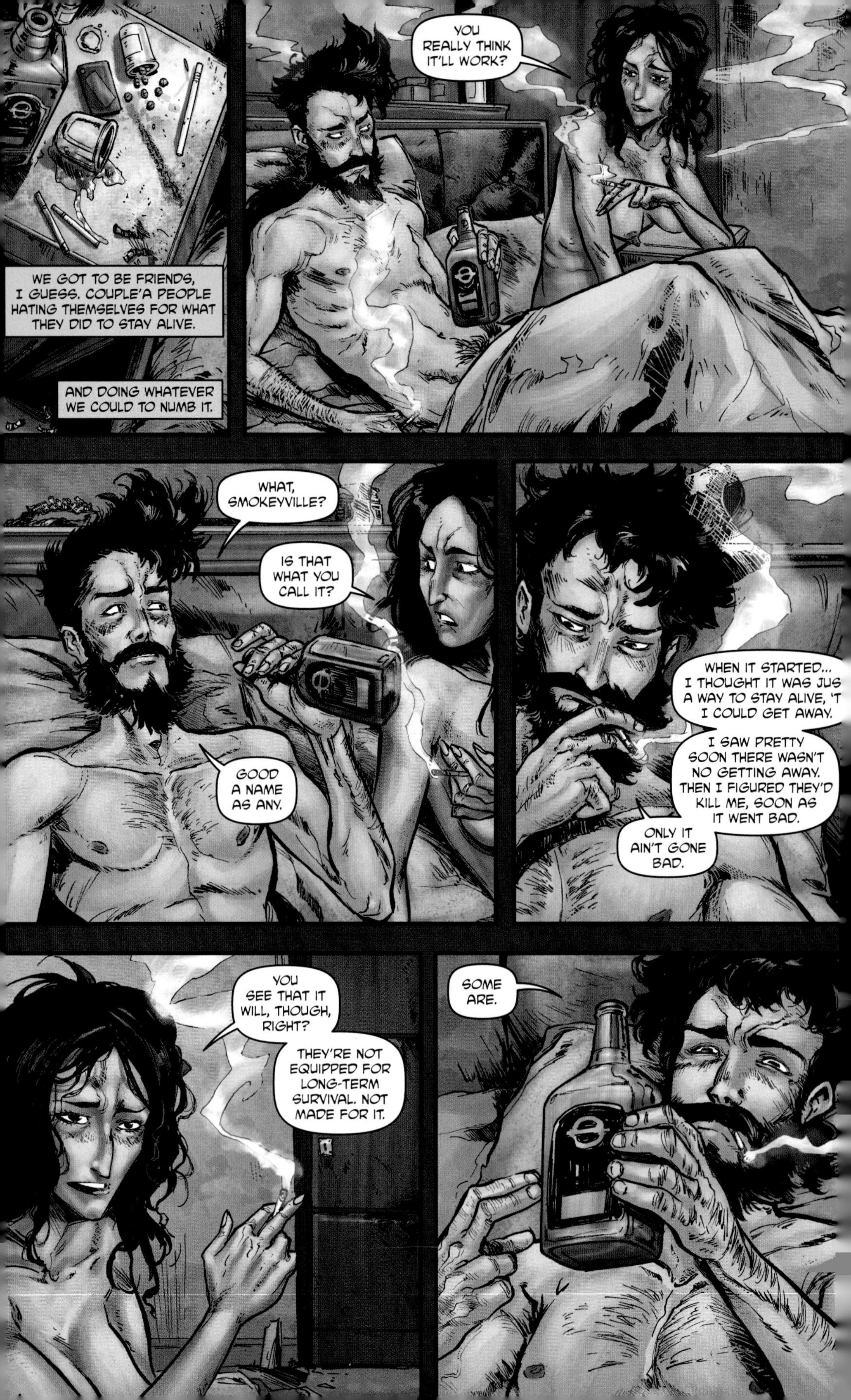
WE GOT TO BE FRIENDS, I GUESS. COUPLE'A PEOPLE HATING THEMSELVES FOR WHAT THEY DID TO STAY ALIVE.
AND DOING WHATEVER WE COULD TO NUMB IT.
YOU REALLY THINK IT'LL WORK?
WHAT, SMOKEYVILLE?
IS THAT WHAT YOU CALL IT?
GOOD A NAME AS ANY.
WHEN IT STARTED... I THOUGHT IT WAS JUS A WAY TO STAY ALIVE, 'T I COULD GET AWAY.
I SAW PRETTY SOON THERE WASN'T NO GETTING AWAY. THEN I FIGURED THEY'D KILL ME, SOON AS IT WENT BAD.
ONLY IT AIN'T GONE BAD.
YOU SEE THAT IT WILL, THOUGH, RIGHT?
THEY'RE NOT EQUIPPED FOR LONG-TERM SURVIVAL. NOT MADE FOR IT.
SOME ARE.

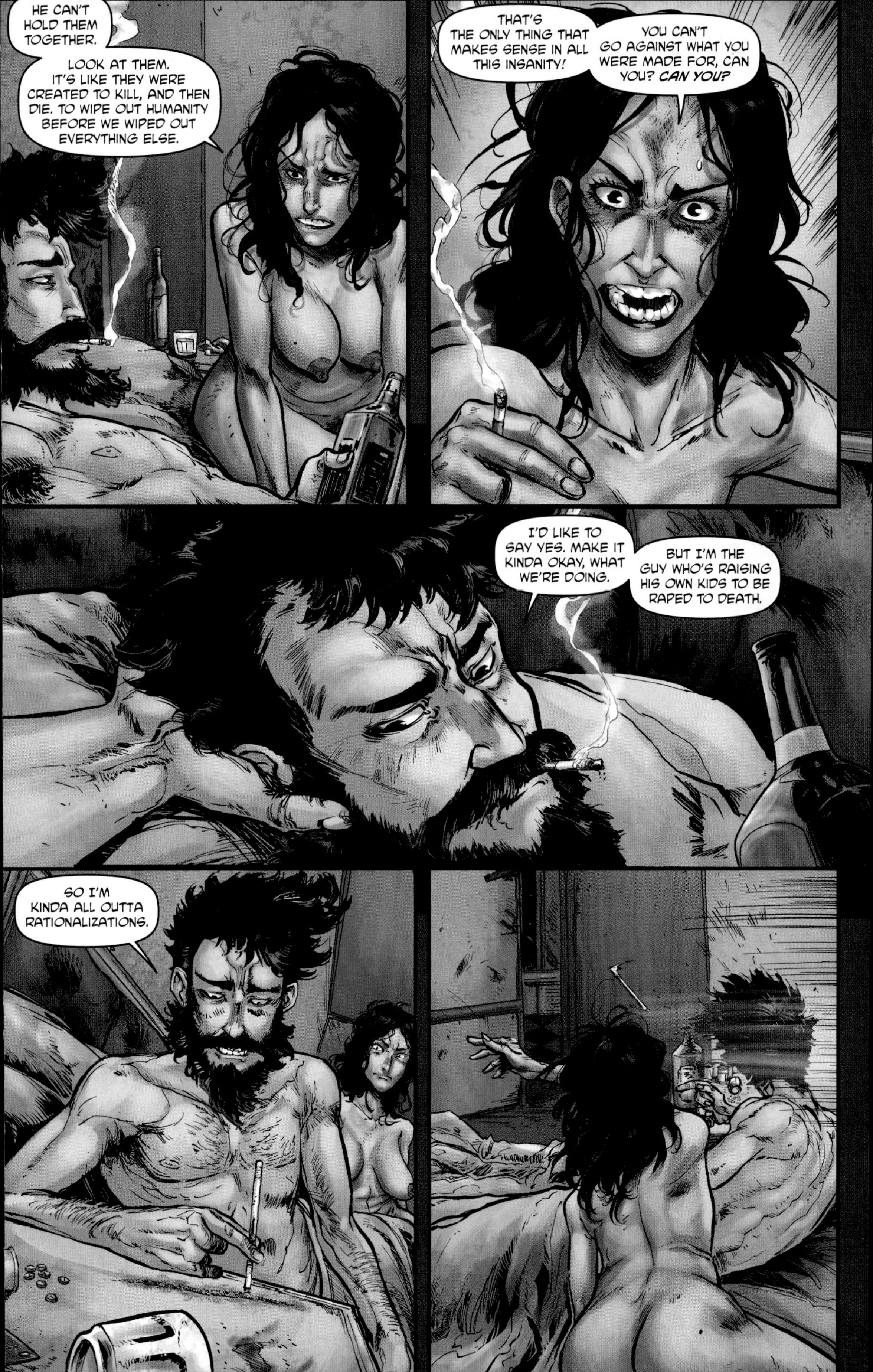

HE CAN'T HOLD THEM TOGETHER.
LOOK AT THEM. IT'S LIKE THEY WERE CREATED TO KILL, AND THEN DIE. TO WIPE OUT HUMANITY BEFORE WE WIPED OUT EVERYTHING ELSE.
THAT'S THE ONLY THING THAT MAKES SENSE IN ALL THIS INSANITY!
YOU CAN'T GO AGAINST WHAT YOU WERE MADE FOR, CAN YOU? CAN YOU?
I'D LIKE TO SAY YES. MAKE IT KINDA OKAY, WHAT WE'RE DOING.
BUT I'M THE GUY WHO'S RAISING HIS OWN KIDS TO BE RAPED TO DEATH.
SO I'M KINDA ALL OUTTA RATIONALIZATIONS.

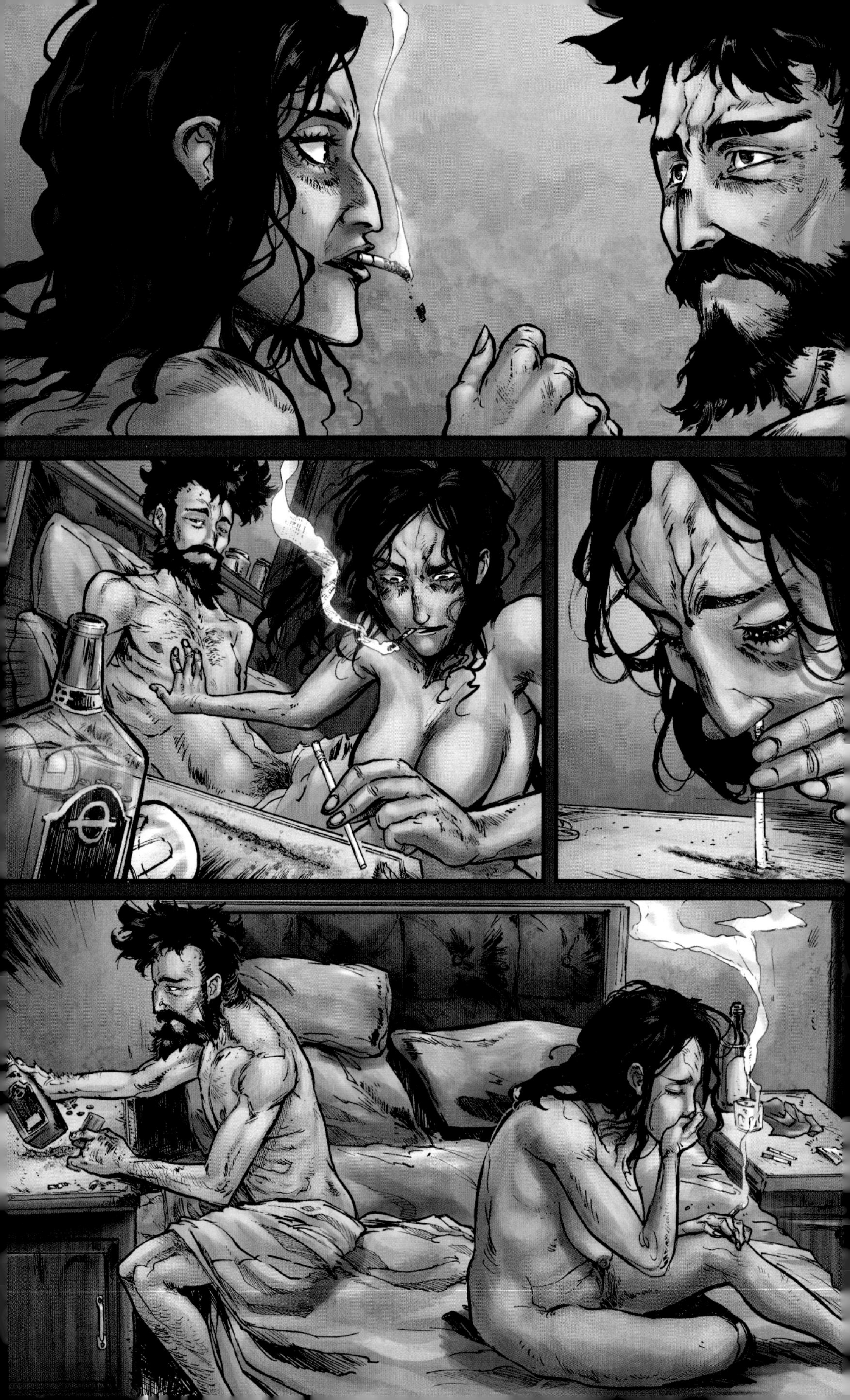

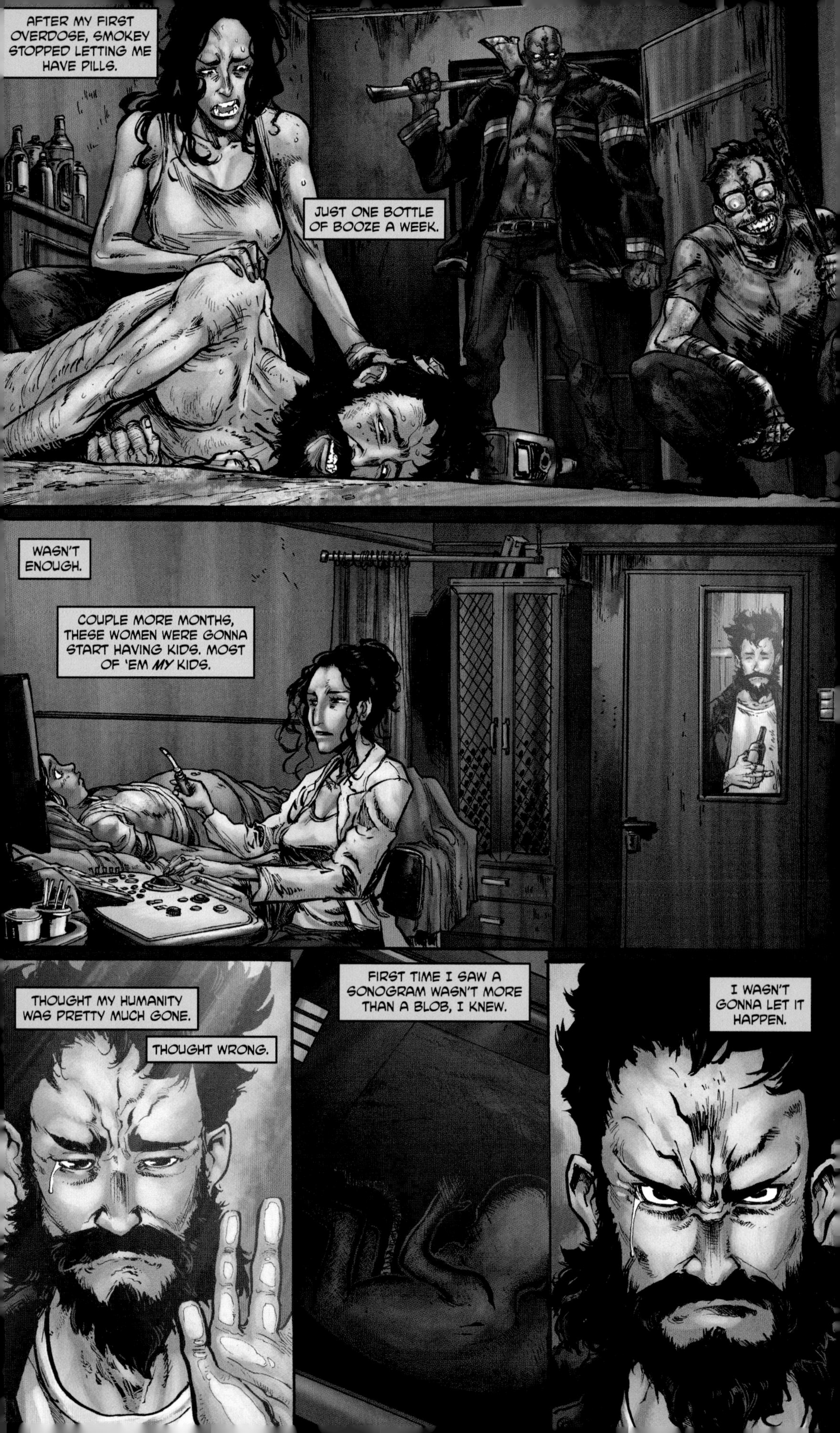
AFTER MY FIRST OVERDOSE, SMOKEY STOPPED LETTING ME HAVE PILLS.
JUST ONE BOTTLE OF BOOZE A WEEK.
WASN'T ENOUGH.
COUPLE MORE MONTHS, THESE WOMEN WERE GONNA START HAVING KIDS. MOST OF 'EM *MY* KIDS.
THOUGHT MY HUMANITY WAS PRETTY MUCH GONE.
THOUGHT WRONG.
FIRST TIME I SAW A SONOGRAM WASN'T MORE THAN A BLOB, I KNEW.
I WASN'T GONNA LET IT HAPPEN.

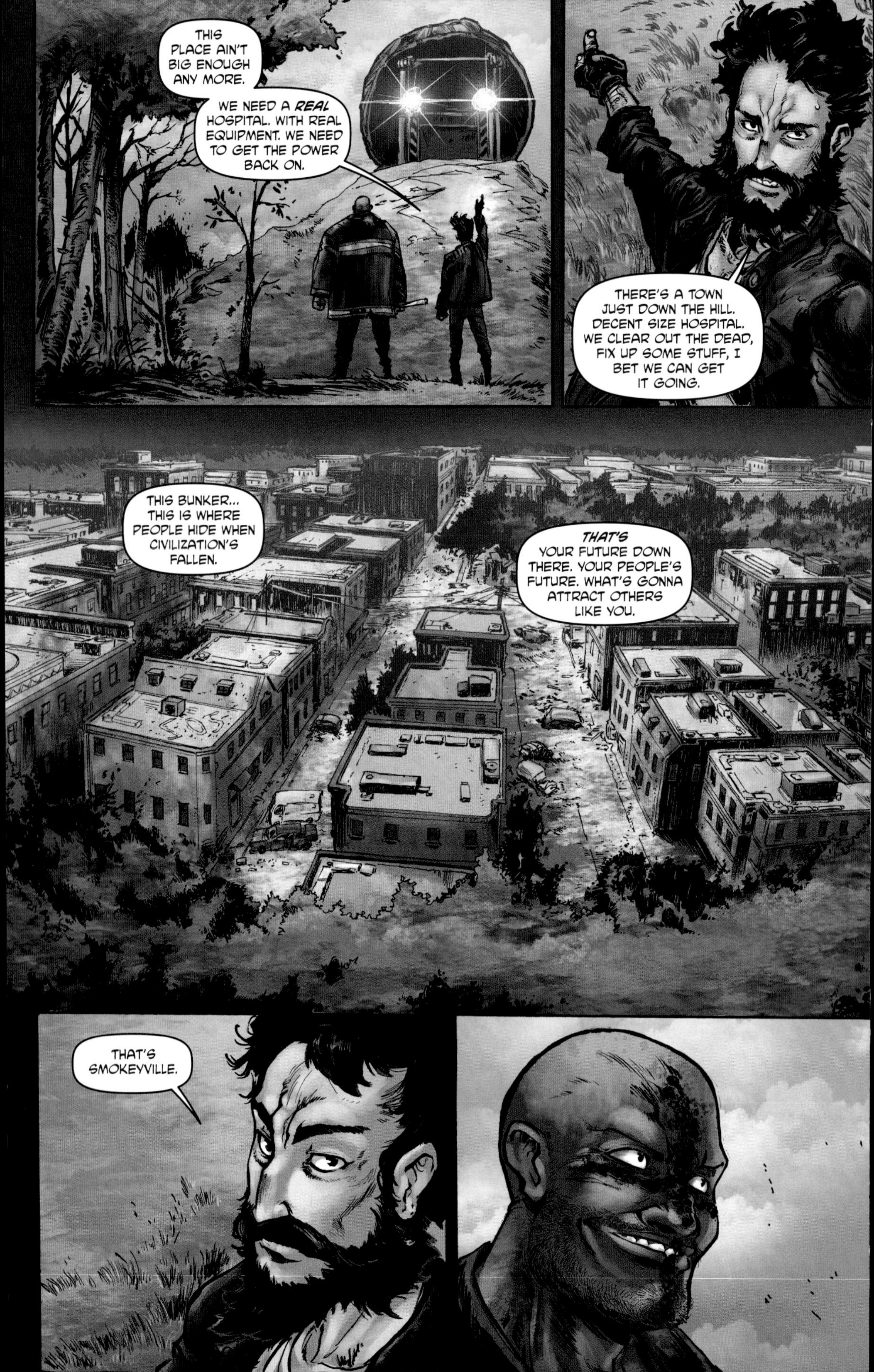
THIS PLACE AIN'T BIG ENOUGH ANY MORE.
WE NEED A *REAL* HOSPITAL. WITH REAL EQUIPMENT. WE NEED TO GET THE POWER BACK ON.
THERE'S A TOWN JUST DOWN THE HILL. DECENT SIZE HOSPITAL. WE CLEAR OUT THE DEAD, FIX UP SOME STUFF, I BET WE CAN GET IT GOING.
THIS BUNKER... THIS IS WHERE PEOPLE HIDE WHEN CIVILIZATION'S FALLEN.
THAT'S YOUR FUTURE DOWN THERE. YOUR PEOPLE'S FUTURE. WHAT'S GONNA ATTRACT OTHERS LIKE YOU.
THAT'S SMOKEYVILLE.

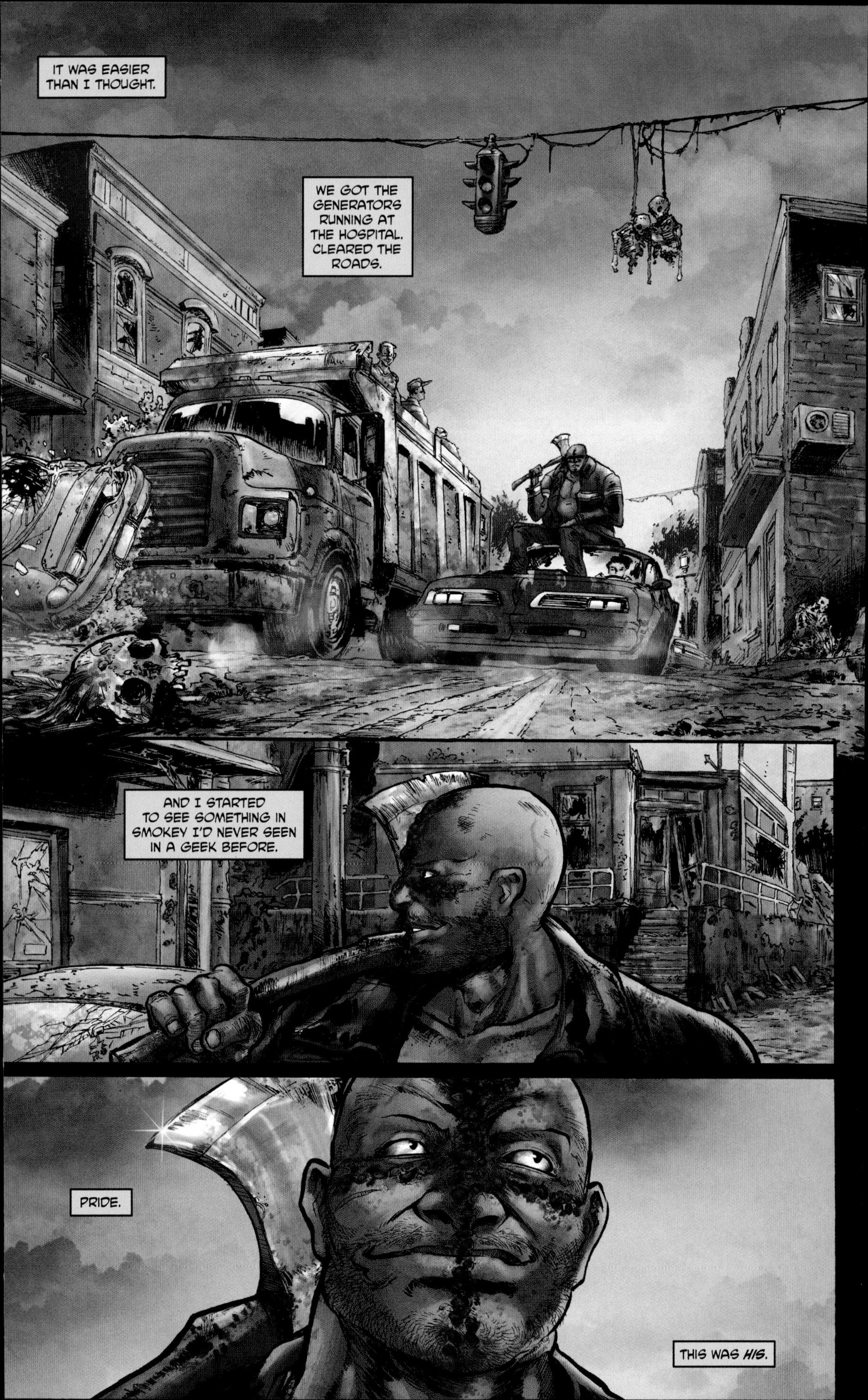
IT WAS EASIER THAN I THOUGHT.
WE GOT THE GENERATORS RUNNING AT THE HOSPITAL. CLEARED THE ROADS.
AND I STARTED TO SEE SOMETHING IN SMOKEY I'D NEVER SEEN IN A GEEK BEFORE.
PRIDE.
THIS WAS *HIS*.

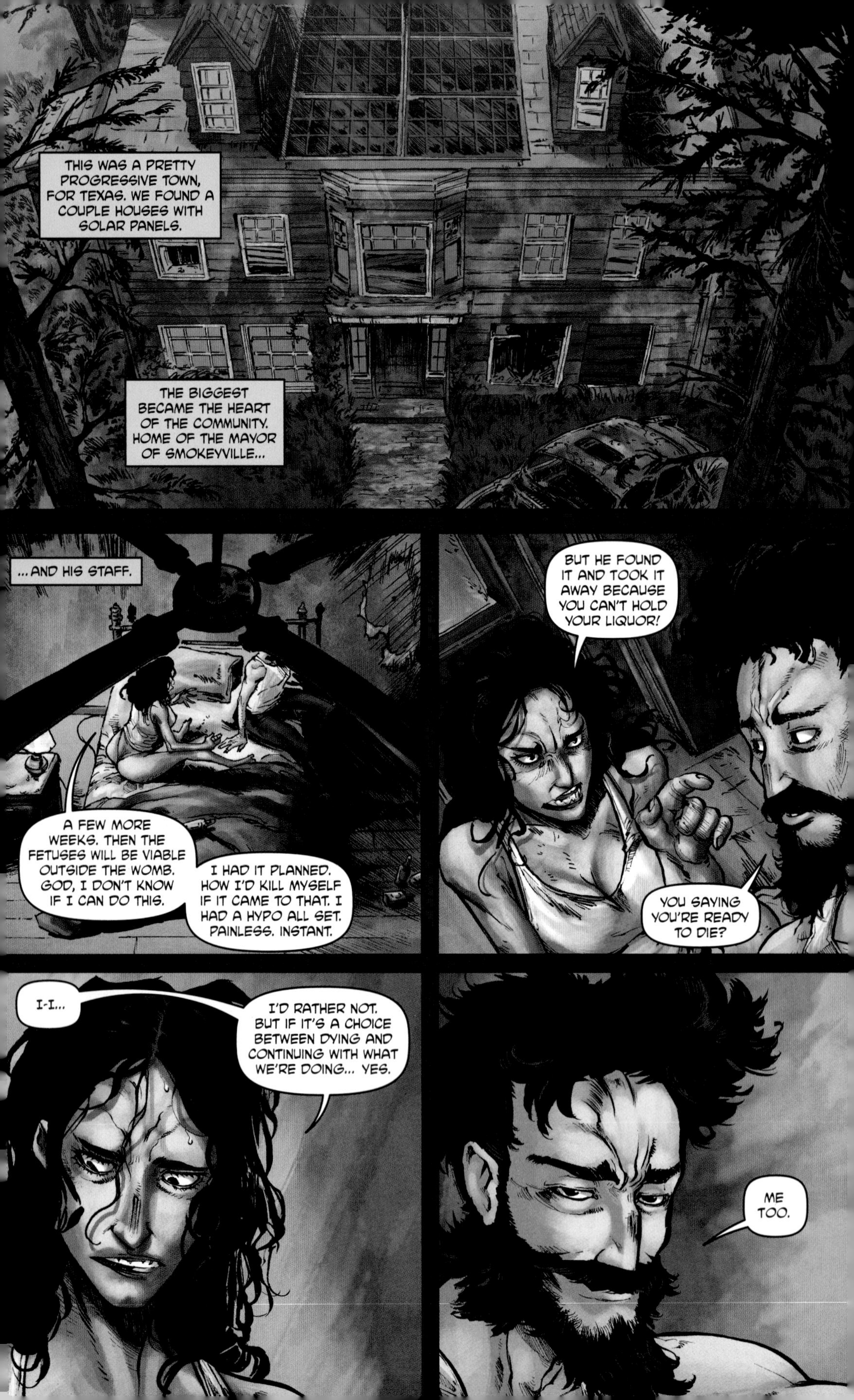
THIS WAS A PRETTY PROGRESSIVE TOWN, FOR TEXAS. WE FOUND A COUPLE HOUSES WITH SOLAR PANELS.
THE BIGGEST BECAME THE HEART OF THE COMMUNITY. HOME OF THE MAYOR OF SMOKEYVILLE...
...AND HIS STAFF.
A FEW MORE WEEKS. THEN THE FETUSES WILL BE VIABLE OUTSIDE THE WOMB. GOD, I DON'T KNOW IF I CAN DO THIS.
I HAD IT PLANNED. HOW I'D KILL MYSELF IF IT CAME TO THAT. I HAD A HYPO ALL SET. PAINLESS. INSTANT.
BUT HE FOUND IT AND TOOK IT AWAY BECAUSE YOU CAN'T HOLD YOUR LIQUOR!
YOU SAYING YOU'RE READY TO DIE?
I-I...
I'D RATHER NOT. BUT IF IT'S A CHOICE BETWEEN DYING AND CONTINUING WITH WHAT WE'RE DOING... YES.
ME TOO.

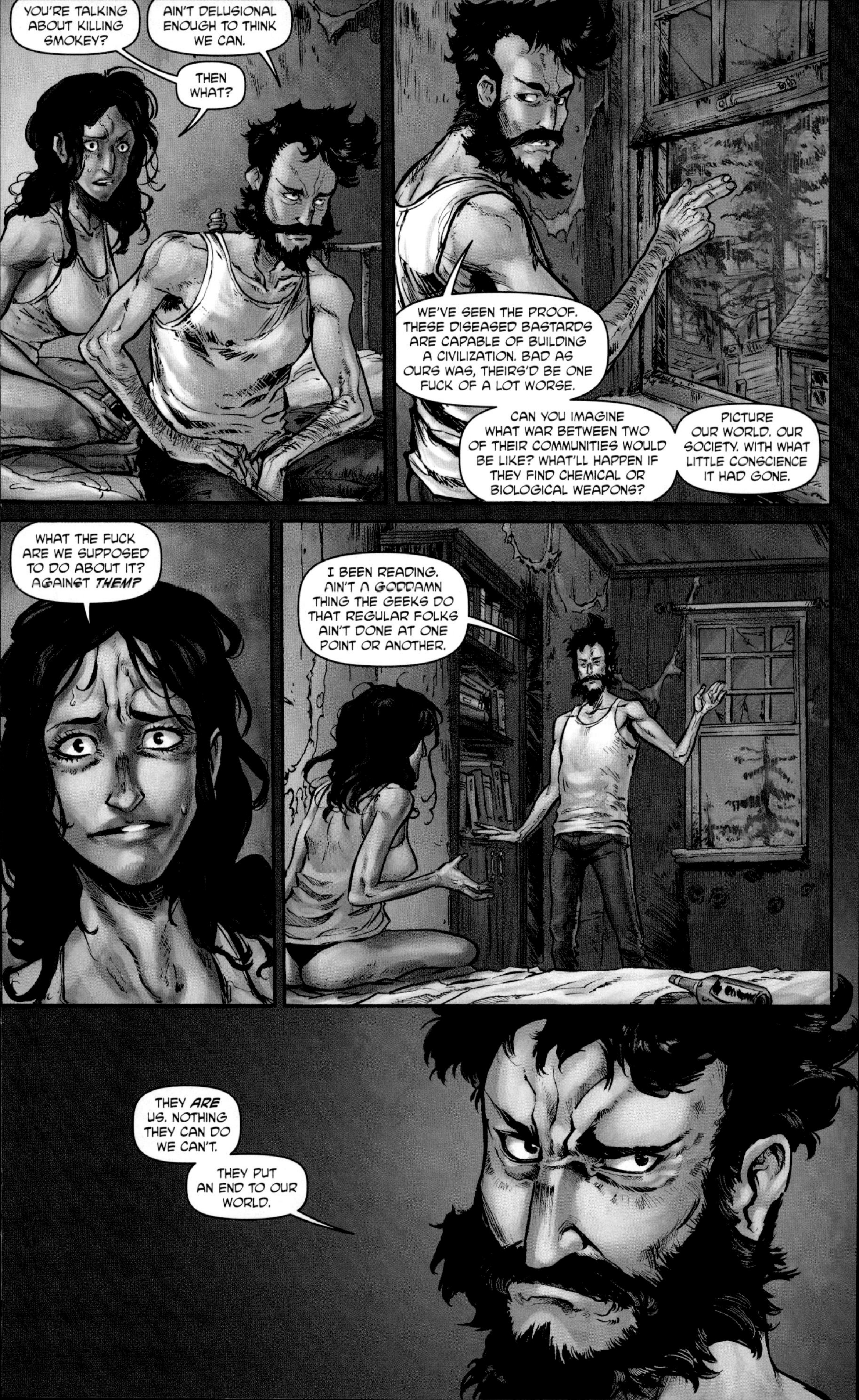
YOU'RE TALKING ABOUT KILLING SMOKEY?
AIN'T DELUSIONAL ENOUGH TO THINK WE CAN.
THEN WHAT?
WE'VE SEEN THE PROOF. THESE DISEASED BASTARDS ARE CAPABLE OF BUILDING A CIVILIZATION. BAD AS OURS WAS, THEIRS'D BE ONE FUCK OF A LOT WORSE.
CAN YOU IMAGINE WHAT WAR BETWEEN TWO OF THEIR COMMUNITIES WOULD BE LIKE? WHAT'LL HAPPEN IF THEY FIND CHEMICAL OR BIOLOGICAL WEAPONS?
PICTURE OUR WORLD. OUR SOCIETY. WITH WHAT LITTLE CONSCIENCE IT HAD GONE.
WHAT THE FUCK ARE WE SUPPOSED TO DO ABOUT IT? AGAINST *THEM?*
I BEEN READING. AIN'T A GODDAMN THING THE GEEKS DO THAT REGULAR FOLKS AIN'T DONE AT ONE POINT OR ANOTHER.
THEY *ARE* US. NOTHING THEY CAN DO WE CAN'T.
THEY PUT AN END TO OUR WORLD.

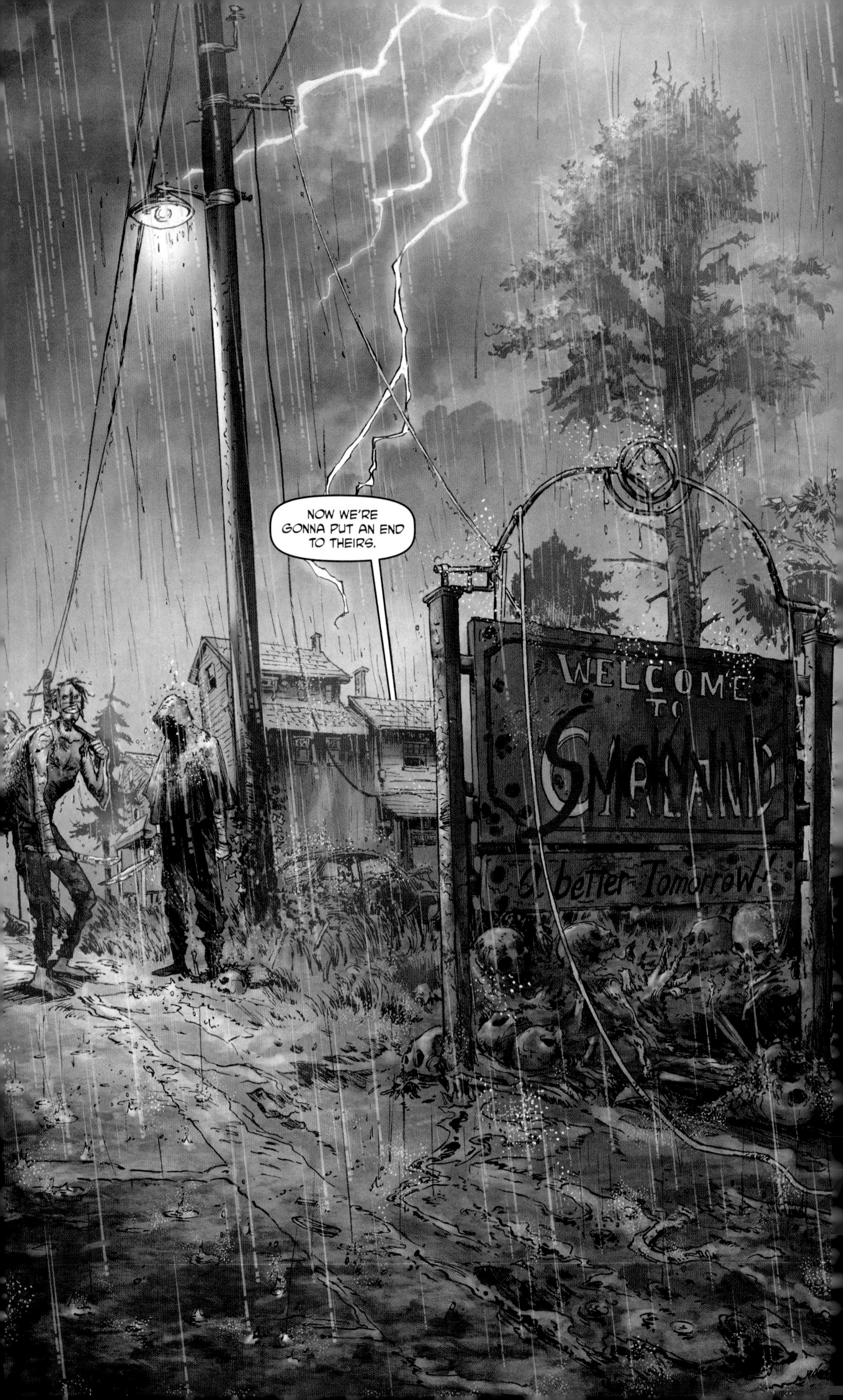
NOW WE'RE GONNA PUT AN END TO THEIRS.
WELCOME TO
better Tomorrow!

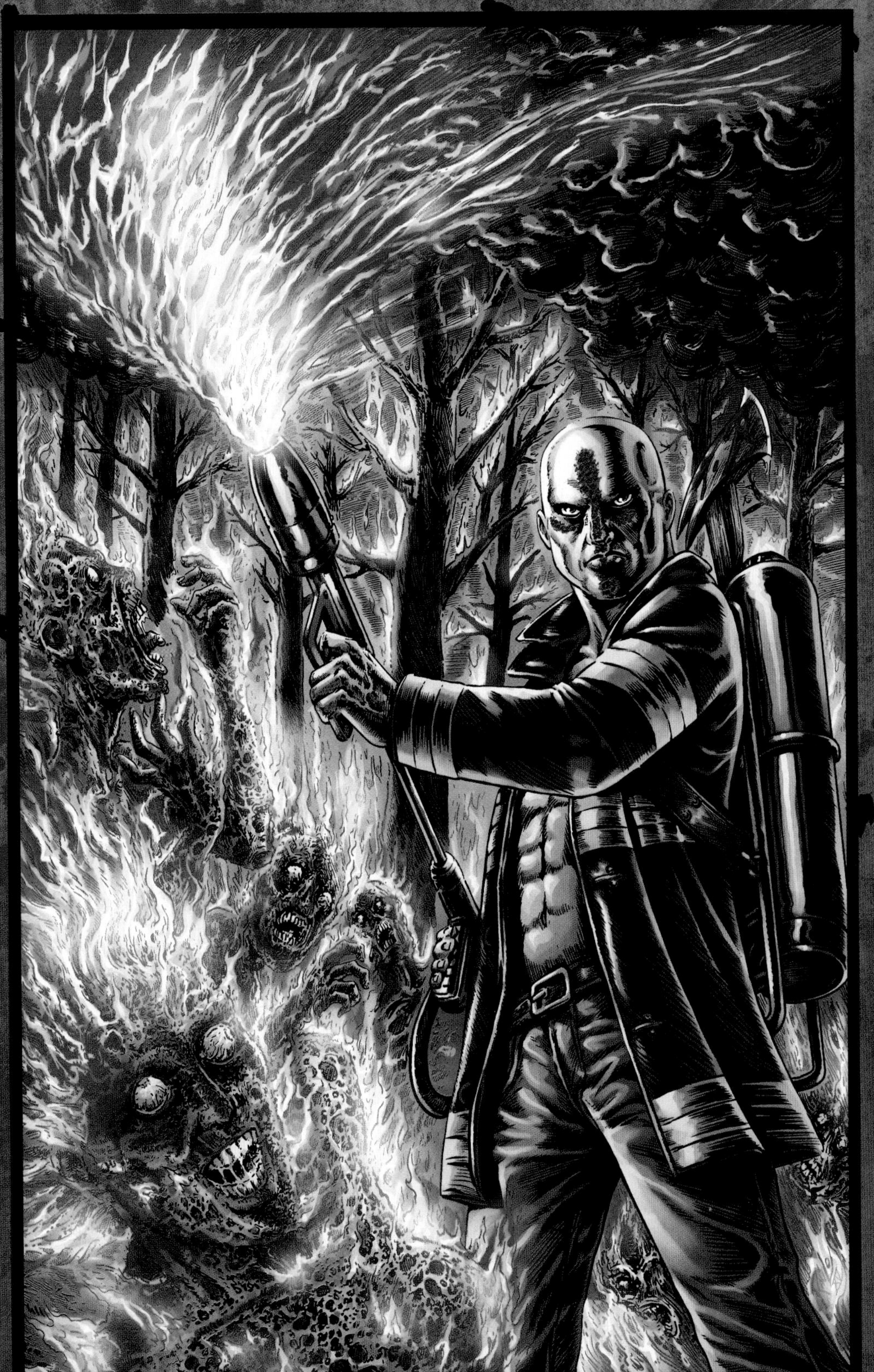

PART 4

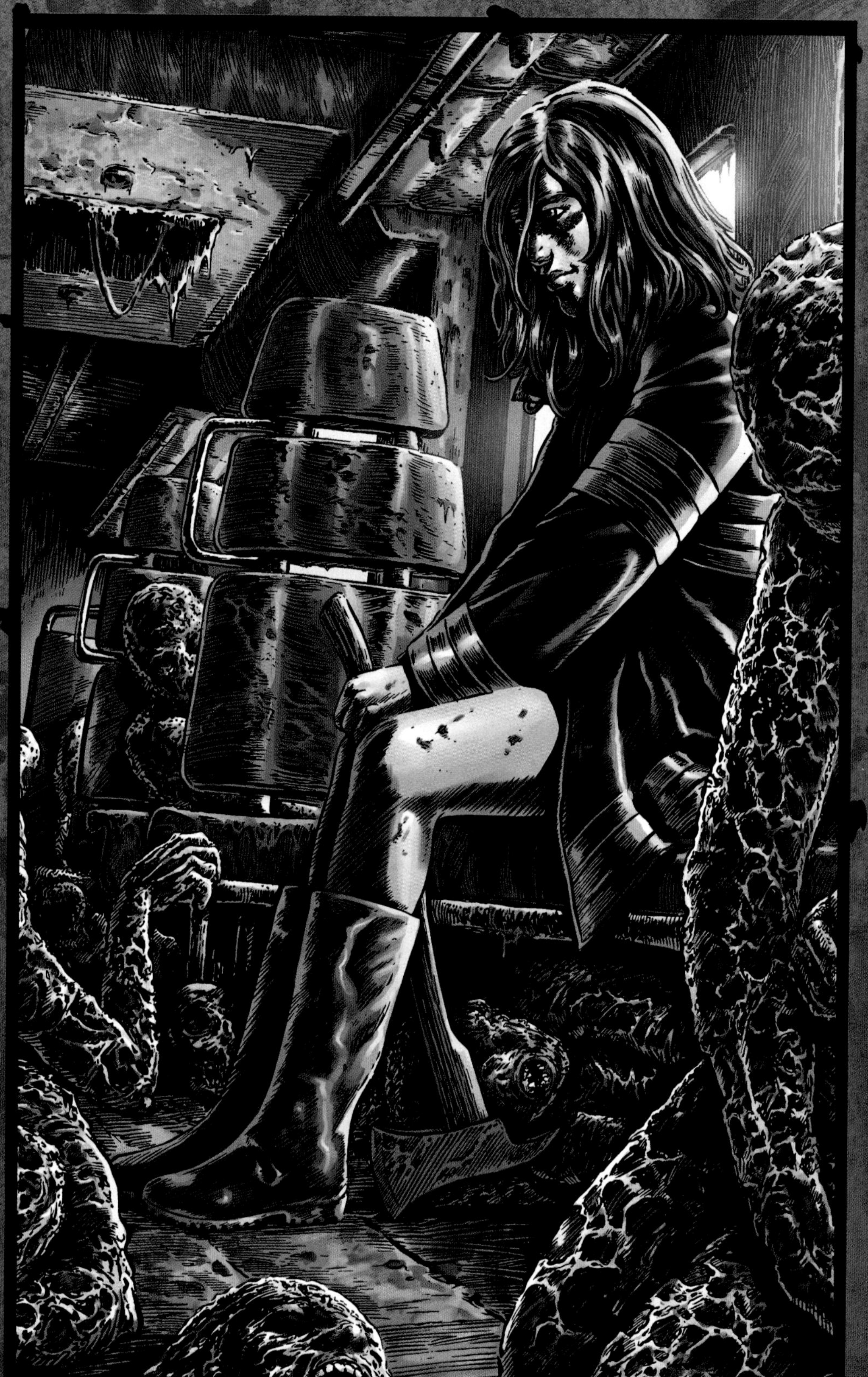

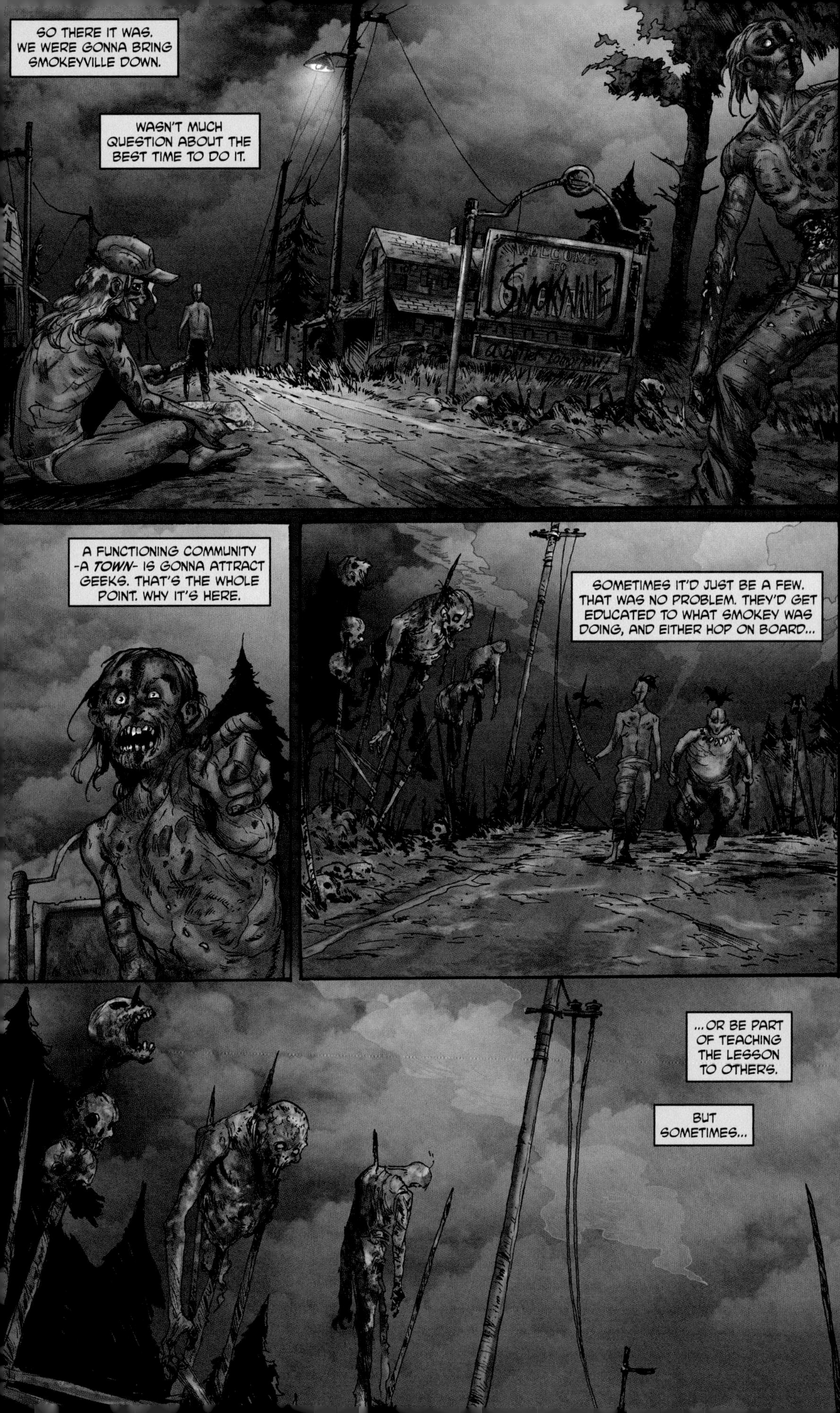
SO THERE IT WAS. WE WERE GONNA BRING SMOKEYVILLE DOWN.
WASN'T MUCH QUESTION ABOUT THE BEST TIME TO DO IT.
WELCOME TO SMOKYVILLE
A FUNCTIONING COMMUNITY -A *TOWN*- IS GONNA ATTRACT GEEKS. THAT'S THE WHOLE POINT. WHY IT'S HERE.
SOMETIMES IT'D JUST BE A FEW. THAT WAS NO PROBLEM. THEY'D GET EDUCATED TO WHAT SMOKEY WAS DOING, AND EITHER HOP ON BOARD...
...OR BE PART OF TEACHING THE LESSON TO OTHERS.
BUT SOMETIMES...

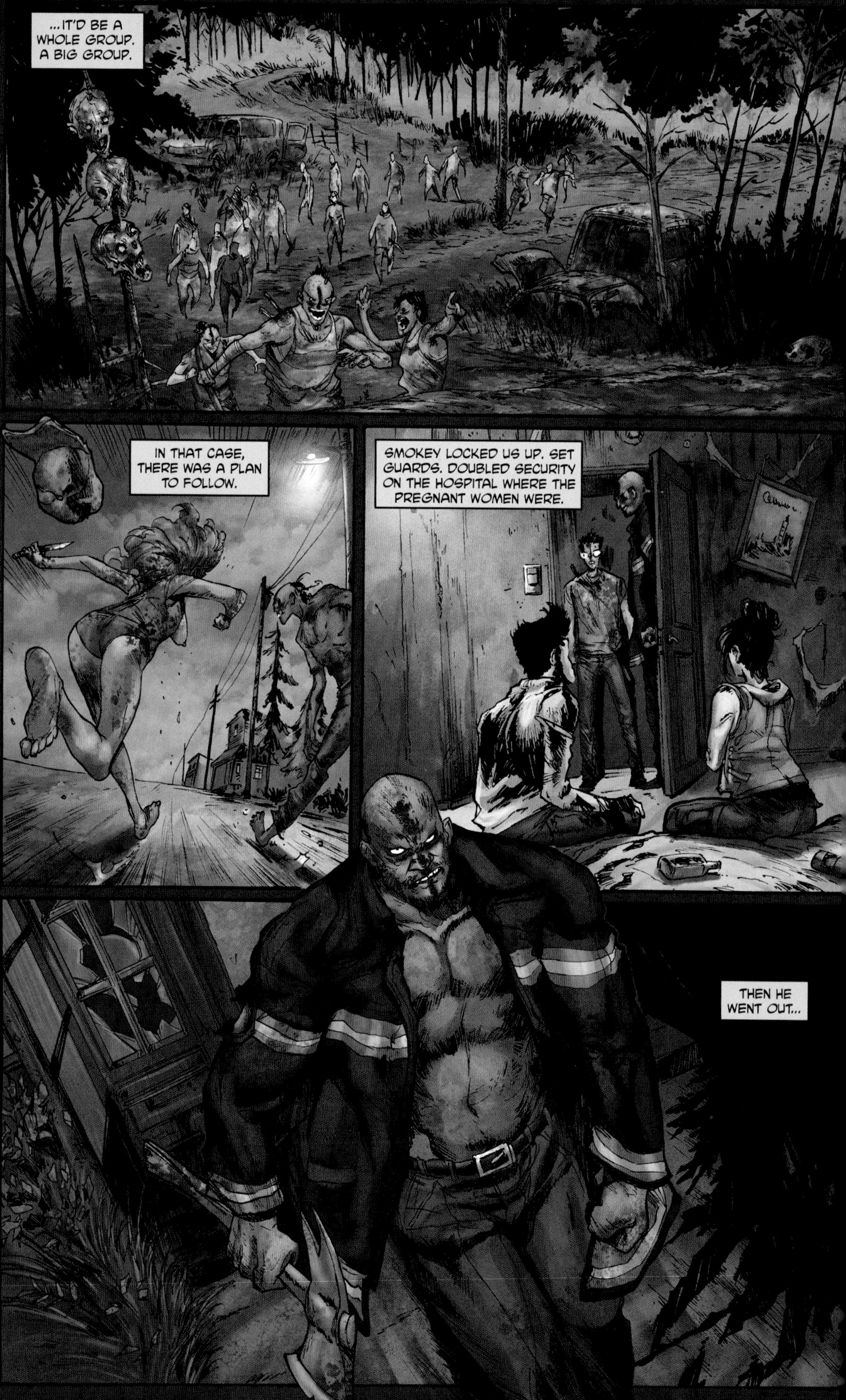
...IT'D BE A WHOLE GROUP. A BIG GROUP.
IN THAT CASE, THERE WAS A PLAN TO FOLLOW.
SMOKEY LOCKED US UP. SET GUARDS. DOUBLED SECURITY ON THE HOSPITAL WHERE THE PREGNANT WOMEN WERE.
THEN HE WENT OUT...

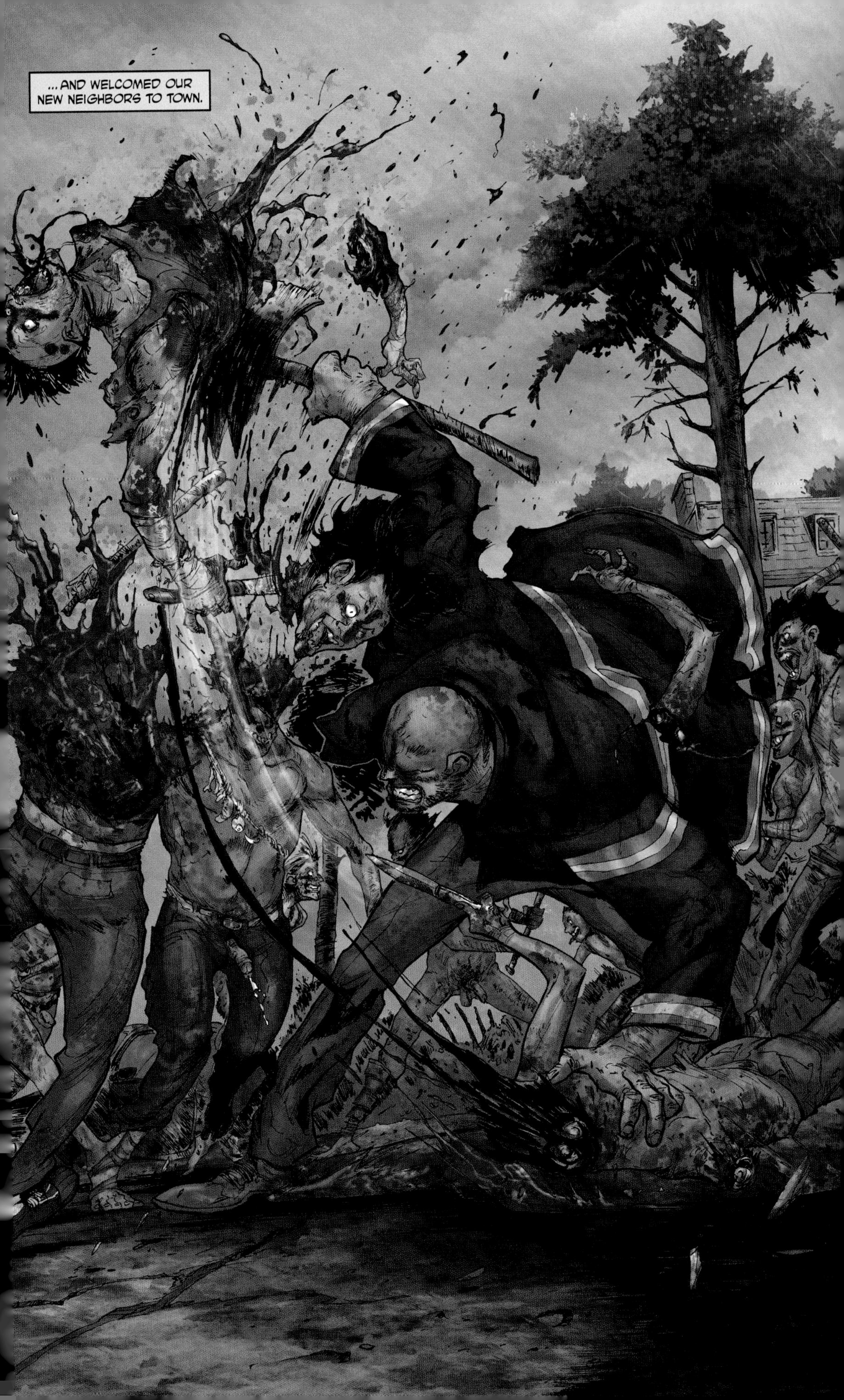
...AND WELCOMED OUR NEW NEIGHBORS TO TOWN.

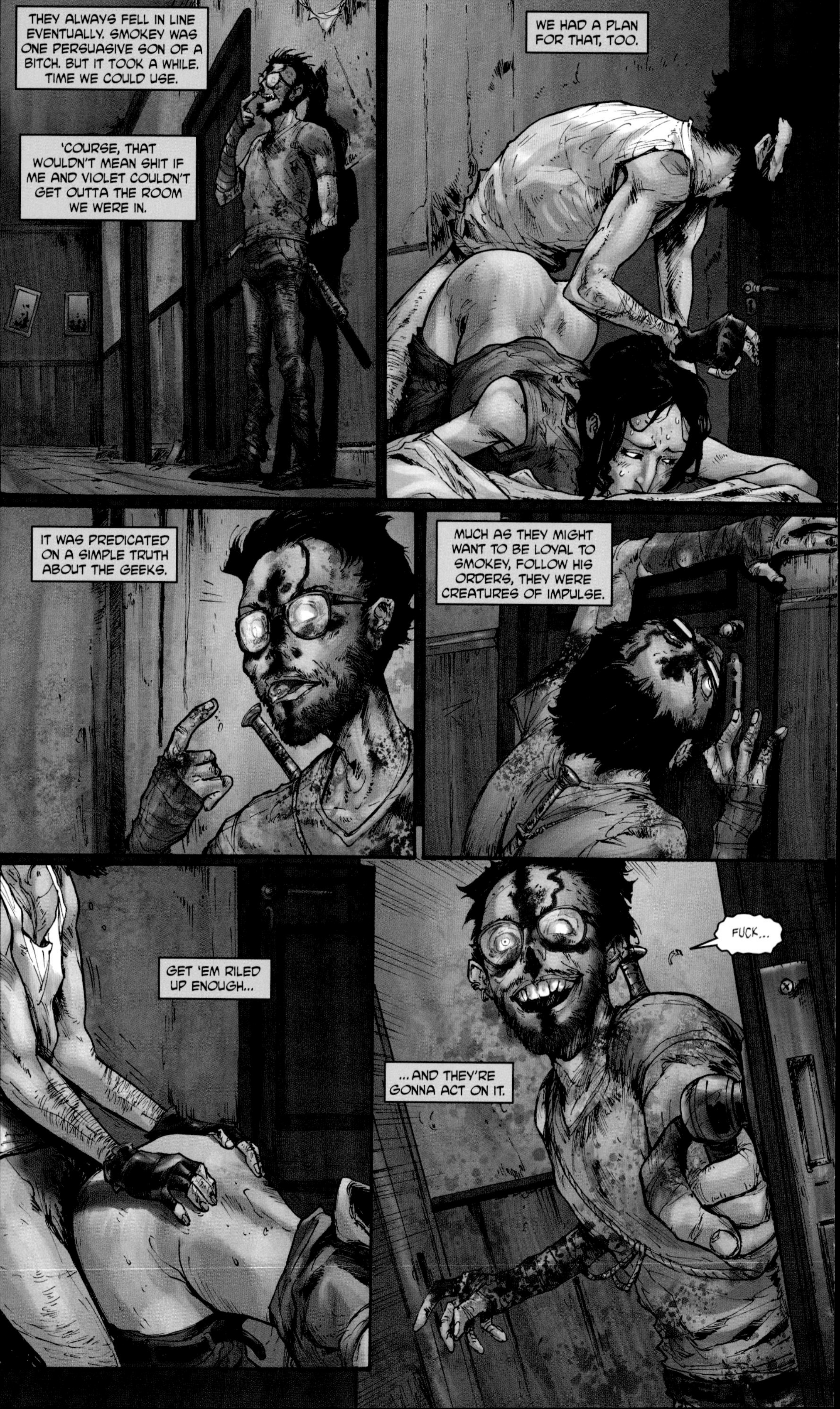
THEY ALWAYS FELL IN LINE EVENTUALLY. SMOKEY WAS ONE PERSUASIVE SON OF A BITCH. BUT IT TOOK A WHILE. TIME WE COULD USE.
'COURSE, THAT WOULDN'T MEAN SHIT IF ME AND VIOLET COULDN'T GET OUTTA THE ROOM WE WERE IN.
WE HAD A PLAN FOR THAT, TOO.
IT WAS PREDICATED ON A SIMPLE TRUTH ABOUT THE GEEKS.
MUCH AS THEY MIGHT WANT TO BE LOYAL TO SMOKEY, FOLLOW HIS ORDERS, THEY WERE CREATURES OF IMPULSE.
GET 'EM RILED UP ENOUGH...
...AND THEY'RE GONNA ACT ON IT.
FUCK...

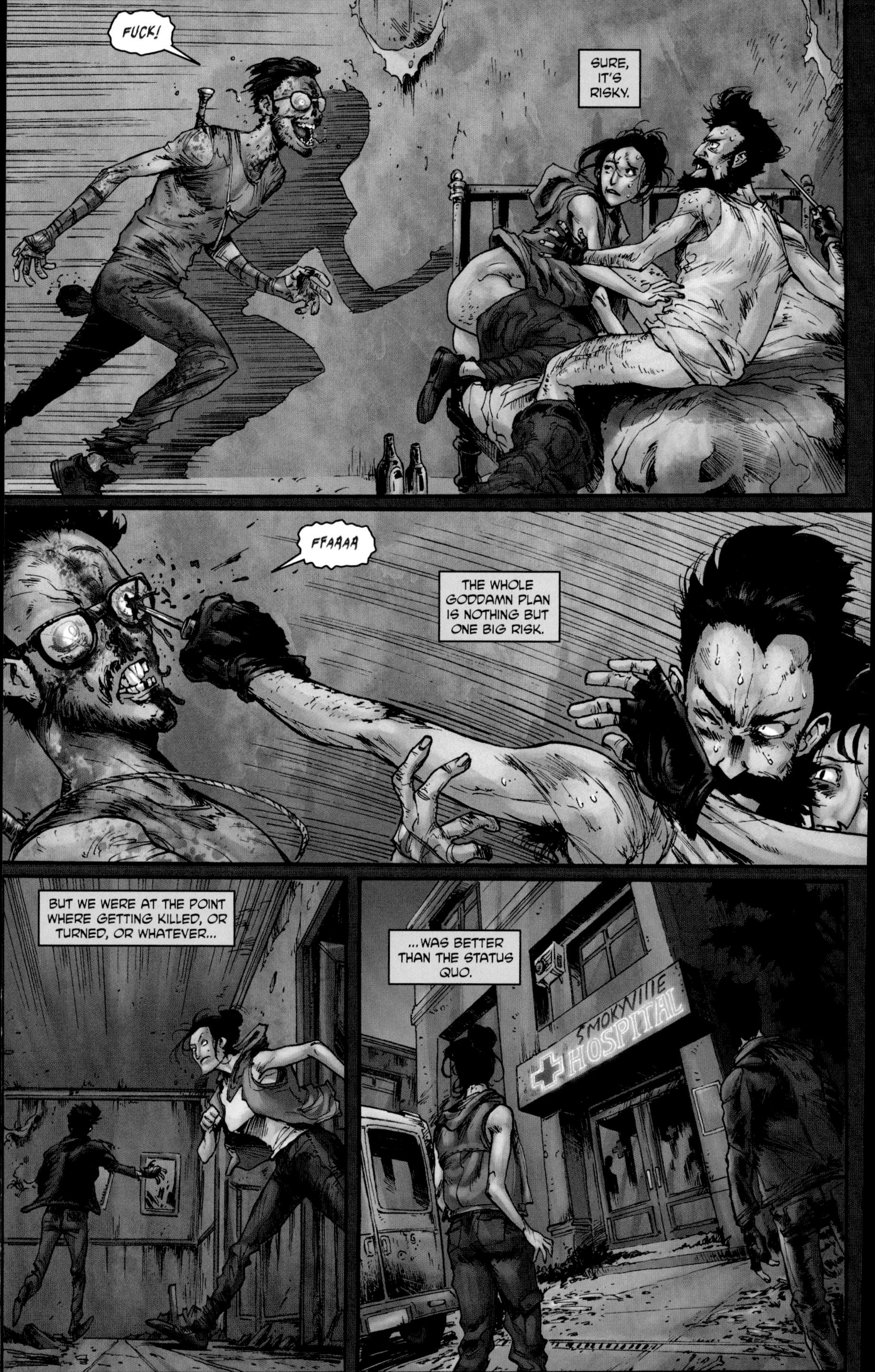
FUCK!
SURE, IT'S RISKY.
FFARAA
THE WHOLE GODDAMN PLAN IS NOTHING BUT ONE BIG RISK.
BUT WE WERE AT THE POINT WHERE GETTING KILLED, OR TURNED, OR WHATEVER...
...WAS BETTER THAN THE STATUS QUO.
SMOKYVILLE HOSPITAL

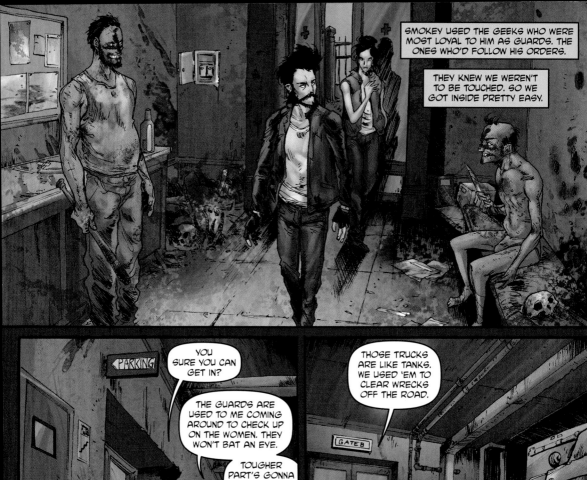

SMOKEY USED THE GEEKS WHO WERE MOST LOYAL TO HIM AS GUARDS. THE ONES WHO'D FOLLOW HIS ORDERS.

THEY KNEW WE WEREN'T TO BE TOUCHED. SO WE GOT INSIDE PRETTY EASY.

YOU SURE YOU CAN GET IN?

THE GUARDS ARE USED TO ME COMING AROUND TO CHECK UP ON THE WOMEN. THEY WON'T BAT AN EYE.

TOUGHER PART'S GONNA BE GETTING US ALL OUT OF THERE.

THOSE TRUCKS ARE LIKE TANKS. WE USED 'EM TO CLEAR WRECKS OFF THE ROAD.

THAT'S NOT WHAT I MEANT.

I'LL GET US GUNS. ENOUGH TO TAKE CARE OF ANY WHO CHASE US.

OR... END THINGS THE OTHER WAY.

YOU'RE NOT A TOTAL BASTARD, CODY.

GOOD LUCK.

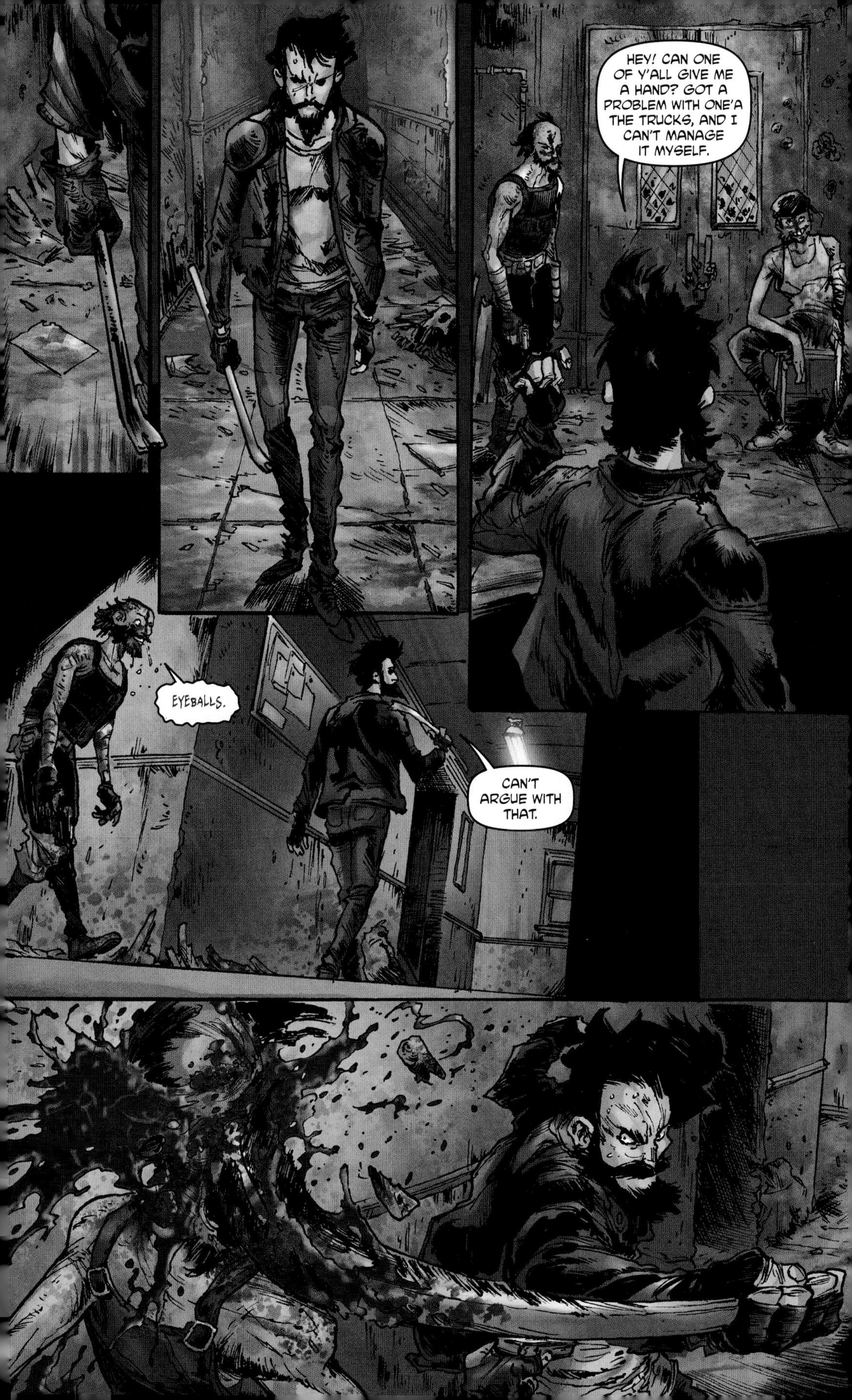
HEY! CAN ONE OF Y'ALL GIVE ME A HAND? GOT A PROBLEM WITH ONE'A THE TRUCKS, AND I CAN'T MANAGE IT MYSELF.
EYEBALLS.
CAN'T ARGUE WITH THAT.

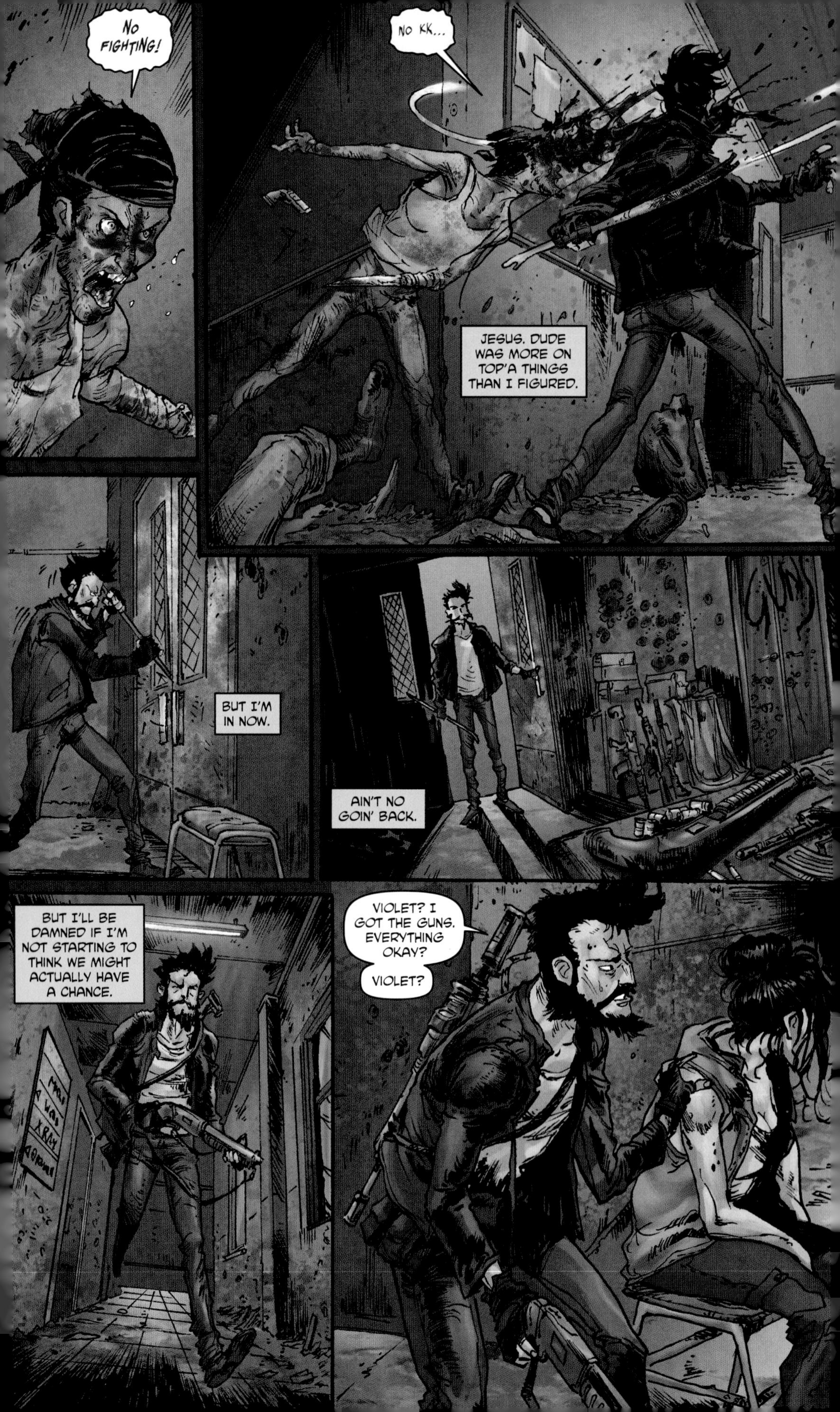
NO FIGHTING!
NO KK...
JESUS. DUDE WAS MORE ON TOP'A THINGS THAN I FIGURED.
BUT I'M IN NOW.
AIN'T NO GOIN' BACK.
BUT I'LL BE DAMNED IF I'M NOT STARTING TO THINK WE MIGHT ACTUALLY HAVE A CHANCE.
VIOLET? I GOT THE GUNS. EVERYTHING OKAY?
VIOLET?

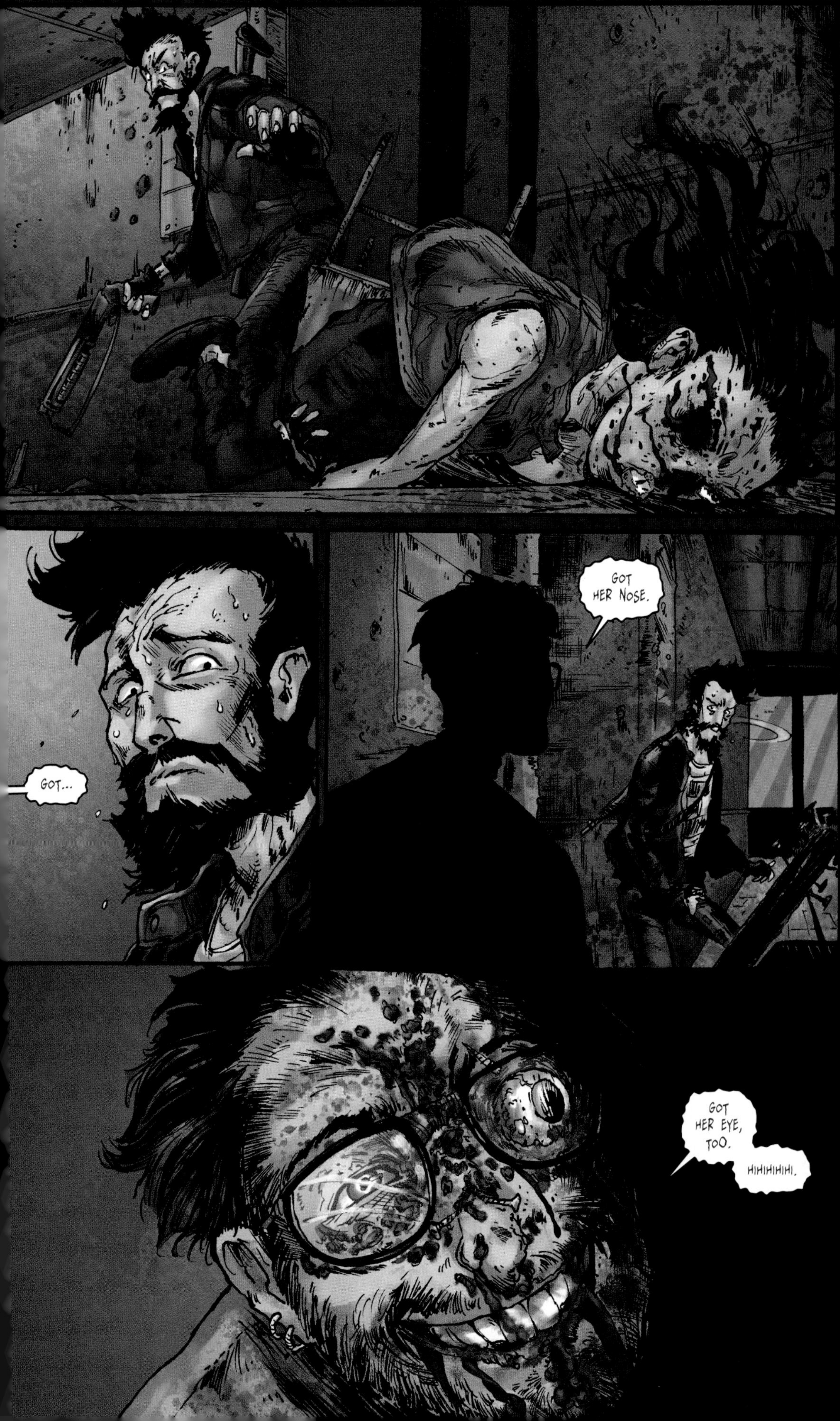
GOT...
GOT HER NOSE.
GOT HER EYE, TOO.
HIHIHIHIHI.

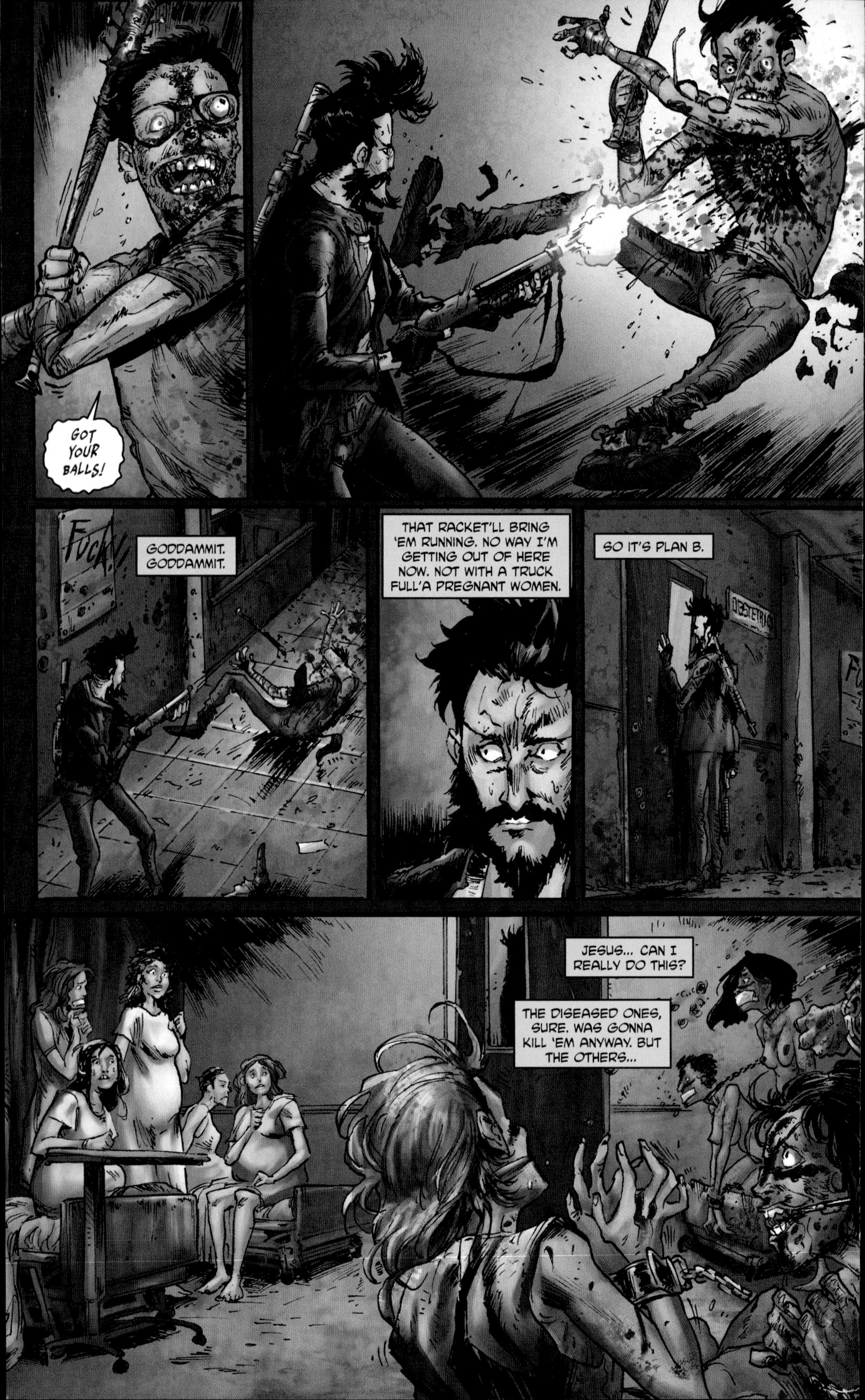

GOT YOUR BALLS!
FUCK
GODDAMMIT. GODDAMMIT.
THAT RACKET'LL BRING 'EM RUNNING. NO WAY I'M GETTING OUT OF HERE NOW. NOT WITH A TRUCK FULL'A PREGNANT WOMEN.
SO IT'S PLAN B.
JESUS... CAN I REALLY DO THIS?
THE DISEASED ONES, SURE. WAS GONNA KILL 'EM ANYWAY. BUT THE OTHERS...

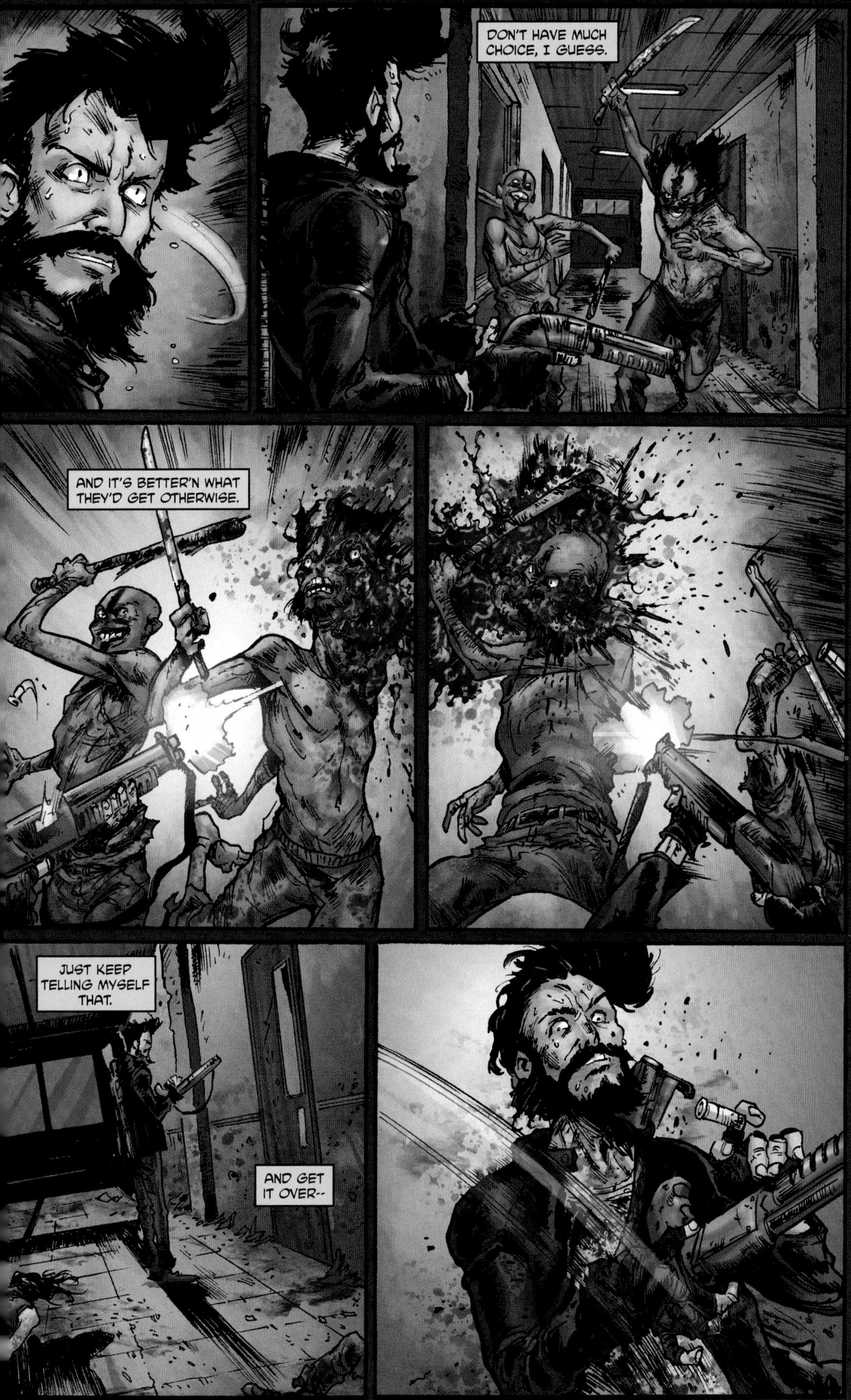
DON'T HAVE MUCH CHOICE, I GUESS.
AND IT'S BETTER'N WHAT THEY'D GET OTHERWISE.
JUST KEEP TELLING MYSELF THAT.
AND GET IT OVER--

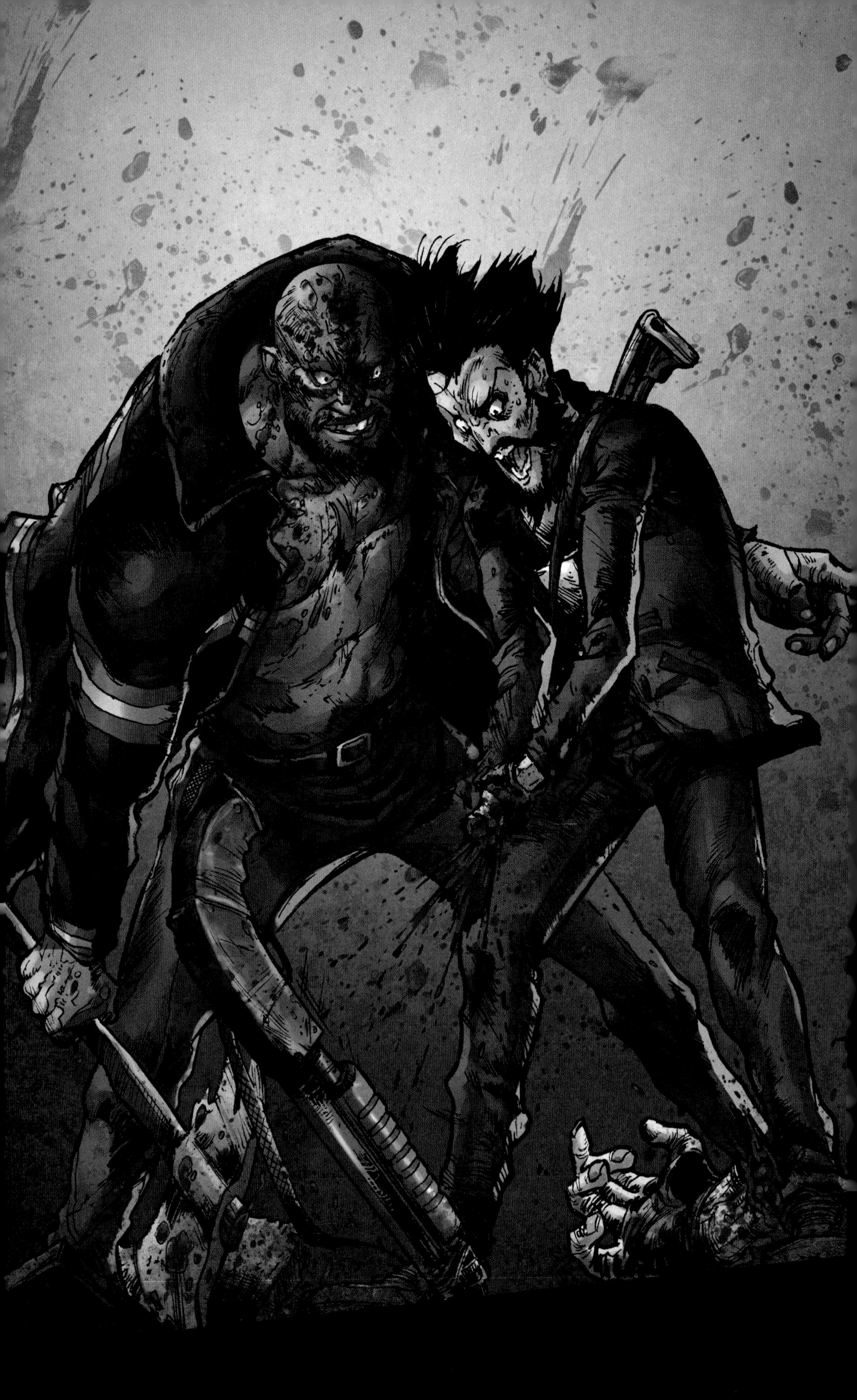

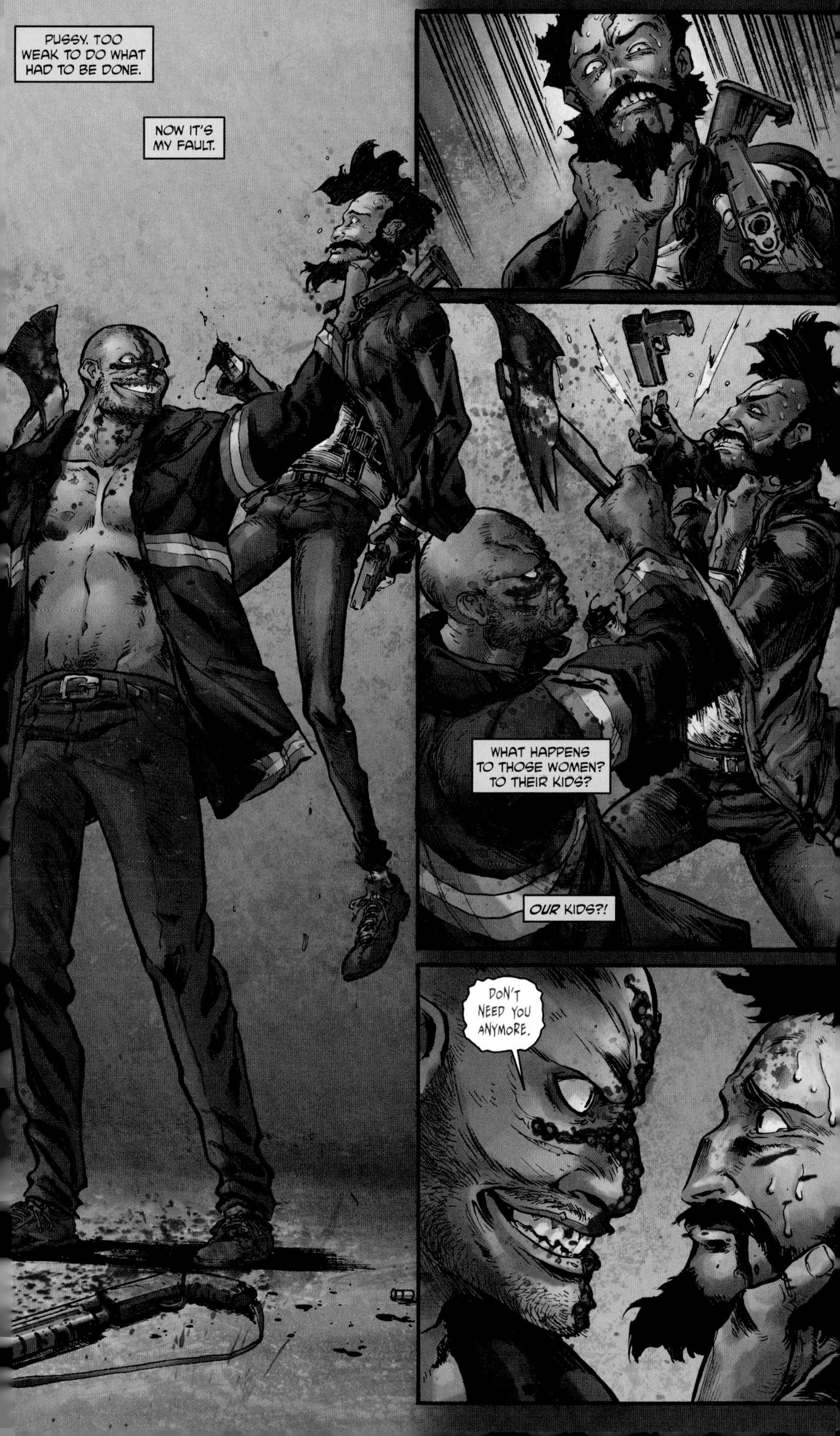
PUSSY. TOO WEAK TO DO WHAT HAD TO BE DONE.
NOW IT'S MY FAULT.
WHAT HAPPENS TO THOSE WOMEN? TO THEIR KIDS?
OUR KIDS?!
DON'T NEED YOU ANYMORE.

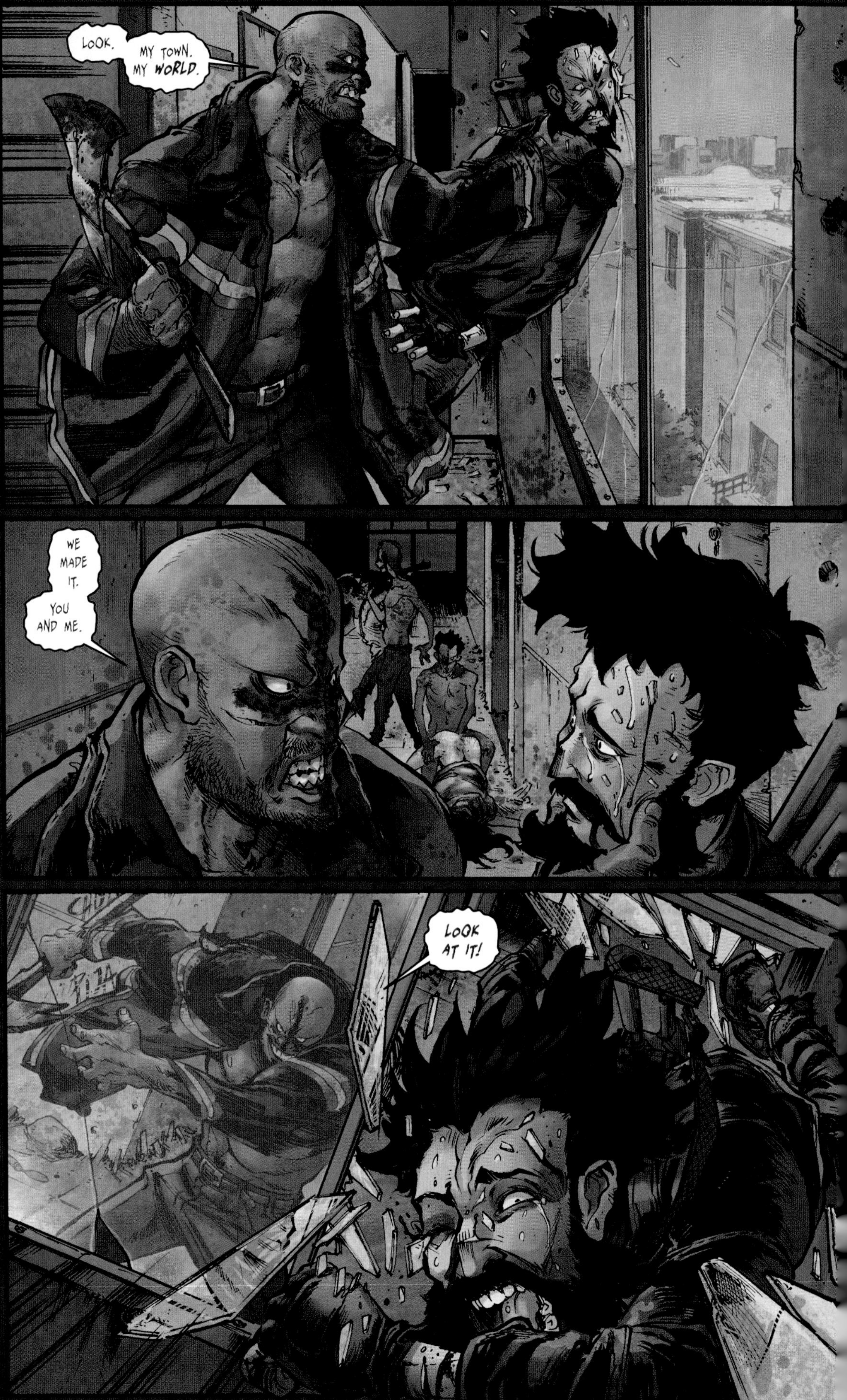
LOOK.
MY TOWN. MY WORLD.
WE MADE IT.
YOU AND ME.
LOOK AT IT!

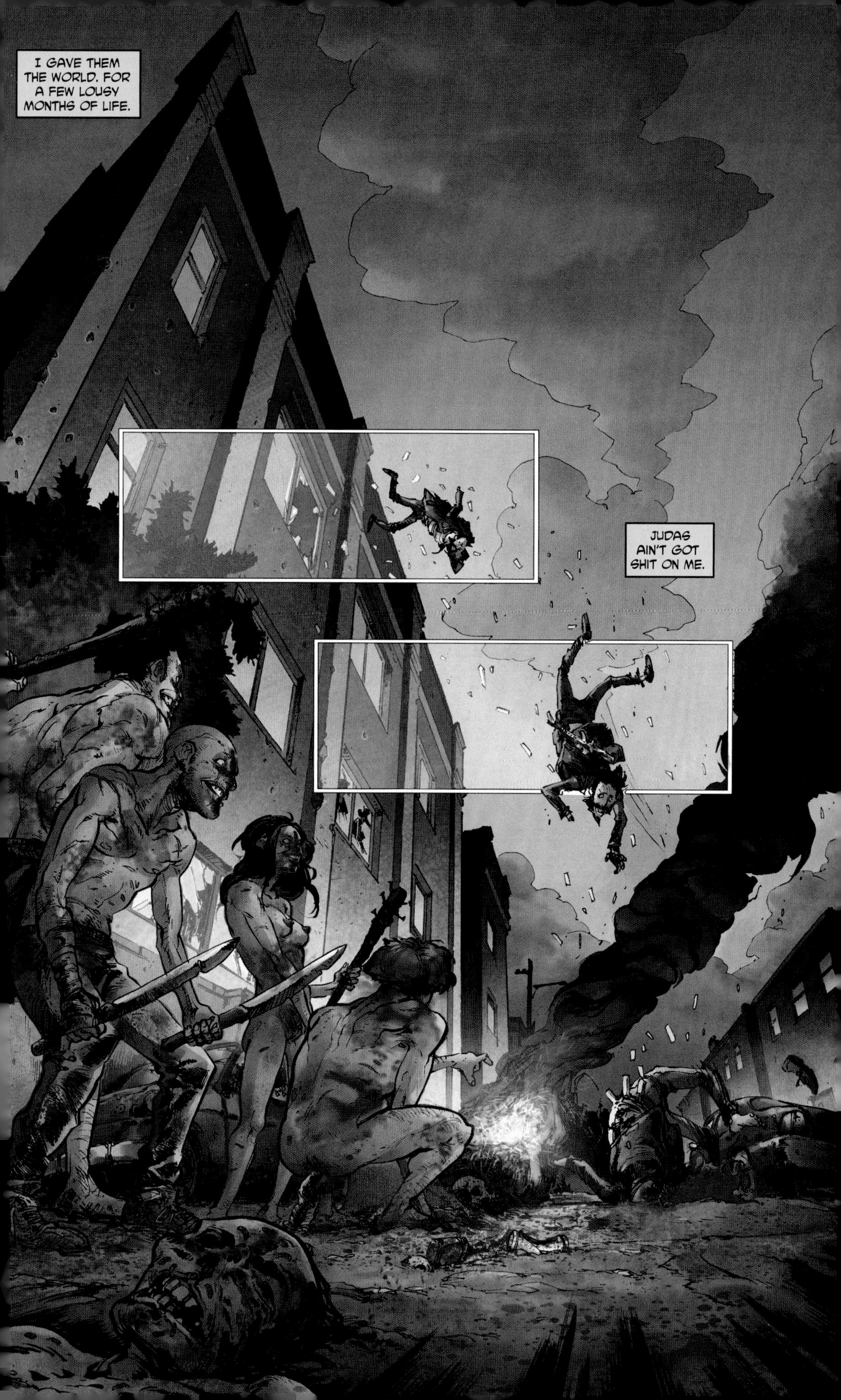
I GAVE THEM THE WORLD. FOR A FEW LOUSY MONTHS OF LIFE.
JUDAS AIN'T GOT SHIT ON ME.

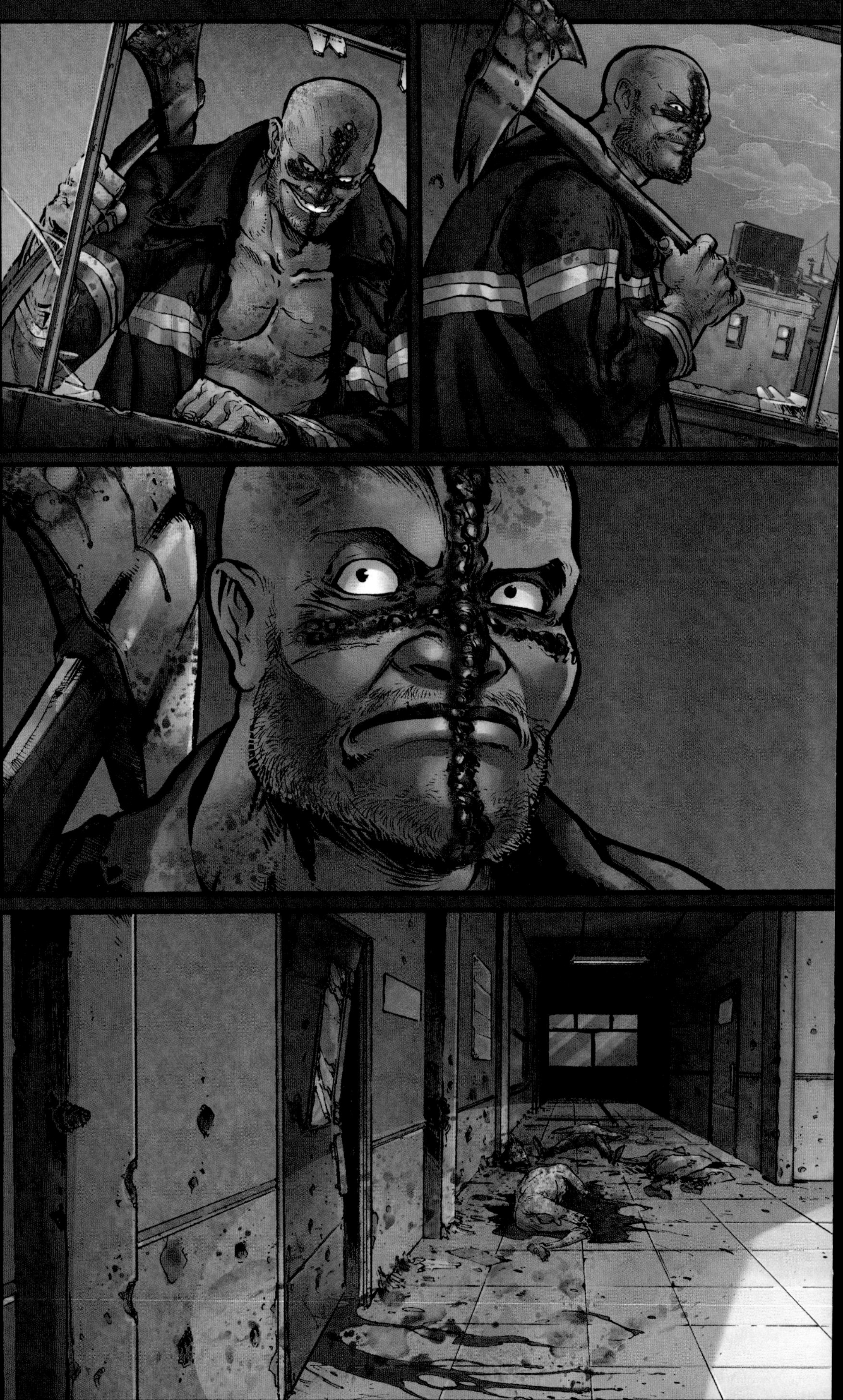

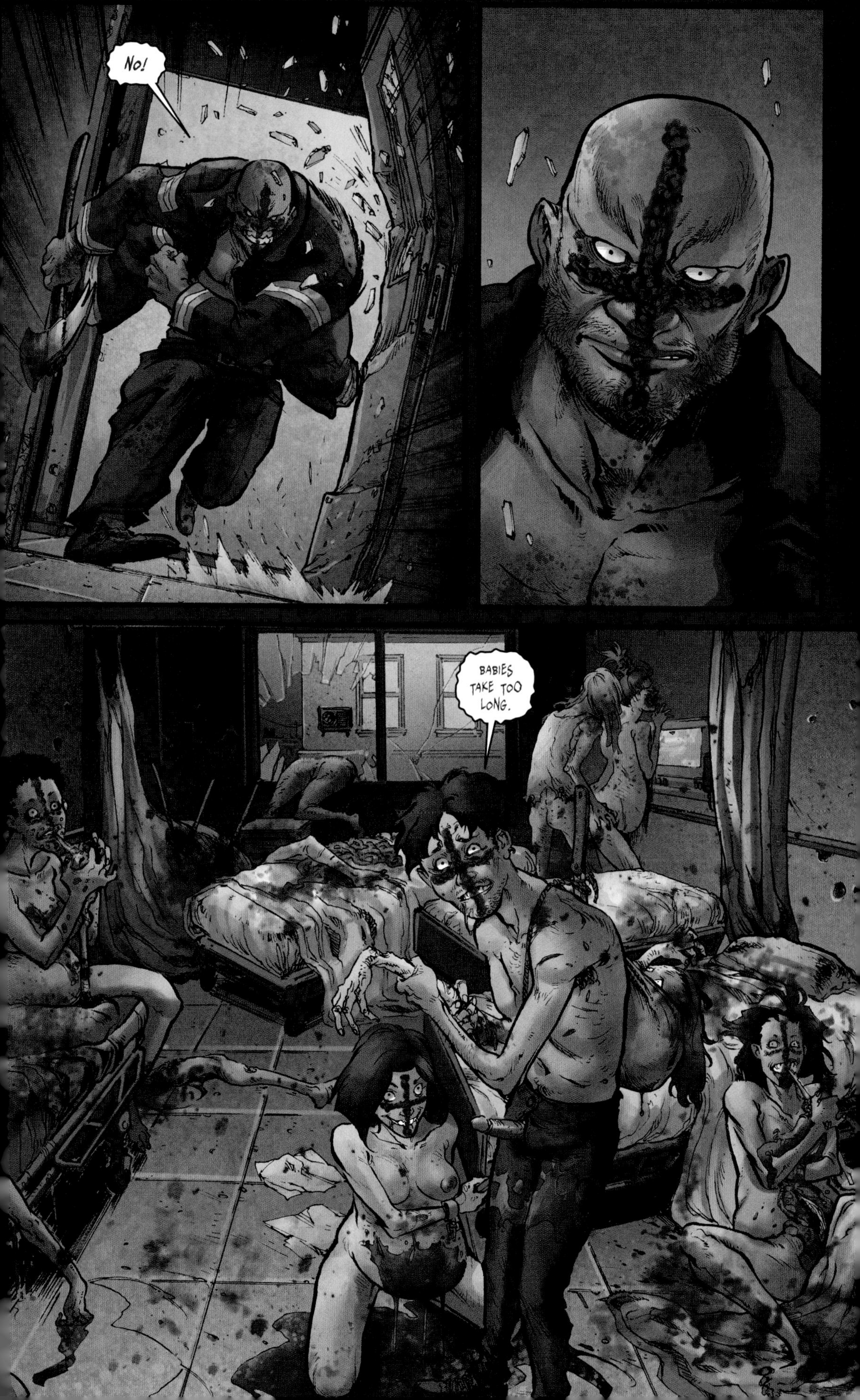
No!
BABIES TAKE TOO LONG.

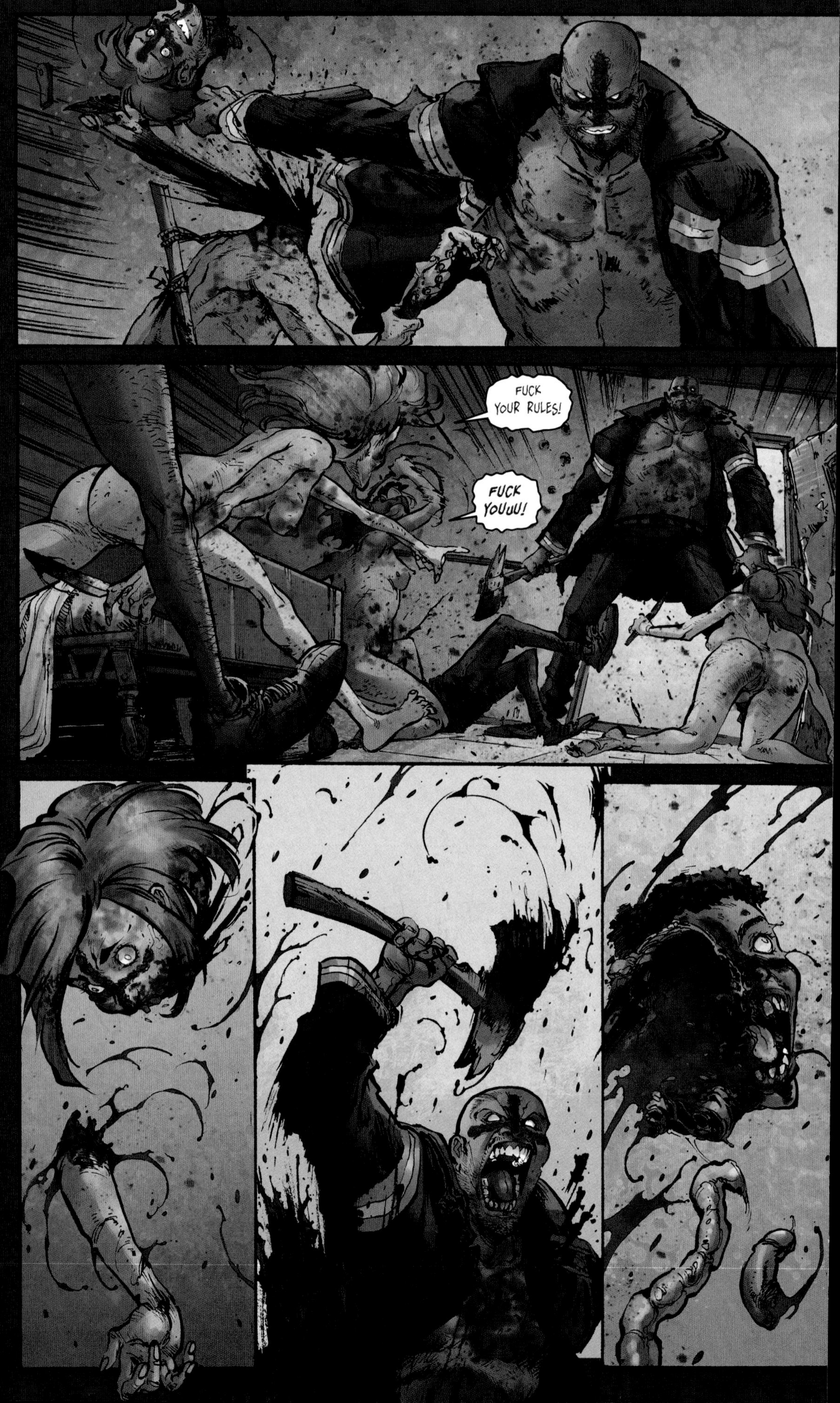
FUCK YOUR RULES!
FUCK YOUUU!

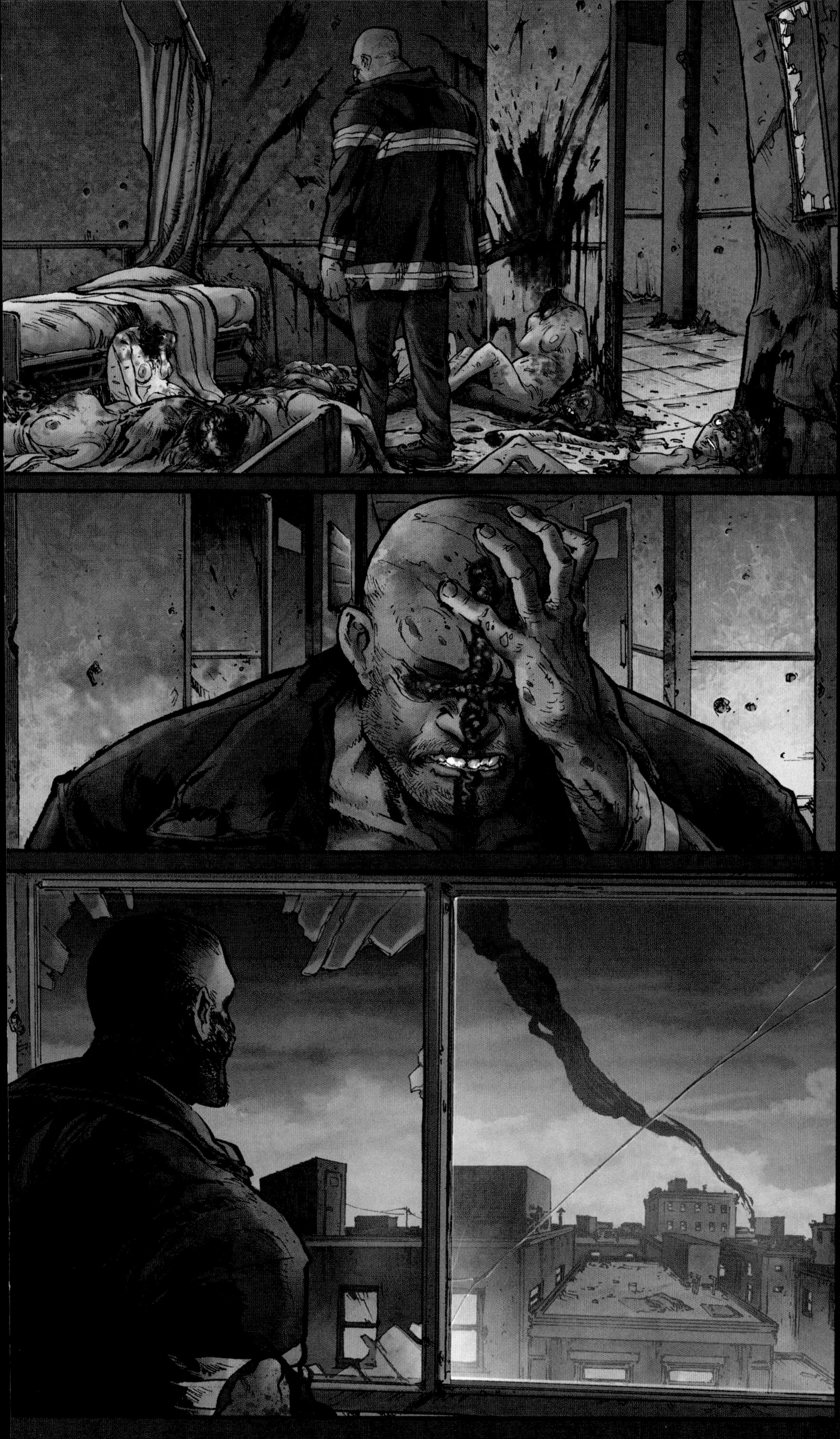

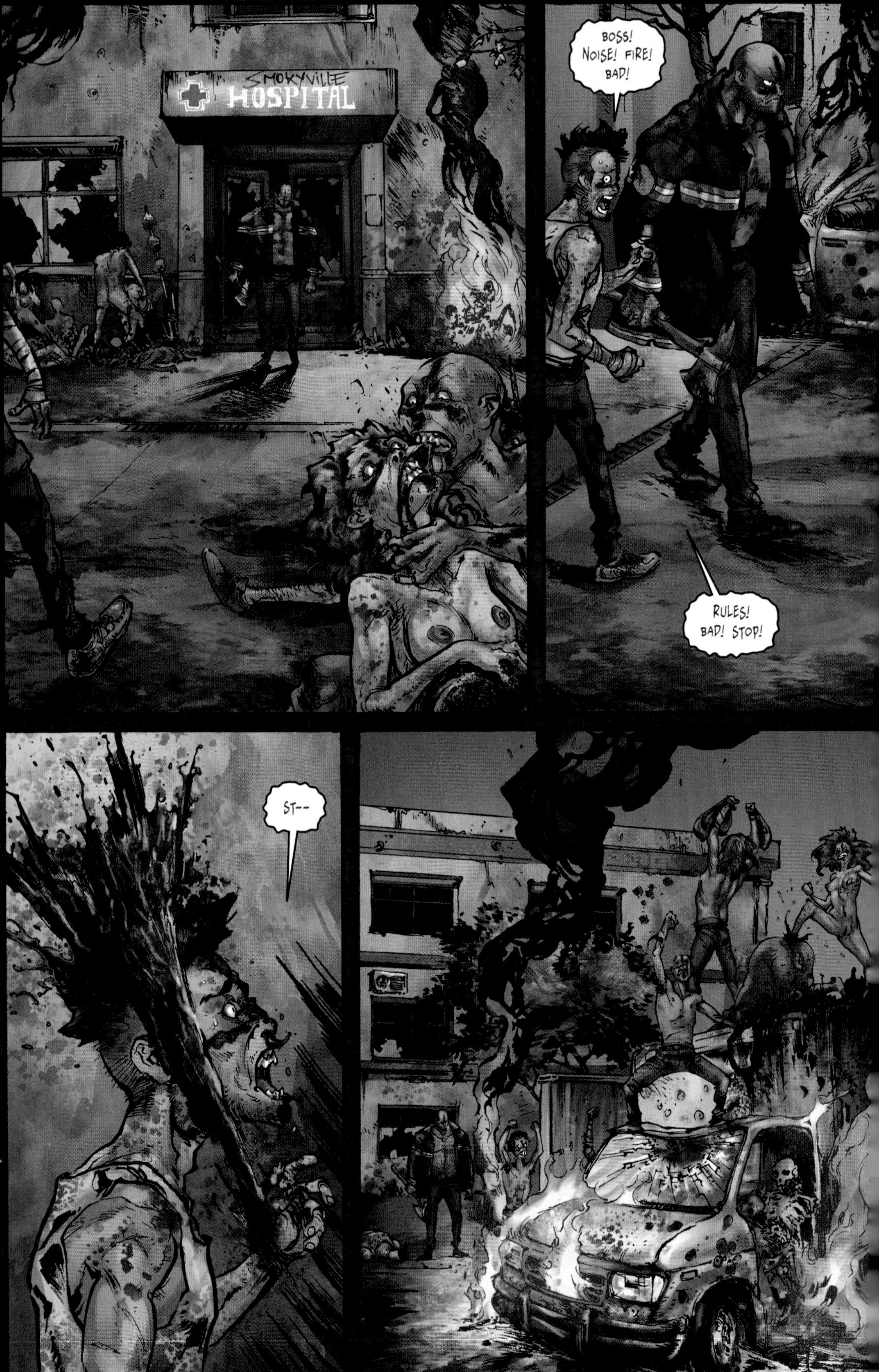
SMOKYVILLE
HOSPITAL
BOSS! NOISE! FIRE! BAD!
RULES! BAD! STOP!
ST--

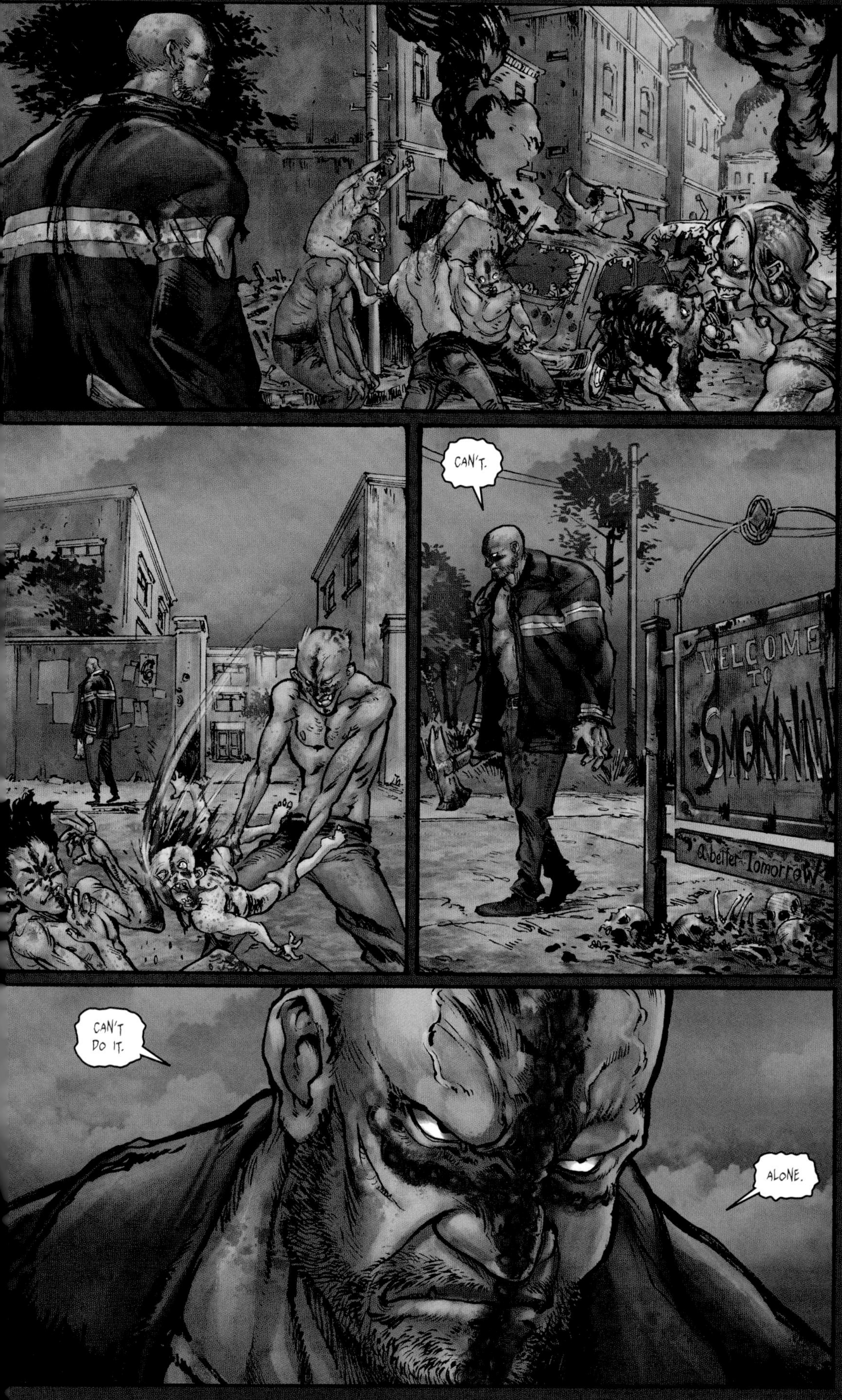
CAN'T.
WELCOME TO
a better Tomorrow
CAN'T DO IT.
ALONE.

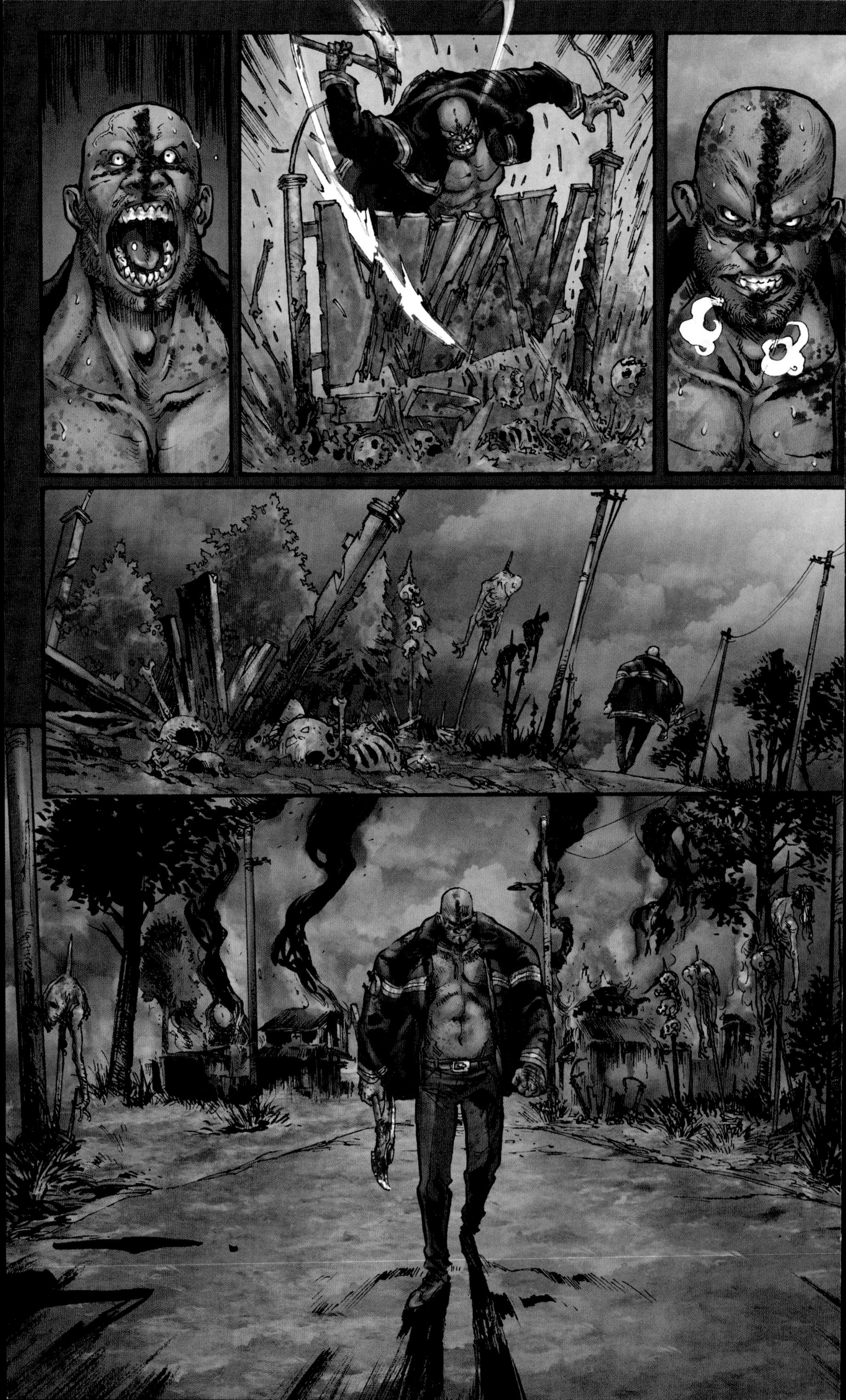

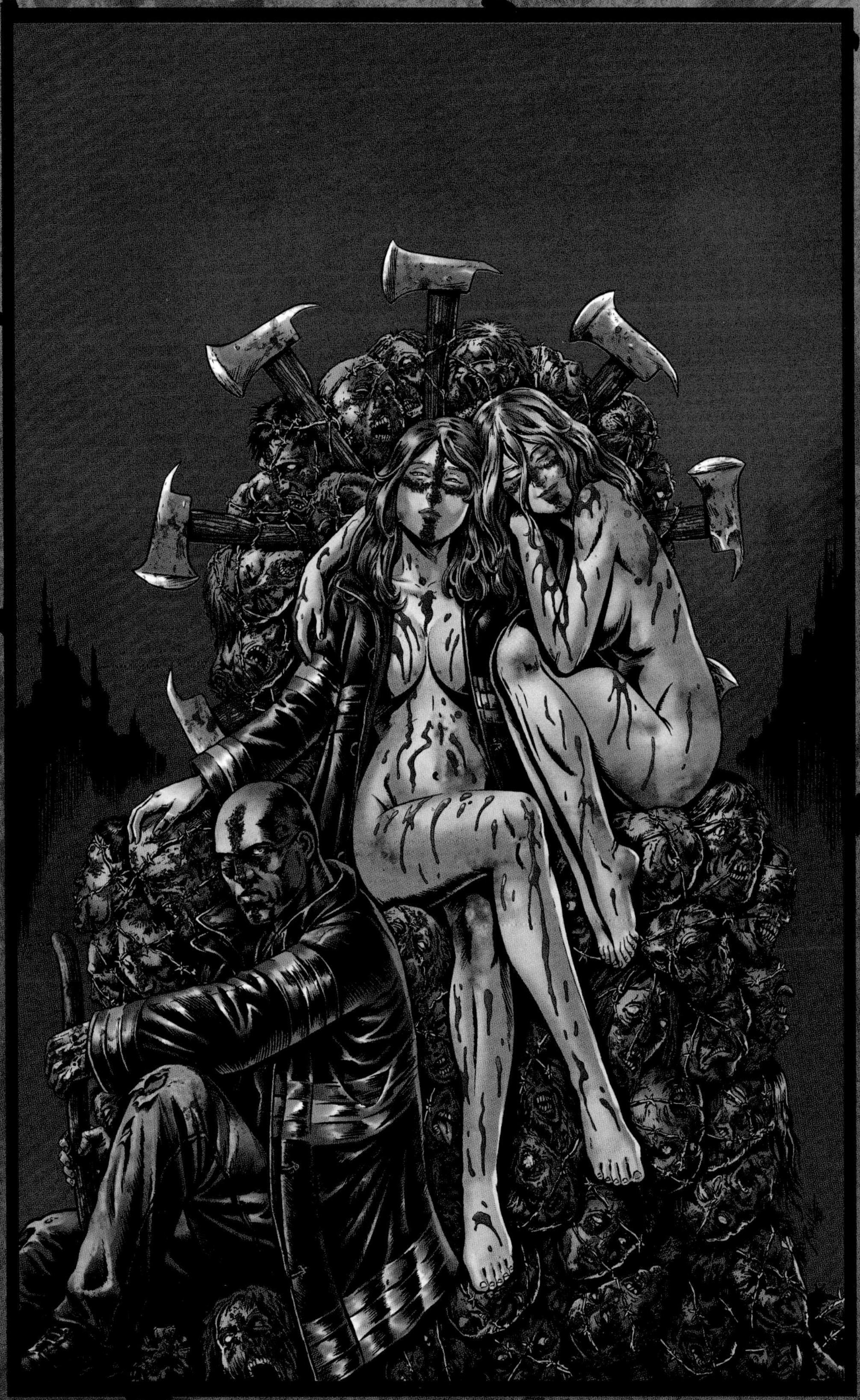

PART 5

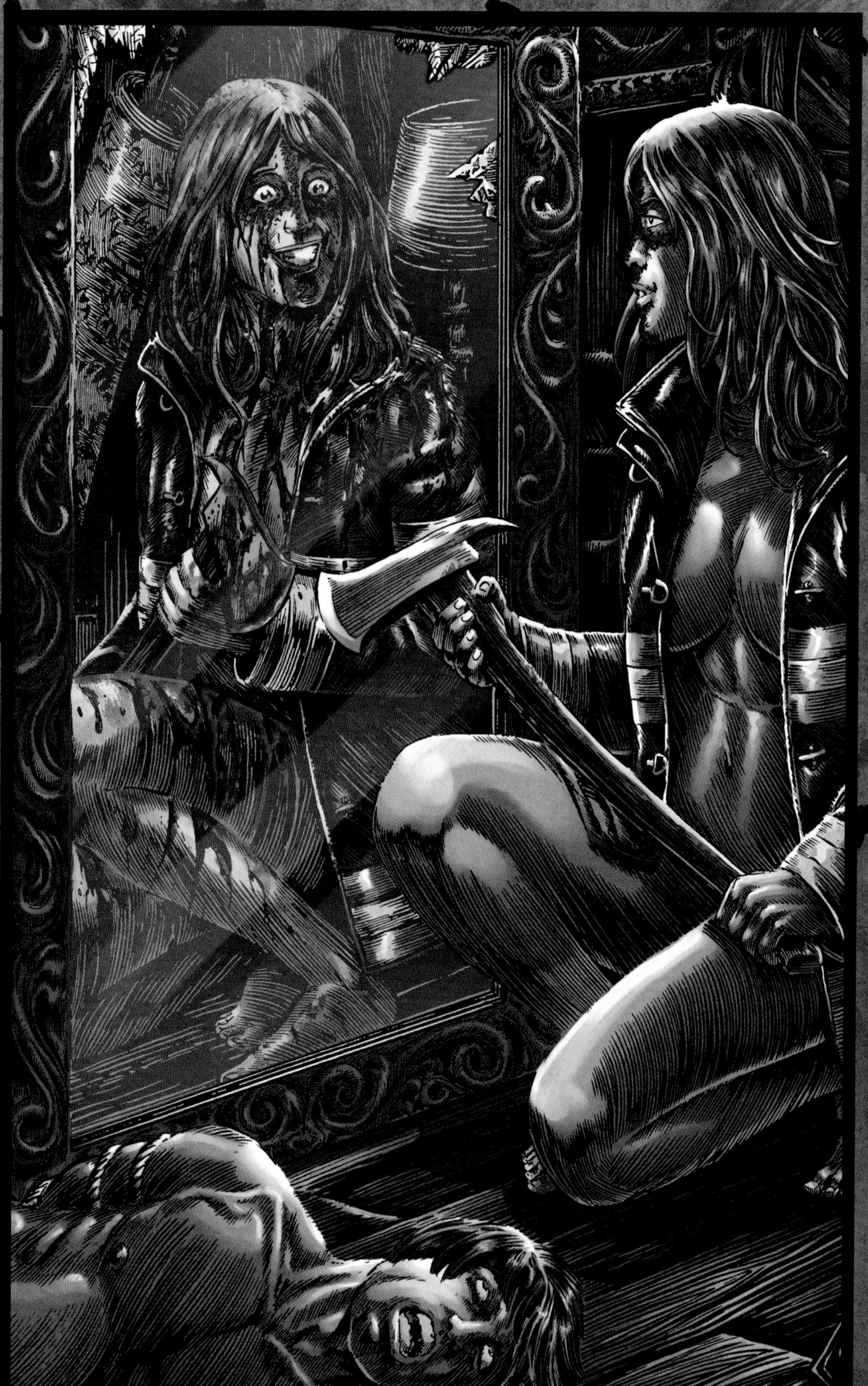

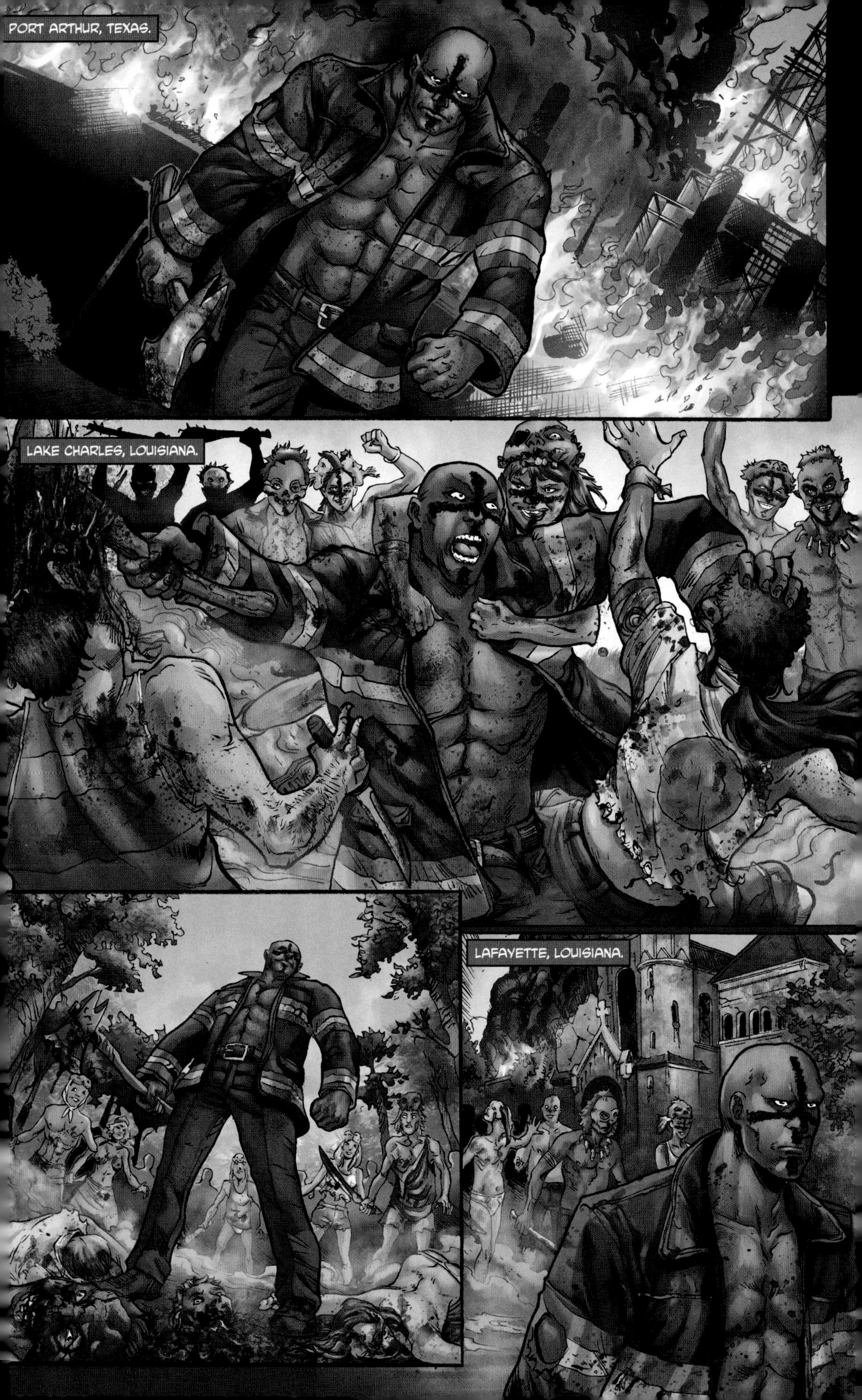
PORT ARTHUR, TEXAS.
LAKE CHARLES, LOUISIANA.
LAFAYETTE, LOUISIANA.

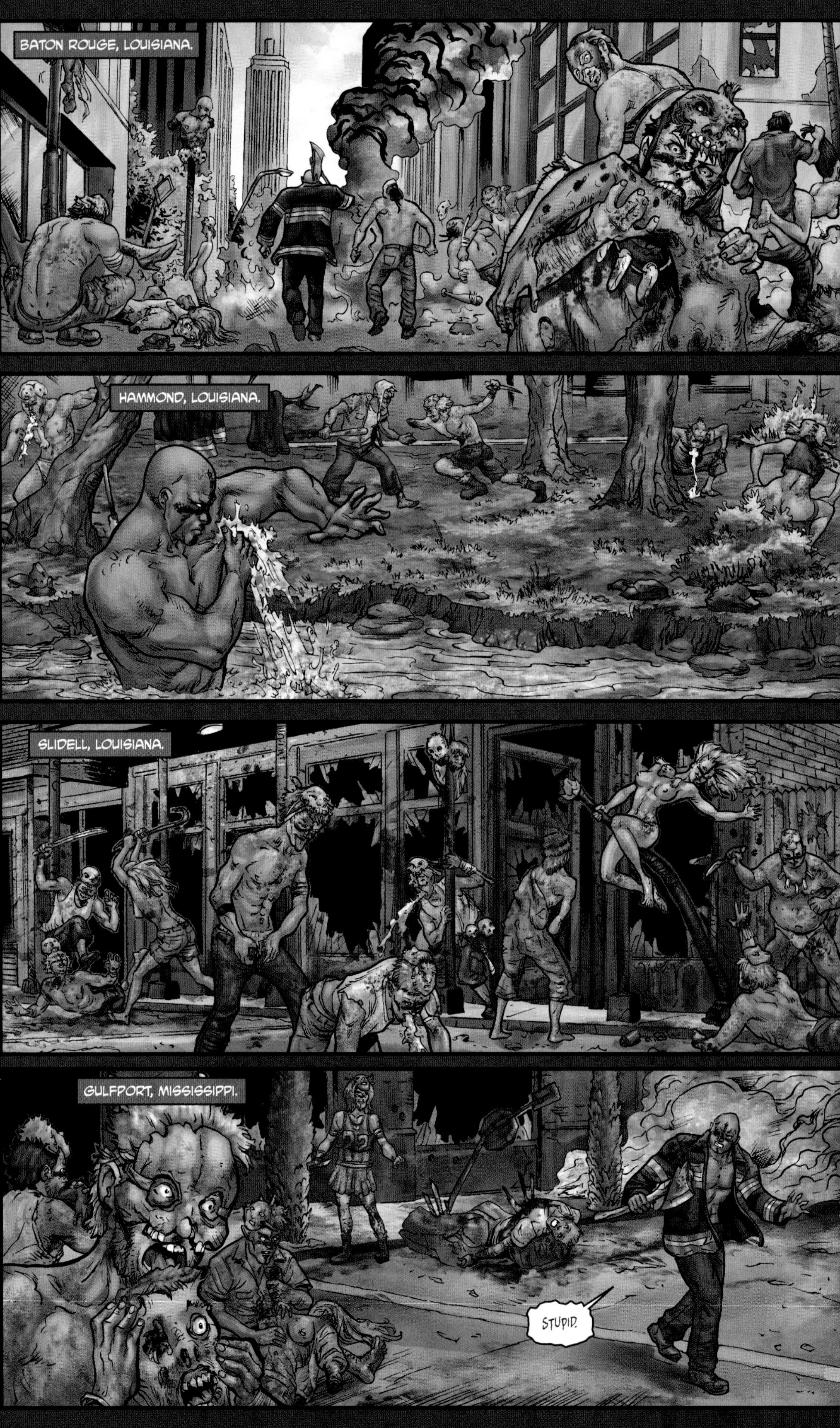
BATON ROUGE, LOUISIANA.
HAMMOND, LOUISIANA.
SLIDELL, LOUISIANA.
GULFPORT, MISSISSIPPI.
STUPID.

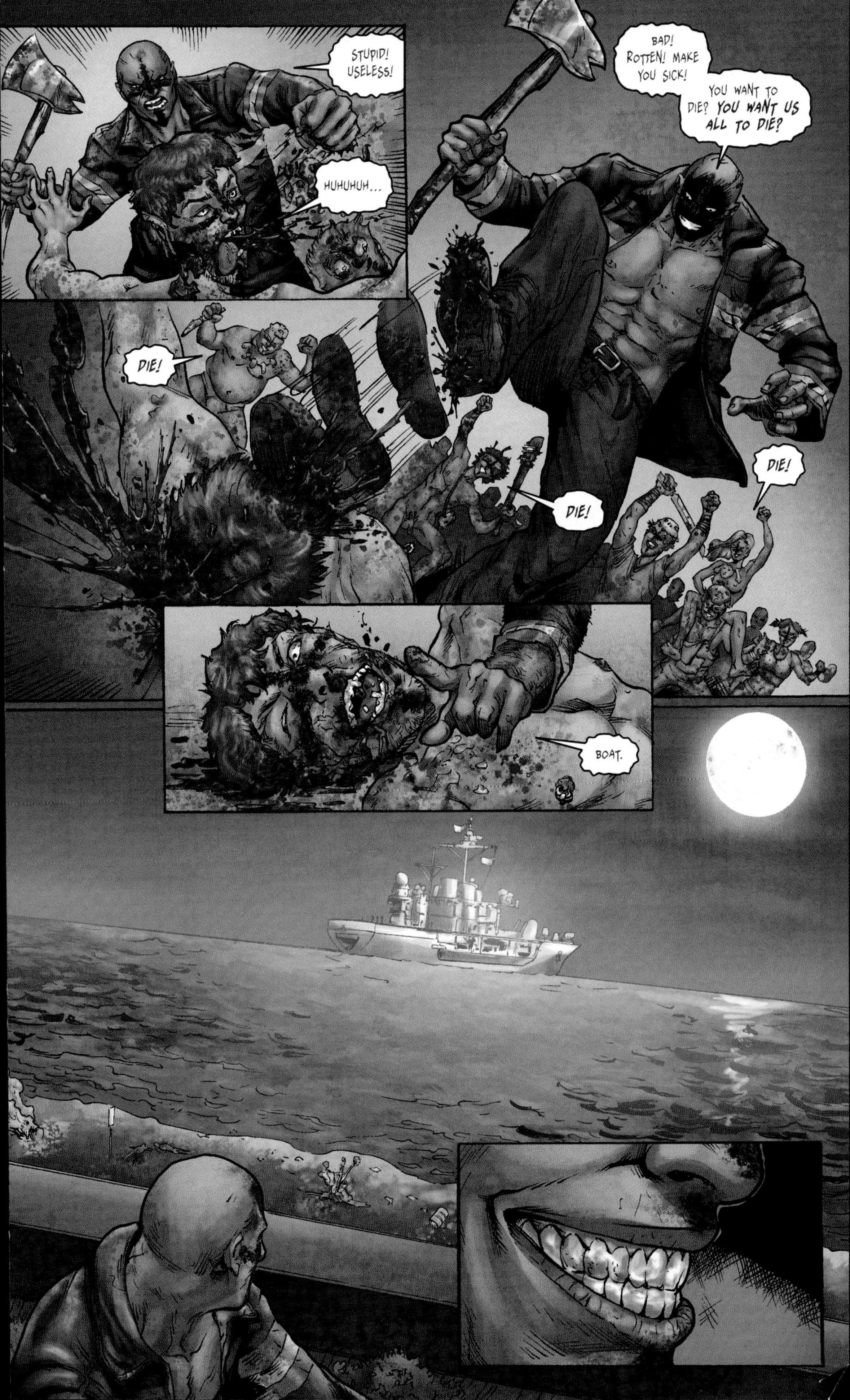
STUPID! USELESS!
HUHUHUH...
BAD! ROTTEN! MAKE YOU SICK!
YOU WANT TO DIE? YOU WANT US ALL TO DIE?
DIE!
DIE!
DIE!
BOAT.

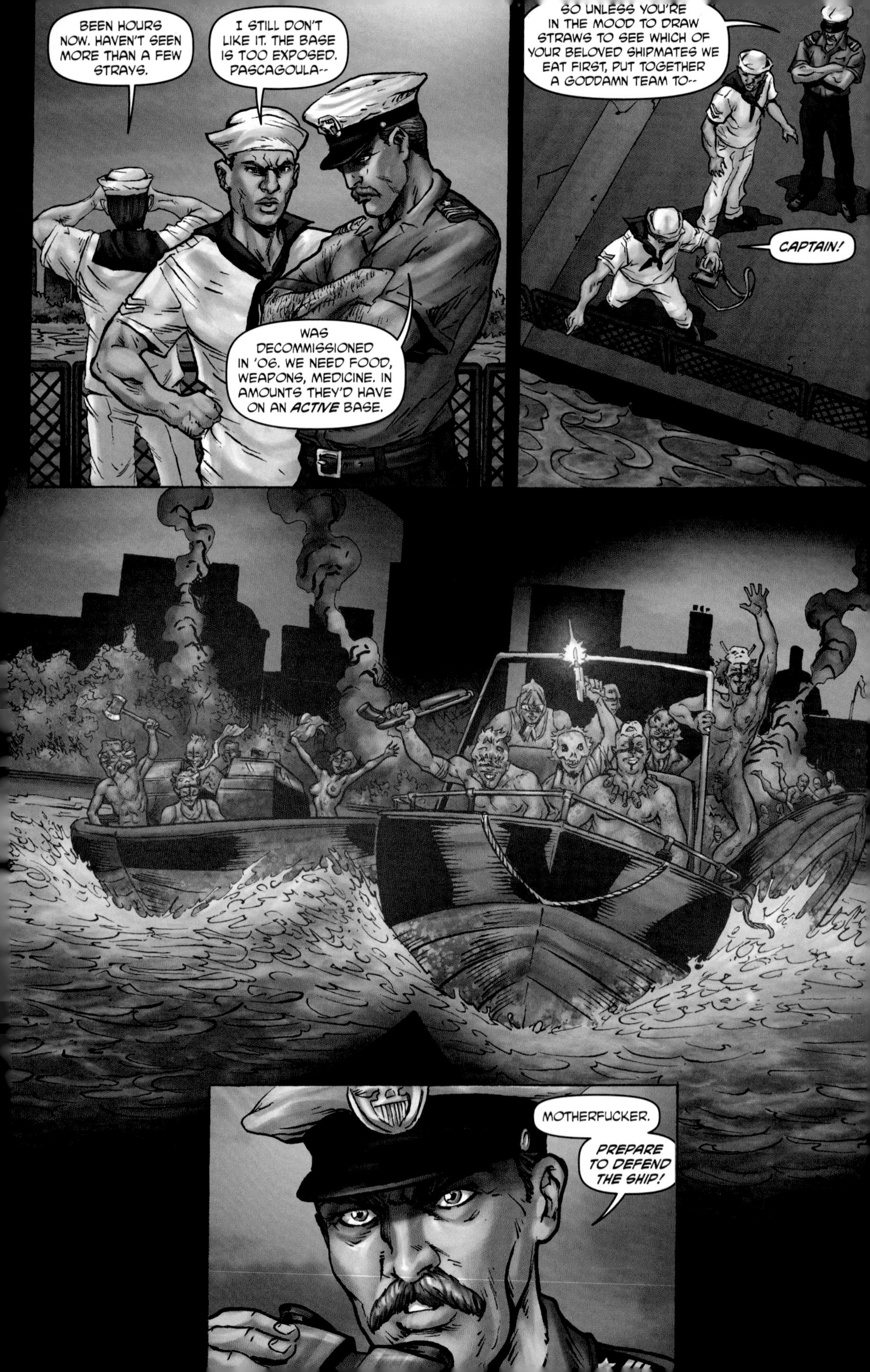

BEEN HOURS NOW. HAVEN'T SEEN MORE THAN A FEW STRAYS.
I STILL DON'T LIKE IT. THE BASE IS TOO EXPOSED. PASCAGOULA--
WAS DECOMMISSIONED IN '06. WE NEED FOOD, WEAPONS, MEDICINE. IN AMOUNTS THEY'D HAVE ON AN *ACTIVE* BASE.
SO UNLESS YOU'RE IN THE MOOD TO DRAW STRAWS TO SEE WHICH OF YOUR BELOVED SHIPMATES WE EAT FIRST, PUT TOGETHER A GODDAMN TEAM TO--
CAPTAIN!
MOTHERFUCKER.
PREPARE TO DEFEND THE SHIP!

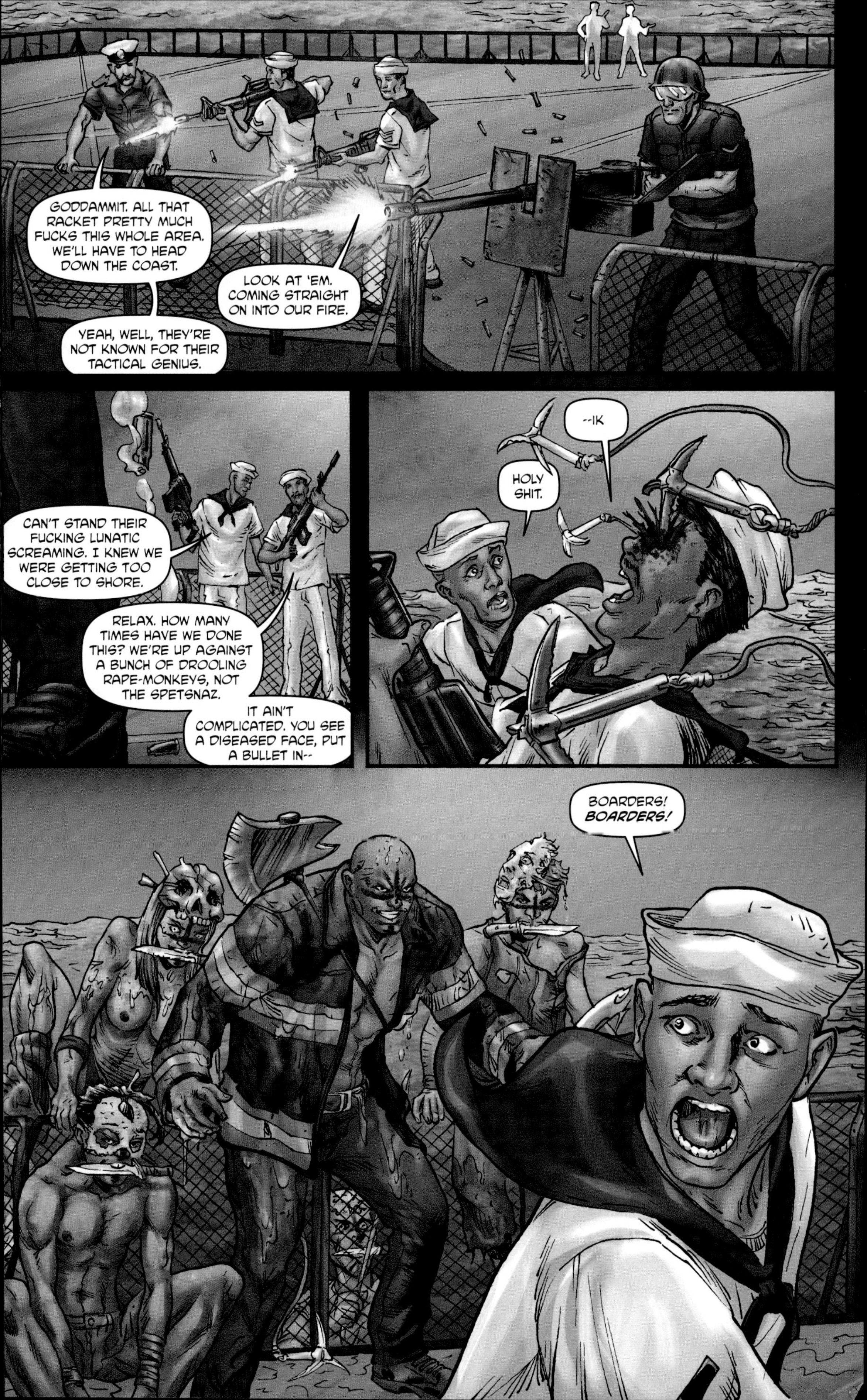
GODDAMMIT. ALL THAT RACKET PRETTY MUCH FUCKS THIS WHOLE AREA. WE'LL HAVE TO HEAD DOWN THE COAST.
LOOK AT 'EM. COMING STRAIGHT ON INTO OUR FIRE.
YEAH, WELL, THEY'RE NOT KNOWN FOR THEIR TACTICAL GENIUS.
CAN'T STAND THEIR FUCKING LUNATIC SCREAMING. I KNEW WE WERE GETTING TOO CLOSE TO SHORE.
RELAX. HOW MANY TIMES HAVE WE DONE THIS? WE'RE UP AGAINST A BUNCH OF DROOLING RAPE-MONKEYS, NOT THE SPETSNAZ.
IT AIN'T COMPLICATED. YOU SEE A DISEASED FACE, PUT A BULLET IN--
--IK
HOLY SHIT.
BOARDERS! *BOARDERS!*

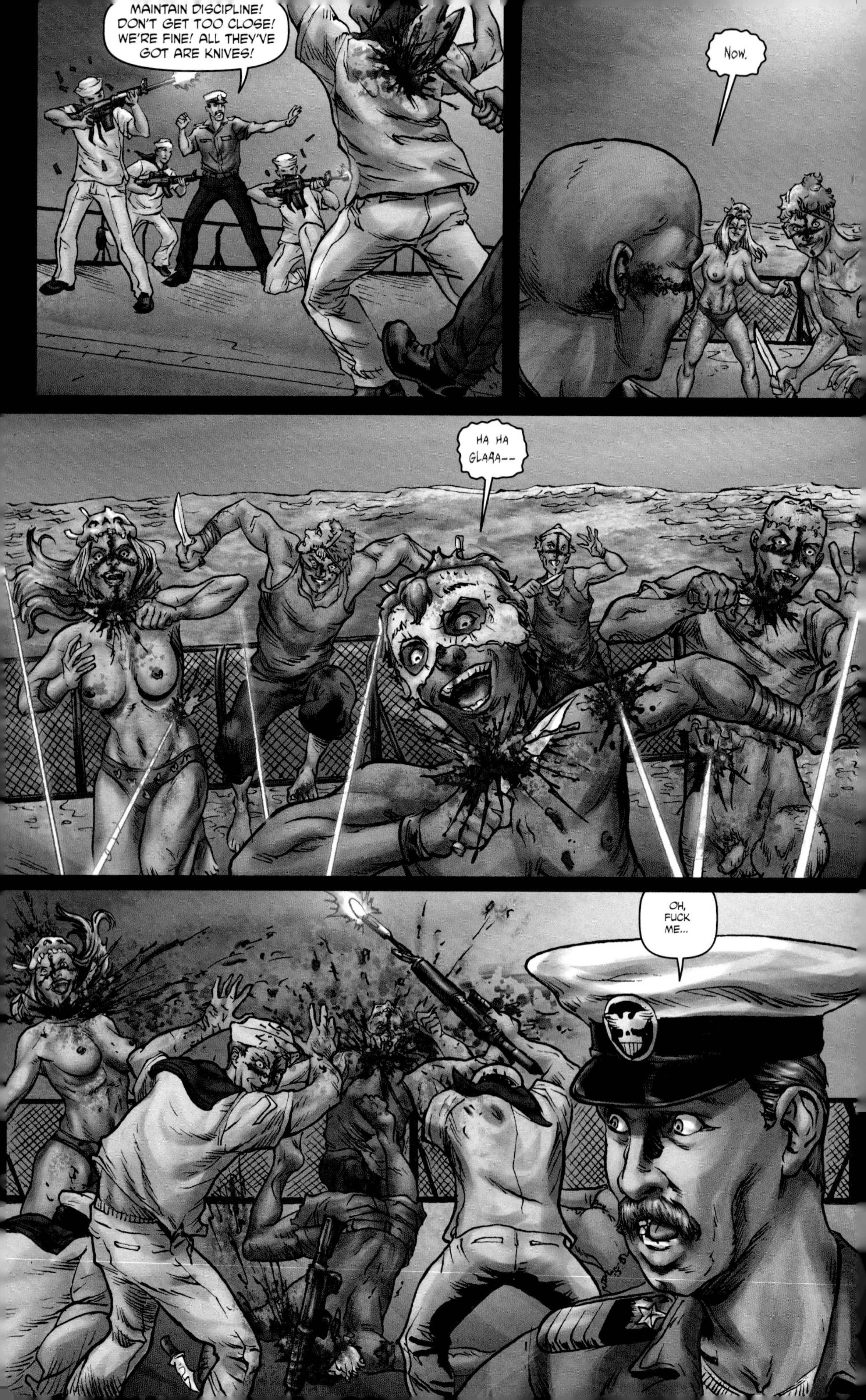
MAINTAIN DISCIPLINE! DON'T GET TOO CLOSE! WE'RE FINE! ALL THEY'VE GOT ARE KNIVES!
NOW.
HA HA GLARA--
OH, FUCK ME...

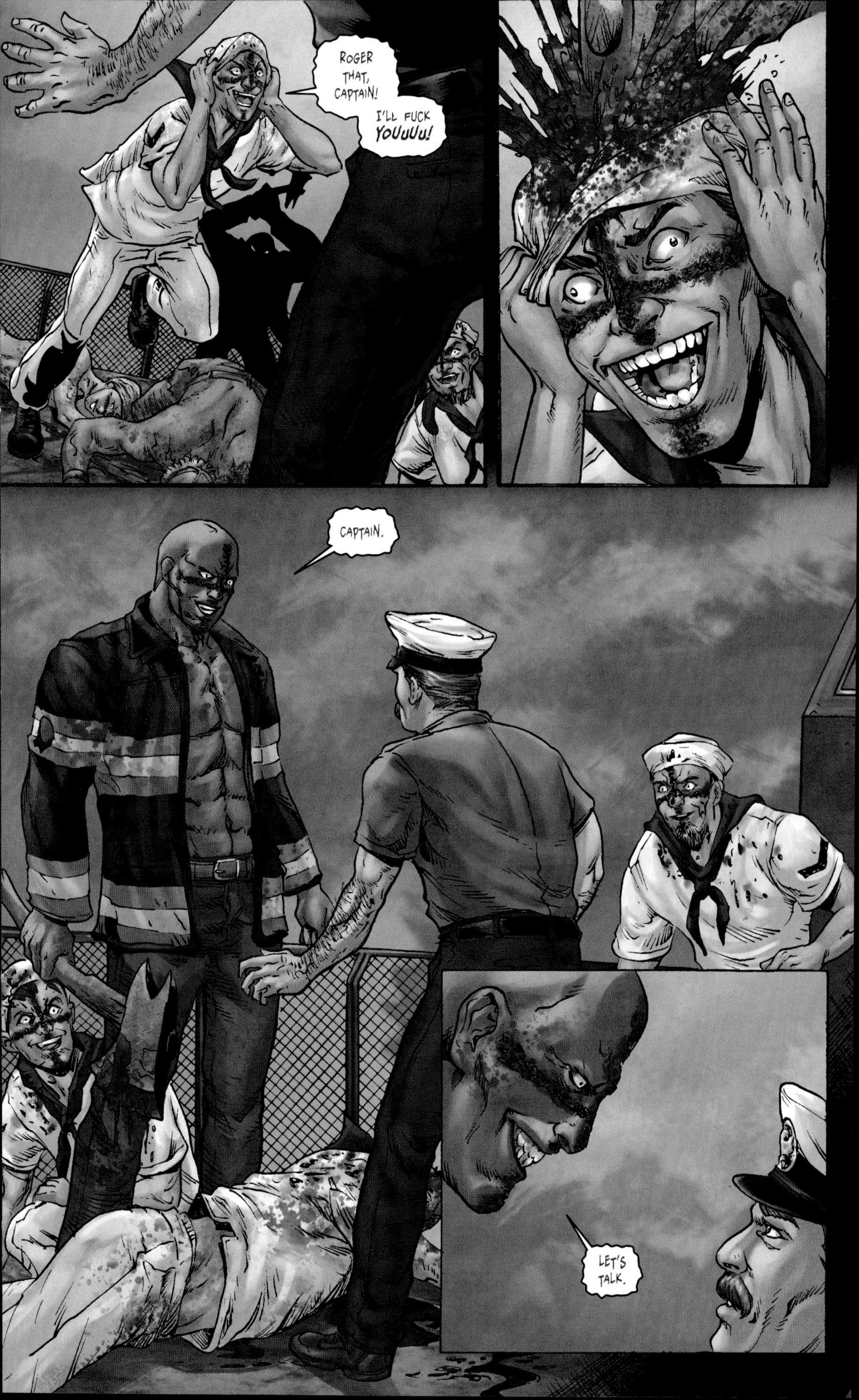
ROGER THAT, CAPTAIN!
I'LL FUCK YOUUUU!
CAPTAIN.
LET'S TALK.

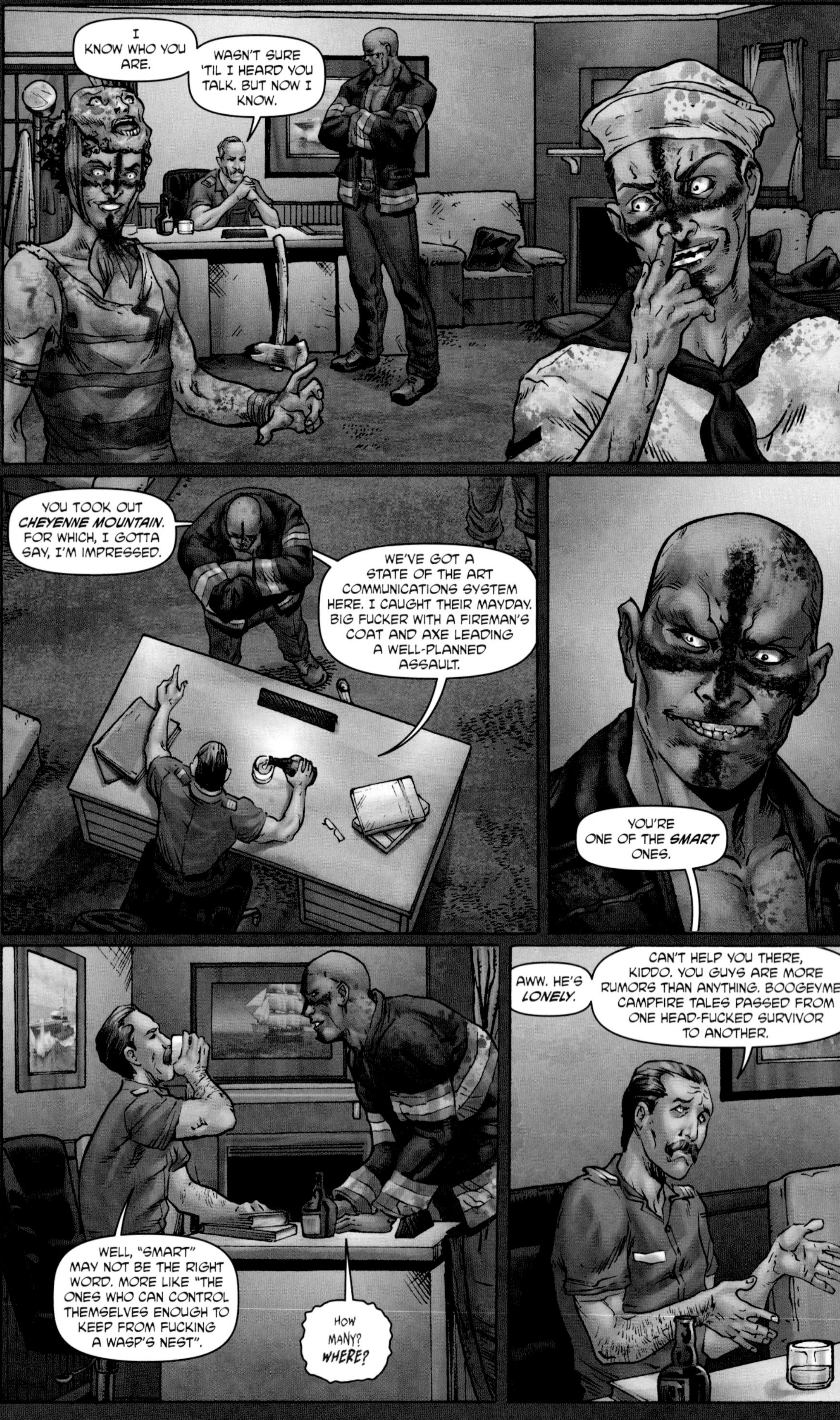
I KNOW WHO YOU ARE.
WASN'T SURE 'TIL I HEARD YOU TALK. BUT NOW I KNOW.
YOU TOOK OUT *CHEYENNE MOUNTAIN*. FOR WHICH, I GOTTA SAY, I'M IMPRESSED.
WE'VE GOT A STATE OF THE ART COMMUNICATIONS SYSTEM HERE. I CAUGHT THEIR MAYDAY. BIG FUCKER WITH A FIREMAN'S COAT AND AXE LEADING A WELL-PLANNED ASSAULT.
YOU'RE ONE OF THE *SMART* ONES.
WELL, "SMART" MAY NOT BE THE RIGHT WORD. MORE LIKE "THE ONES WHO CAN CONTROL THEMSELVES ENOUGH TO KEEP FROM FUCKING A WASP'S NEST".
HOW MANY? **WHERE?**
AWW. HE'S *LONELY*.
CAN'T HELP YOU THERE, KIDDO. YOU GUYS ARE MORE RUMORS THAN ANYTHING. BOOGEYMEN. CAMPFIRE TALES PASSED FROM ONE HEAD-FUCKED SURVIVOR TO ANOTHER.

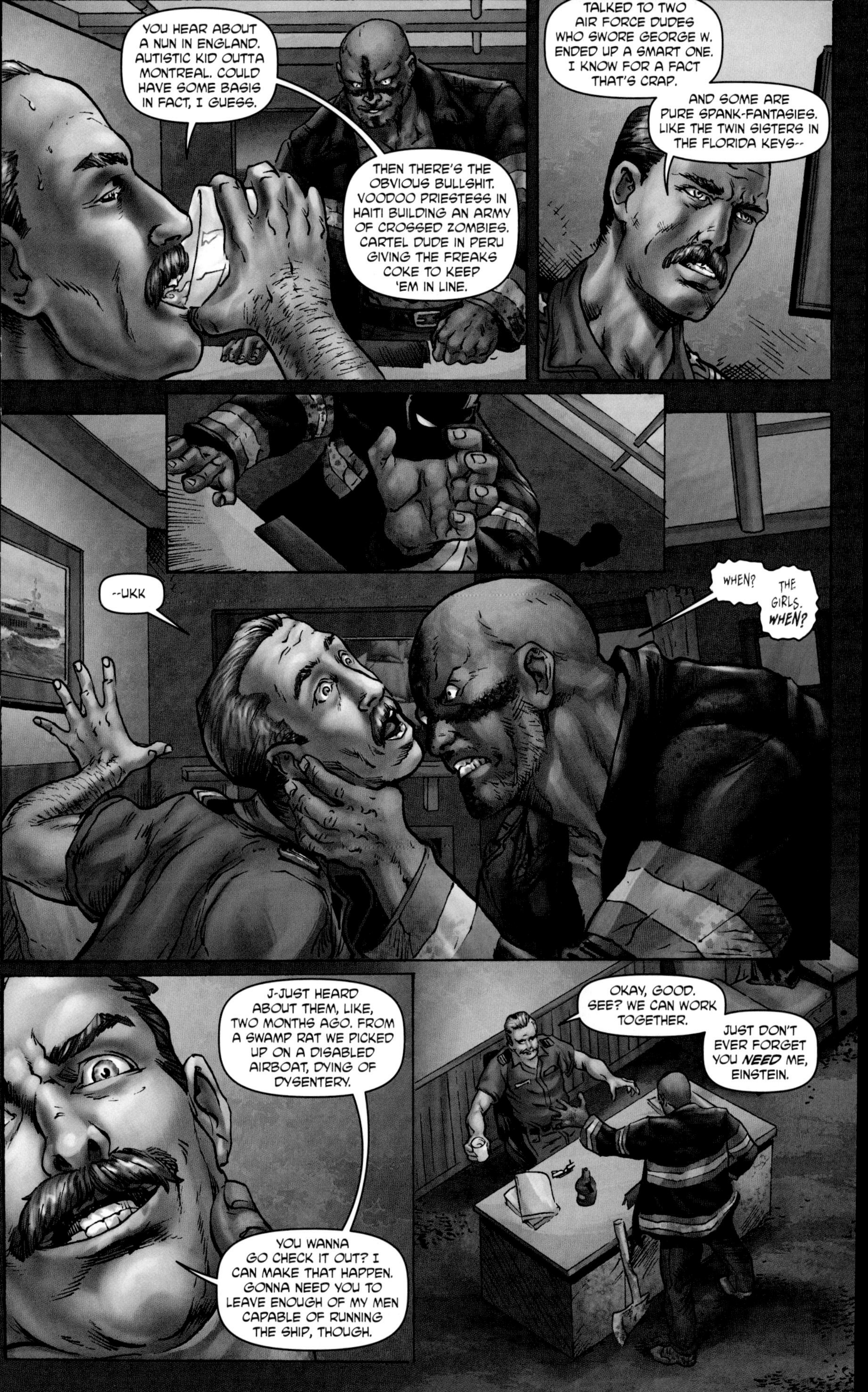
YOU HEAR ABOUT A NUN IN ENGLAND. AUTISTIC KID OUTTA MONTREAL. COULD HAVE SOME BASIS IN FACT, I GUESS.
THEN THERE'S THE OBVIOUS BULLSHIT. VOODOO PRIESTESS IN HAITI BUILDING AN ARMY OF CROSSED ZOMBIES. CARTEL DUDE IN PERU GIVING THE FREAKS COKE TO KEEP 'EM IN LINE.
TALKED TO TWO AIR FORCE DUDES WHO SWORE GEORGE W. ENDED UP A SMART ONE. I KNOW FOR A FACT THAT'S CRAP.
AND SOME ARE PURE SPANK-FANTASIES. LIKE THE TWIN SISTERS IN THE FLORIDA KEYS--
--UKK
WHEN?
THE GIRLS. *WHEN?*
J-JUST HEARD ABOUT THEM, LIKE, TWO MONTHS AGO. FROM A SWAMP RAT WE PICKED UP ON A DISABLED AIRBOAT, DYING OF DYSENTERY.
YOU WANNA GO CHECK IT OUT? I CAN MAKE THAT HAPPEN. GONNA NEED YOU TO LEAVE ENOUGH OF MY MEN CAPABLE OF RUNNING THE SHIP, THOUGH.
OKAY, GOOD. SEE? WE CAN WORK TOGETHER.
JUST DON'T EVER FORGET YOU *NEED* ME, EINSTEIN.

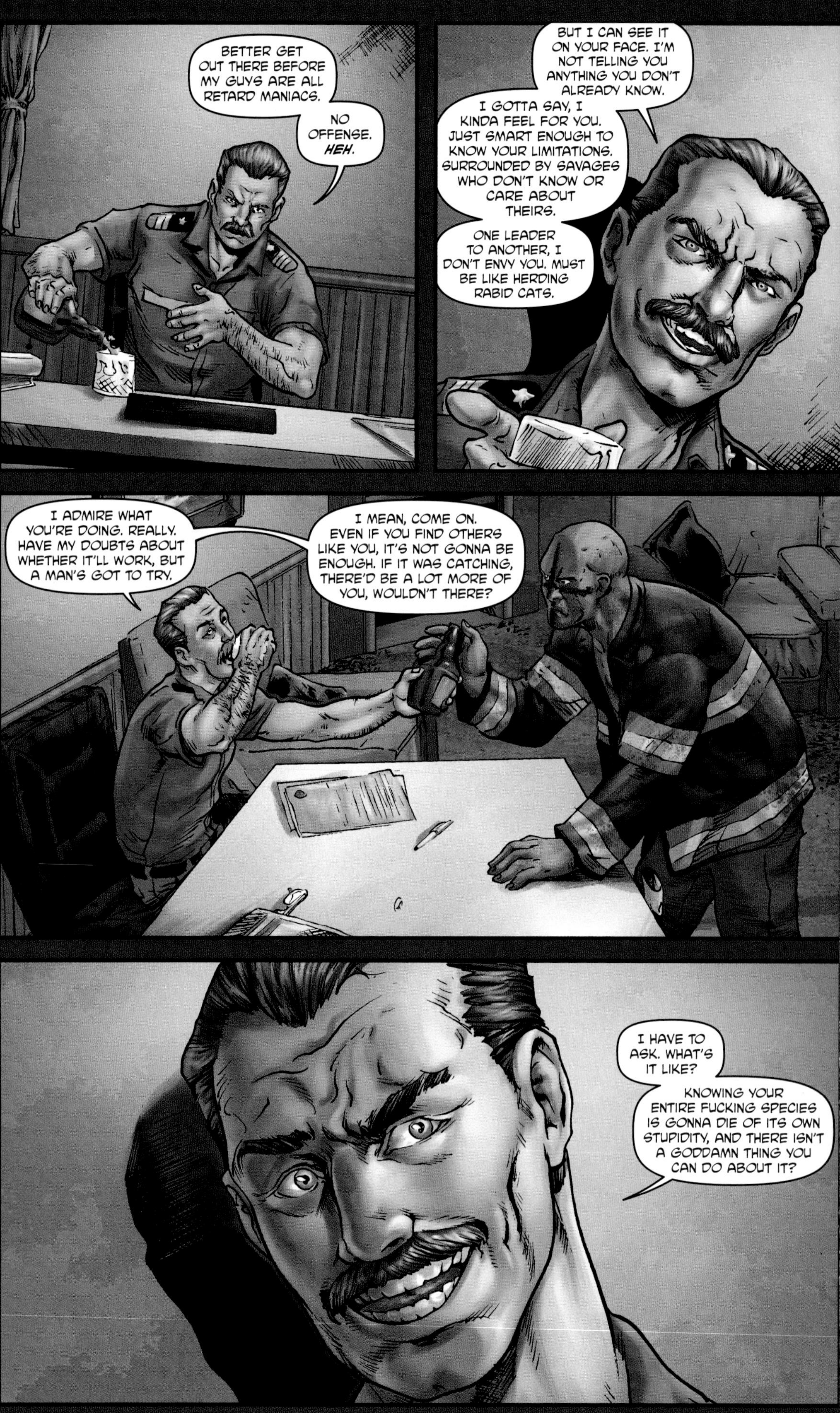
BETTER GET OUT THERE BEFORE MY GUYS ARE ALL RETARD MANIACS.
NO OFFENSE. *HEH*.
BUT I CAN SEE IT ON YOUR FACE. I'M NOT TELLING YOU ANYTHING YOU DON'T ALREADY KNOW.
I GOTTA SAY, I KINDA FEEL FOR YOU. JUST SMART ENOUGH TO KNOW YOUR LIMITATIONS. SURROUNDED BY SAVAGES WHO DON'T KNOW OR CARE ABOUT THEIRS.
ONE LEADER TO ANOTHER, I DON'T ENVY YOU. MUST BE LIKE HERDING RABID CATS.
I ADMIRE WHAT YOU'RE DOING. REALLY. HAVE MY DOUBTS ABOUT WHETHER IT'LL WORK, BUT A MAN'S GOT TO TRY.
I MEAN, COME ON. EVEN IF YOU FIND OTHERS LIKE YOU, IT'S NOT GONNA BE ENOUGH. IF IT WAS CATCHING, THERE'D BE A LOT MORE OF YOU, WOULDN'T THERE?
I HAVE TO ASK. WHAT'S IT LIKE?
KNOWING YOUR ENTIRE FUCKING SPECIES IS GONNA DIE OF ITS OWN STUPIDITY, AND THERE ISN'T A GODDAMN THING YOU CAN DO ABOUT IT?

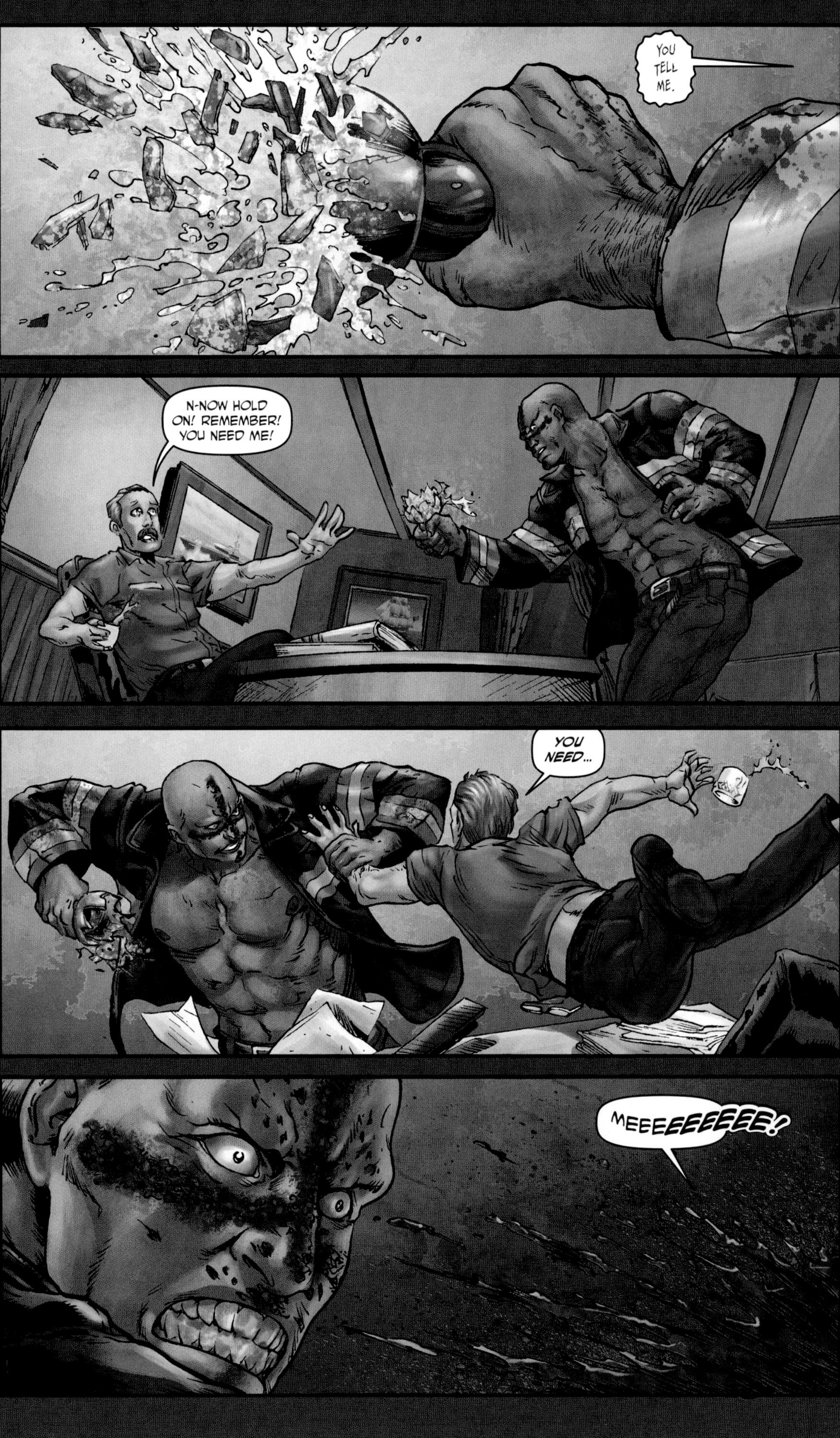
YOU TELL ME.
N-NOW HOLD ON! REMEMBER! YOU NEED ME!
YOU NEED...
MEEEEEEEEEE!

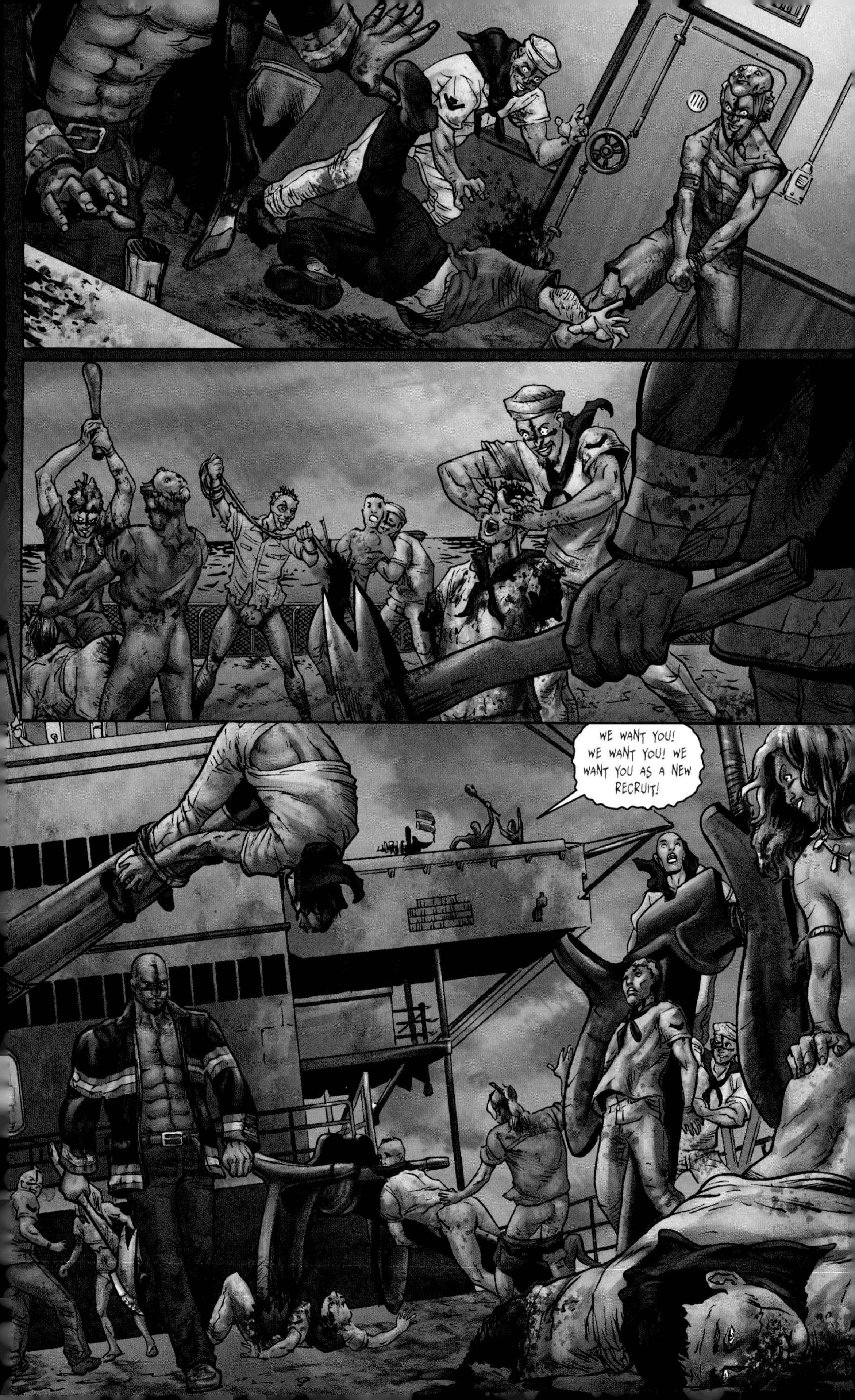
WE WANT YOU! WE WANT YOU! WE WANT YOU AS A NEW RECRUIT!

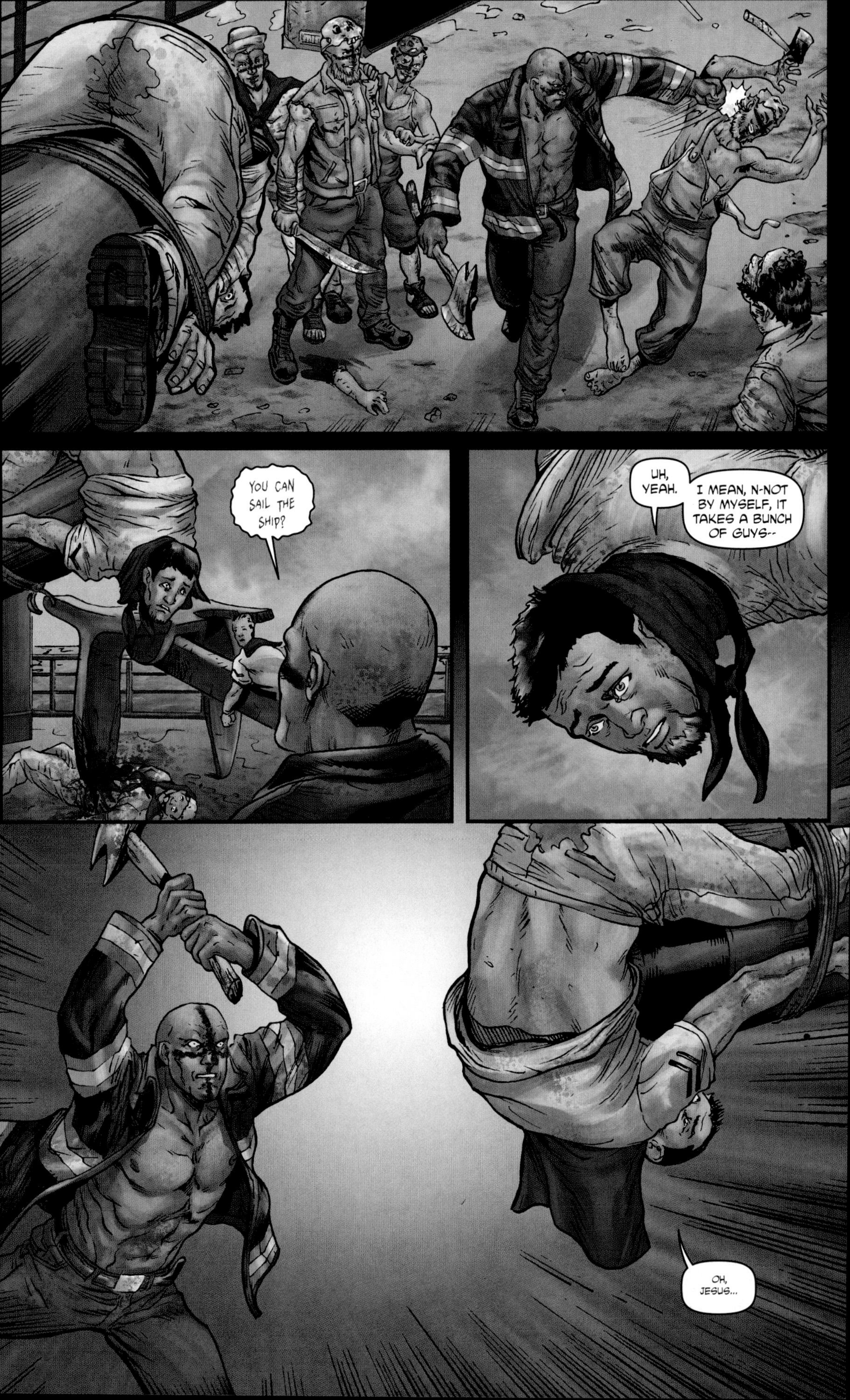
YOU CAN SAIL THE SHIP?
UH, YEAH.
I MEAN, N-NOT BY MYSELF, IT TAKES A BUNCH OF GUYS--
OH, JESUS...

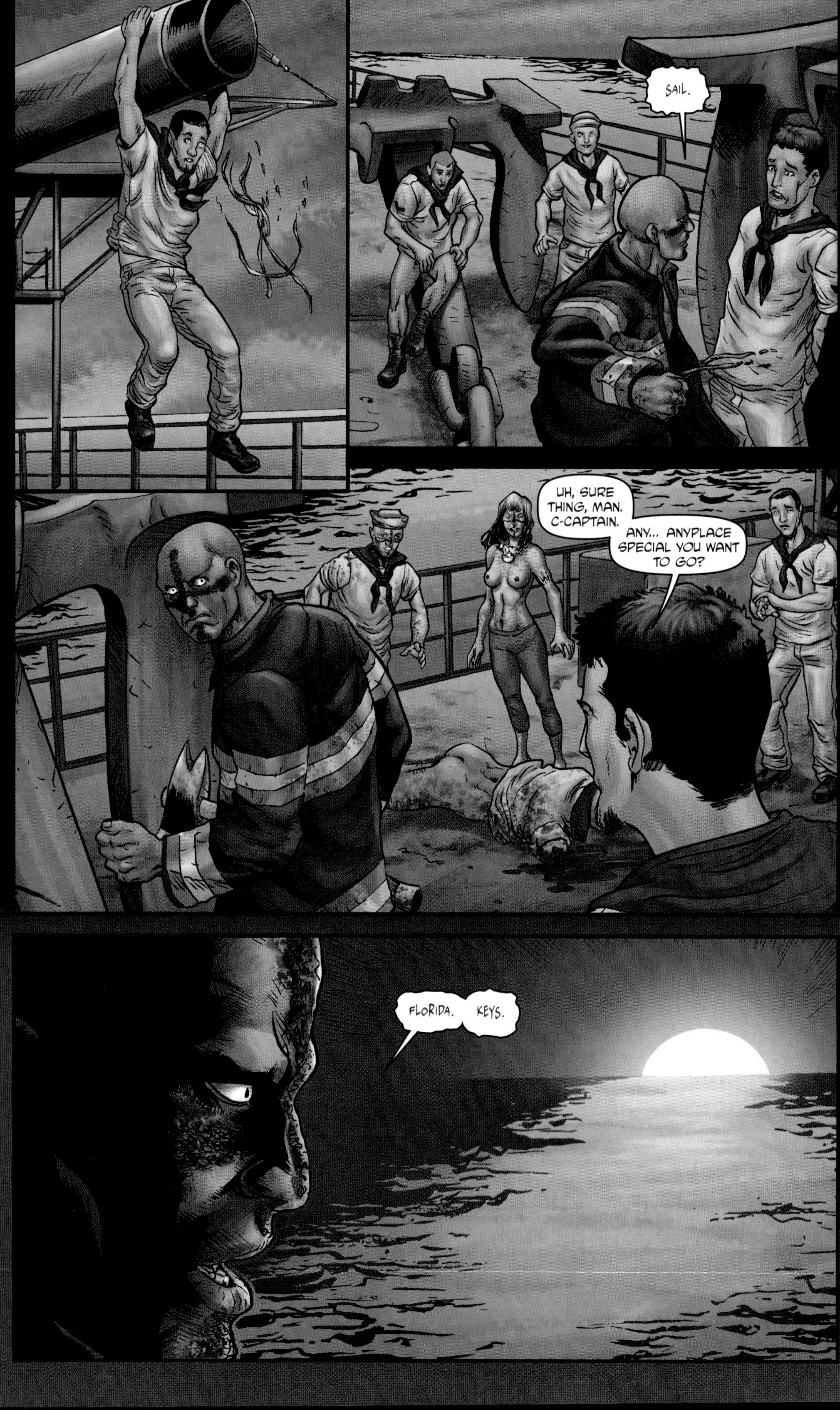
SAIL.
UH, SURE THING, MAN. C-CAPTAIN.
ANY... ANYPLACE SPECIAL YOU WANT TO GO?
FLORIDA.
KEYS.

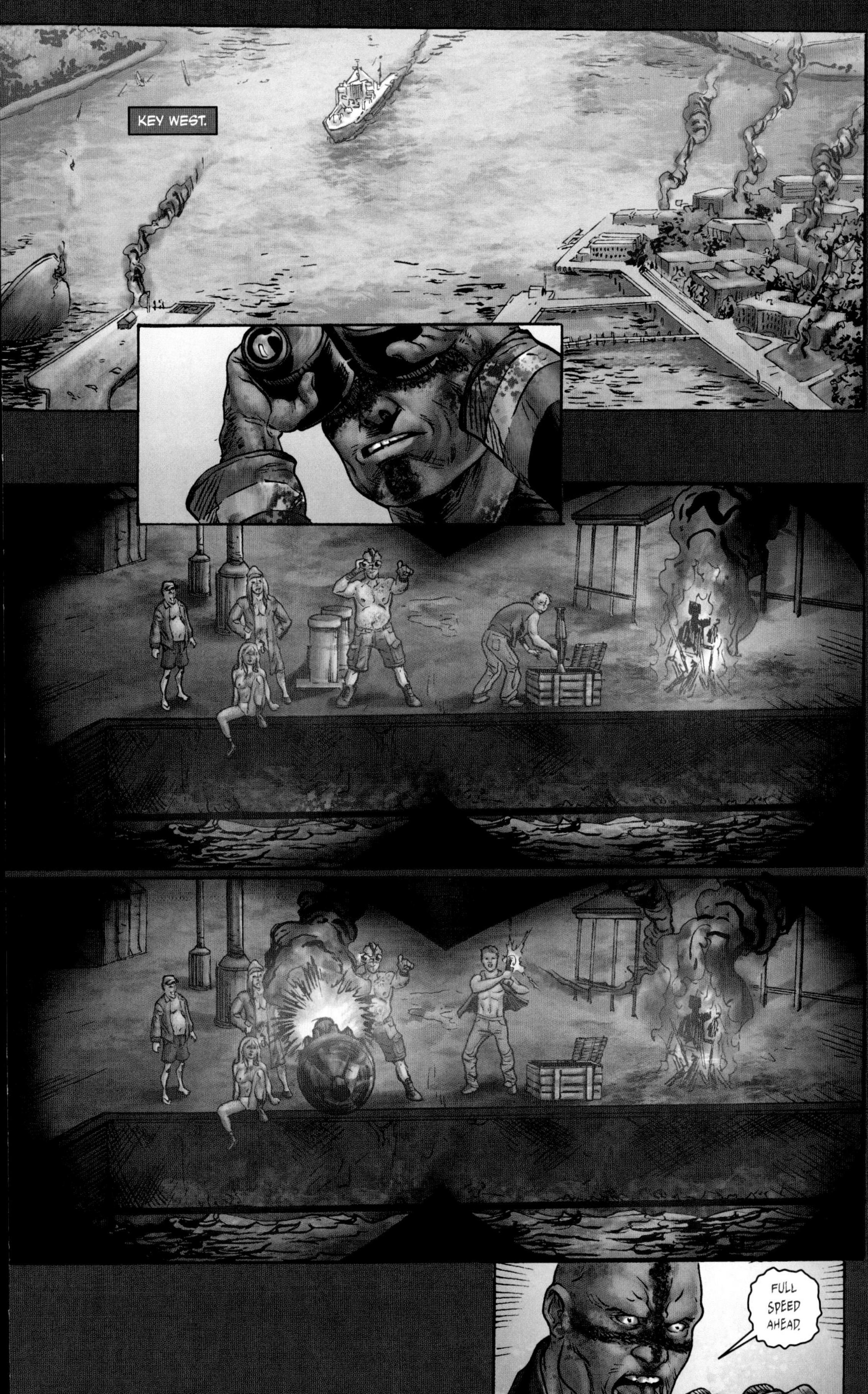
KEY WEST.
FULL SPEED AHEAD.

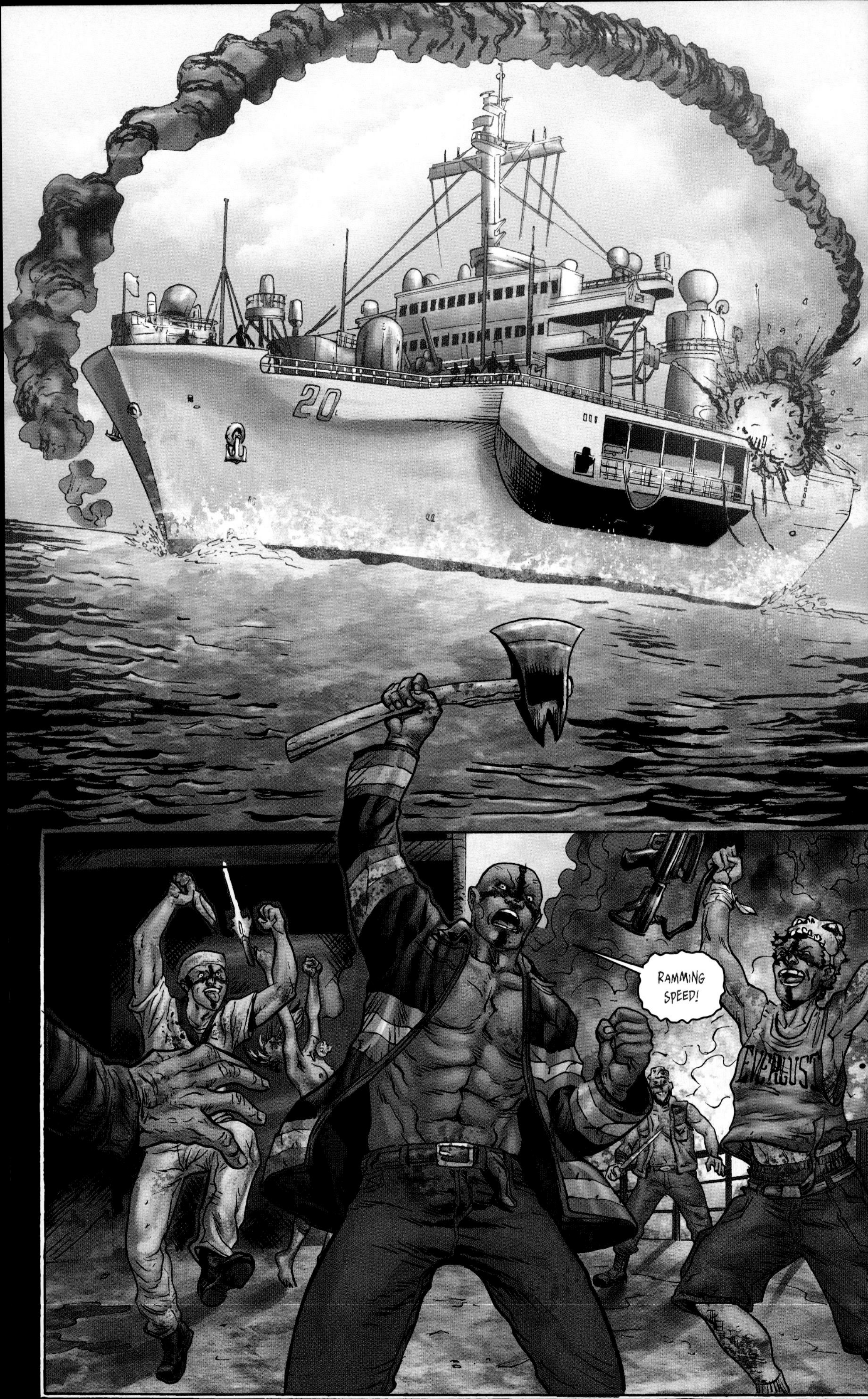
RAMMING SPEED!

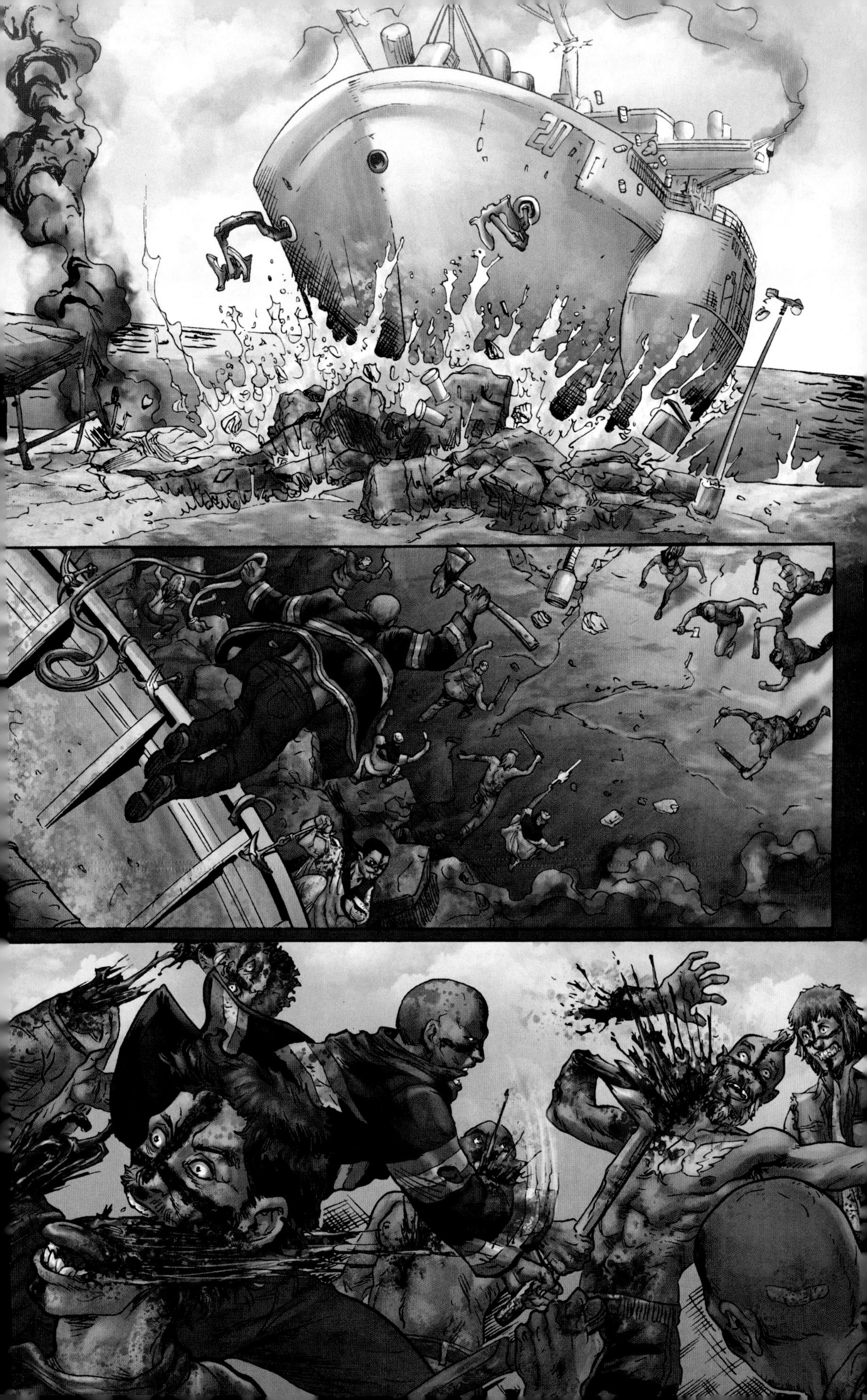

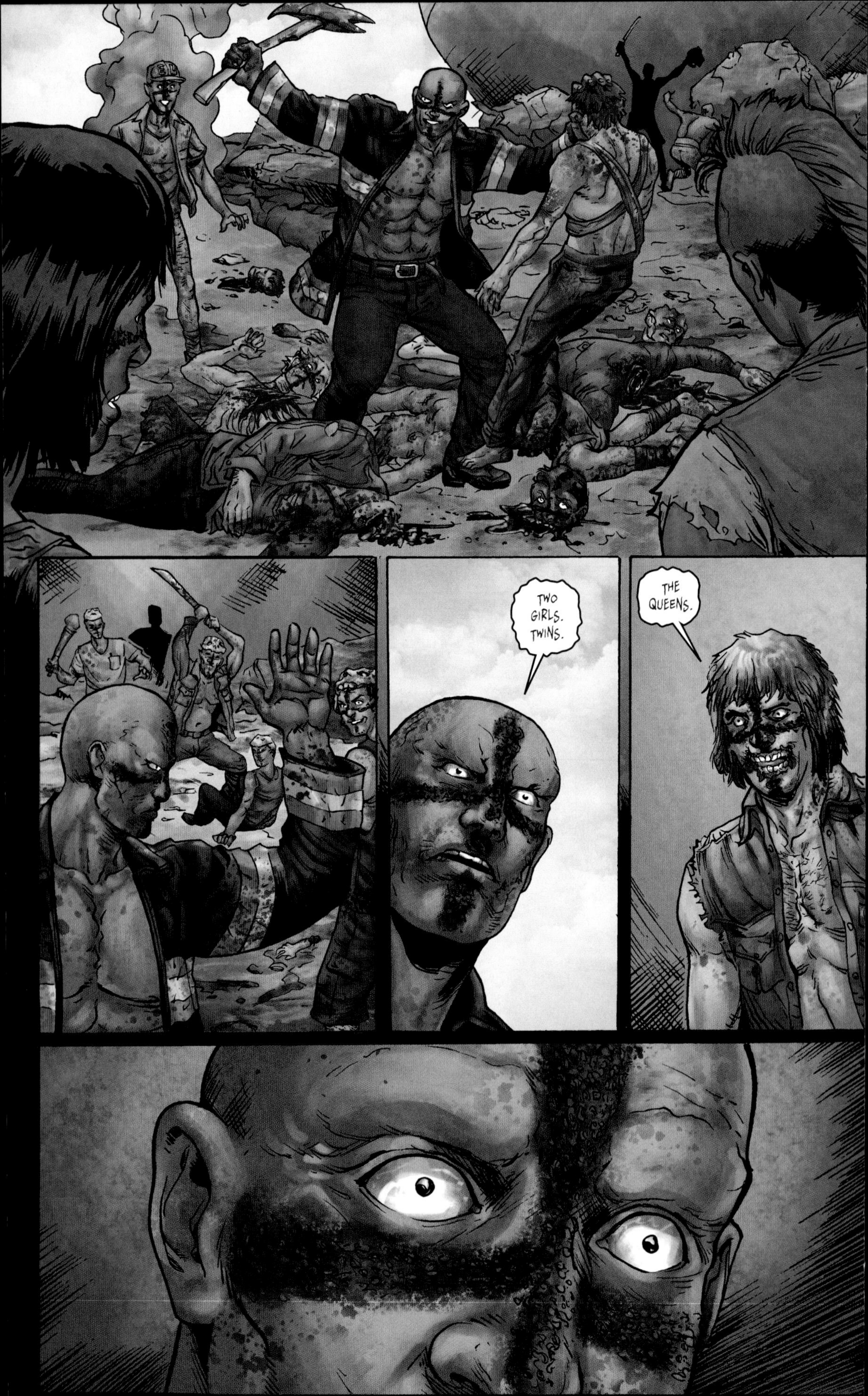
TWO GIRLS. TWINS.
THE QUEENS.

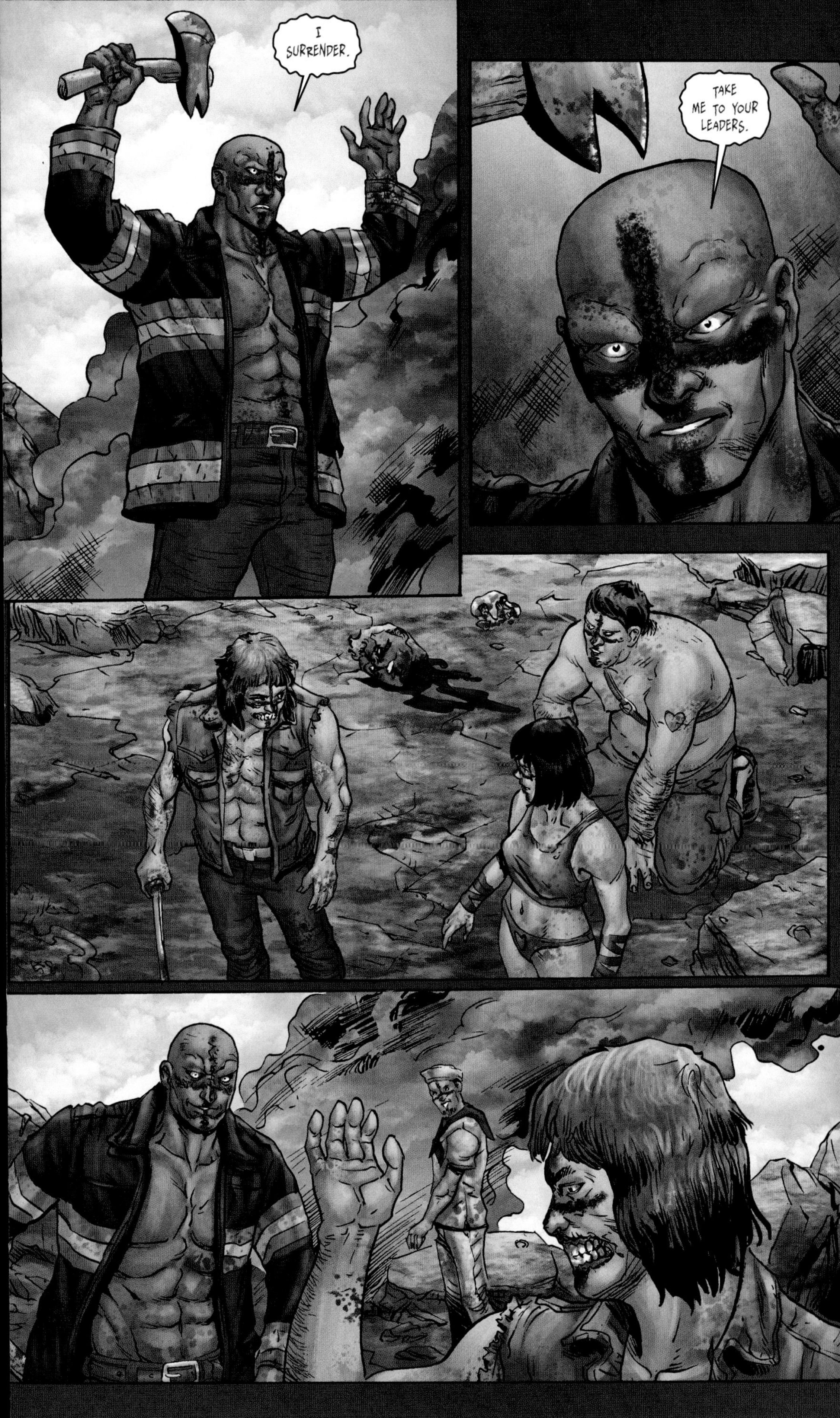
I SURRENDER.
TAKE ME TO YOUR LEADERS.

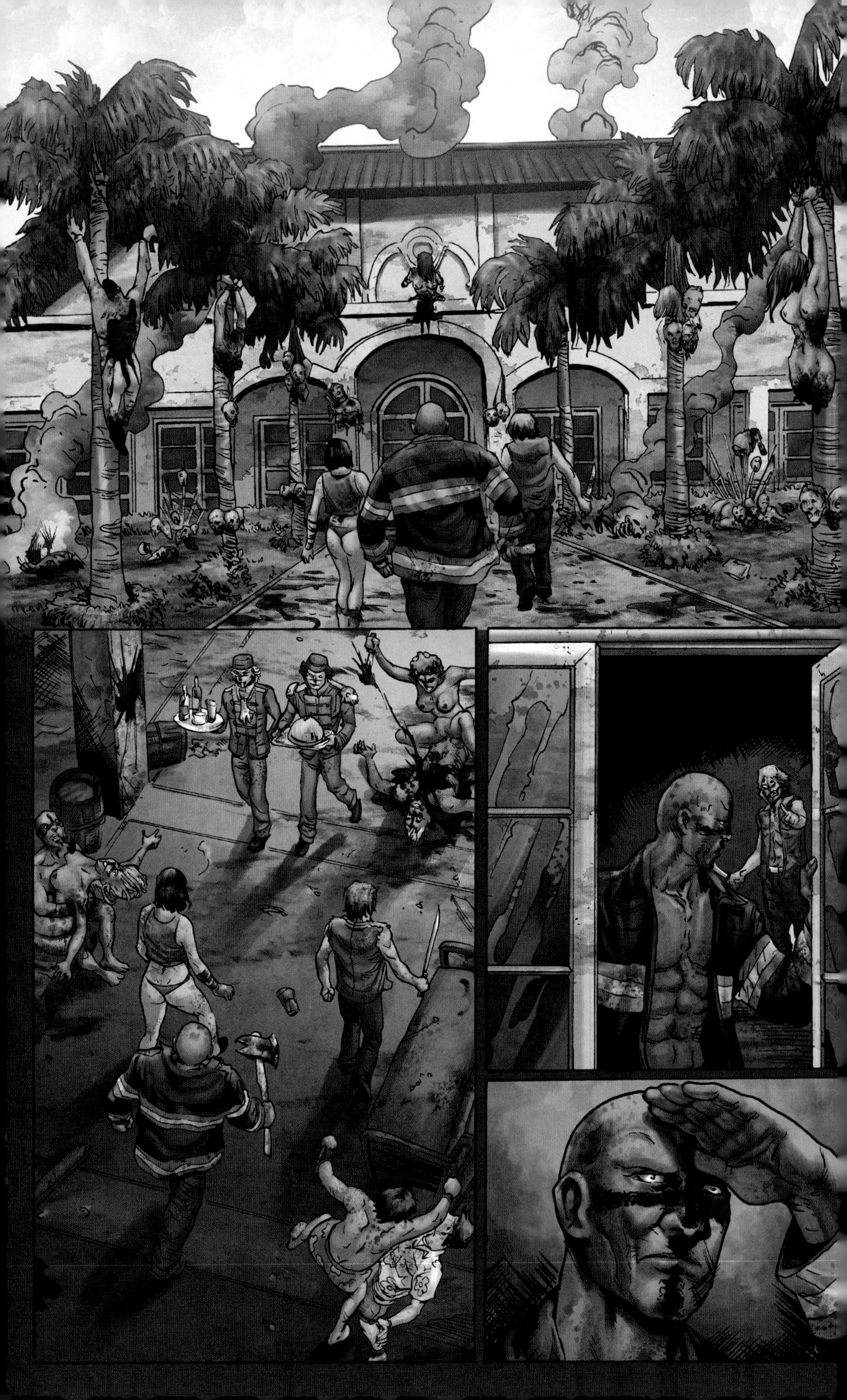

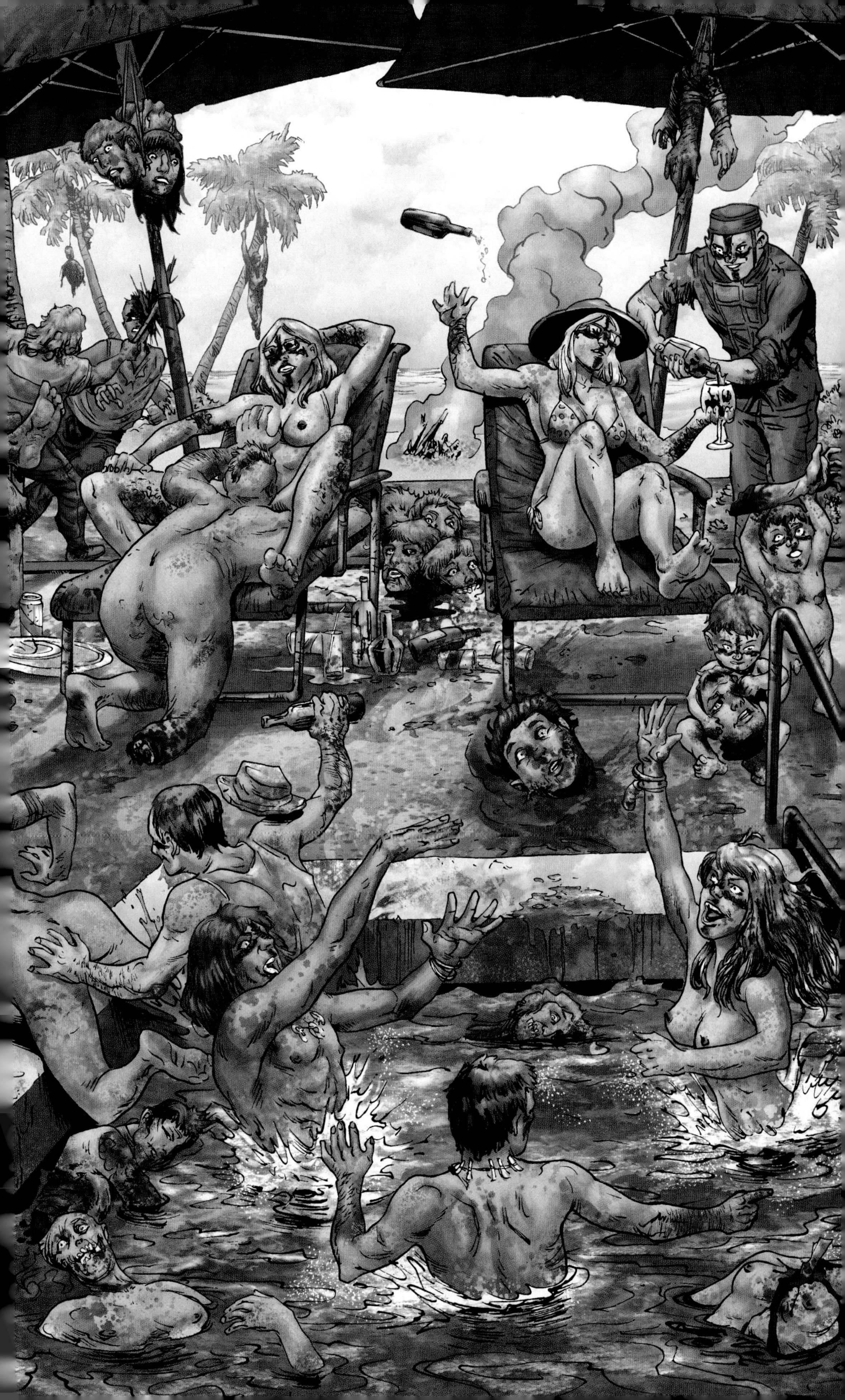

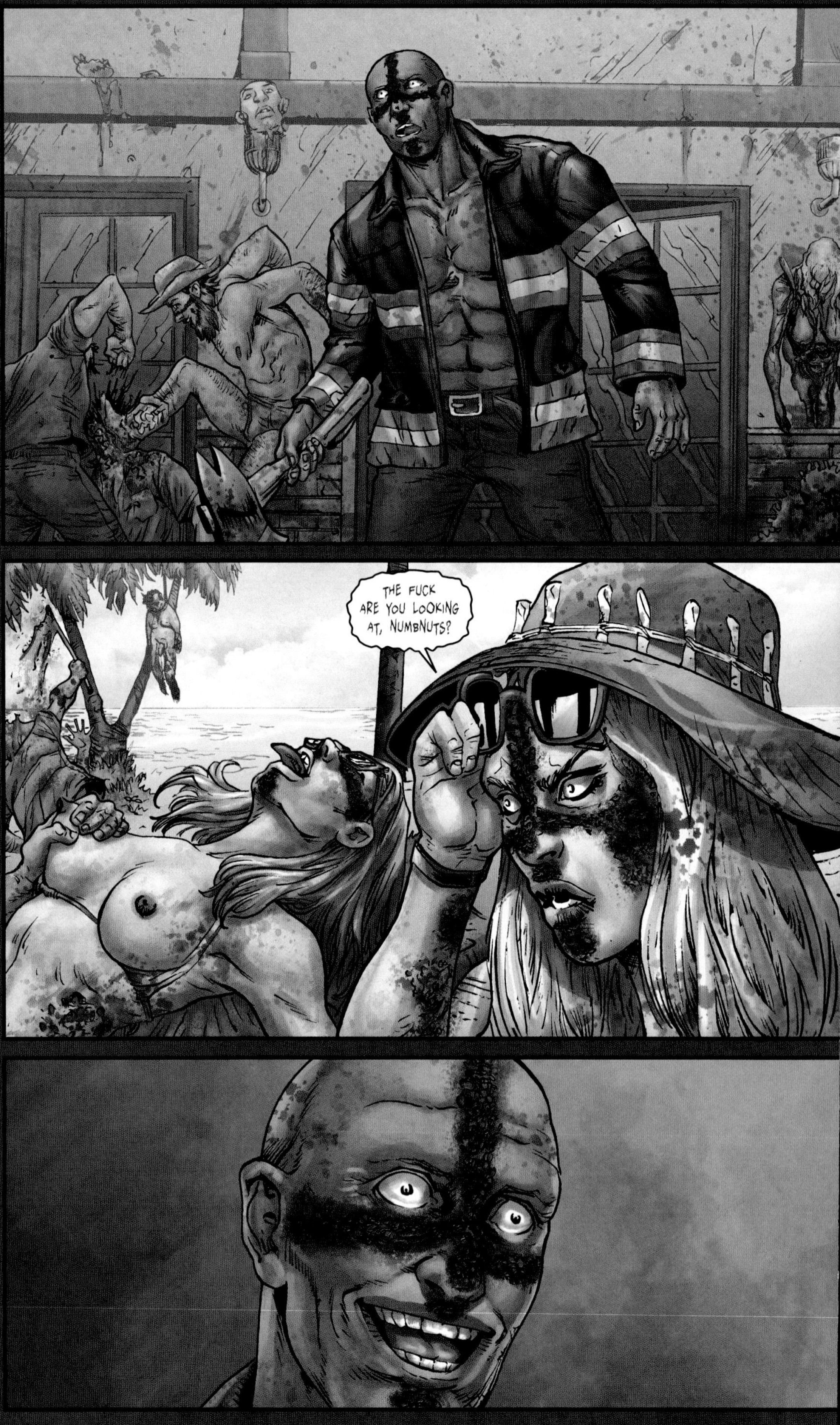
THE FUCK ARE YOU LOOKING AT, NUMBNUTS?

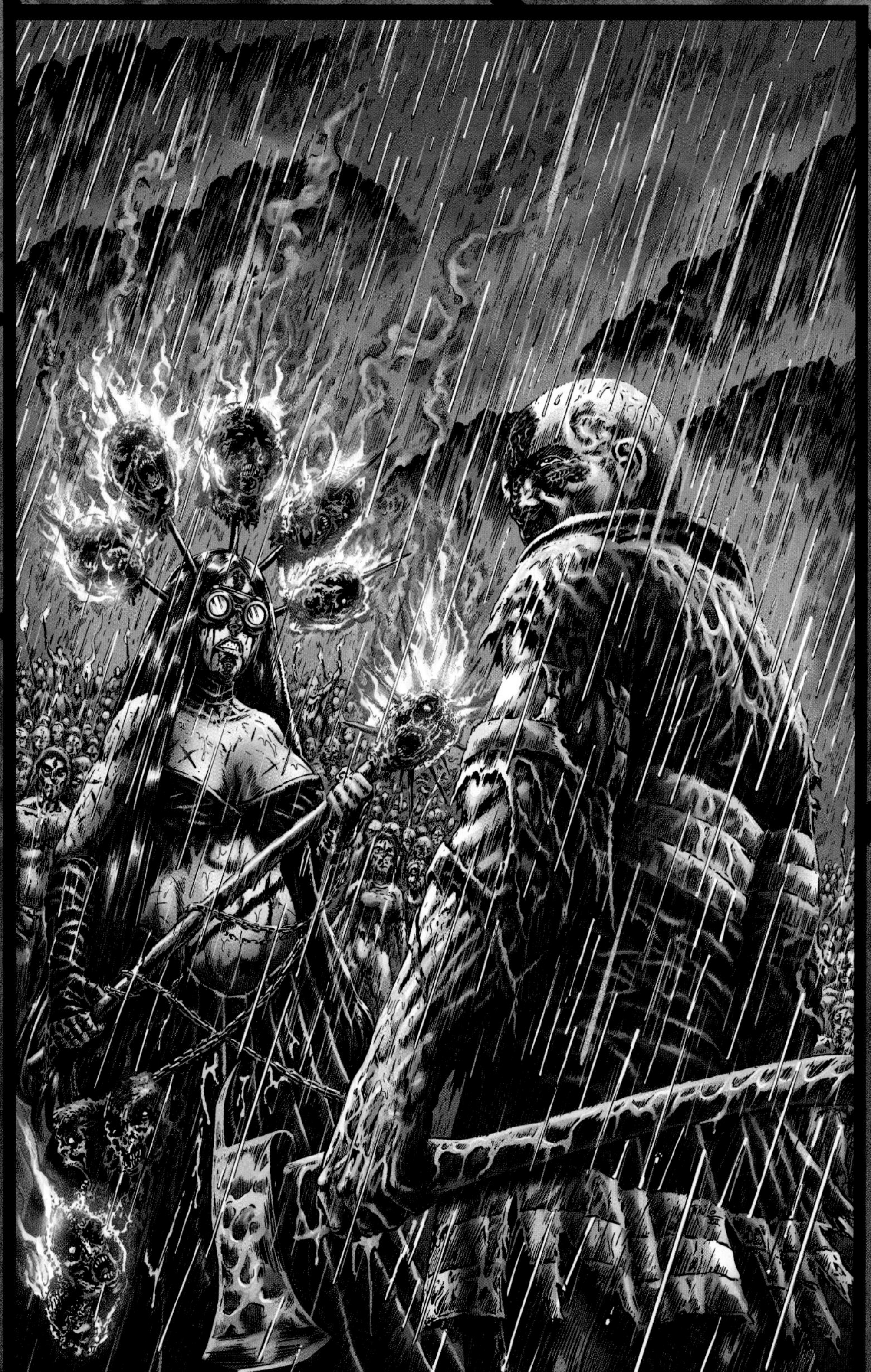

PART 6

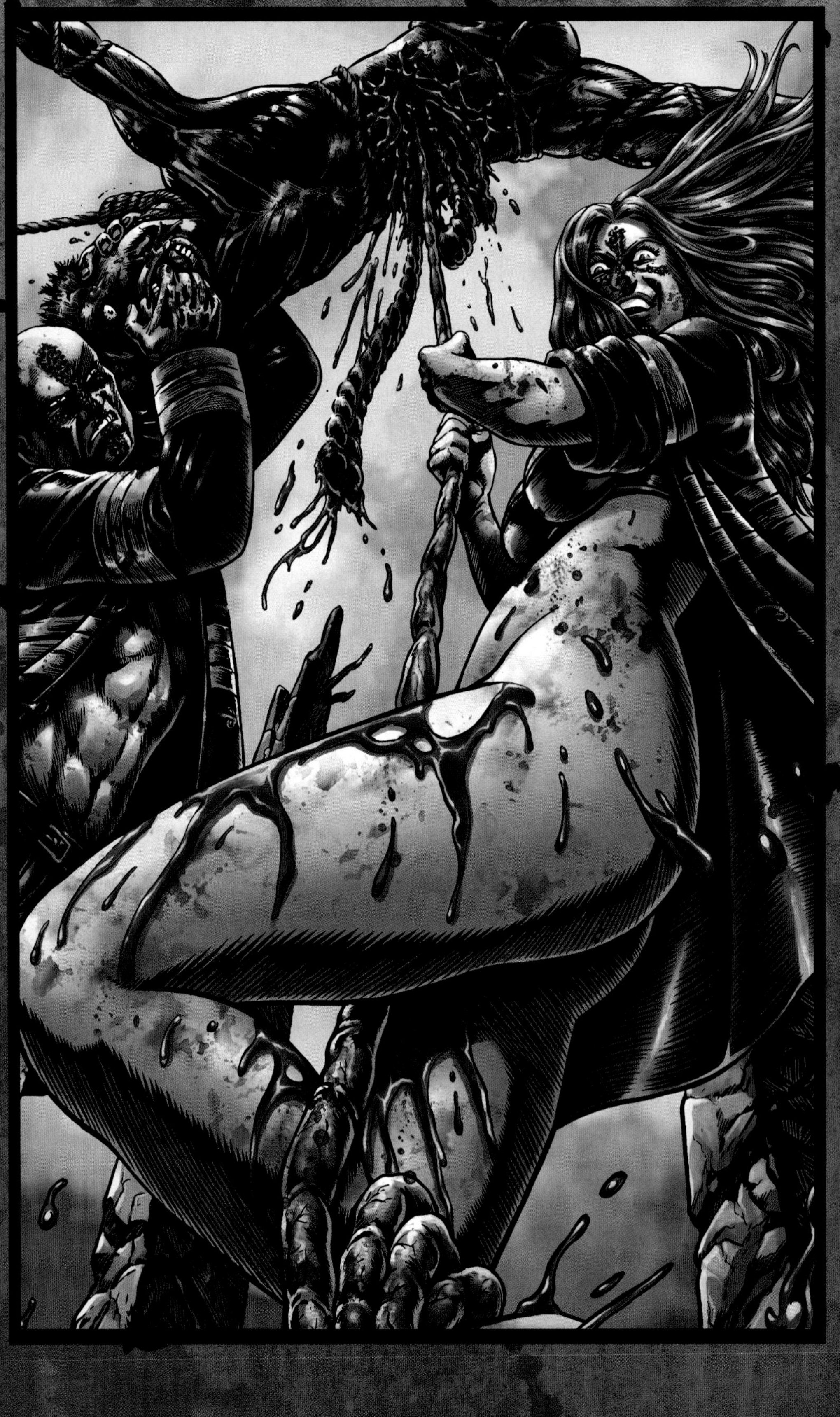

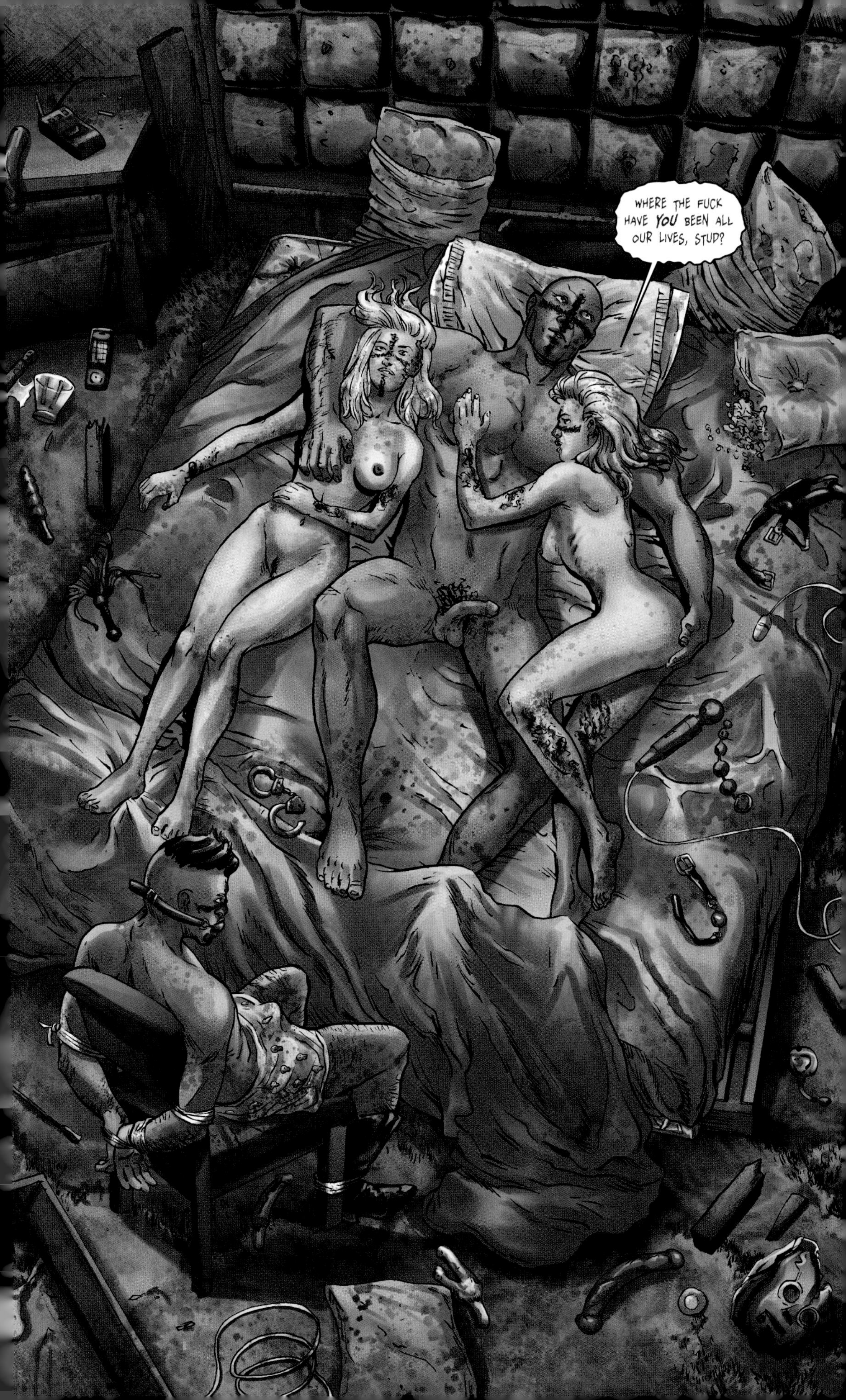
WHERE THE FUCK HAVE *YOU* BEEN ALL OUR LIVES, STUD?

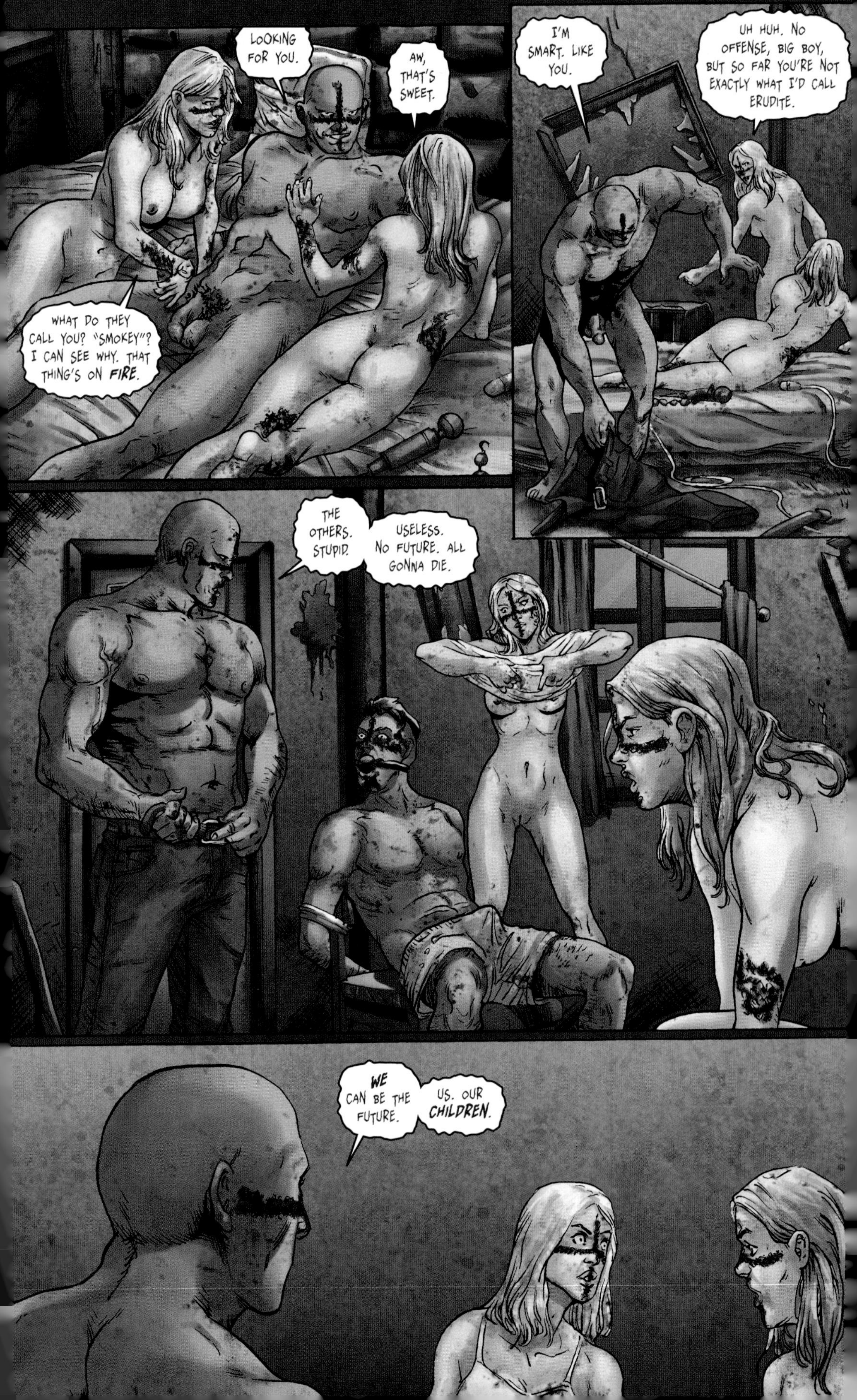
LOOKING FOR YOU.
AW, THAT'S SWEET.
WHAT DO THEY CALL YOU? "SMOKEY"? I CAN SEE WHY. THAT THING'S ON **FIRE**.
I'M SMART. LIKE YOU.
UH HUH. NO OFFENSE, BIG BOY, BUT SO FAR YOU'RE NOT EXACTLY WHAT I'D CALL ERUDITE.
THE OTHERS. STUPID.
USELESS. NO FUTURE. ALL GONNA DIE.
WE CAN BE THE FUTURE.
US. OUR **CHILDREN**.

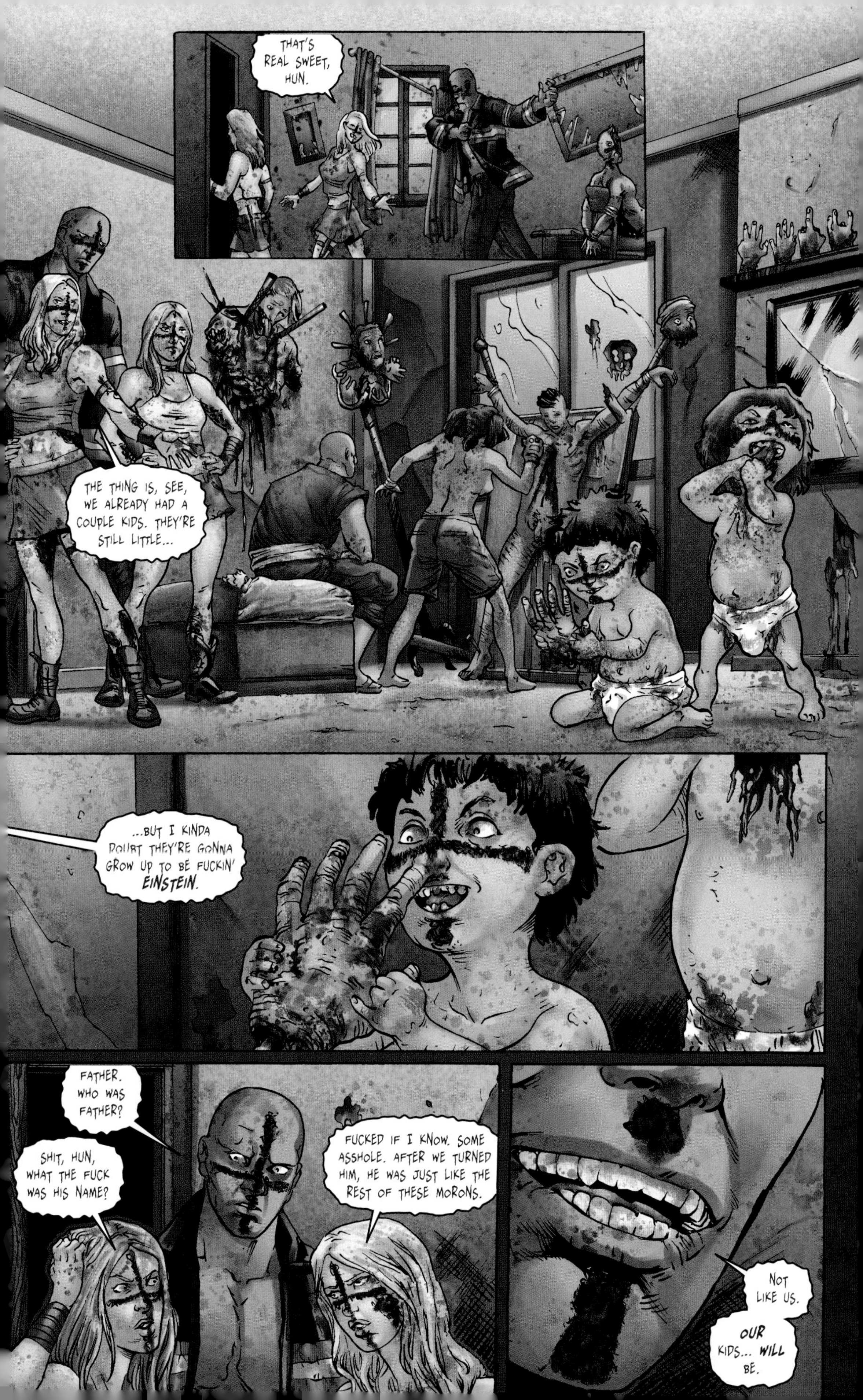
THAT'S REAL SWEET, HUN.
THE THING IS, SEE, WE ALREADY HAD A COUPLE KIDS. THEY'RE STILL LITTLE...
...BUT I KINDA DOUBT THEY'RE GONNA GROW UP TO BE FUCKIN' EINSTEIN.
FATHER. WHO WAS FATHER?
SHIT, HUN, WHAT THE FUCK WAS HIS NAME?
FUCKED IF I KNOW. SOME ASSHOLE. AFTER WE TURNED HIM, HE WAS JUST LIKE THE REST OF THESE MORONS.
NOT LIKE US.
OUR KIDS... WILL BE.

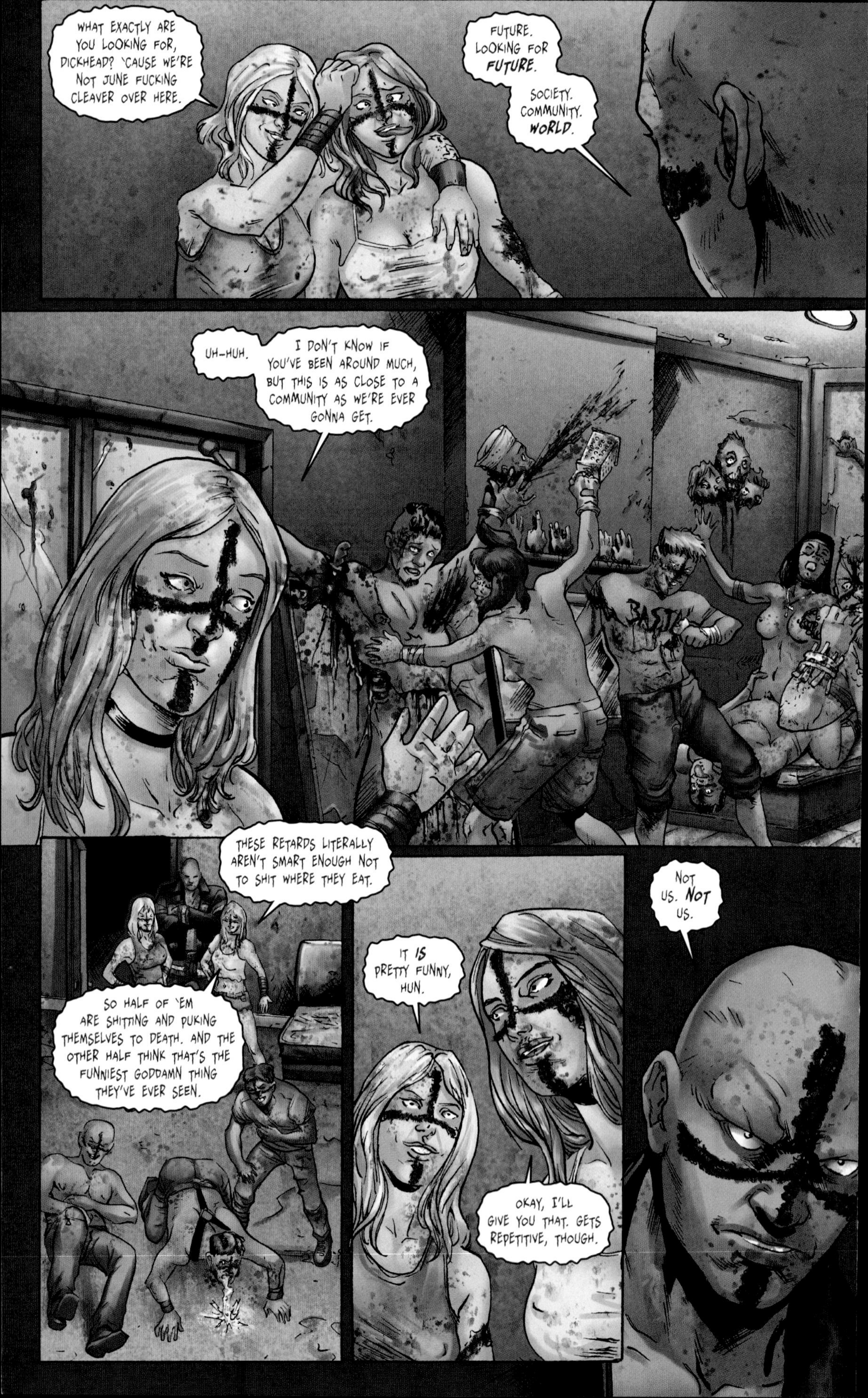
WHAT EXACTLY ARE YOU LOOKING FOR, DICKHEAD? 'CAUSE WE'RE NOT JUNE FUCKING CLEAVER OVER HERE.
FUTURE. LOOKING FOR *FUTURE*.
SOCIETY. COMMUNITY. *WORLD*.
UH-HUH.
I DON'T KNOW IF YOU'VE BEEN AROUND MUCH, BUT THIS IS AS CLOSE TO A COMMUNITY AS WE'RE EVER GONNA GET.
THESE RETARDS LITERALLY AREN'T SMART ENOUGH NOT TO SHIT WHERE THEY EAT.
SO HALF OF 'EM ARE SHITTING AND PUKING THEMSELVES TO DEATH. AND THE OTHER HALF THINK THAT'S THE FUNNIEST GODDAMN THING THEY'VE EVER SEEN.
IT *IS* PRETTY FUNNY, HUN.
OKAY, I'LL GIVE YOU THAT. GETS REPETITIVE, THOUGH.
NOT US. *NOT* US.

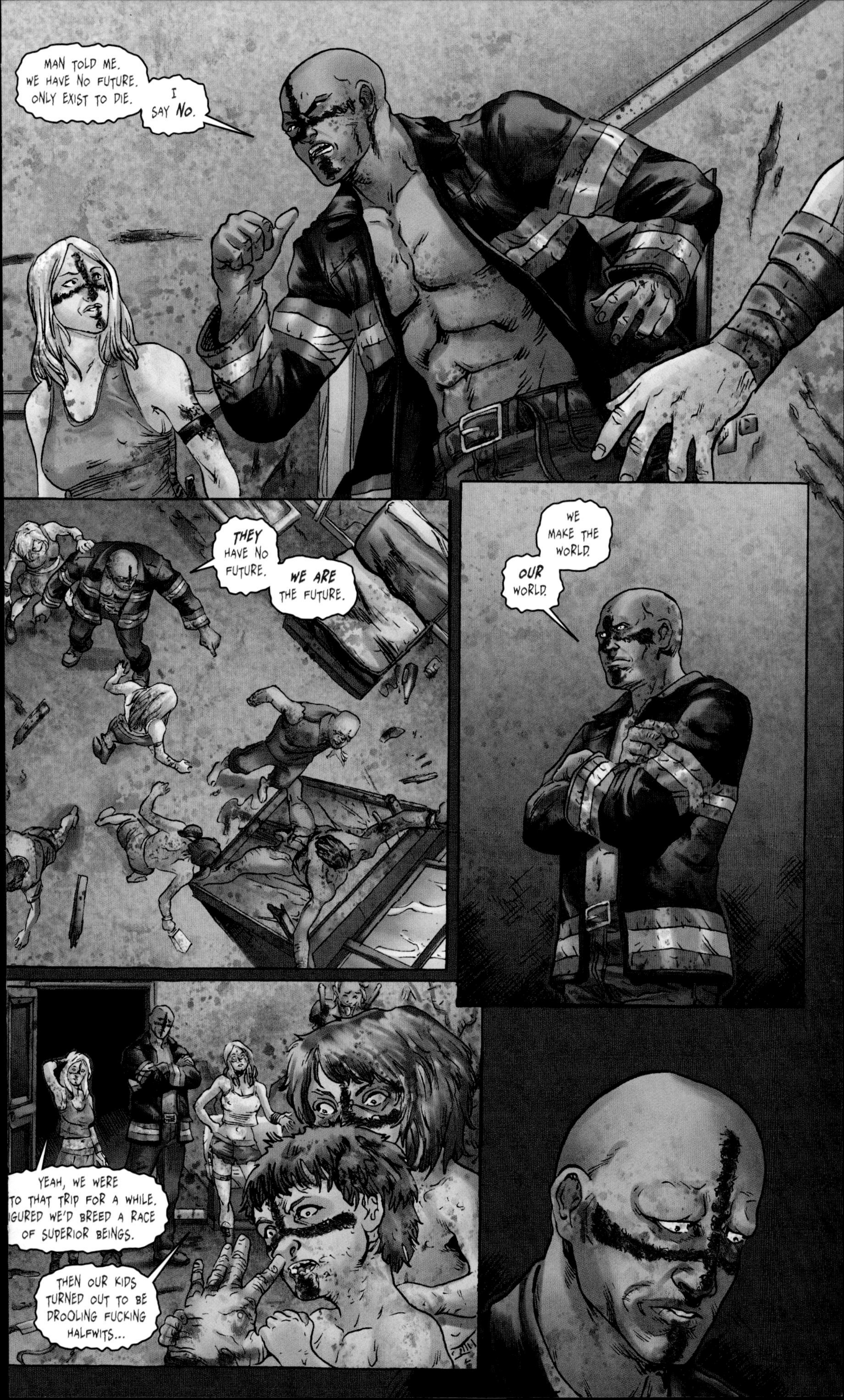
MAN TOLD ME. WE HAVE NO FUTURE. ONLY EXIST TO DIE.
I SAY NO.
THEY HAVE NO FUTURE.
WE ARE THE FUTURE.
WE MAKE THE WORLD.
OUR WORLD.
YEAH, WE WERE TO THAT TRIP FOR A WHILE. IGURED WE'D BREED A RACE OF SUPERIOR BEINGS.
THEN OUR KIDS TURNED OUT TO BE DROOLING FUCKING HALFWITS...

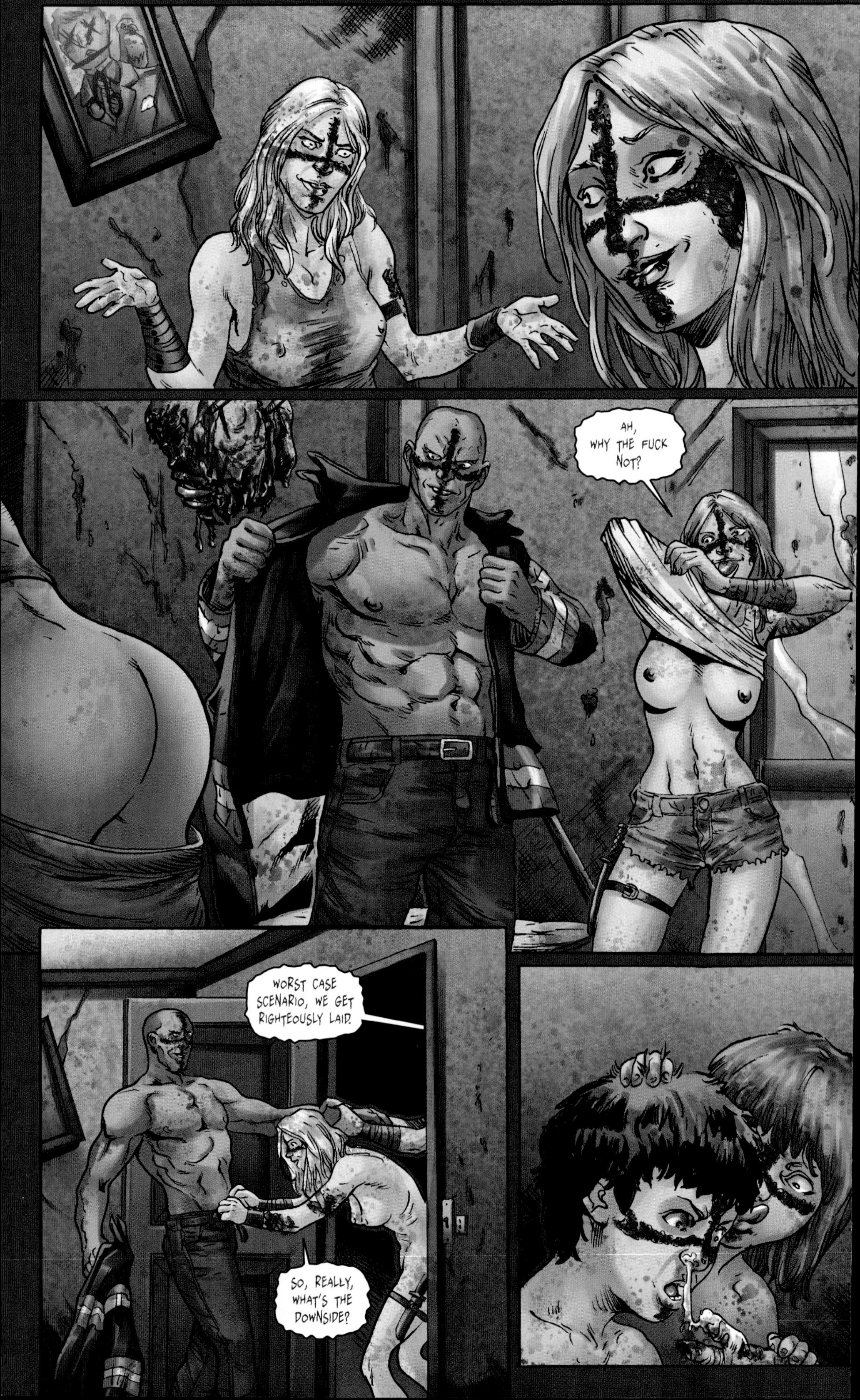
AH, WHY THE FUCK NOT?
WORST CASE SCENARIO, WE GET RIGHTEOUSLY LAID.
SO, REALLY, WHAT'S THE DOWNSIDE?

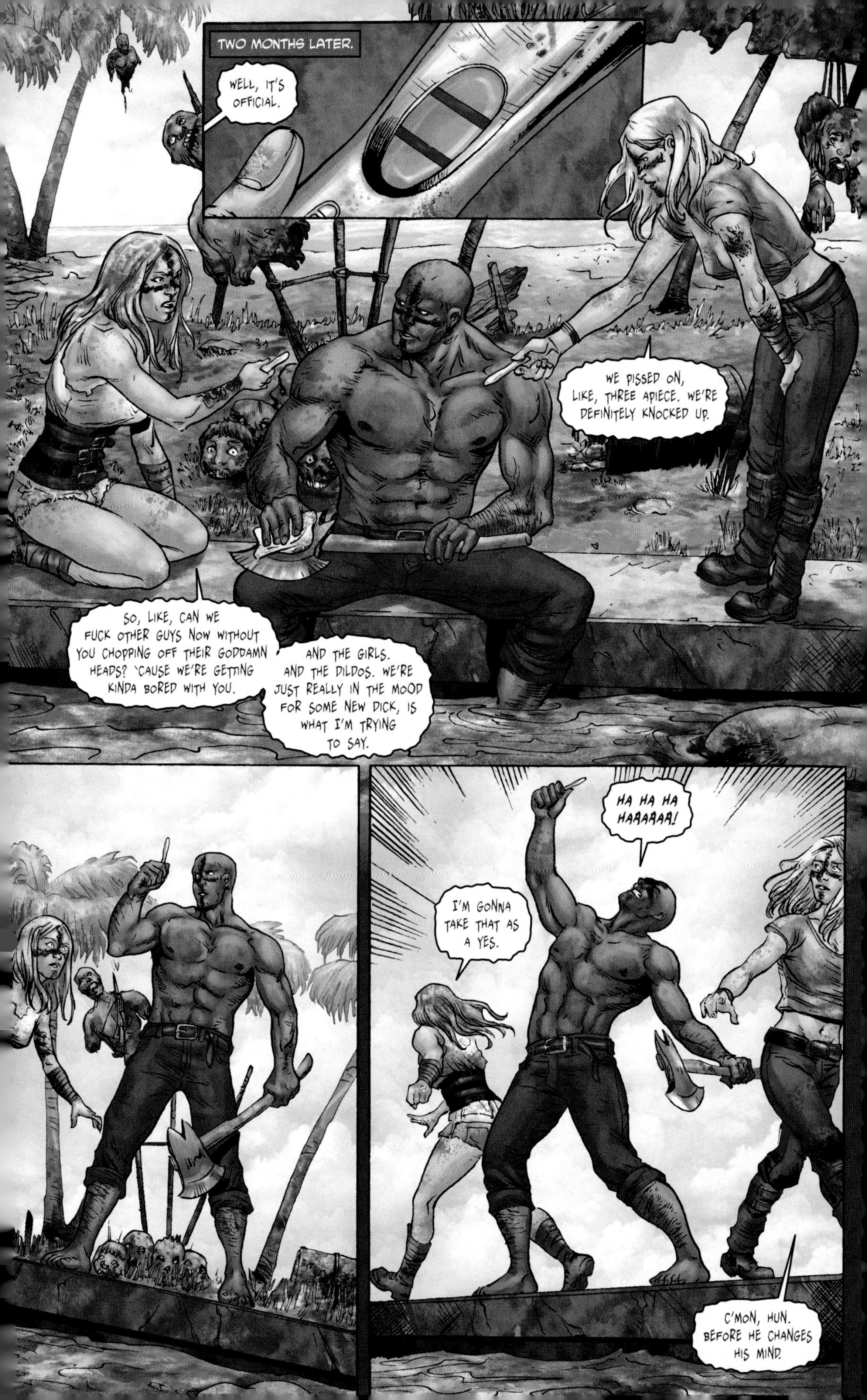
TWO MONTHS LATER.
WELL, IT'S OFFICIAL.
WE PISSED ON, LIKE, THREE APIECE. WE'RE DEFINITELY KNOCKED UP.
SO, LIKE, CAN WE FUCK OTHER GUYS NOW WITHOUT YOU CHOPPING OFF THEIR GODDAMN HEADS? 'CAUSE WE'RE GETTING KINDA BORED WITH YOU.
AND THE GIRLS. AND THE DILDOS. WE'RE JUST REALLY IN THE MOOD FOR SOME NEW DICK, IS WHAT I'M TRYING TO SAY.
HA HA HA HARAAAA!
I'M GONNA TAKE THAT AS A YES.
C'MON, HUN. BEFORE HE CHANGES HIS MIND.

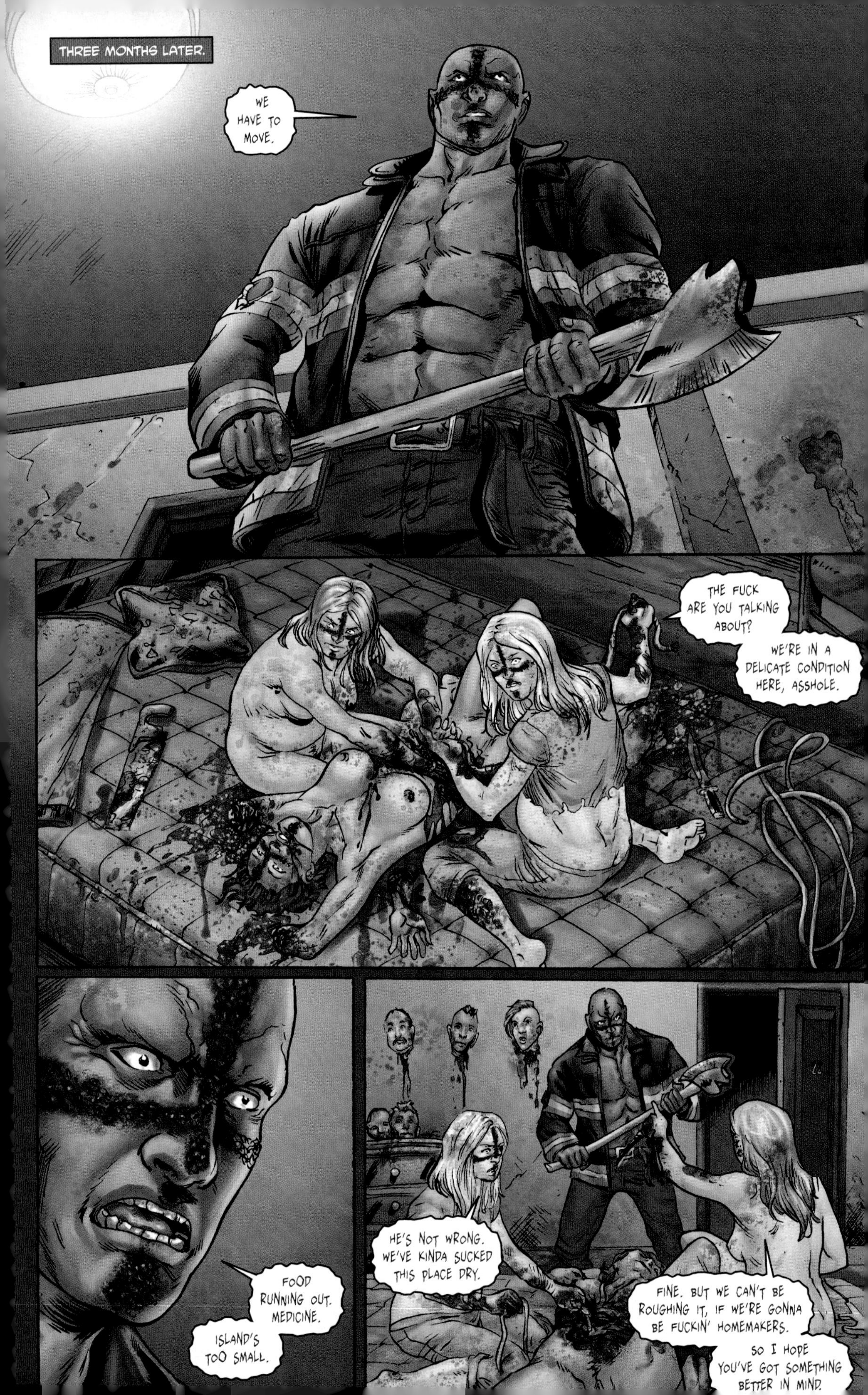
THREE MONTHS LATER.
WE HAVE TO MOVE.
THE FUCK ARE YOU TALKING ABOUT?
WE'RE IN A DELICATE CONDITION HERE, ASSHOLE.
FOOD RUNNING OUT. MEDICINE.
ISLAND'S TOO SMALL.
HE'S NOT WRONG. WE'VE KINDA SUCKED THIS PLACE DRY.
FINE. BUT WE CAN'T BE ROUGHING IT, IF WE'RE GONNA BE FUCKIN' HOMEMAKERS.
SO I HOPE YOU'VE GOT SOMETHING BETTER IN MIND.

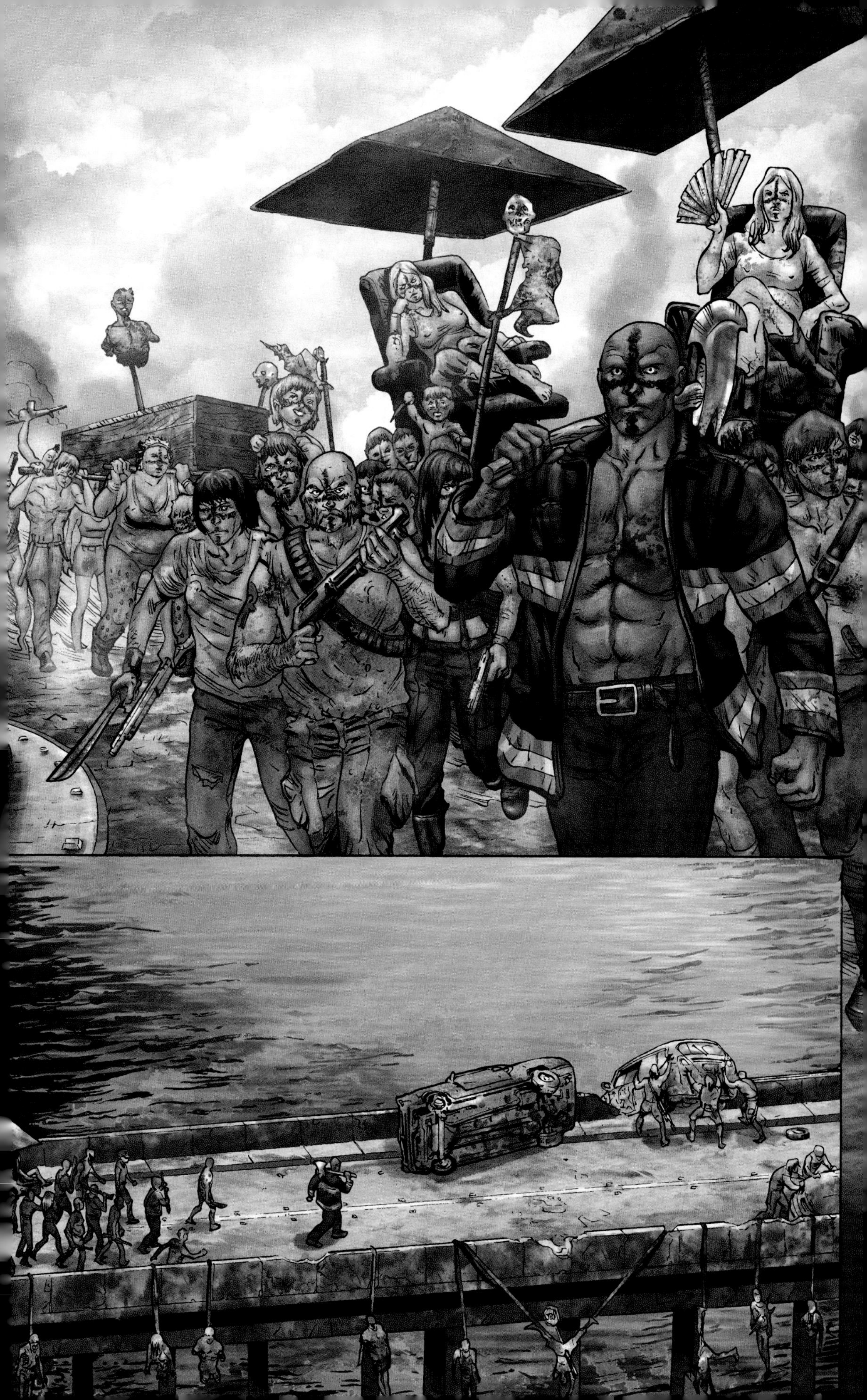

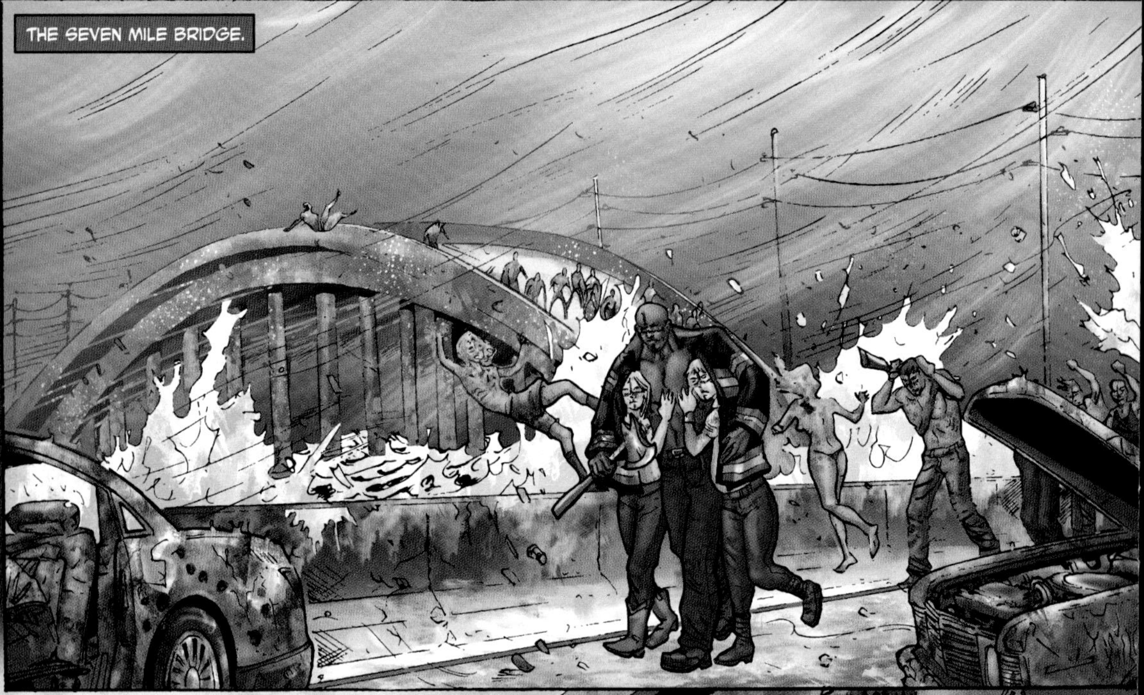
THE SEVEN MILE BRIDGE.

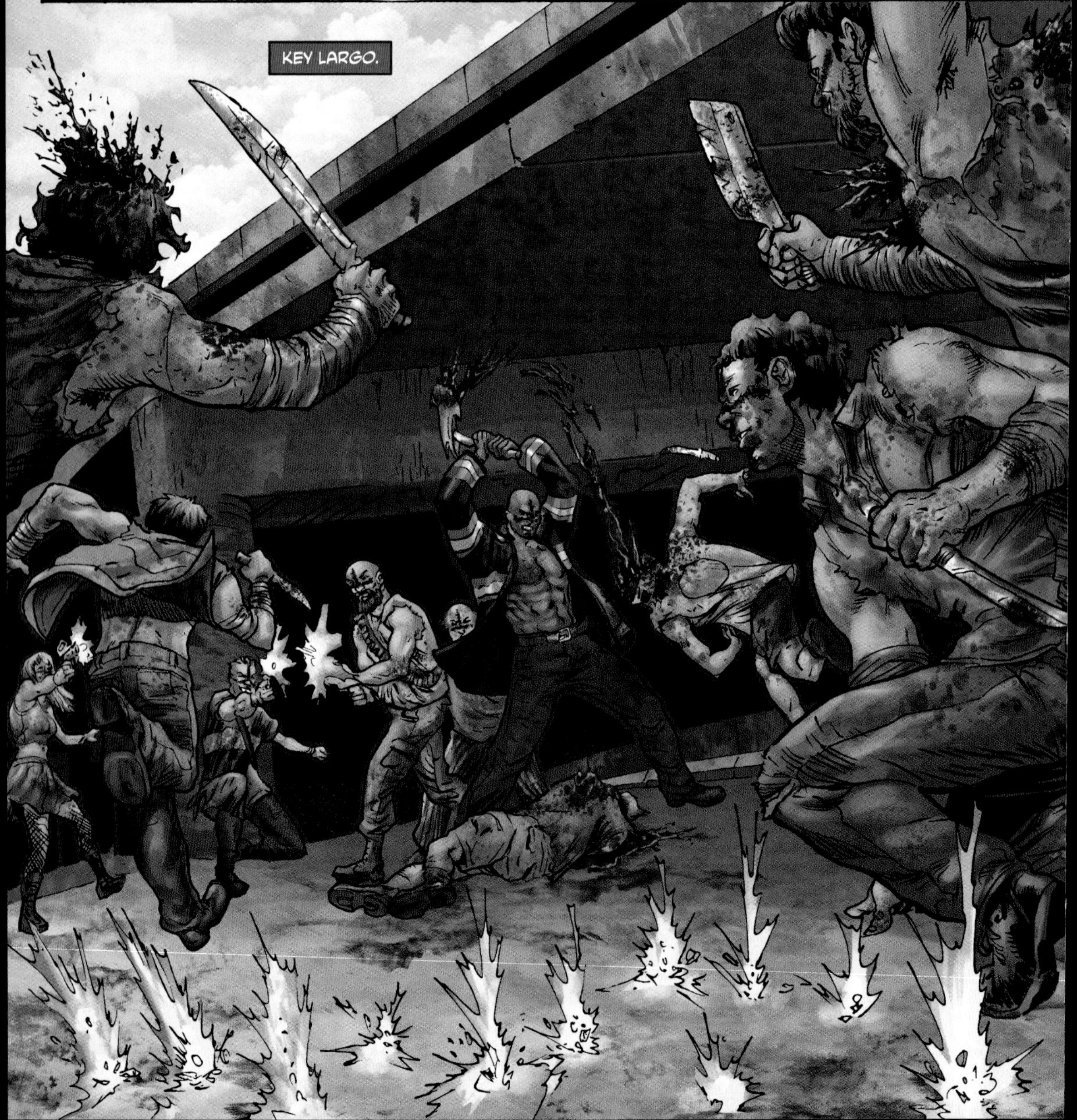
KEY LARGO.

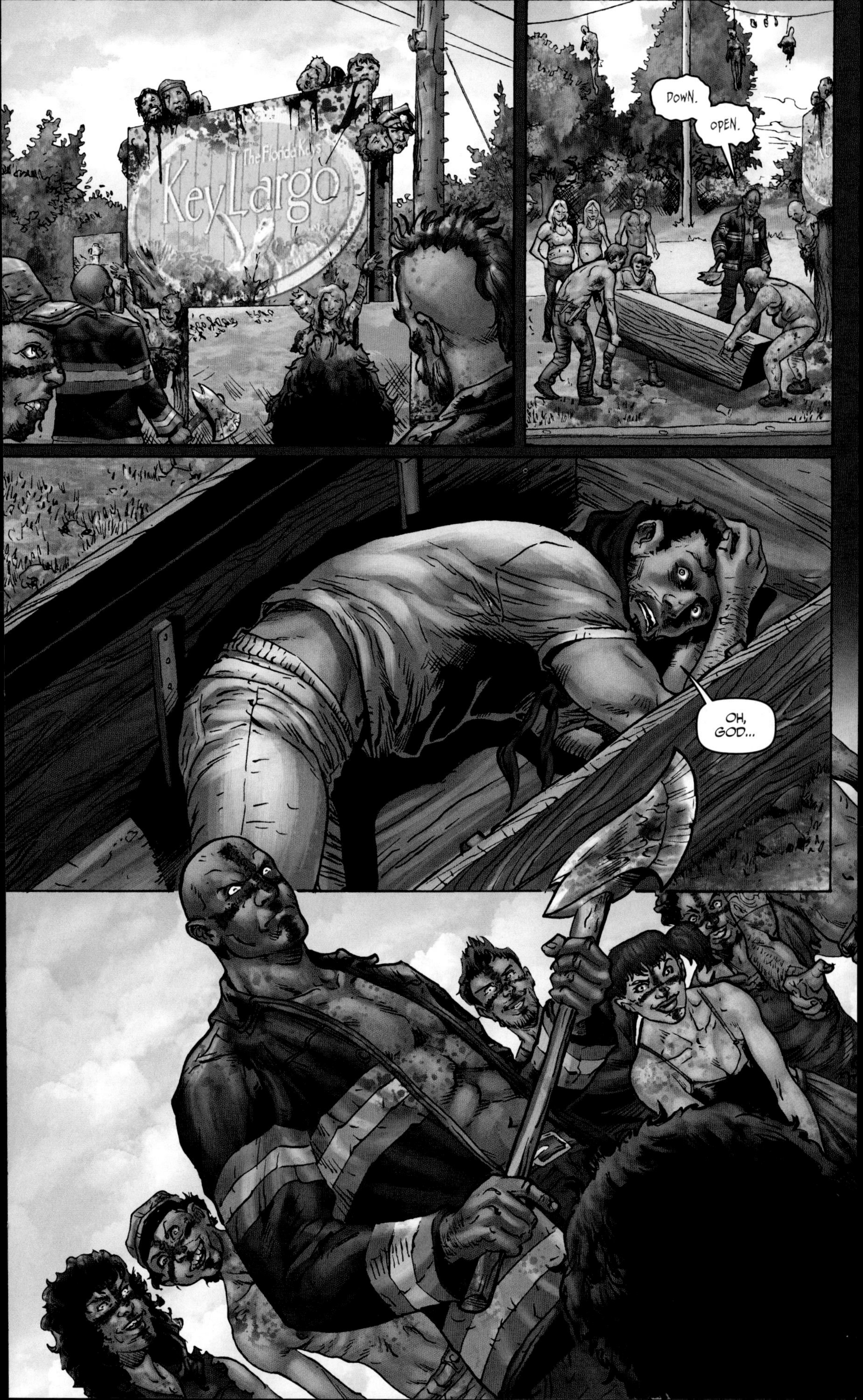
The Florida Keys
Key Largo
DOWN.
OPEN.
OH, GOD...

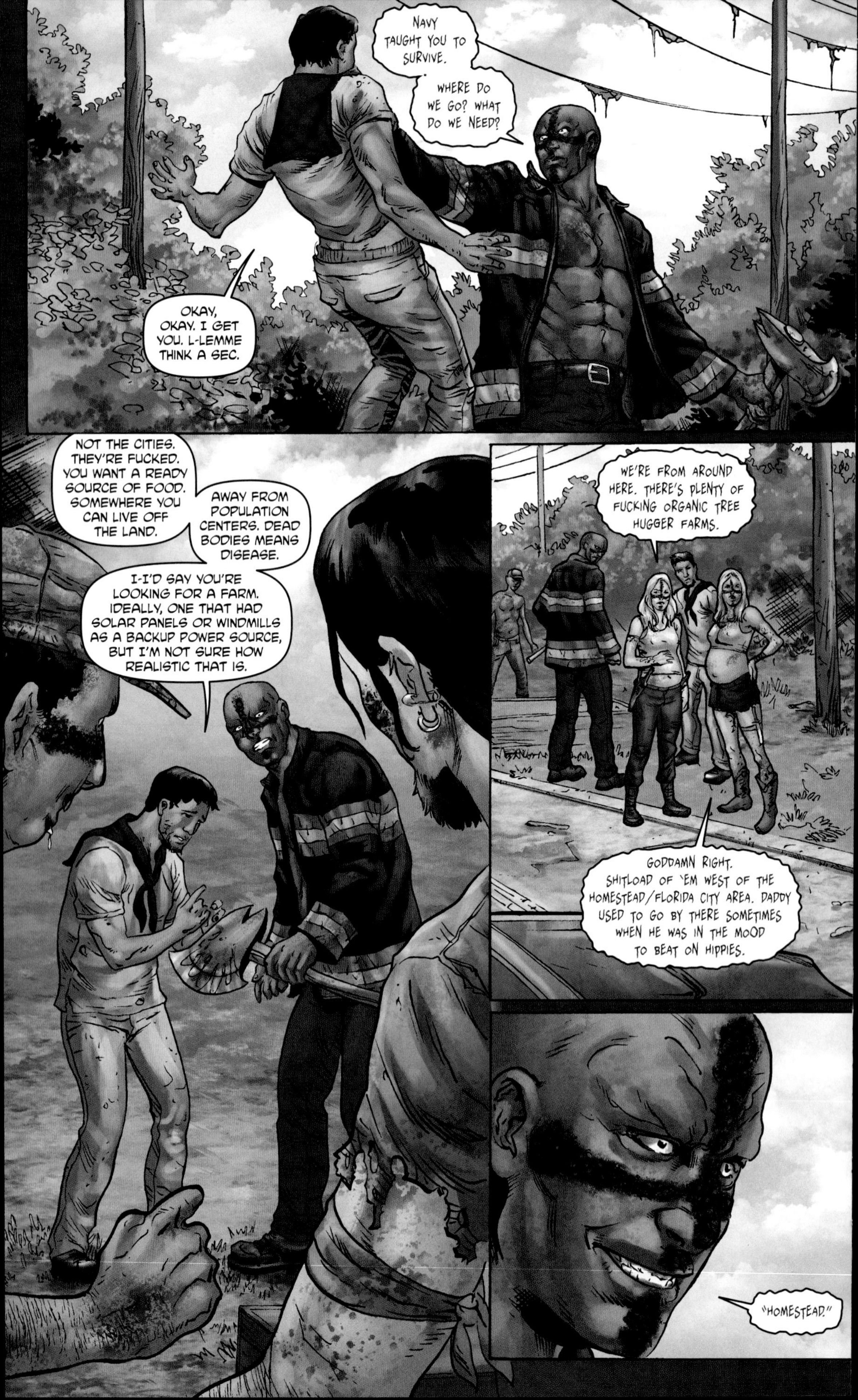
NAVY TAUGHT YOU TO SURVIVE.
WHERE DO WE GO? WHAT DO WE NEED?
OKAY, OKAY. I GET YOU. L-LEMME THINK A SEC.
NOT THE CITIES. THEY'RE FUCKED. YOU WANT A READY SOURCE OF FOOD. SOMEWHERE YOU CAN LIVE OFF THE LAND.
AWAY FROM POPULATION CENTERS. DEAD BODIES MEANS DISEASE.
I-I'D SAY YOU'RE LOOKING FOR A FARM. IDEALLY, ONE THAT HAD SOLAR PANELS OR WINDMILLS AS A BACKUP POWER SOURCE, BUT I'M NOT SURE HOW REALISTIC THAT IS.
WE'RE FROM AROUND HERE. THERE'S PLENTY OF FUCKING ORGANIC TREE HUGGER FARMS.
GODDAMN RIGHT. SHITLOAD OF 'EM WEST OF THE HOMESTEAD/FLORIDA CITY AREA. DADDY USED TO GO BY THERE SOMETIMES WHEN HE WAS IN THE MOOD TO BEAT ON HIPPIES.
"HOMESTEAD."

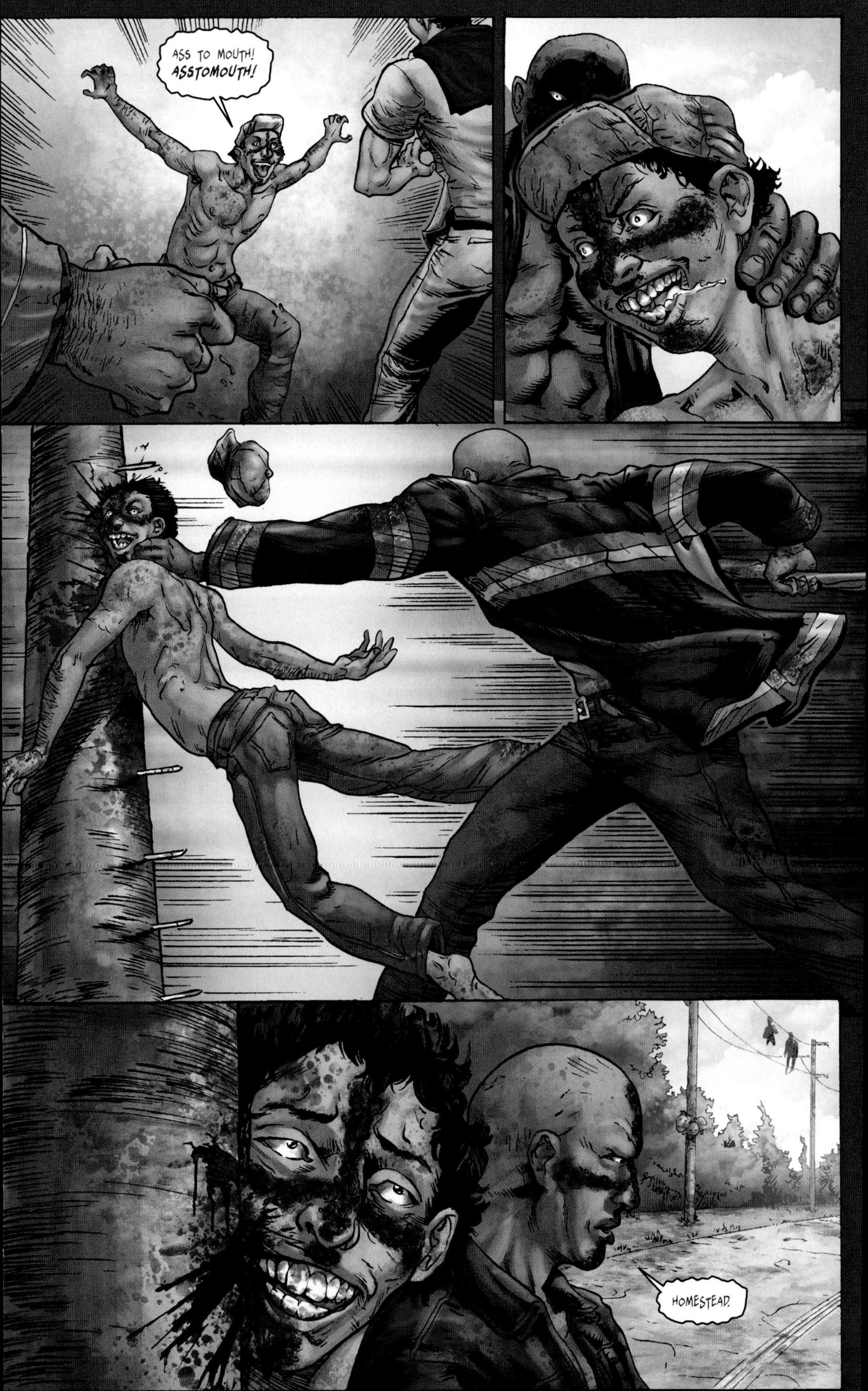
ASS TO MOUTH!
ASSTOMOUTH!
HOMESTEAD.

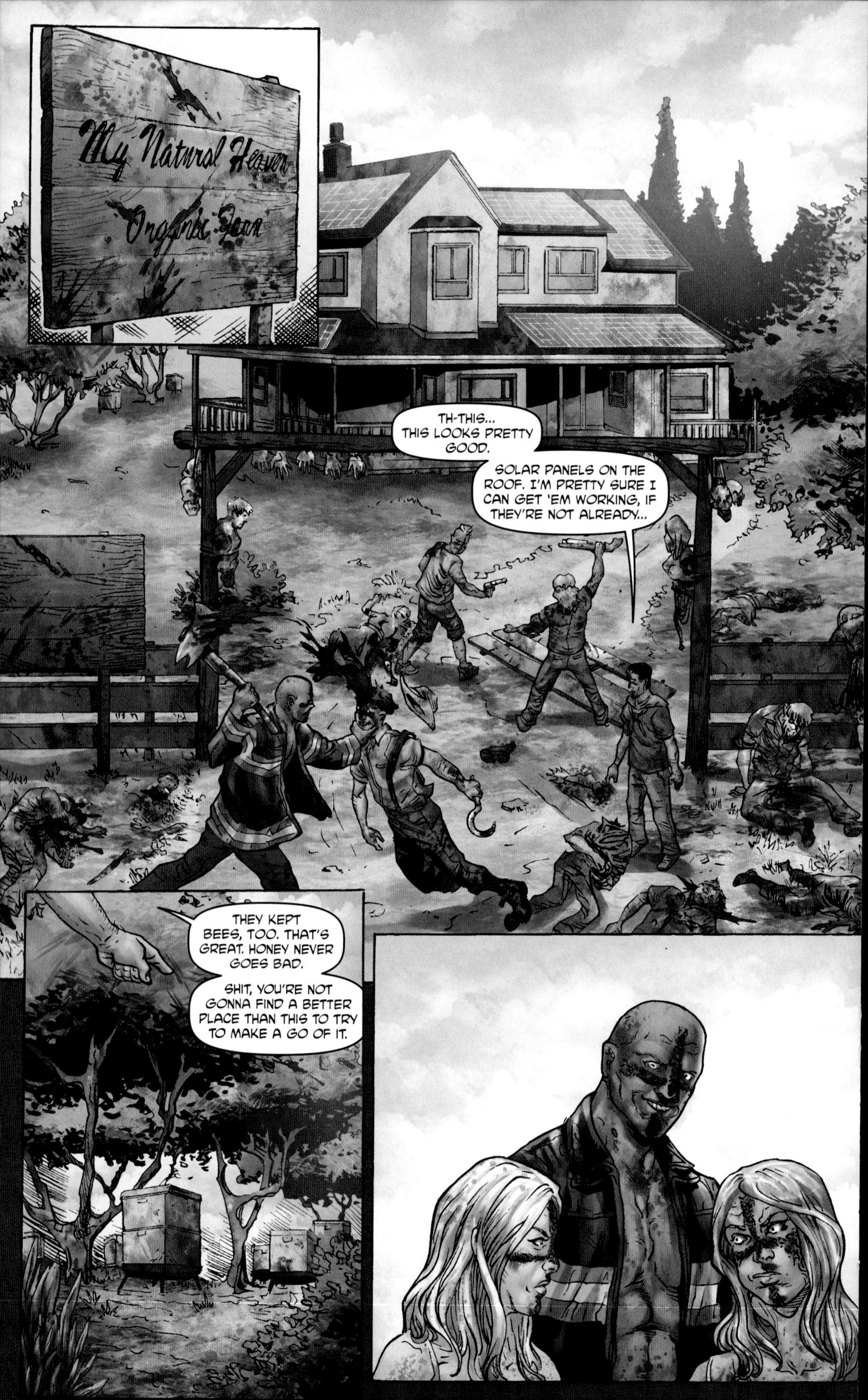

My Natural Heaven
Organic Farm
TH-THIS... THIS LOOKS PRETTY GOOD.
SOLAR PANELS ON THE ROOF. I'M PRETTY SURE I CAN GET 'EM WORKING, IF THEY'RE NOT ALREADY...
THEY KEPT BEES, TOO. THAT'S GREAT. HONEY NEVER GOES BAD.
SHIT, YOU'RE NOT GONNA FIND A BETTER PLACE THAN THIS TO TRY TO MAKE A GO OF IT.

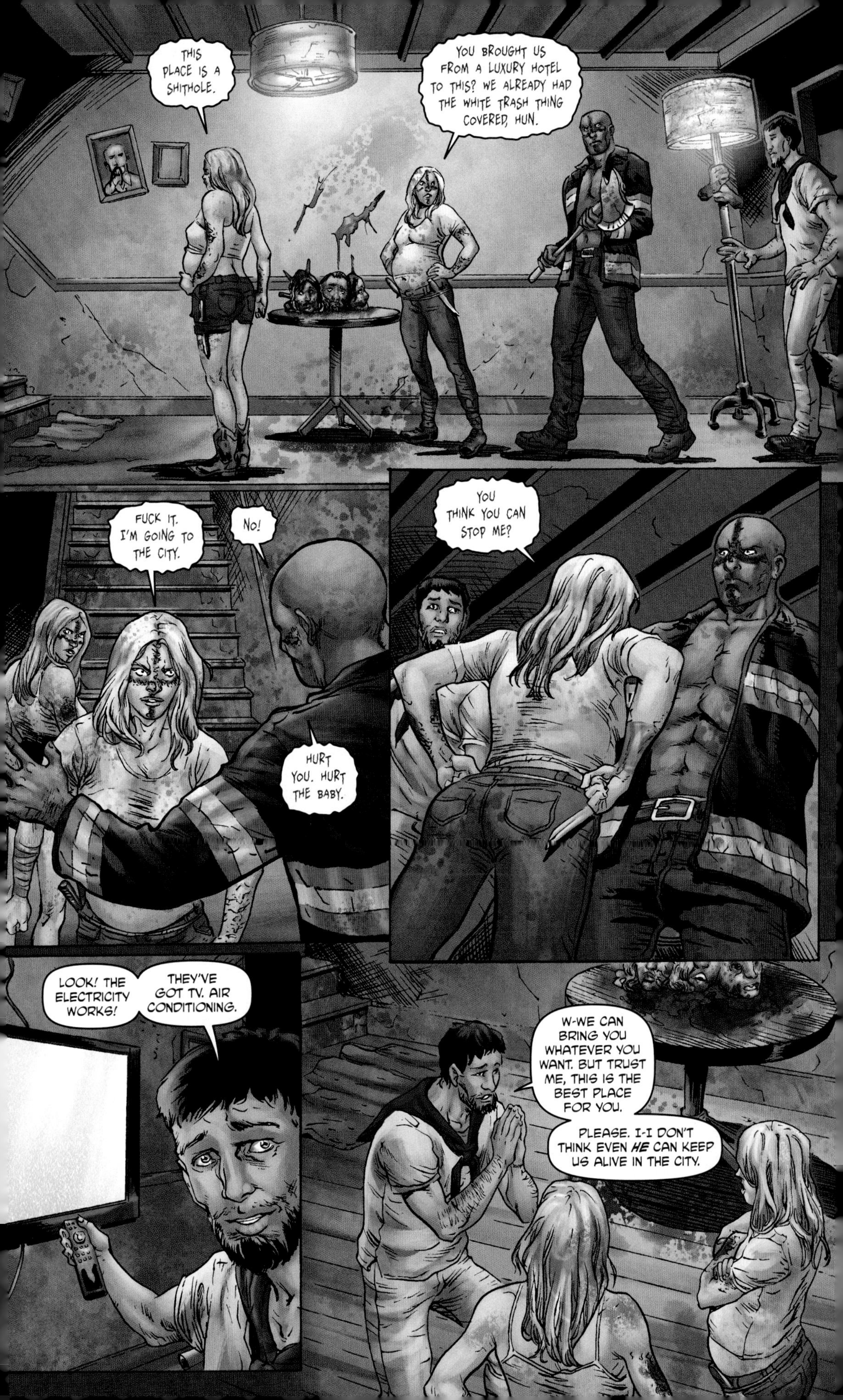
THIS PLACE IS A SHITHOLE.
YOU BROUGHT US FROM A LUXURY HOTEL TO THIS? WE ALREADY HAD THE WHITE TRASH THING COVERED, HUN.
FUCK IT. I'M GOING TO THE CITY.
NO!
HURT YOU. HURT THE BABY.
YOU THINK YOU CAN STOP ME?
LOOK! THE ELECTRICITY WORKS!
THEY'VE GOT TV. AIR CONDITIONING.
W-WE CAN BRING YOU WHATEVER YOU WANT. BUT TRUST ME, THIS IS THE BEST PLACE FOR YOU.
PLEASE. I-I DON'T THINK EVEN ***HE*** CAN KEEP US ALIVE IN THE CITY.

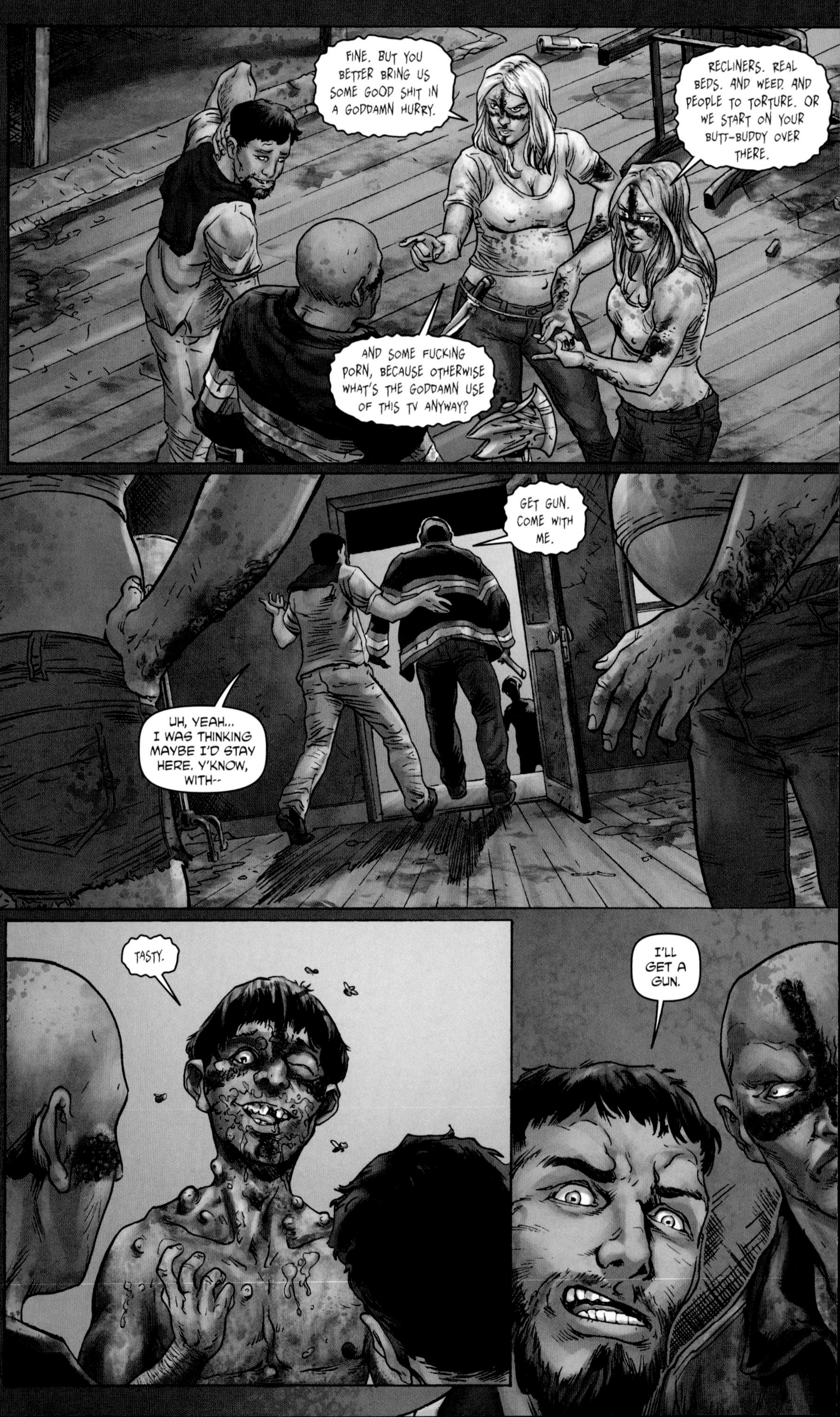

FINE. BUT YOU BETTER BRING US SOME GOOD SHIT IN A GODDAMN HURRY.
RECLINERS. REAL BEDS. AND WEED. AND PEOPLE TO TORTURE. OR WE START ON YOUR BUTT-BUDDY OVER THERE.
AND SOME FUCKING PORN, BECAUSE OTHERWISE WHAT'S THE GODDAMN USE OF THIS TV ANYWAY?
GET GUN. COME WITH ME.
UH, YEAH... I WAS THINKING MAYBE I'D STAY HERE. Y'KNOW, WITH--
TASTY.
I'LL GET A GUN.

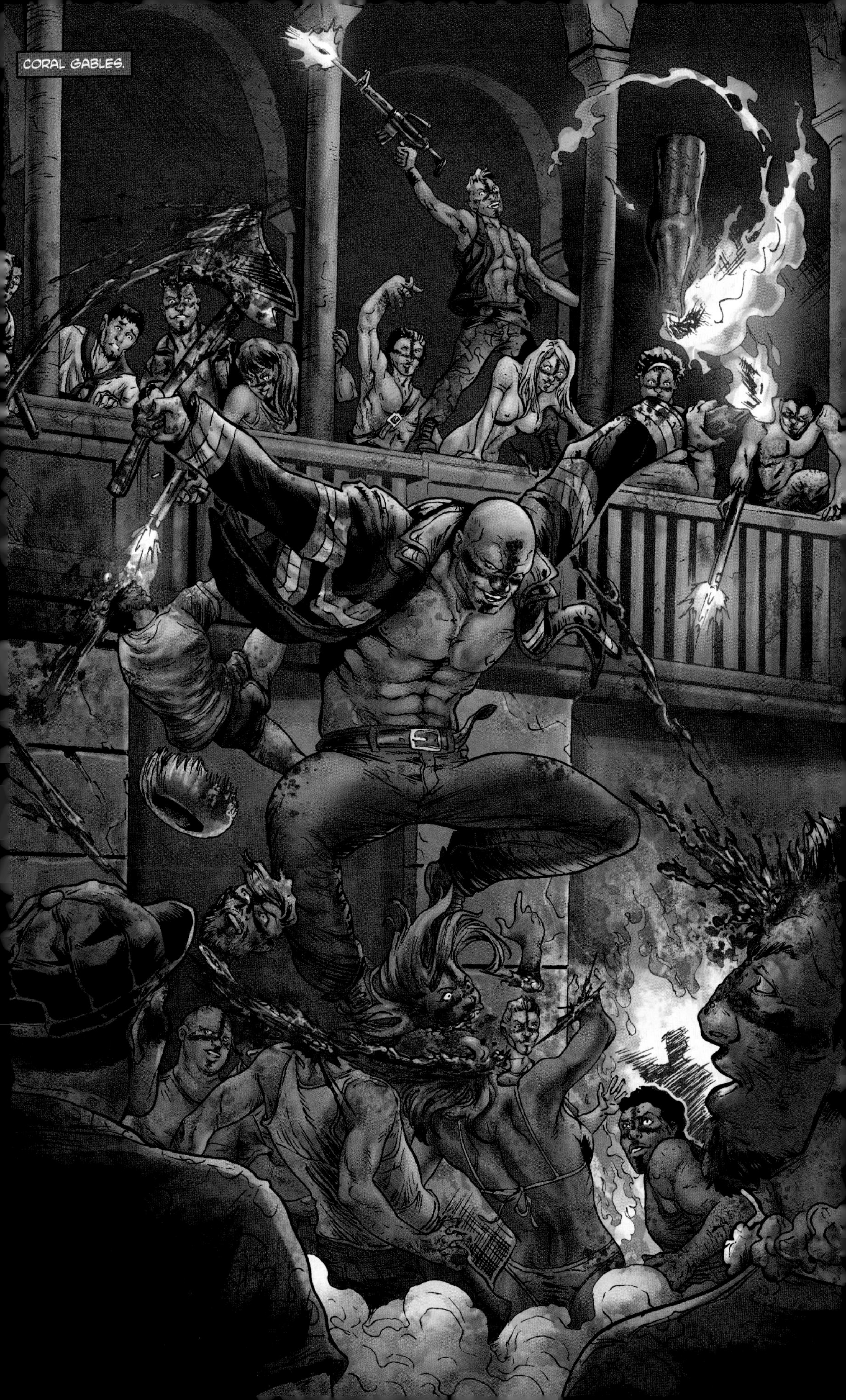
CORAL GABLES.

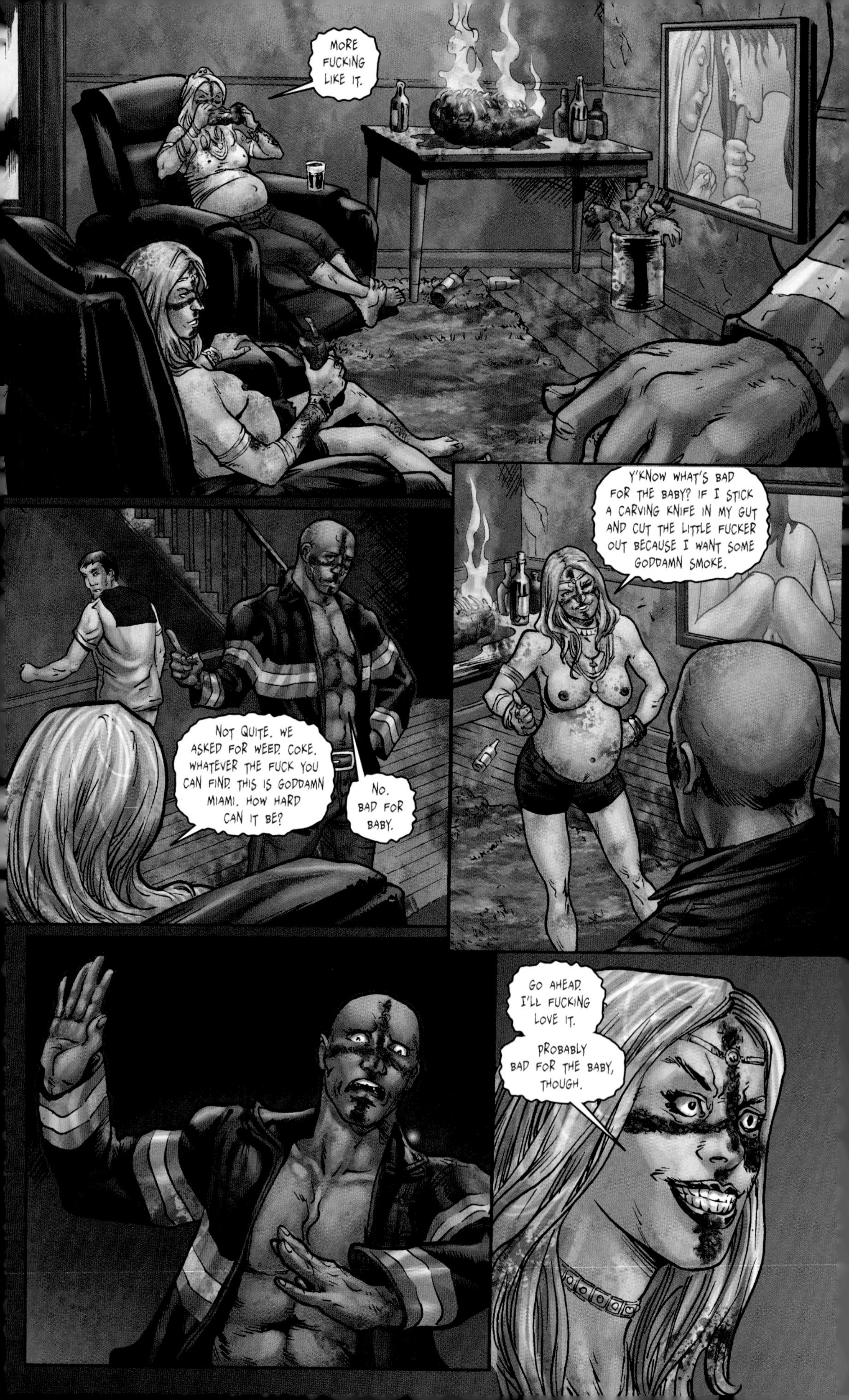
MORE FUCKING LIKE IT.
NOT QUITE. WE ASKED FOR WEED. COKE. WHATEVER THE FUCK YOU CAN FIND. THIS IS GODDAMN MIAMI. HOW HARD CAN IT BE?
NO. BAD FOR BABY.
Y'KNOW WHAT'S BAD FOR THE BABY? IF I STICK A CARVING KNIFE IN MY GUT AND CUT THE LITTLE FUCKER OUT BECAUSE I WANT SOME GODDAMN SMOKE.
GO AHEAD. I'LL FUCKING LOVE IT.
PROBABLY BAD FOR THE BABY, THOUGH.

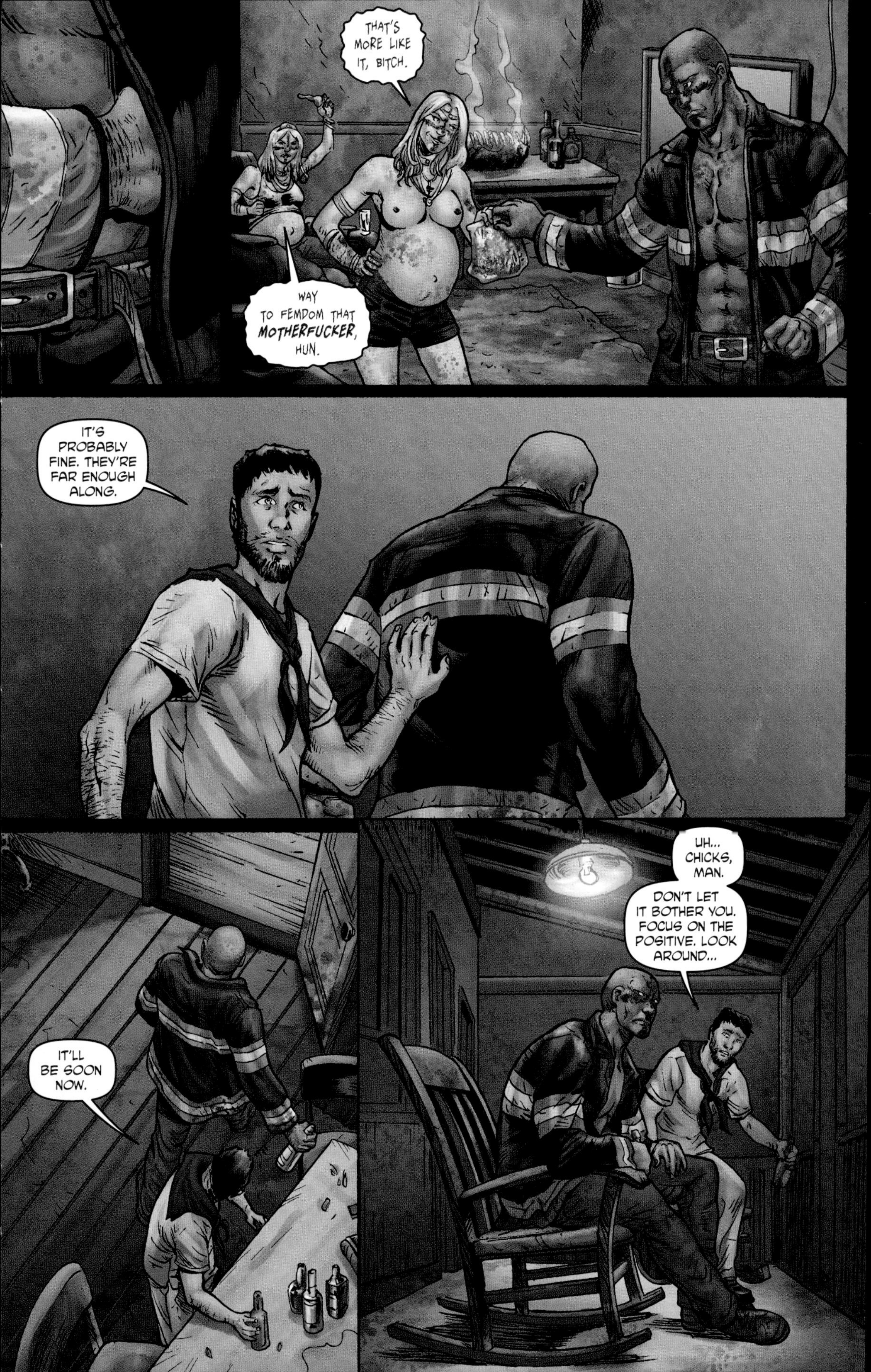
THAT'S MORE LIKE IT, BITCH.
WAY TO FEMDOM THAT MOTHERFUCKER, HUN.
IT'S PROBABLY FINE. THEY'RE FAR ENOUGH ALONG.
IT'LL BE SOON NOW.
UH... CHICKS, MAN.
DON'T LET IT BOTHER YOU. FOCUS ON THE POSITIVE. LOOK AROUND...

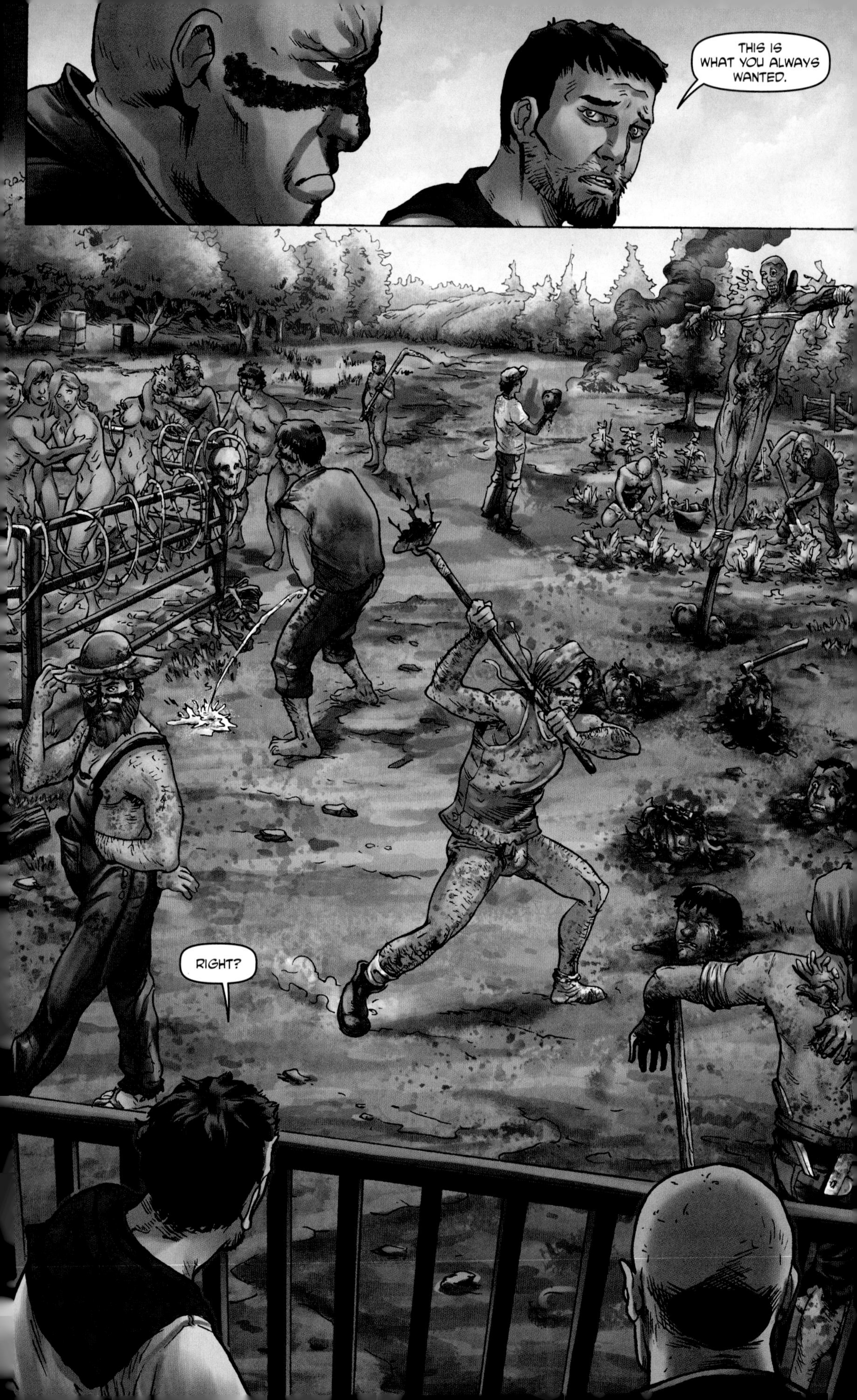
THIS IS WHAT YOU ALWAYS WANTED.
RIGHT?

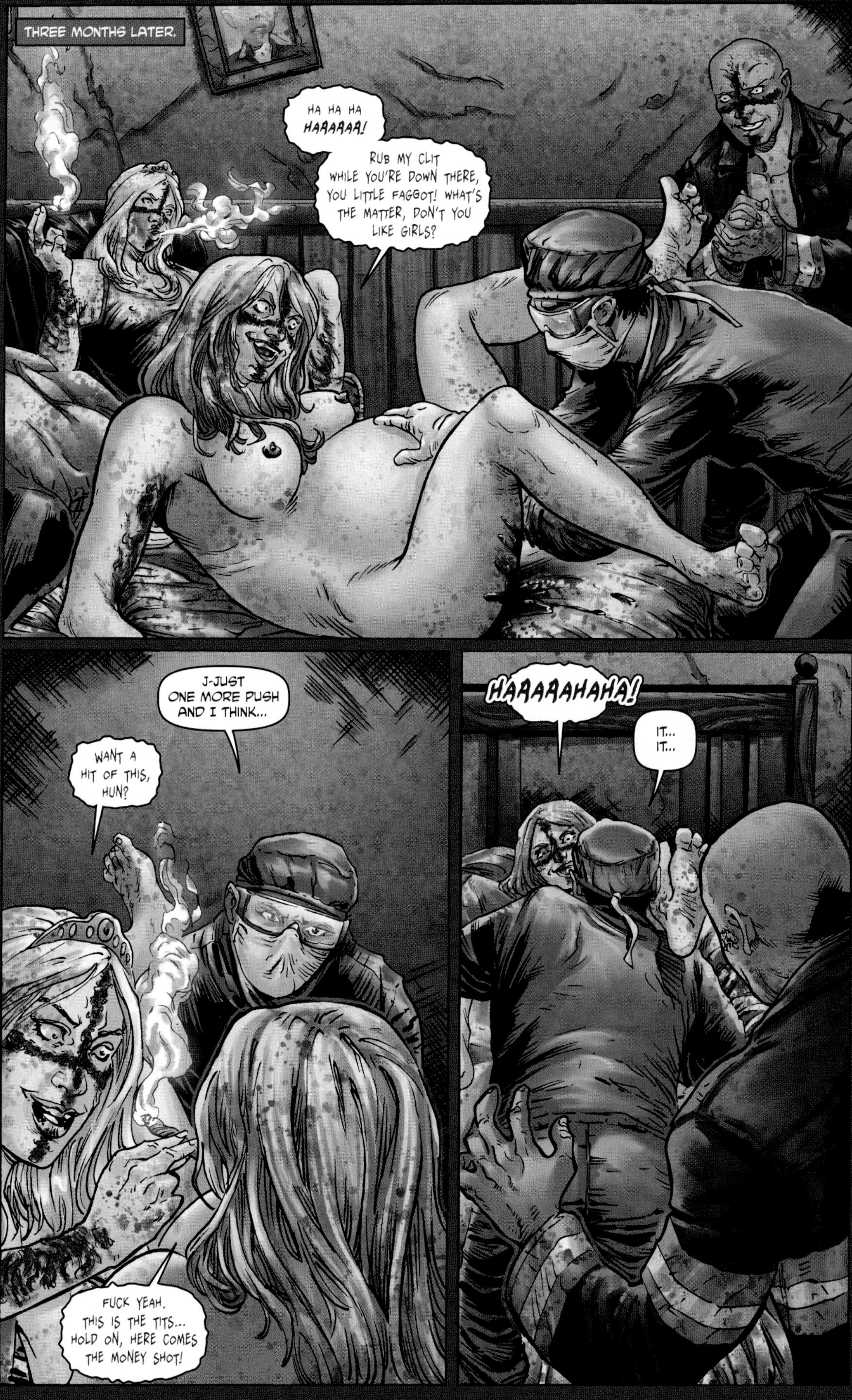

THREE MONTHS LATER.
HA HA HA HAAAAAA!
RUB MY CLIT WHILE YOU'RE DOWN THERE, YOU LITTLE FAGGOT! WHAT'S THE MATTER, DON'T YOU LIKE GIRLS?
J-JUST ONE MORE PUSH AND I THINK...
WANT A HIT OF THIS, HUN?
FUCK YEAH. THIS IS THE TITS... HOLD ON, HERE COMES THE MONEY SHOT!
HAAAAAHAHA!
IT... IT...

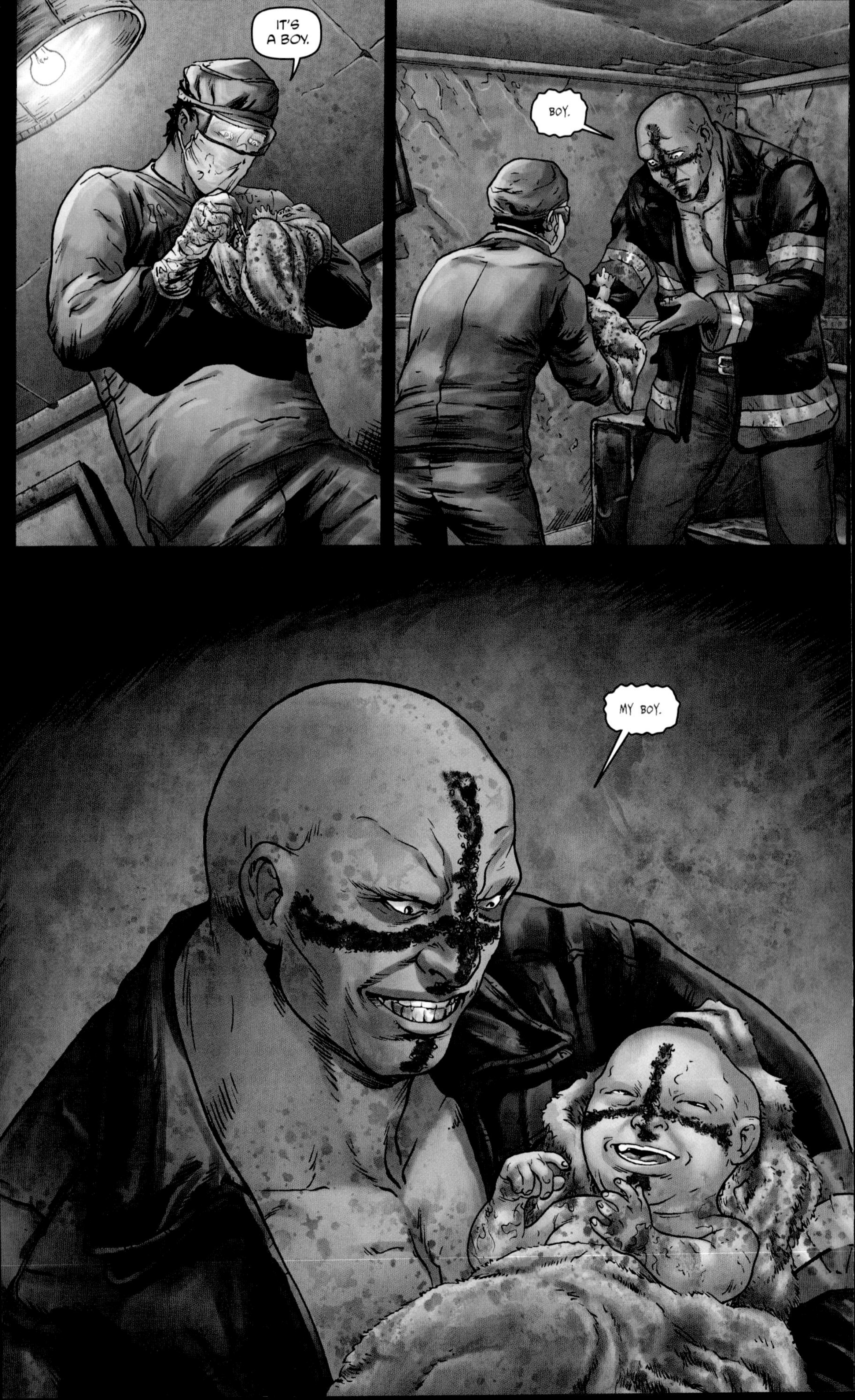
IT'S A BOY.
BOY.
MY BOY.

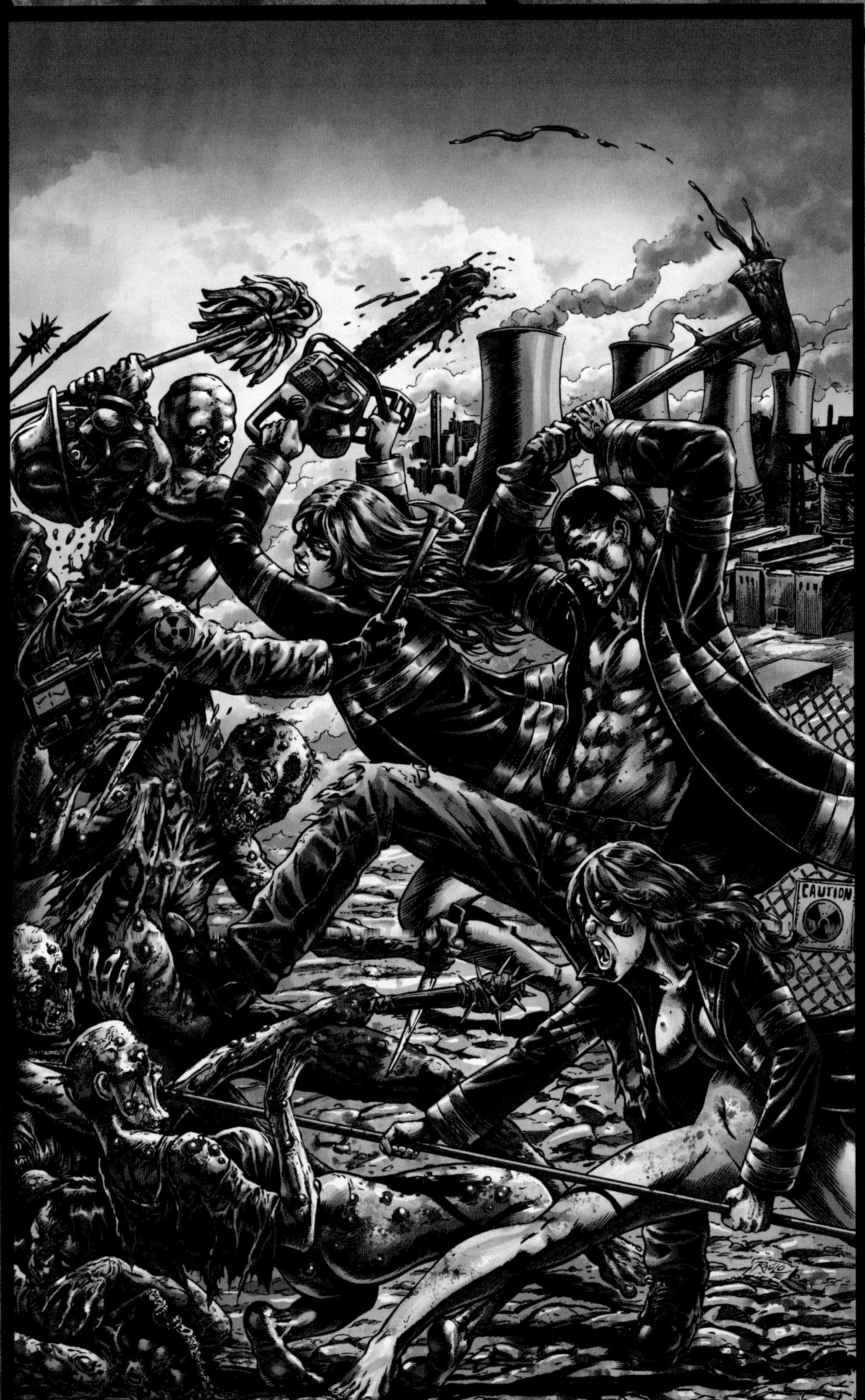
CAUTION

PART 7

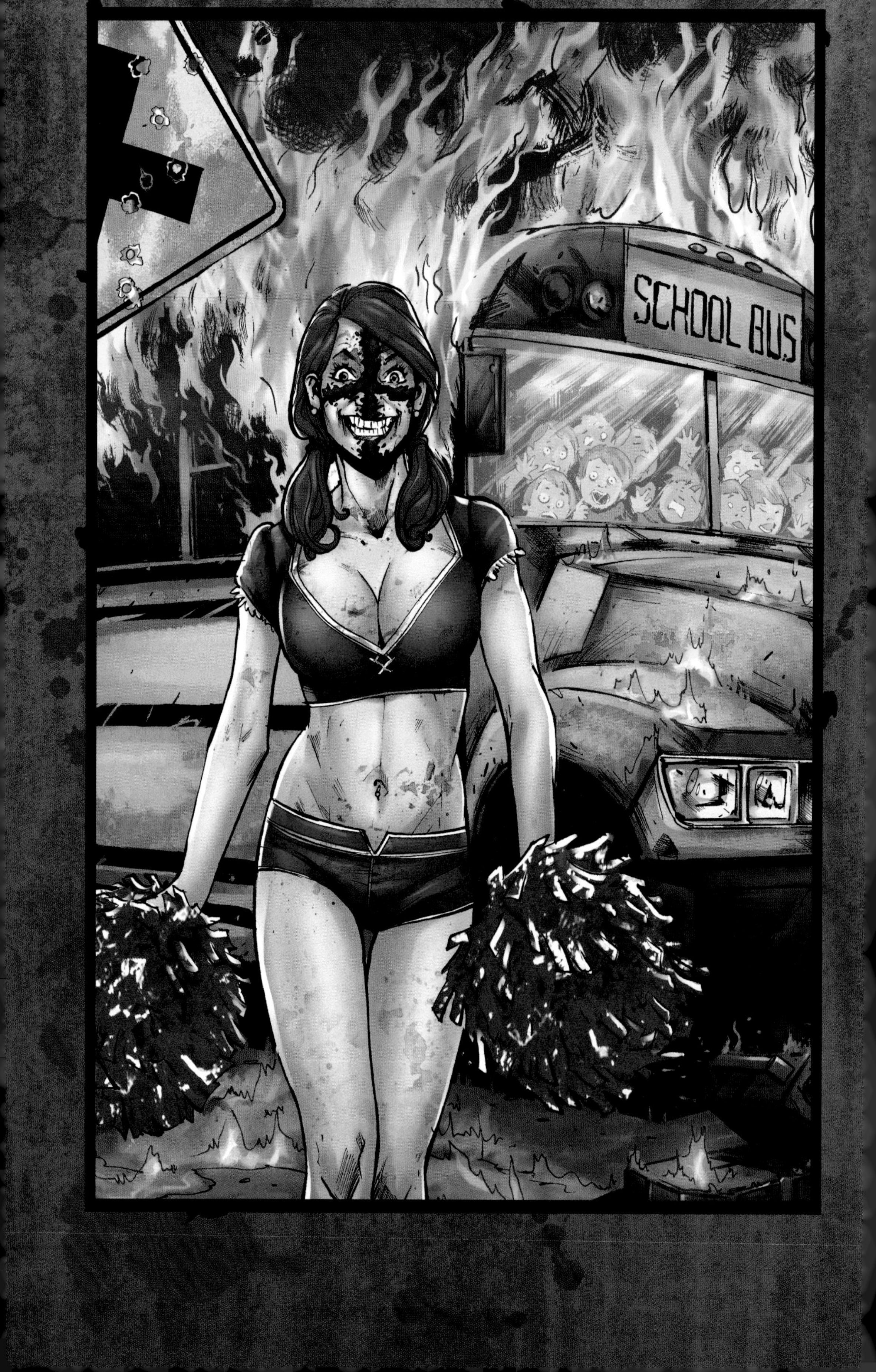
SCHOOL BUS

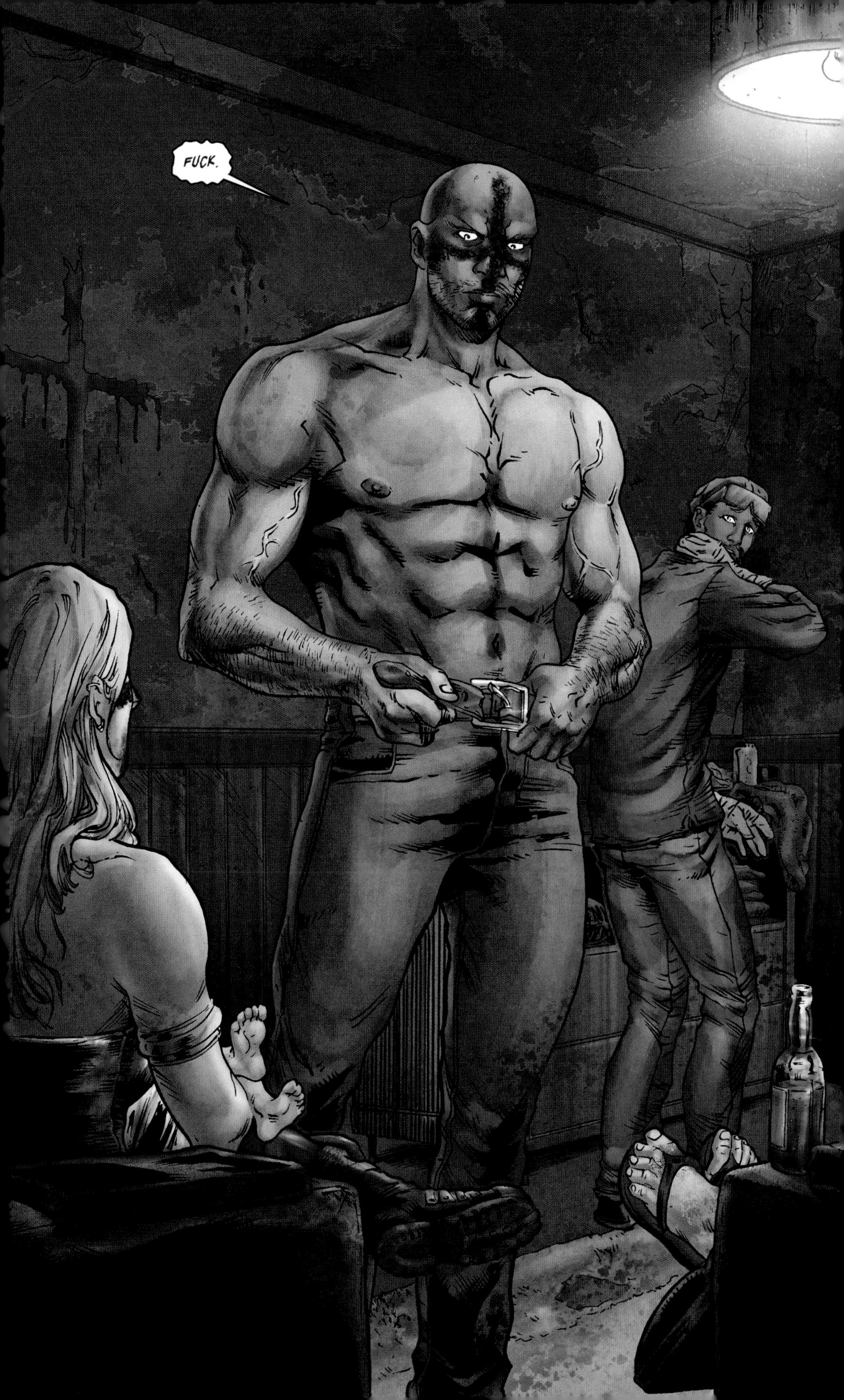
FUCK.

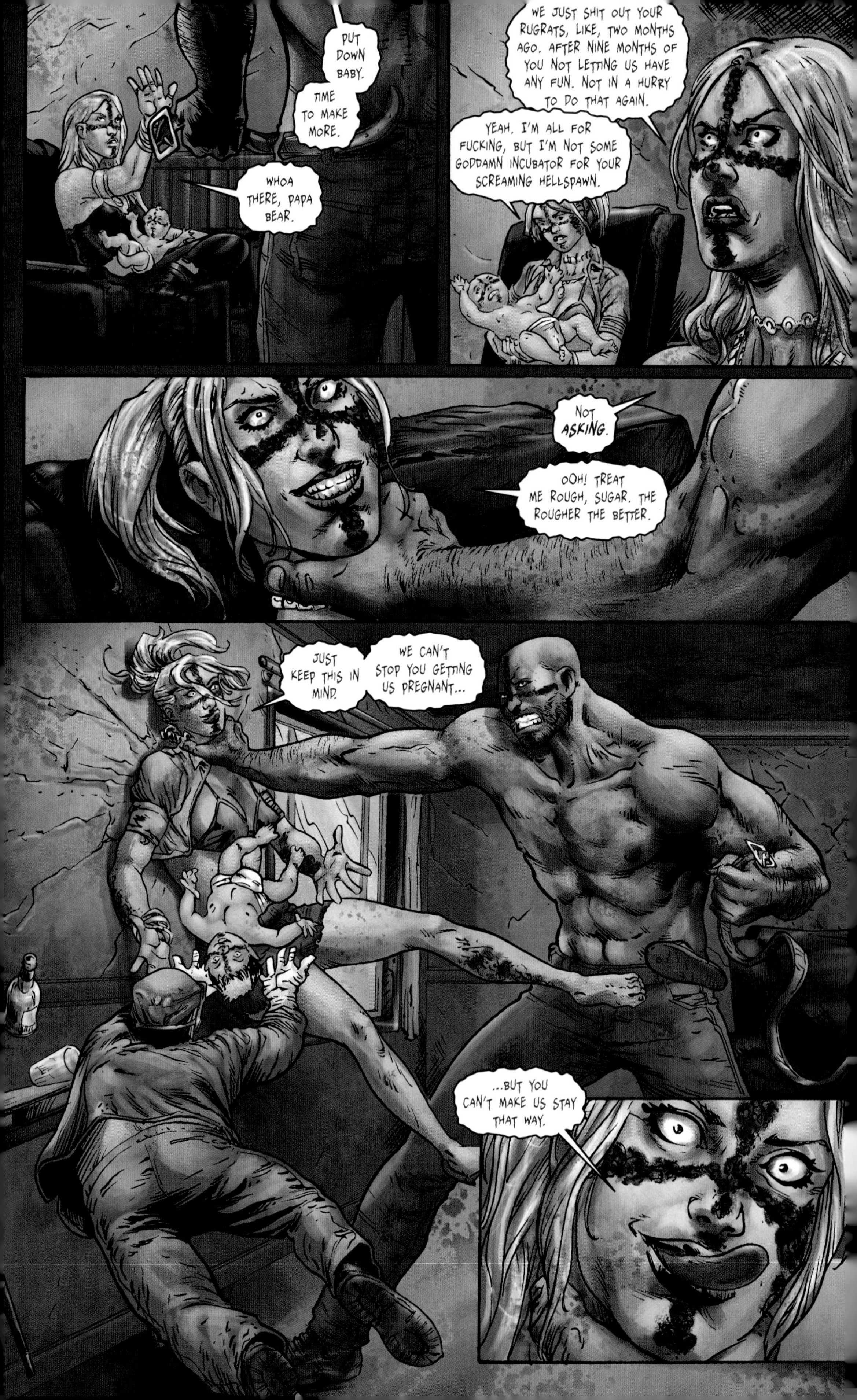
PUT DOWN BABY.
TIME TO MAKE MORE.
WHOA THERE, PAPA BEAR.
WE JUST SHIT OUT YOUR RUGRATS, LIKE, TWO MONTHS AGO. AFTER NINE MONTHS OF YOU NOT LETTING US HAVE ANY FUN. NOT IN A HURRY TO DO THAT AGAIN.
YEAH. I'M ALL FOR FUCKING, BUT I'M NOT SOME GODDAMN INCUBATOR FOR YOUR SCREAMING HELLSPAWN.
NOT ASKING.
OOH! TREAT ME ROUGH, SUGAR. THE ROUGHER THE BETTER.
JUST KEEP THIS IN MIND.
WE CAN'T STOP YOU GETTING US PREGNANT...
...BUT YOU CAN'T MAKE US STAY THAT WAY.

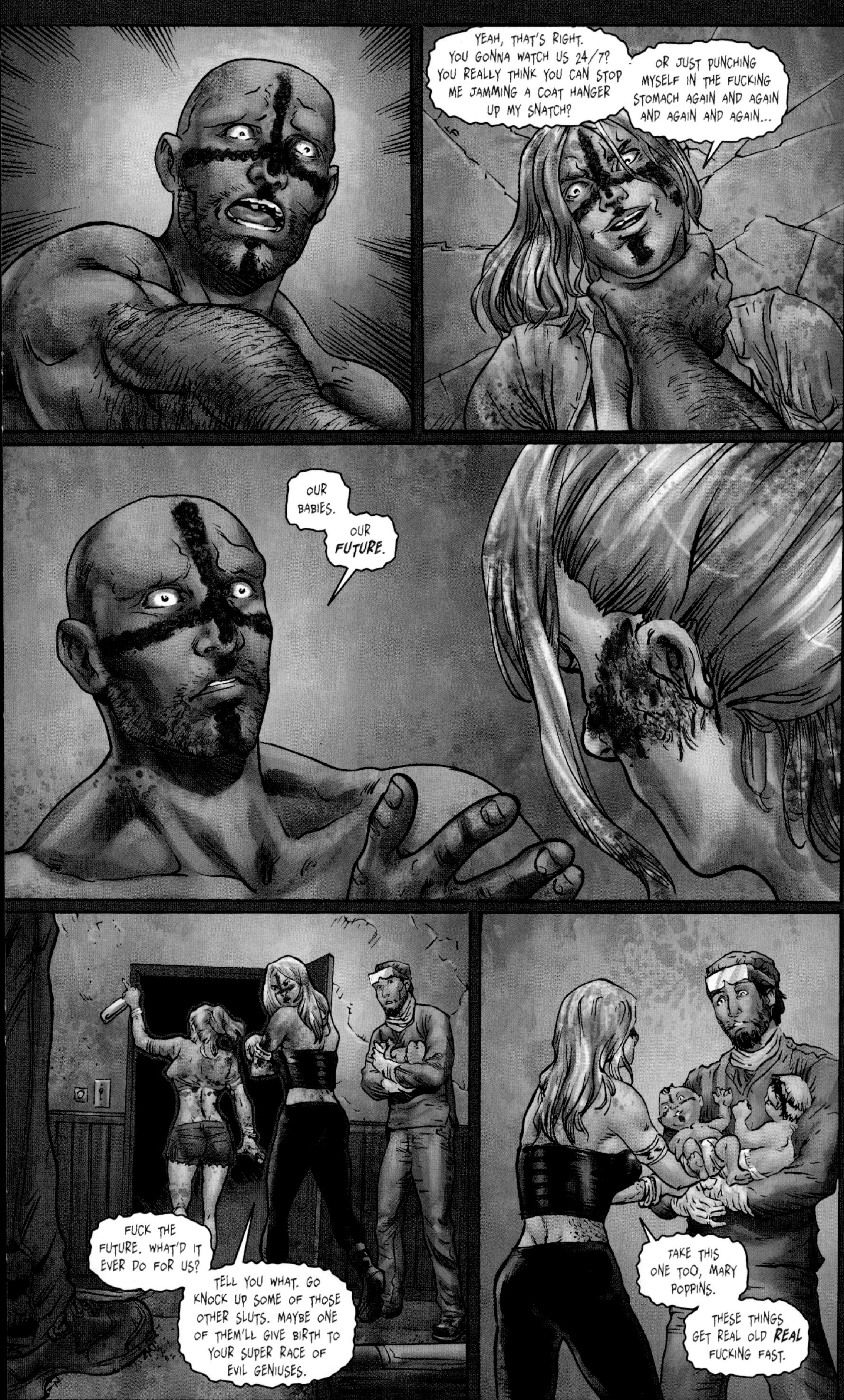
YEAH, THAT'S RIGHT. YOU GONNA WATCH US 24/7? YOU REALLY THINK YOU CAN STOP ME JAMMING A COAT HANGER UP MY SNATCH?
OR JUST PUNCHING MYSELF IN THE FUCKING STOMACH AGAIN AND AGAIN AND AGAIN AND AGAIN...
OUR BABIES.
OUR FUTURE.
FUCK THE FUTURE. WHAT'D IT EVER DO FOR US?
TELL YOU WHAT. GO KNOCK UP SOME OF THOSE OTHER SLUTS. MAYBE ONE OF THEM'LL GIVE BIRTH TO YOUR SUPER RACE OF EVIL GENIUSES.
TAKE THIS ONE TOO, MARY POPPINS.
THESE THINGS GET REAL OLD REAL FUCKING FAST.

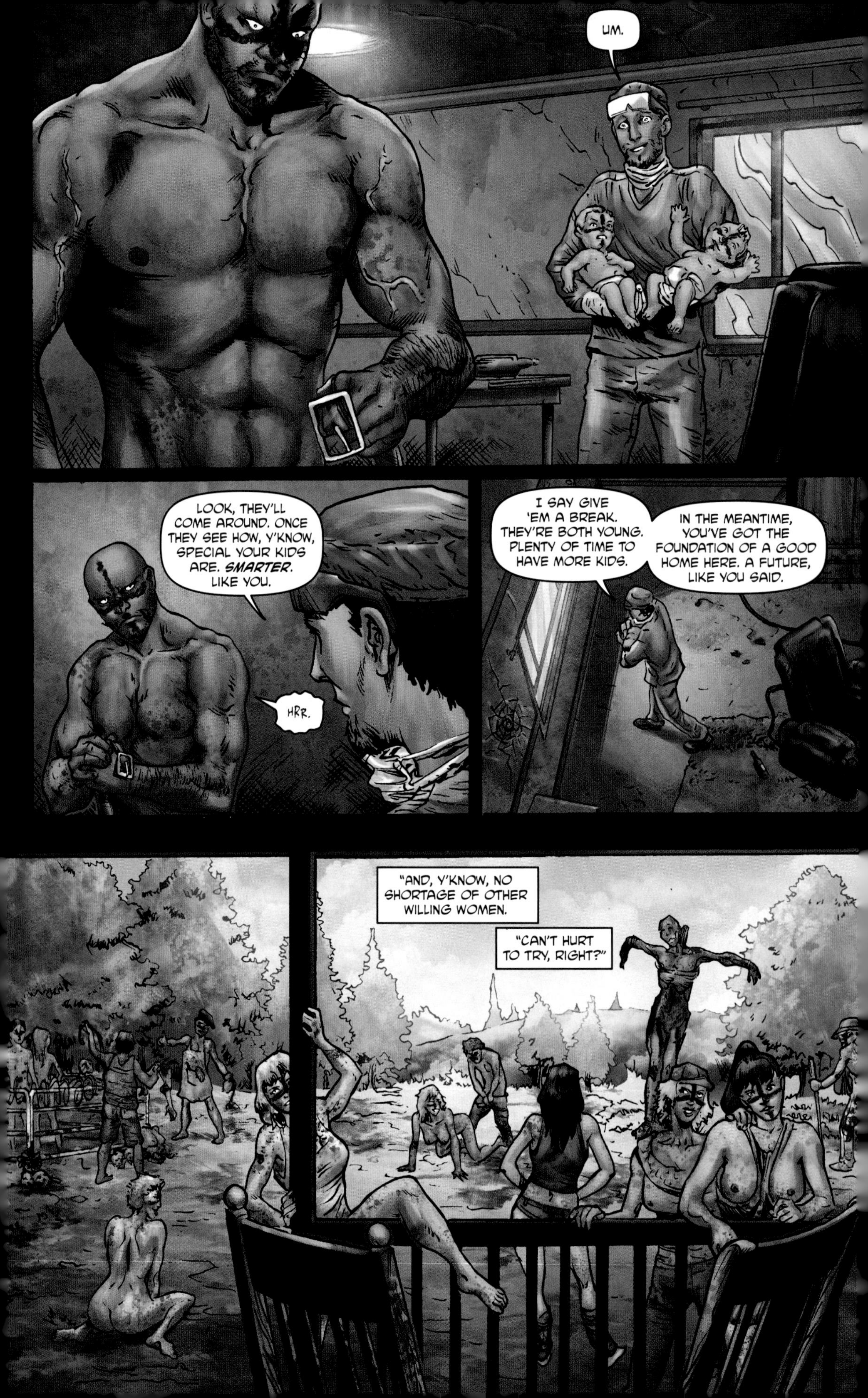
UM.
LOOK, THEY'LL COME AROUND. ONCE THEY SEE HOW, Y'KNOW, SPECIAL YOUR KIDS ARE. *SMARTER.* LIKE YOU.
HRR.
I SAY GIVE 'EM A BREAK. THEY'RE BOTH YOUNG. PLENTY OF TIME TO HAVE MORE KIDS.
IN THE MEANTIME, YOU'VE GOT THE FOUNDATION OF A GOOD HOME HERE. A FUTURE, LIKE YOU SAID.
"AND, Y'KNOW, NO SHORTAGE OF OTHER WILLING WOMEN.
"CAN'T HURT TO TRY, RIGHT?"

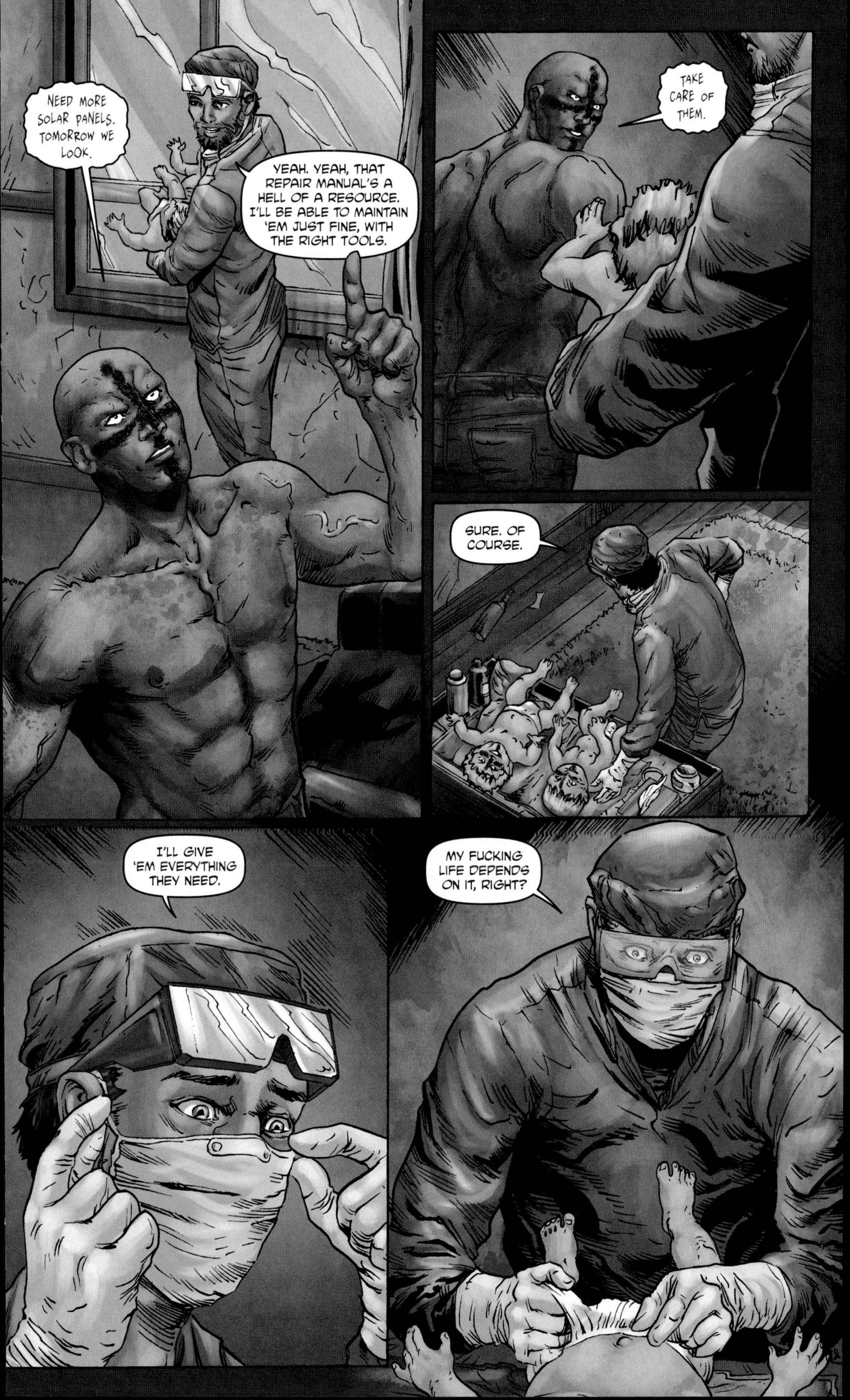
NEED MORE SOLAR PANELS. TOMORROW WE LOOK.
YEAH. YEAH, THAT REPAIR MANUAL'S A HELL OF A RESOURCE. I'LL BE ABLE TO MAINTAIN 'EM JUST FINE, WITH THE RIGHT TOOLS.
TAKE CARE OF THEM.
SURE. OF COURSE.
I'LL GIVE 'EM EVERYTHING THEY NEED.
MY FUCKING LIFE DEPENDS ON IT, RIGHT?

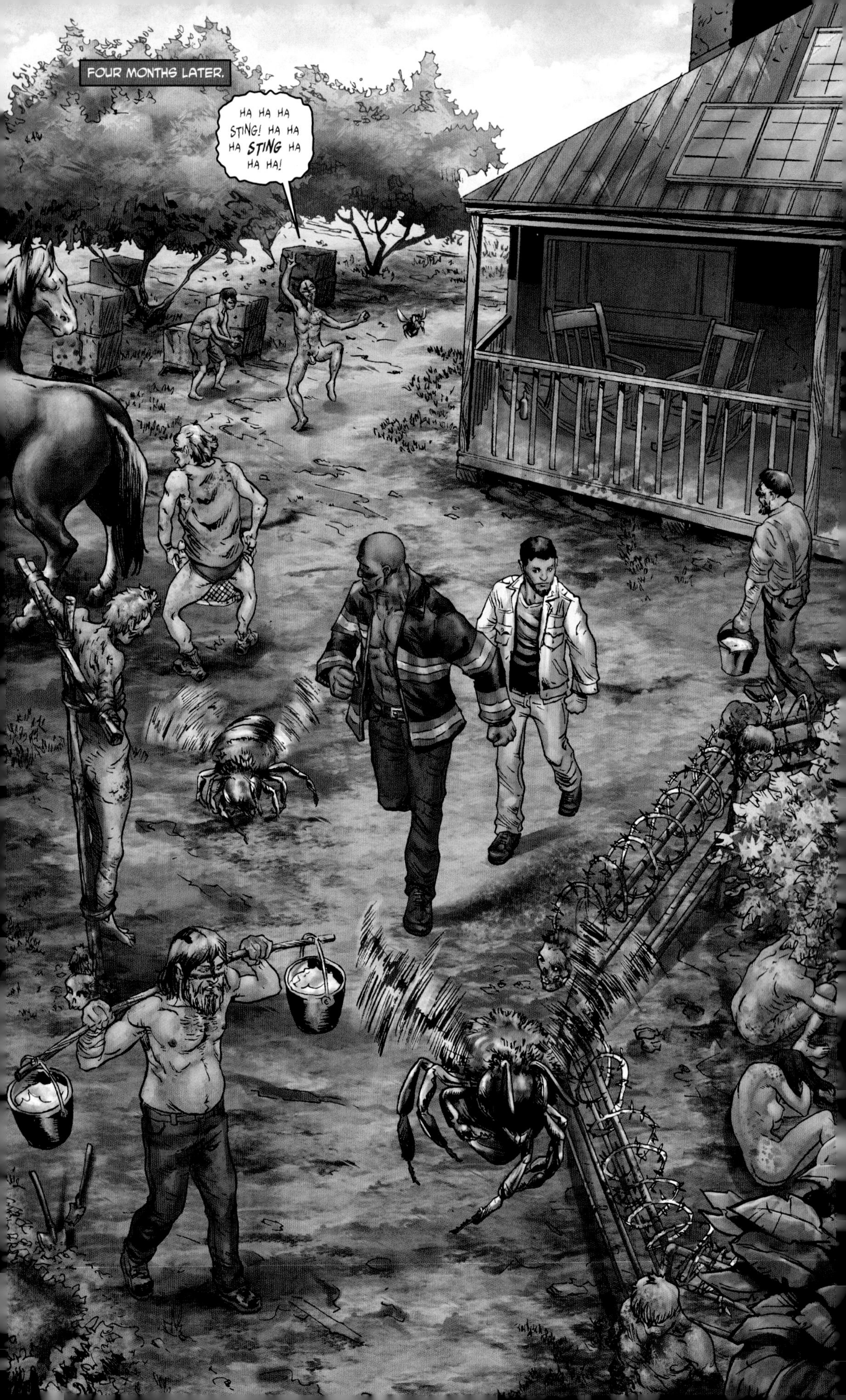
FOUR MONTHS LATER.
HA HA HA STING! HA HA HA STING HA HA HA!

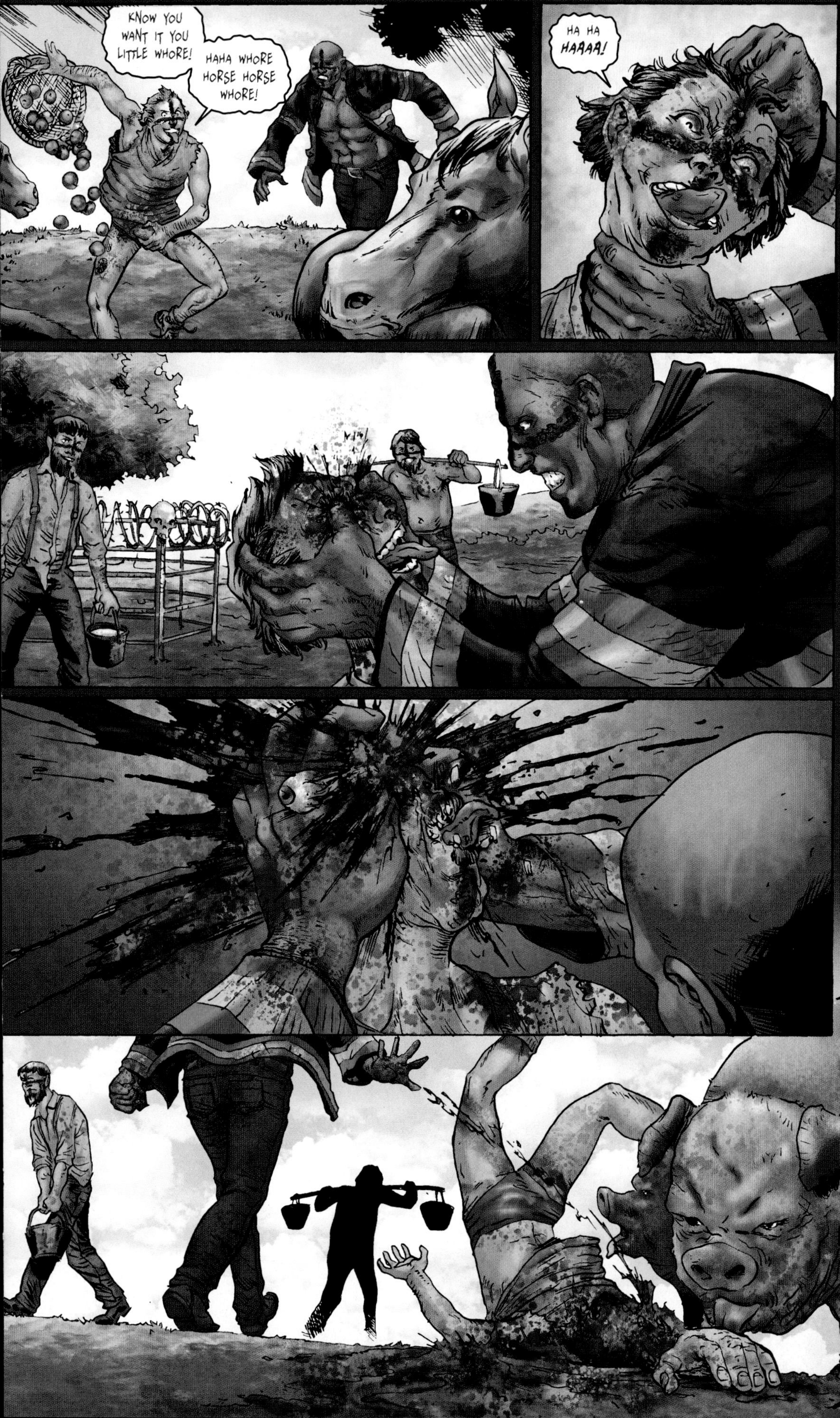
KNOW YOU WANT IT YOU LITTLE WHORE!
HAHA WHORE HORSE HORSE WHORE!
HA HA HAAAA!

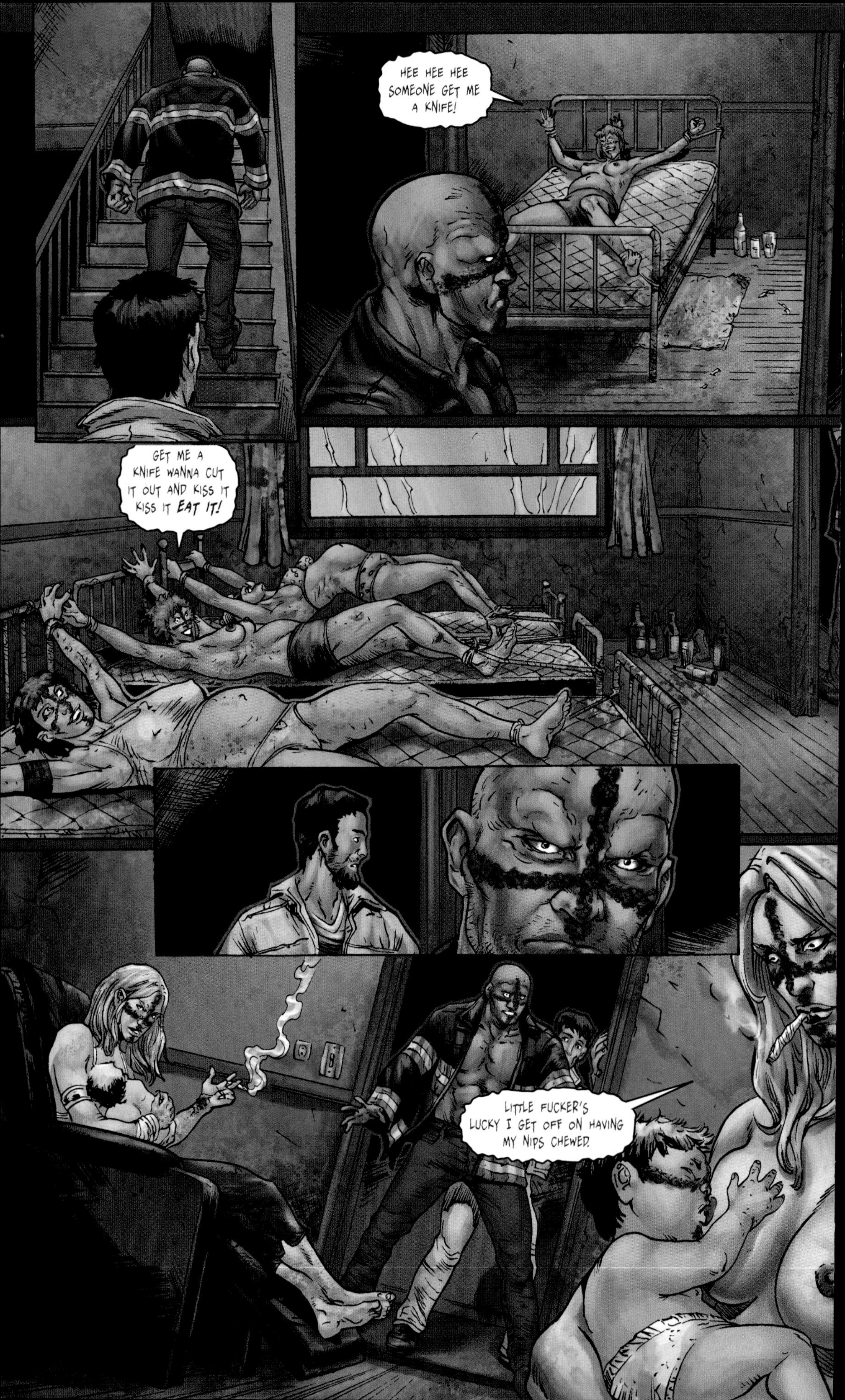
HEE HEE HEE
SOMEONE GET ME
A KNIFE!
GET ME A
KNIFE WANNA CUT
IT OUT AND KISS IT
KISS IT EAT IT!
LITTLE FUCKER'S
LUCKY I GET OFF ON HAVING
MY NIPS CHEWED.

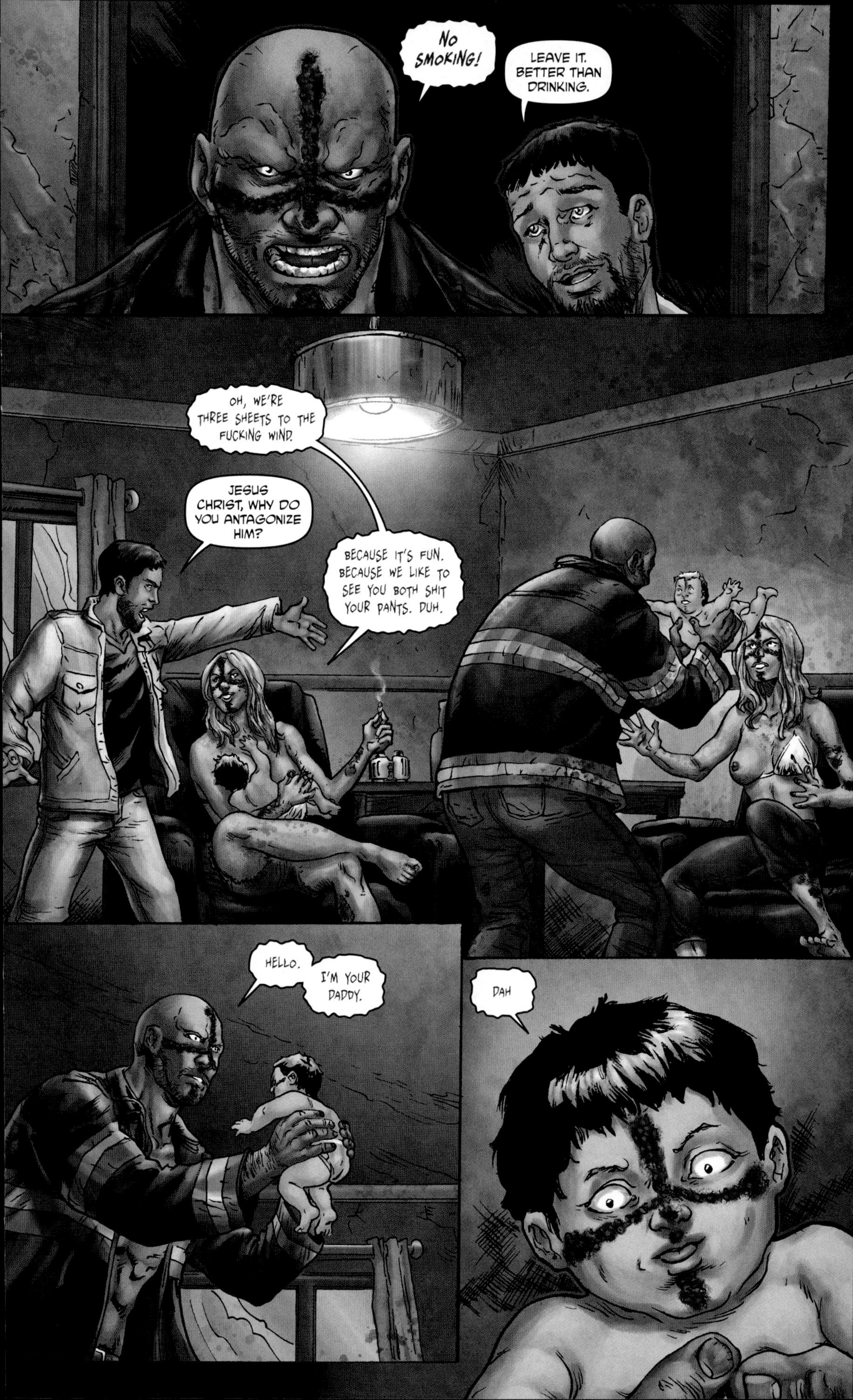
NO SMOKING!
LEAVE IT. BETTER THAN DRINKING.
OH, WE'RE THREE SHEETS TO THE FUCKING WIND.
JESUS CHRIST, WHY DO YOU ANTAGONIZE HIM?
BECAUSE IT'S FUN. BECAUSE WE LIKE TO SEE YOU BOTH SHIT YOUR PANTS. DUH.
HELLO.
I'M YOUR DADDY.
DAH

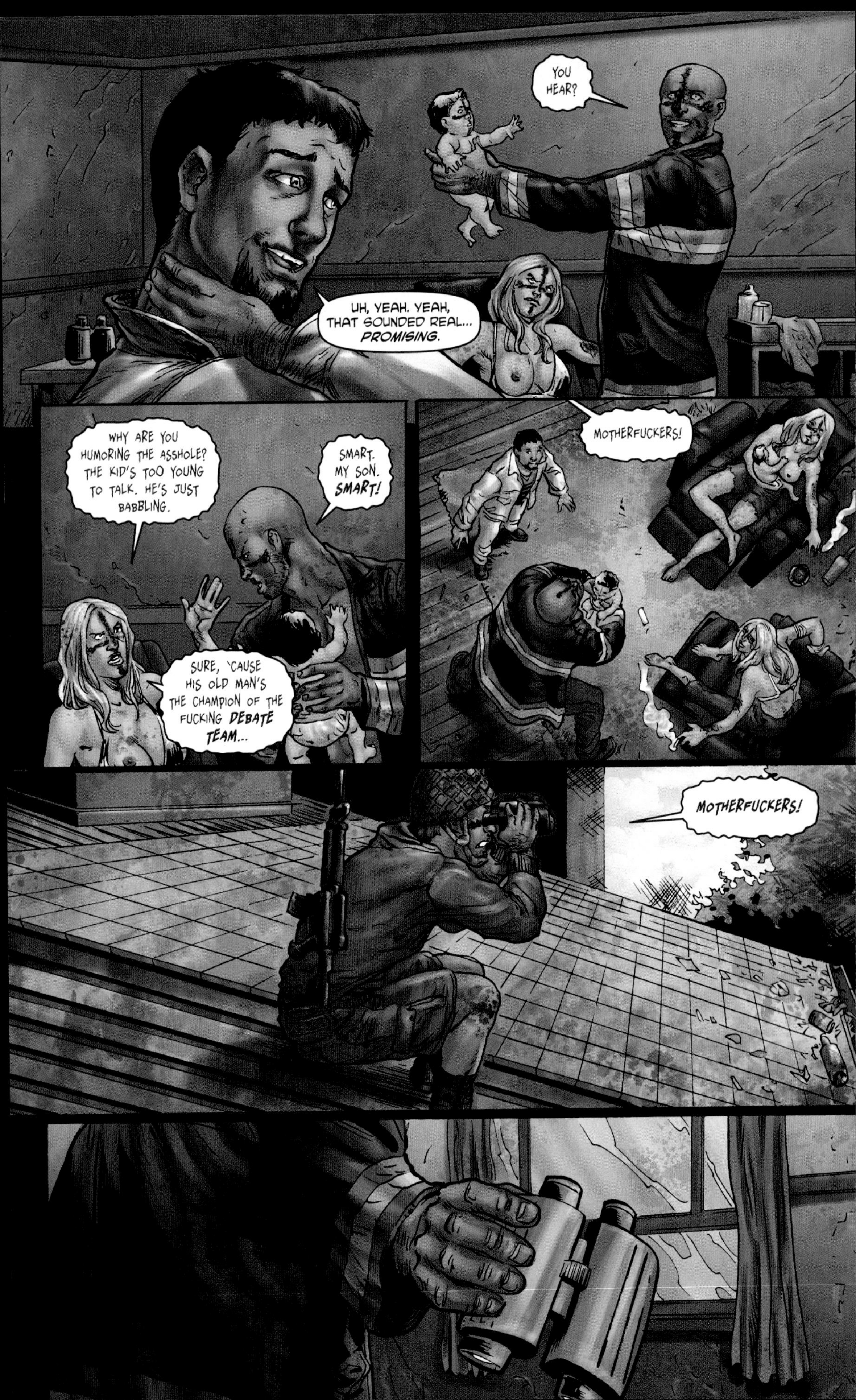
YOU HEAR?
UH, YEAH. YEAH, THAT SOUNDED REAL... PROMISING.
WHY ARE YOU HUMORING THE ASSHOLE? THE KID'S TOO YOUNG TO TALK. HE'S JUST BABBLING.
SMART. MY SON. SMART!
SURE, 'CAUSE HIS OLD MAN'S THE CHAMPION OF THE FUCKING DEBATE TEAM...
MOTHERFUCKERS!
MOTHERFUCKERS!

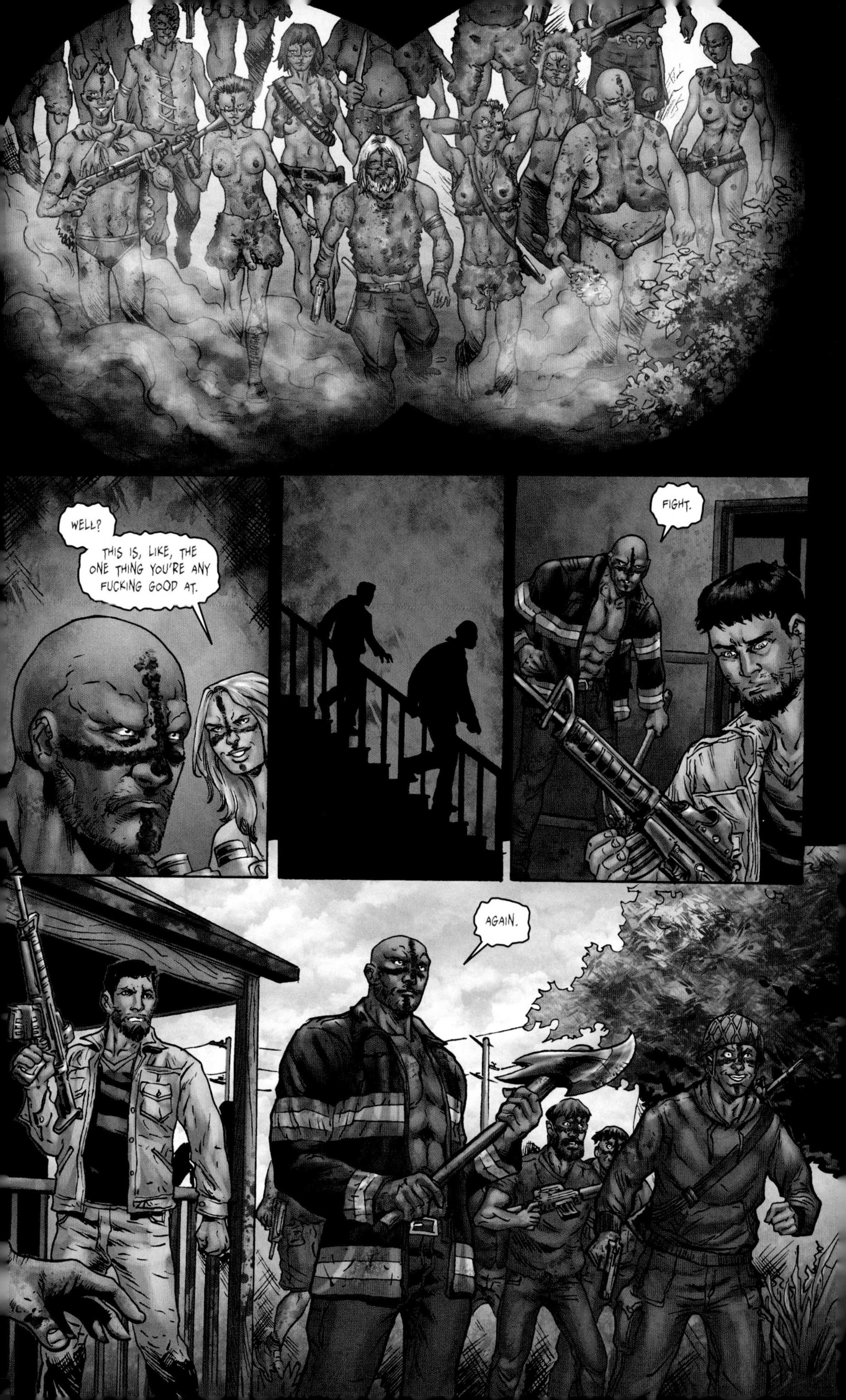
WELL?
THIS IS, LIKE, THE ONE THING YOU'RE ANY FUCKING GOOD AT.
FIGHT.
AGAIN.

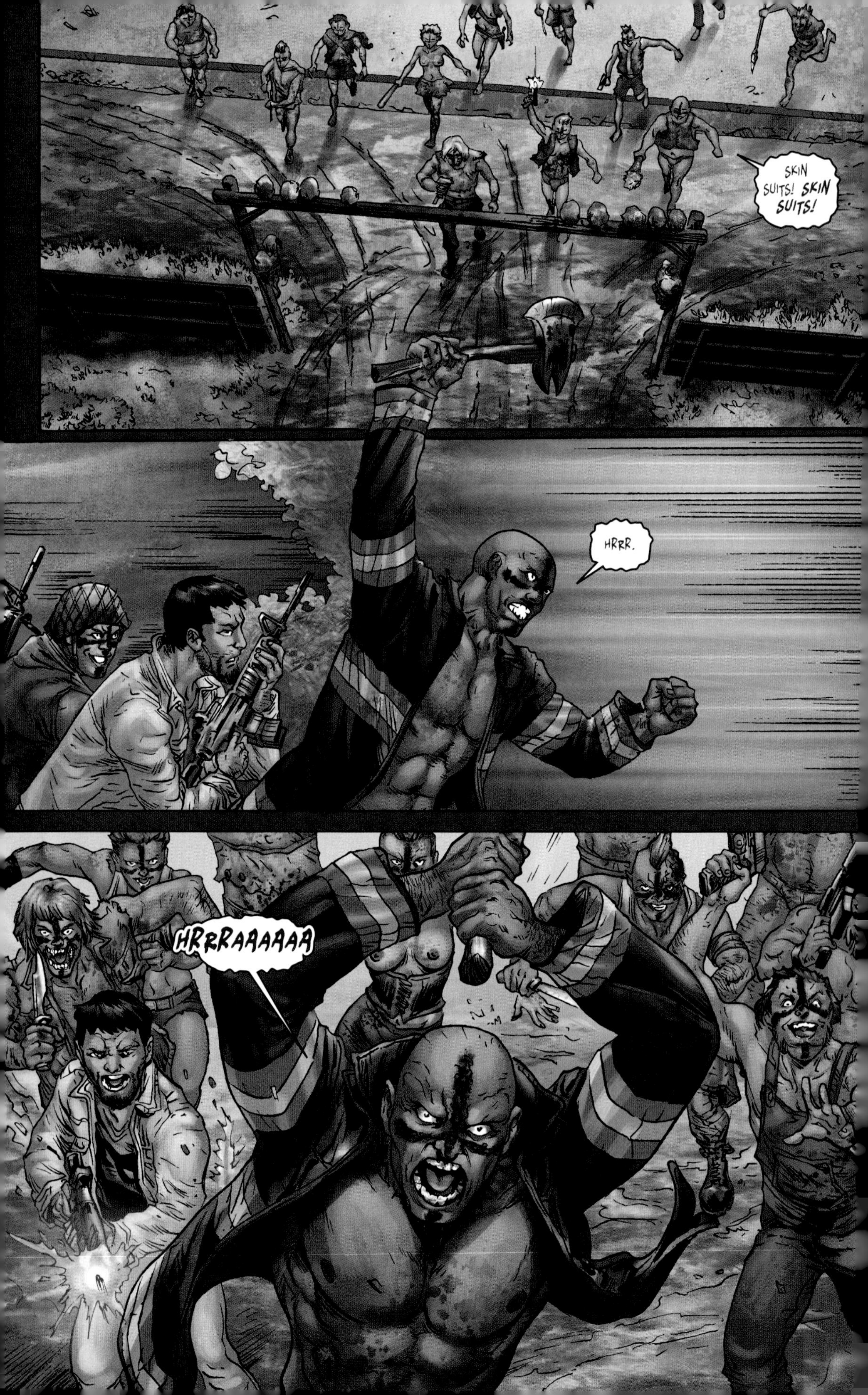
SKIN SUITS! SKIN SUITS!
HRRR.
HRRRAAAAAA

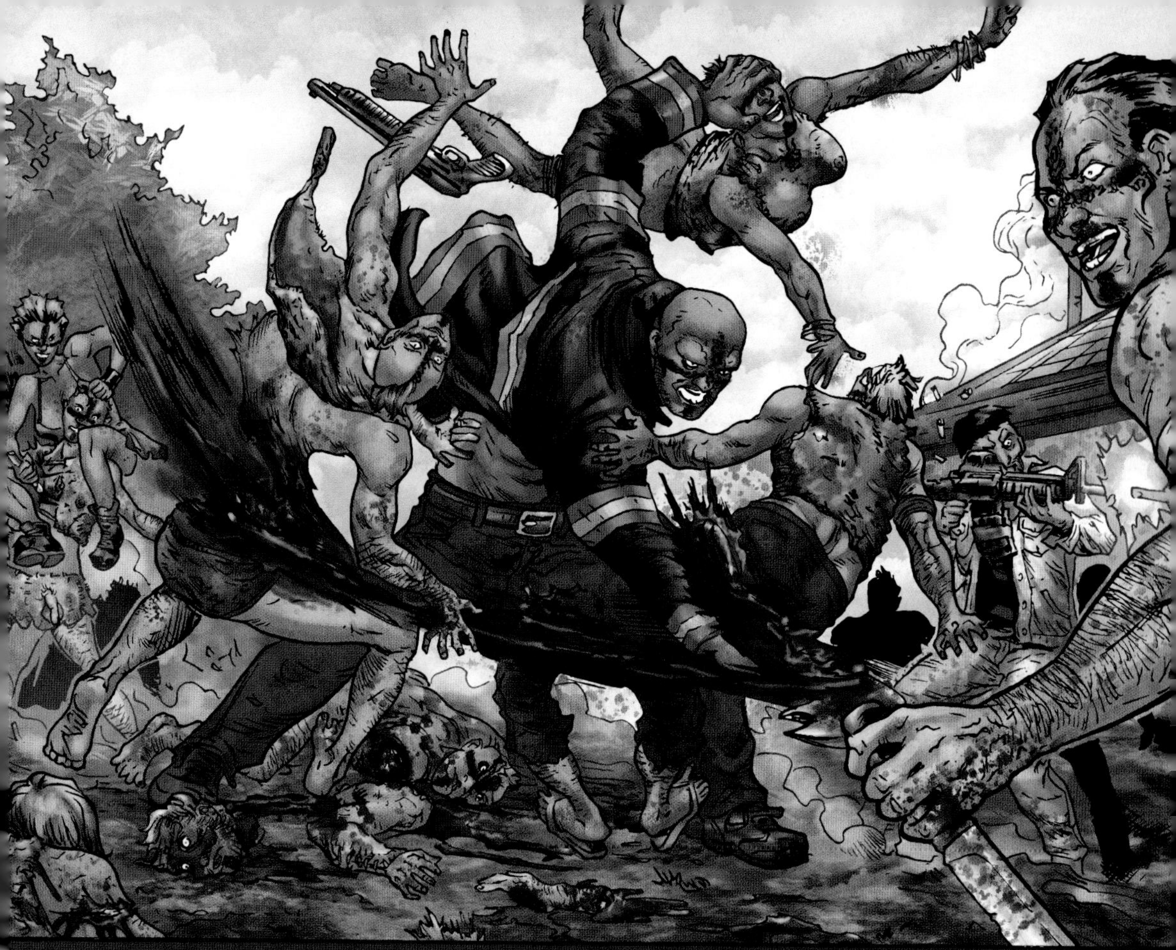

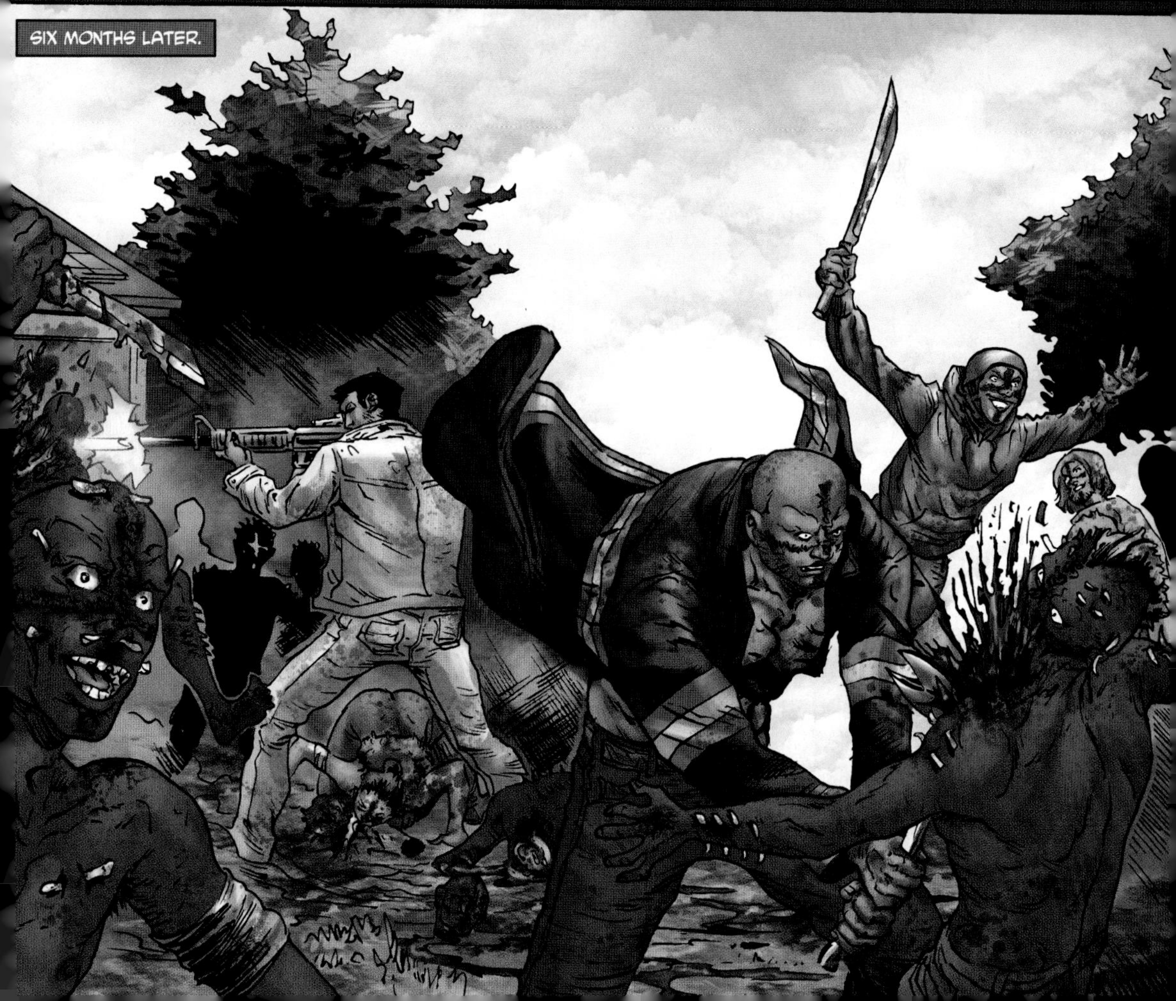
SIX MONTHS LATER.

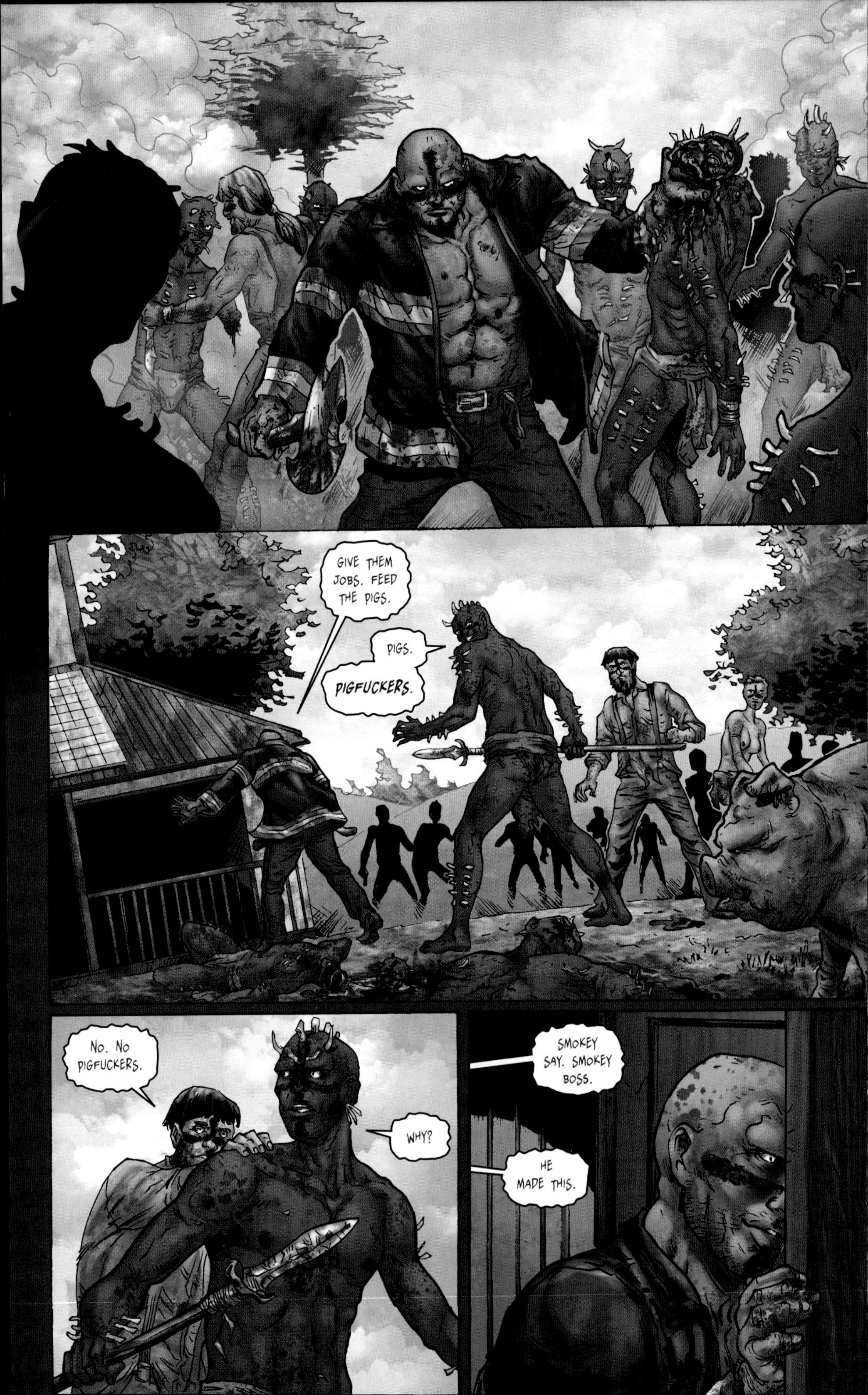
GIVE THEM JOBS. FEED THE PIGS.
PIGS.
PIGFUCKERS.
No. No PIGFUCKERS.
WHY?
SMOKEY SAY. SMOKEY BOSS.
HE MADE THIS.

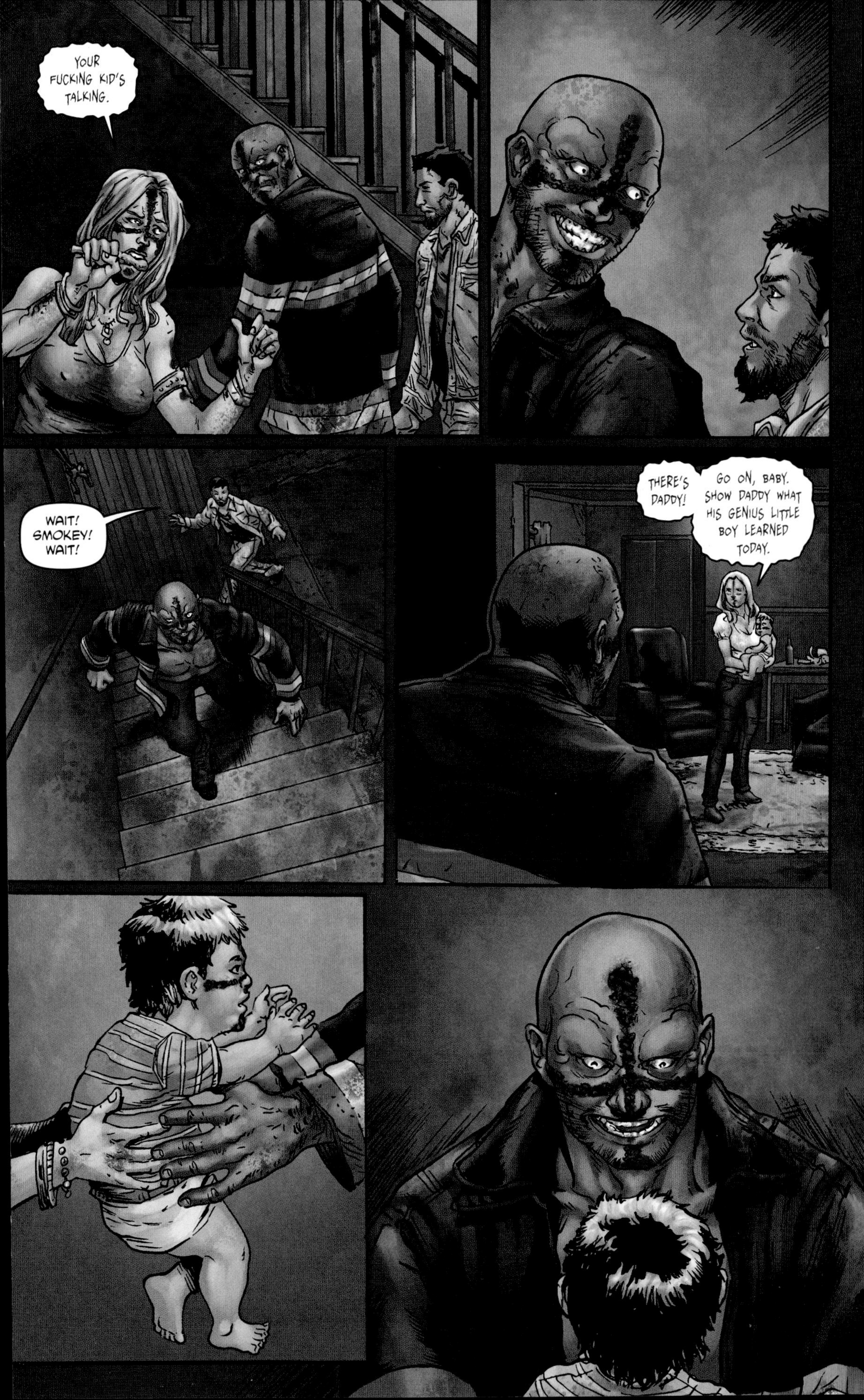
YOUR FUCKING KID'S TALKING.
WAIT! SMOKEY! WAIT!
THERE'S DADDY!
GO ON, BABY. SHOW DADDY WHAT HIS GENIUS LITTLE BOY LEARNED TODAY.

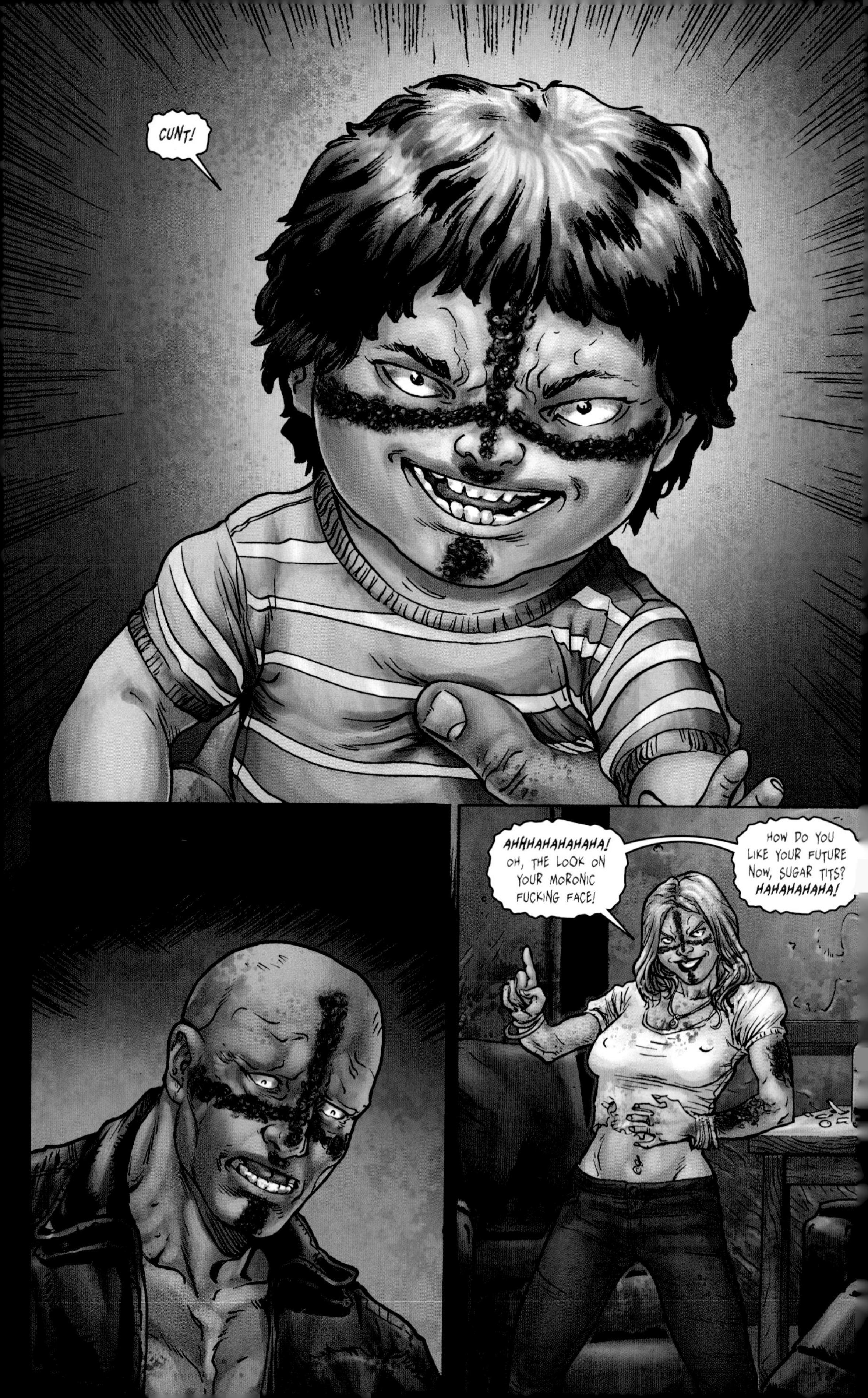
CUNT!
AHHHAHAHAHAHA! OH, THE LOOK ON YOUR MORONIC FUCKING FACE!
HOW DO YOU LIKE YOUR FUTURE NOW, SUGAR TITS? HAHAHAHAHA!

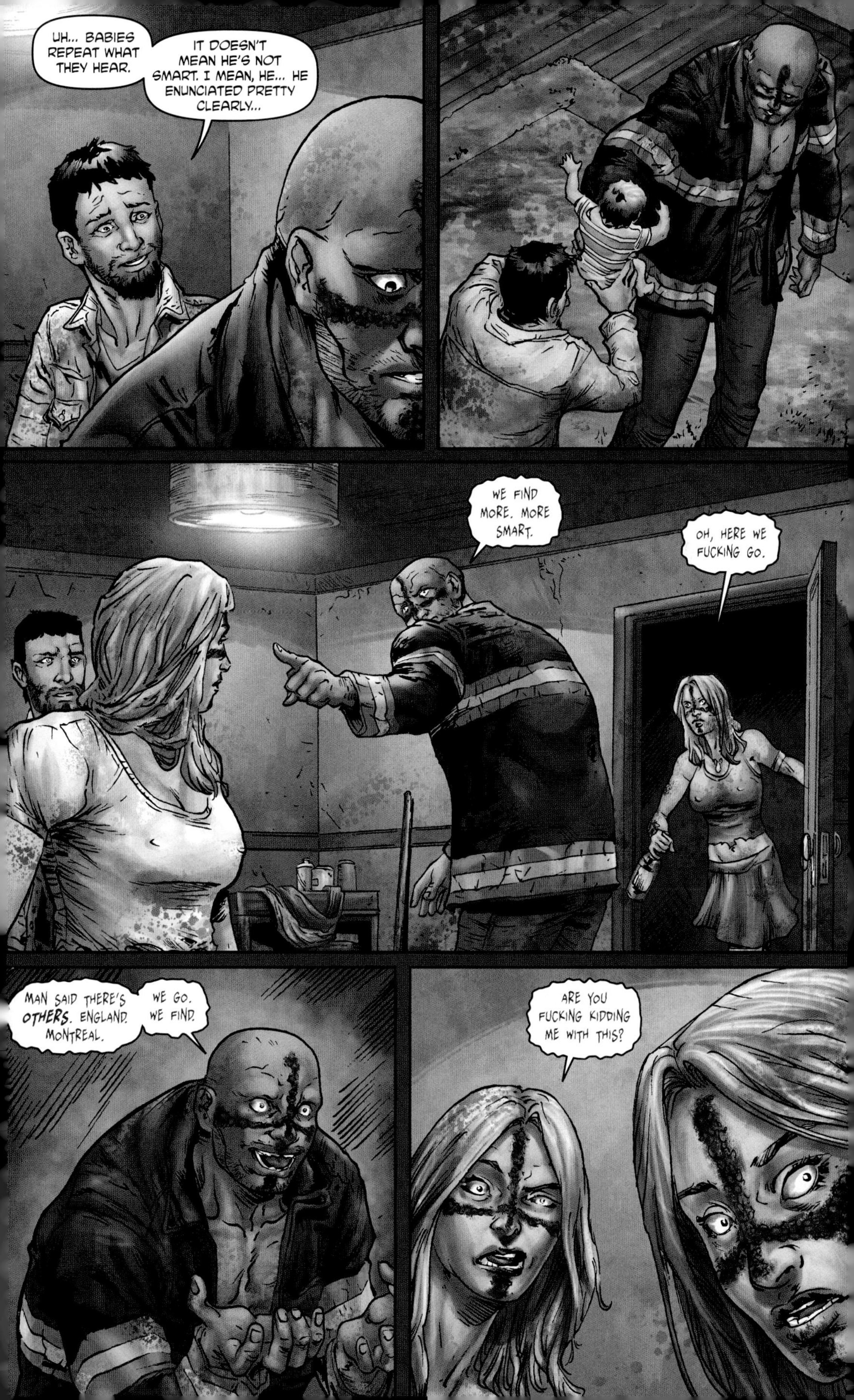
UH... BABIES REPEAT WHAT THEY HEAR.
IT DOESN'T MEAN HE'S NOT SMART. I MEAN, HE... HE ENUNCIATED PRETTY CLEARLY...
WE FIND MORE. MORE SMART.
OH, HERE WE FUCKING GO.
MAN SAID THERE'S OTHERS. ENGLAND. MONTREAL.
WE GO. WE FIND.
ARE YOU FUCKING KIDDING ME WITH THIS?

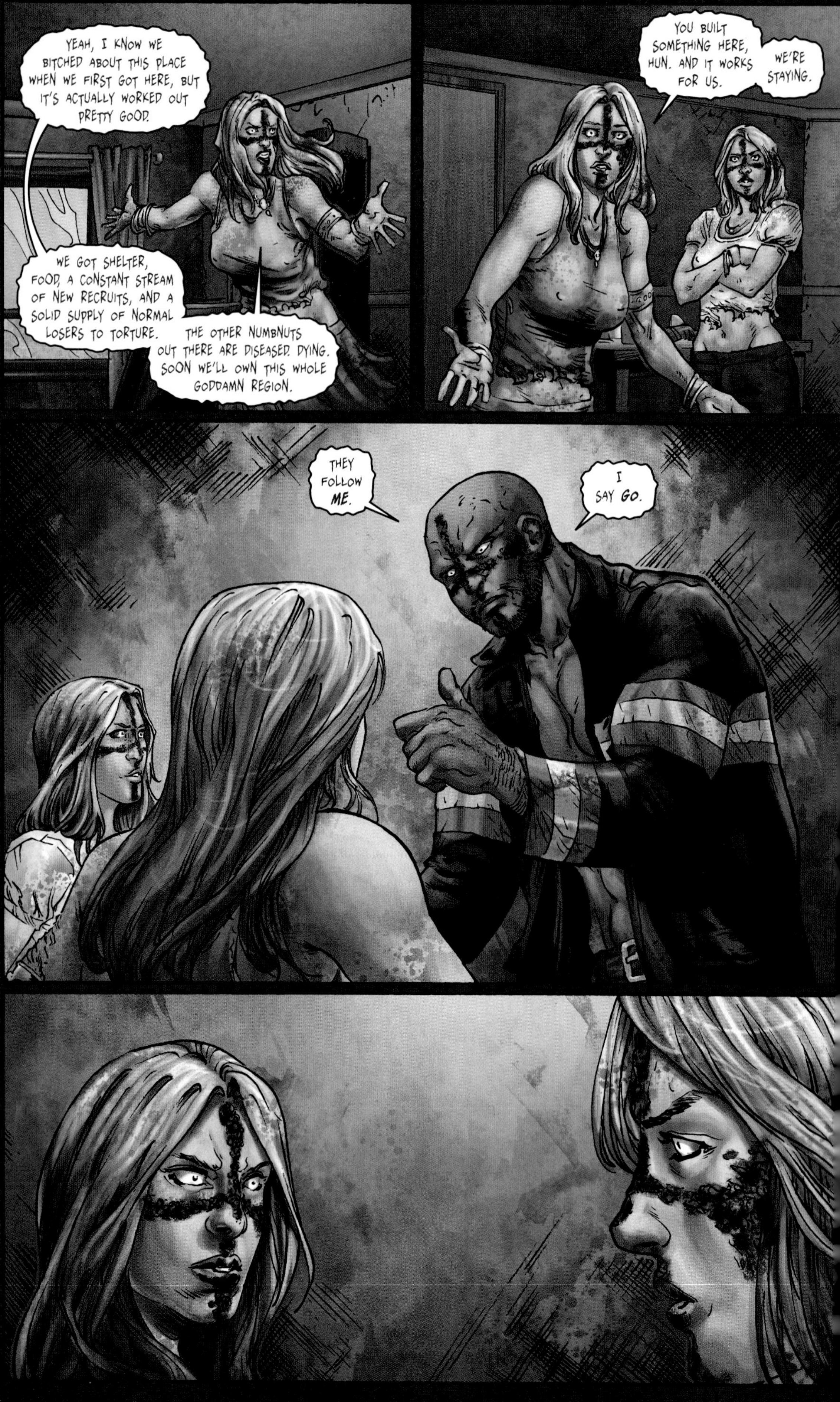
YEAH, I KNOW WE BITCHED ABOUT THIS PLACE WHEN WE FIRST GOT HERE, BUT IT'S ACTUALLY WORKED OUT PRETTY GOOD.
WE GOT SHELTER, FOOD, A CONSTANT STREAM OF NEW RECRUITS, AND A SOLID SUPPLY OF NORMAL LOSERS TO TORTURE.
THE OTHER NUMBNUTS OUT THERE ARE DISEASED. DYING. SOON WE'LL OWN THIS WHOLE GODDAMN REGION.
YOU BUILT SOMETHING HERE, HUN. AND IT WORKS FOR US.
WE'RE STAYING.
THEY FOLLOW ME.
I SAY GO.

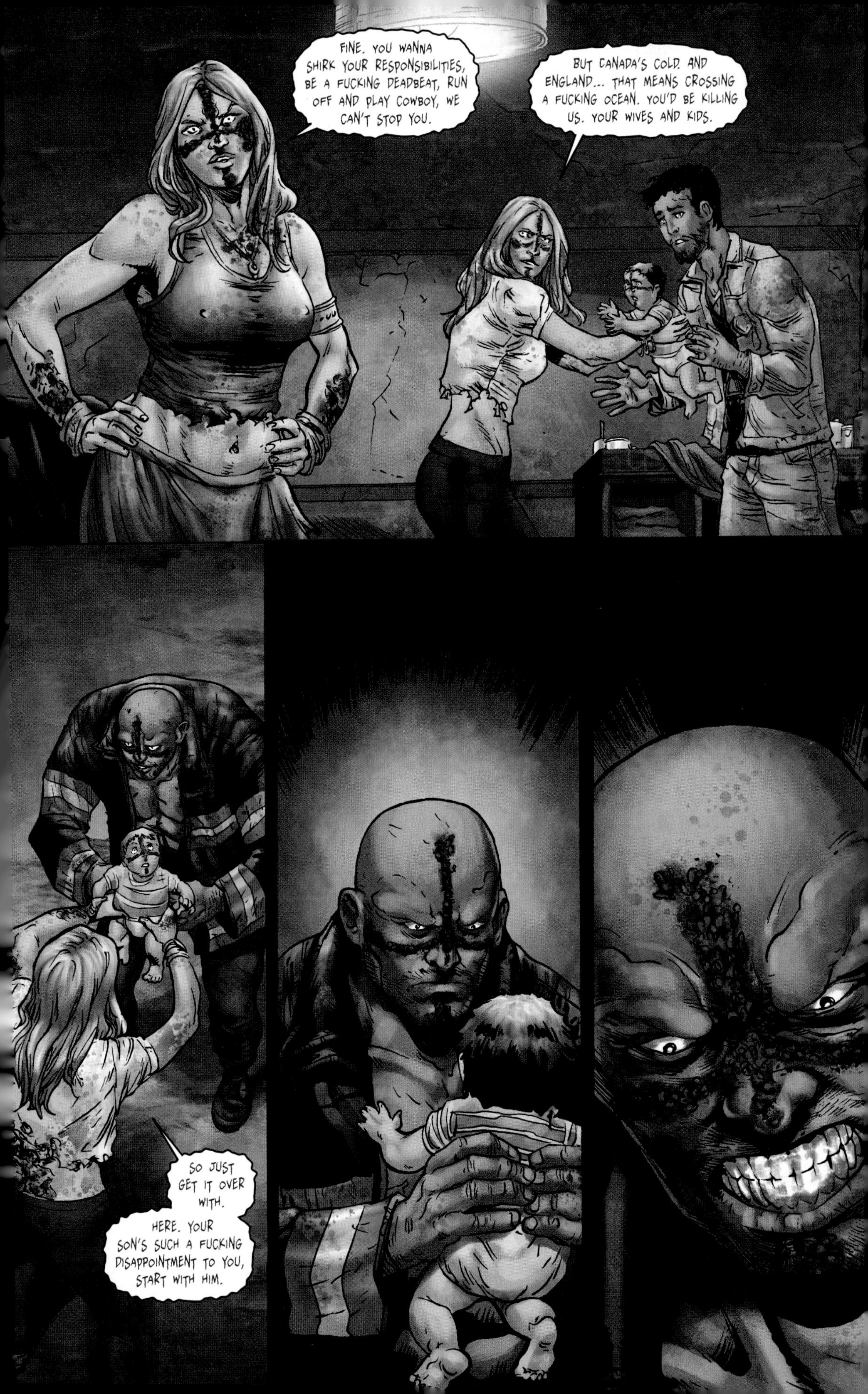
FINE. YOU WANNA SHIRK YOUR RESPONSIBILITIES, BE A FUCKING DEADBEAT, RUN OFF AND PLAY COWBOY, WE CAN'T STOP YOU.
BUT CANADA'S COLD. AND ENGLAND... THAT MEANS CROSSING A FUCKING OCEAN. YOU'D BE KILLING US. YOUR WIVES AND KIDS.
SO JUST GET IT OVER WITH.
HERE. YOUR SON'S SUCH A FUCKING DISAPPOINTMENT TO YOU, START WITH HIM.

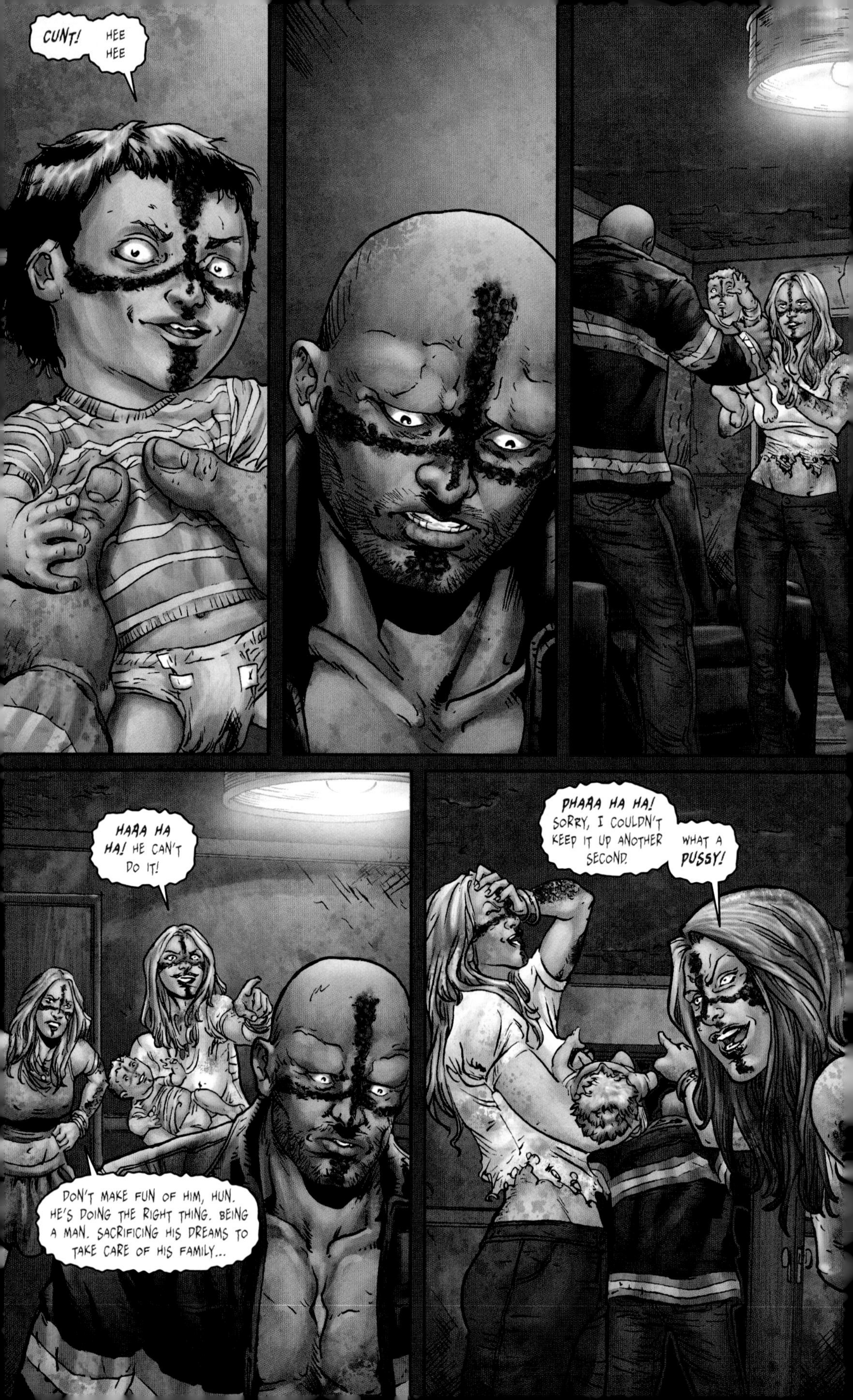
CUNT!
HEE HEE
HAAA HA HA! HE CAN'T DO IT!
DON'T MAKE FUN OF HIM, HUN. HE'S DOING THE RIGHT THING. BEING A MAN. SACRIFICING HIS DREAMS TO TAKE CARE OF HIS FAMILY...
PHAAA HA HA! SORRY, I COULDN'T KEEP IT UP ANOTHER SECOND.
WHAT A PUSSY!

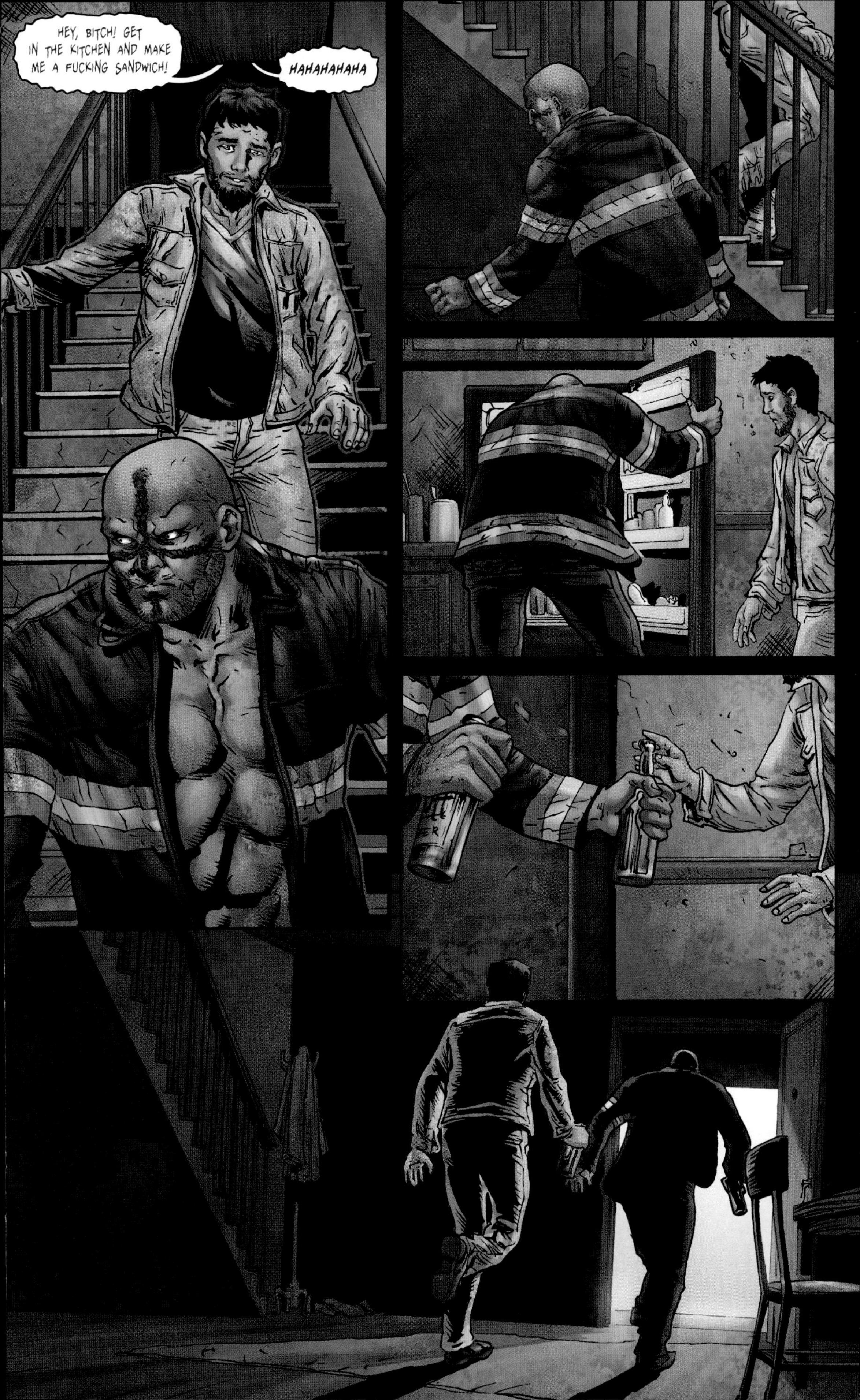
HEY, BITCH! GET IN THE KITCHEN AND MAKE ME A FUCKING SANDWICH!
HAHAHAHAHA

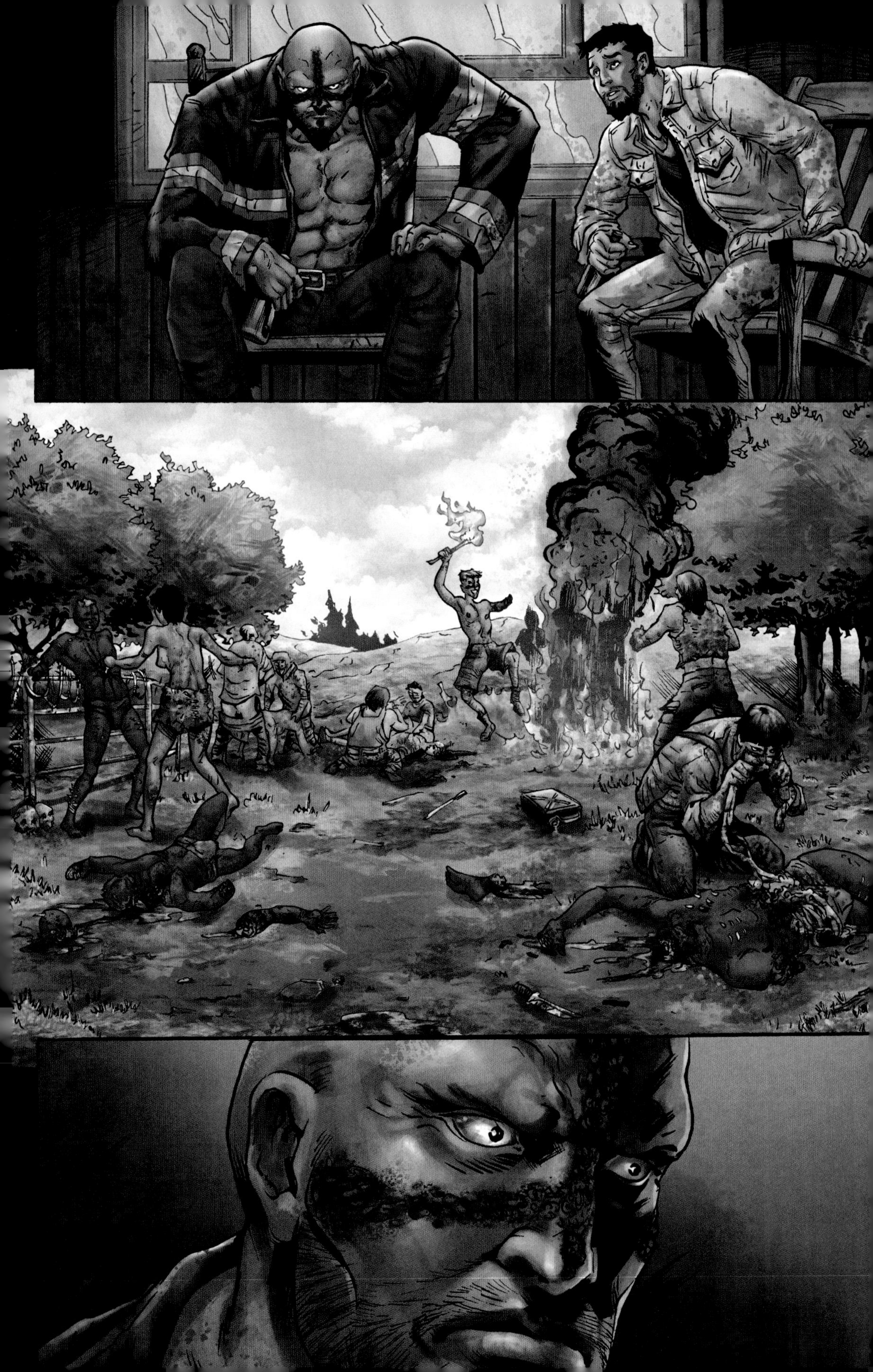

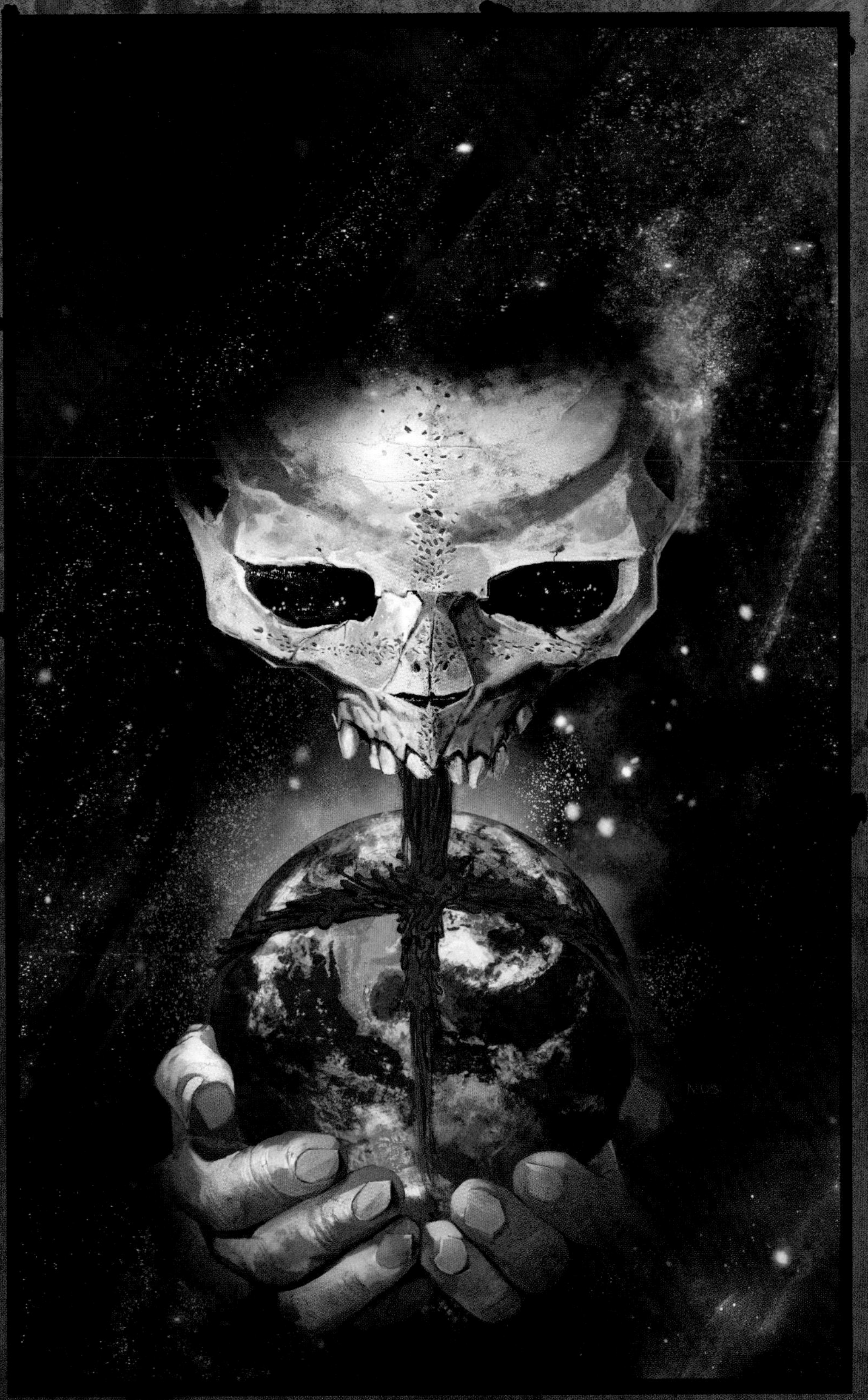

PART 8

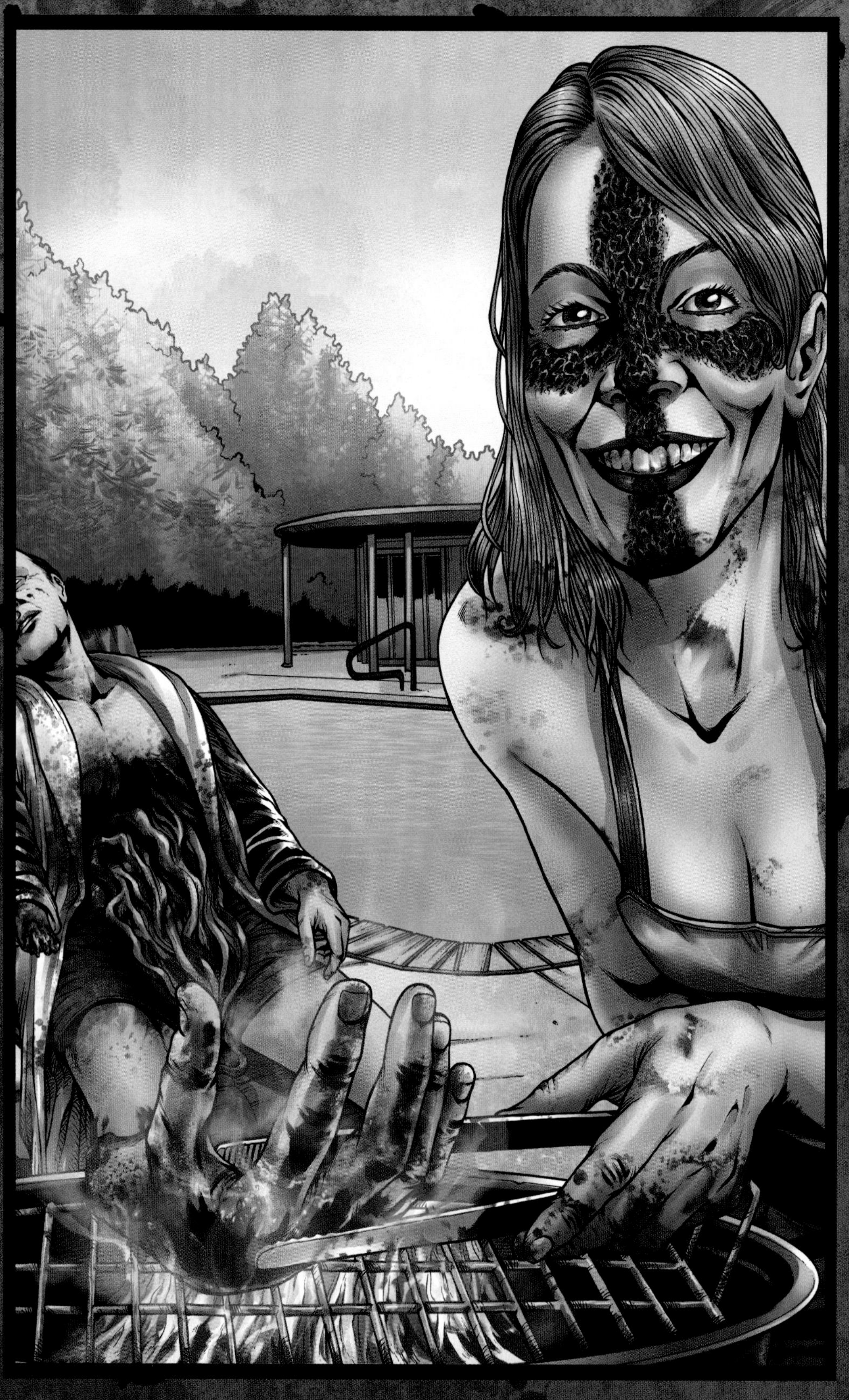

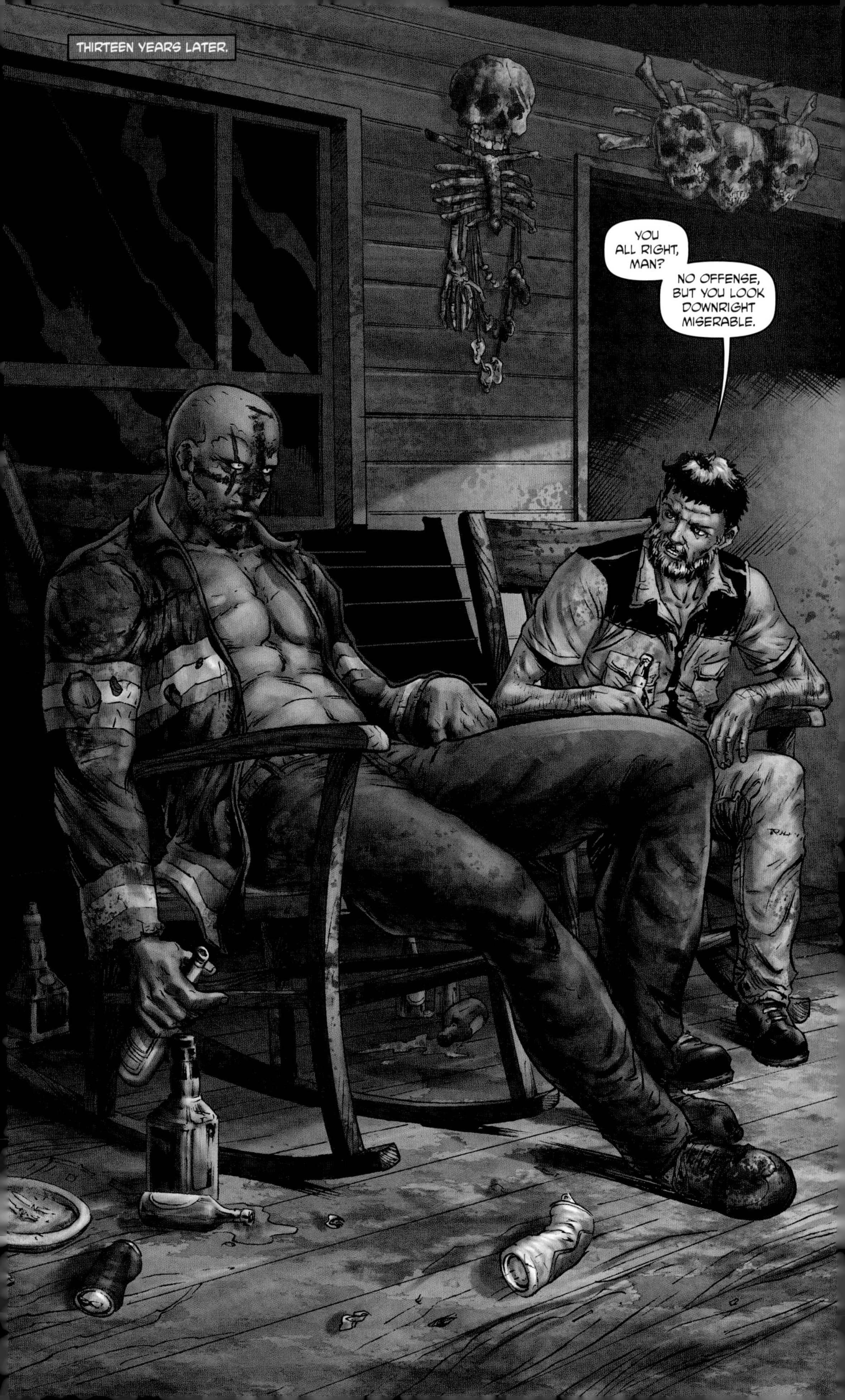
THIRTEEN YEARS LATER.
YOU ALL RIGHT, MAN?
NO OFFENSE, BUT YOU LOOK DOWNRIGHT MISERABLE.

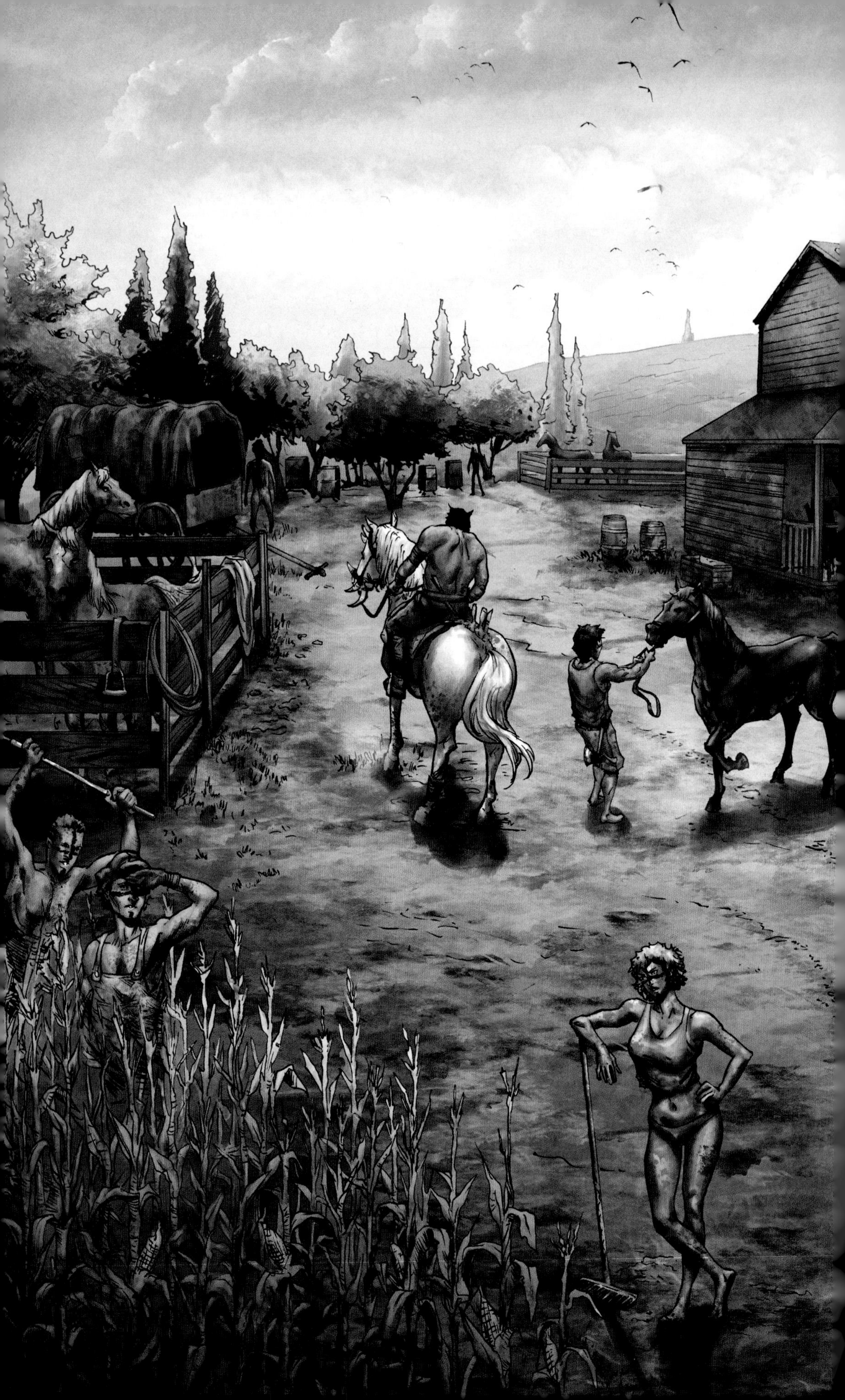

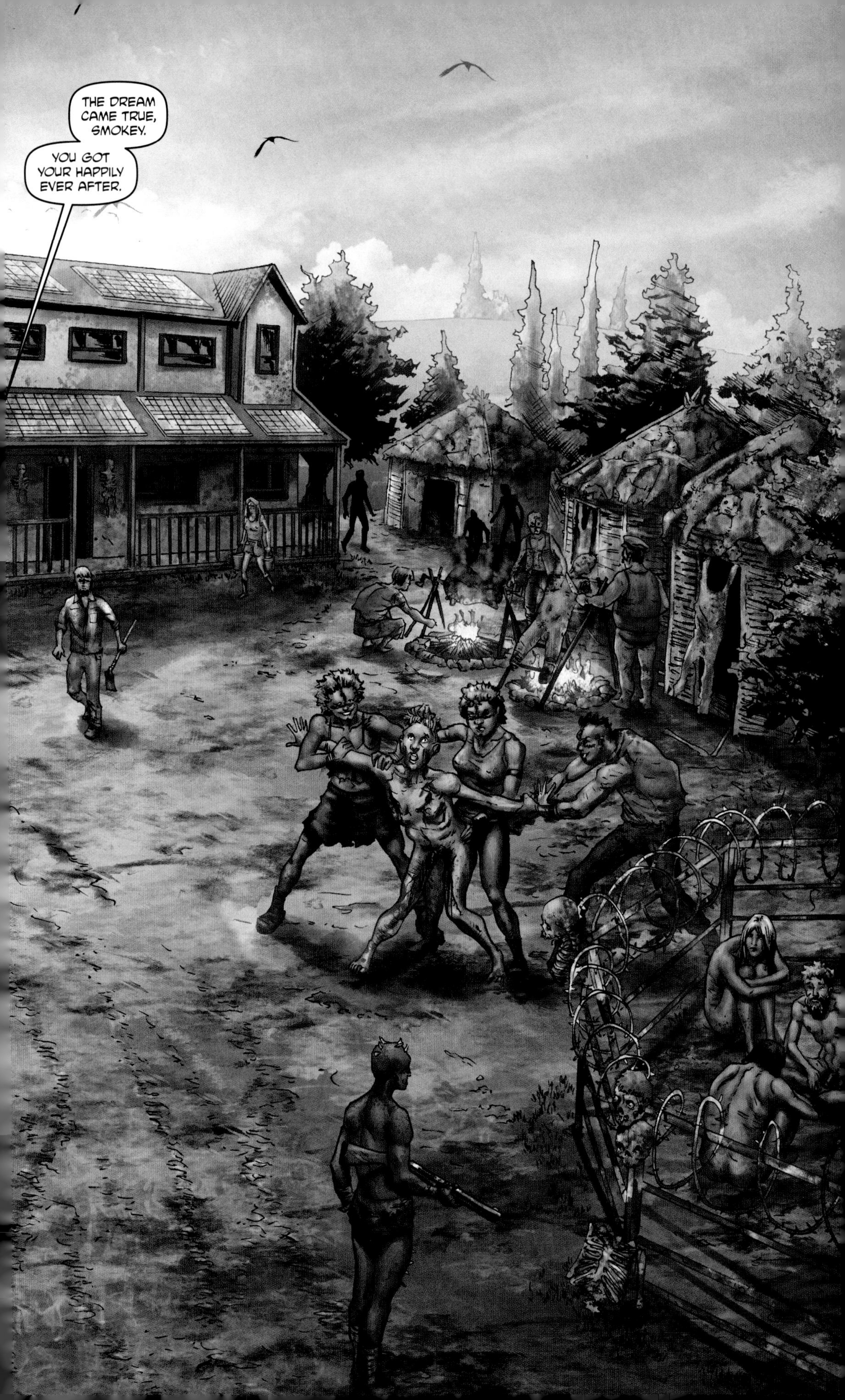
THE DREAM CAME TRUE, SMOKEY.
YOU GOT YOUR HAPPILY EVER AFTER.

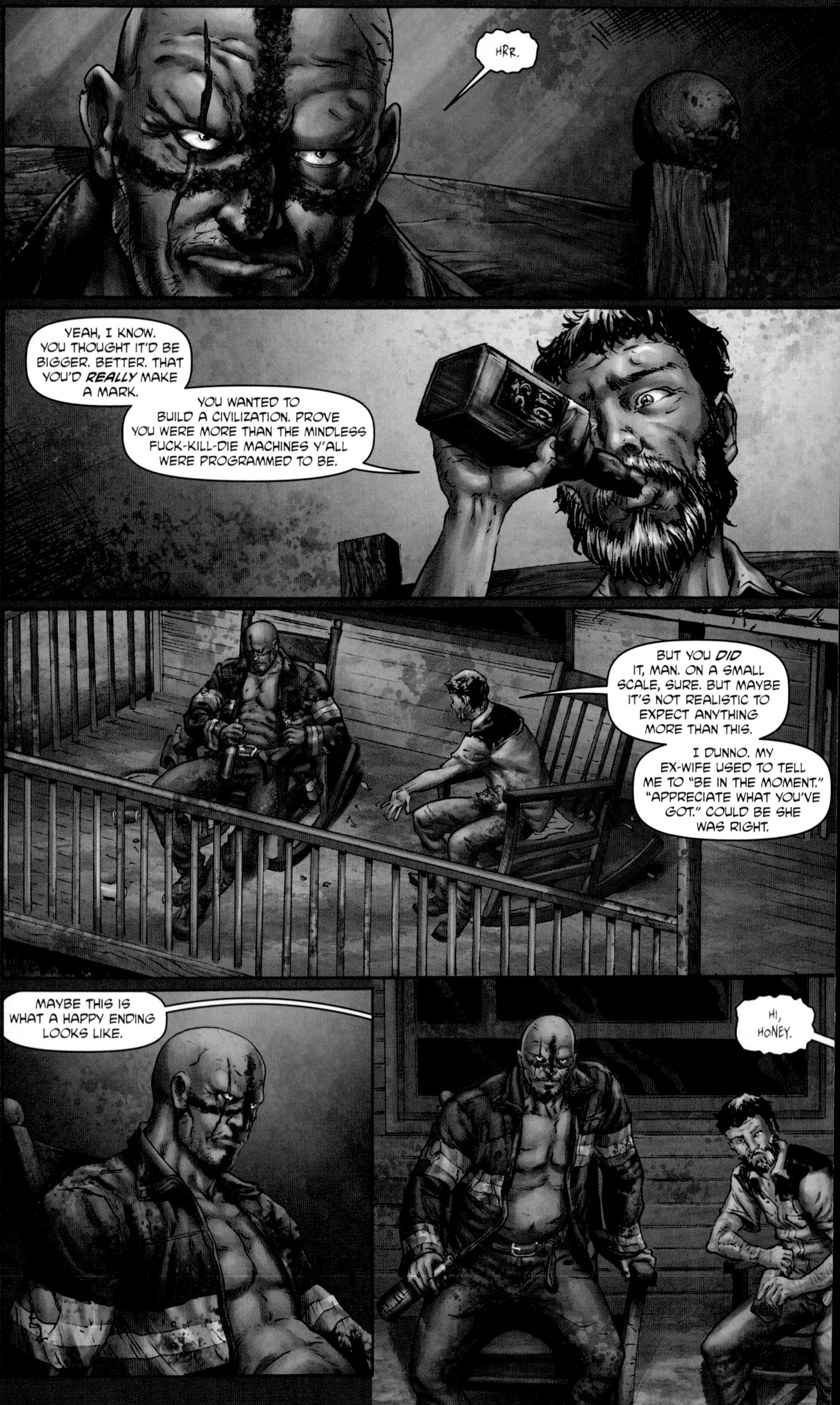
HRR.
YEAH, I KNOW. YOU THOUGHT IT'D BE BIGGER. BETTER. THAT YOU'D *REALLY* MAKE A MARK.
YOU WANTED TO BUILD A CIVILIZATION. PROVE YOU WERE MORE THAN THE MINDLESS FUCK-KILL-DIE MACHINES Y'ALL WERE PROGRAMMED TO BE.
BUT YOU *DID* IT, MAN. ON A SMALL SCALE, SURE. BUT MAYBE IT'S NOT REALISTIC TO EXPECT ANYTHING MORE THAN THIS.
I DUNNO. MY EX-WIFE USED TO TELL ME TO "BE IN THE MOMENT." "APPRECIATE WHAT YOU'VE GOT." COULD BE SHE WAS RIGHT.
MAYBE THIS IS WHAT A HAPPY ENDING LOOKS LIKE.
HI, HONEY.

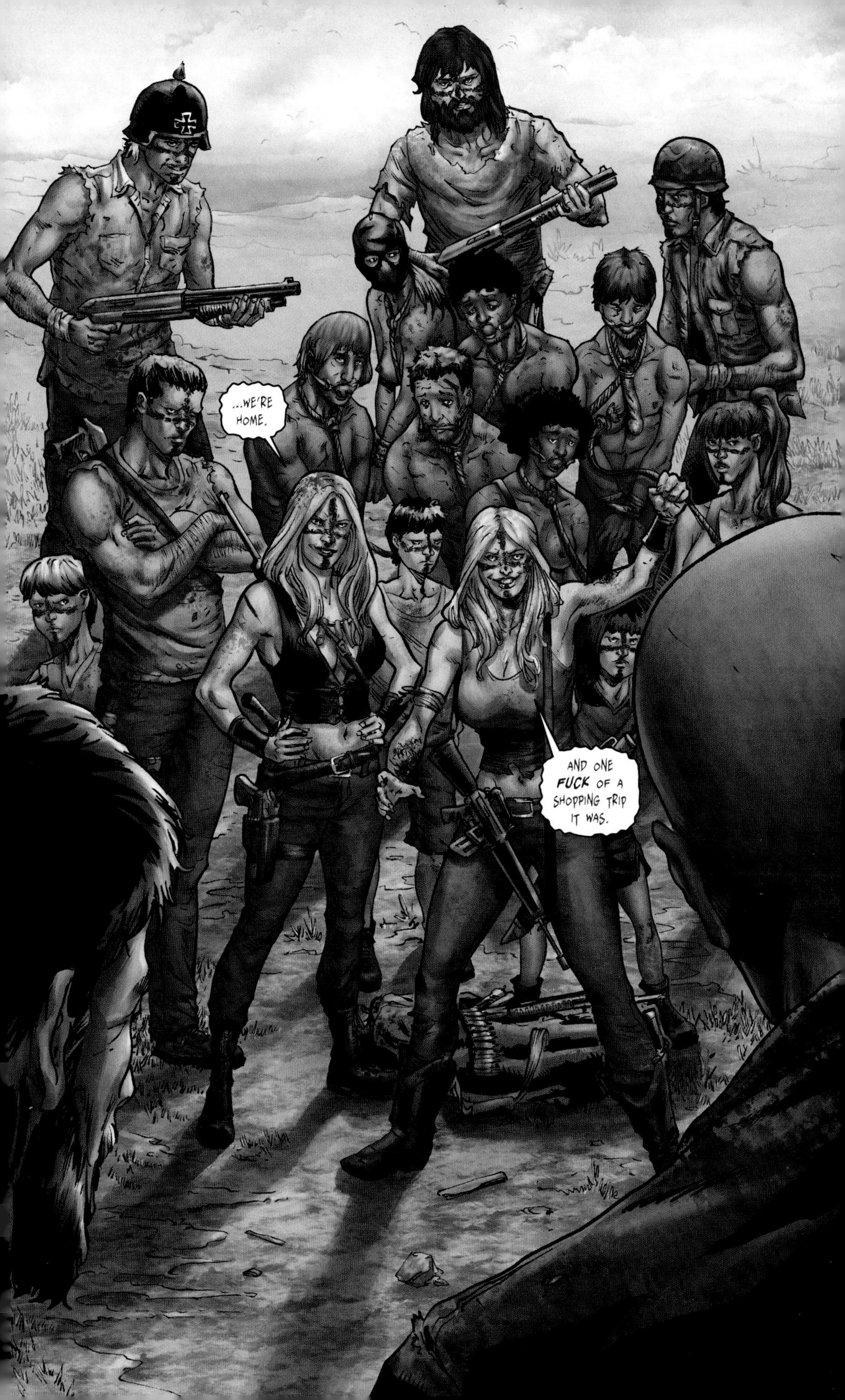
...WE'RE HOME.
AND ONE FUCK OF A SHOPPING TRIP IT WAS.

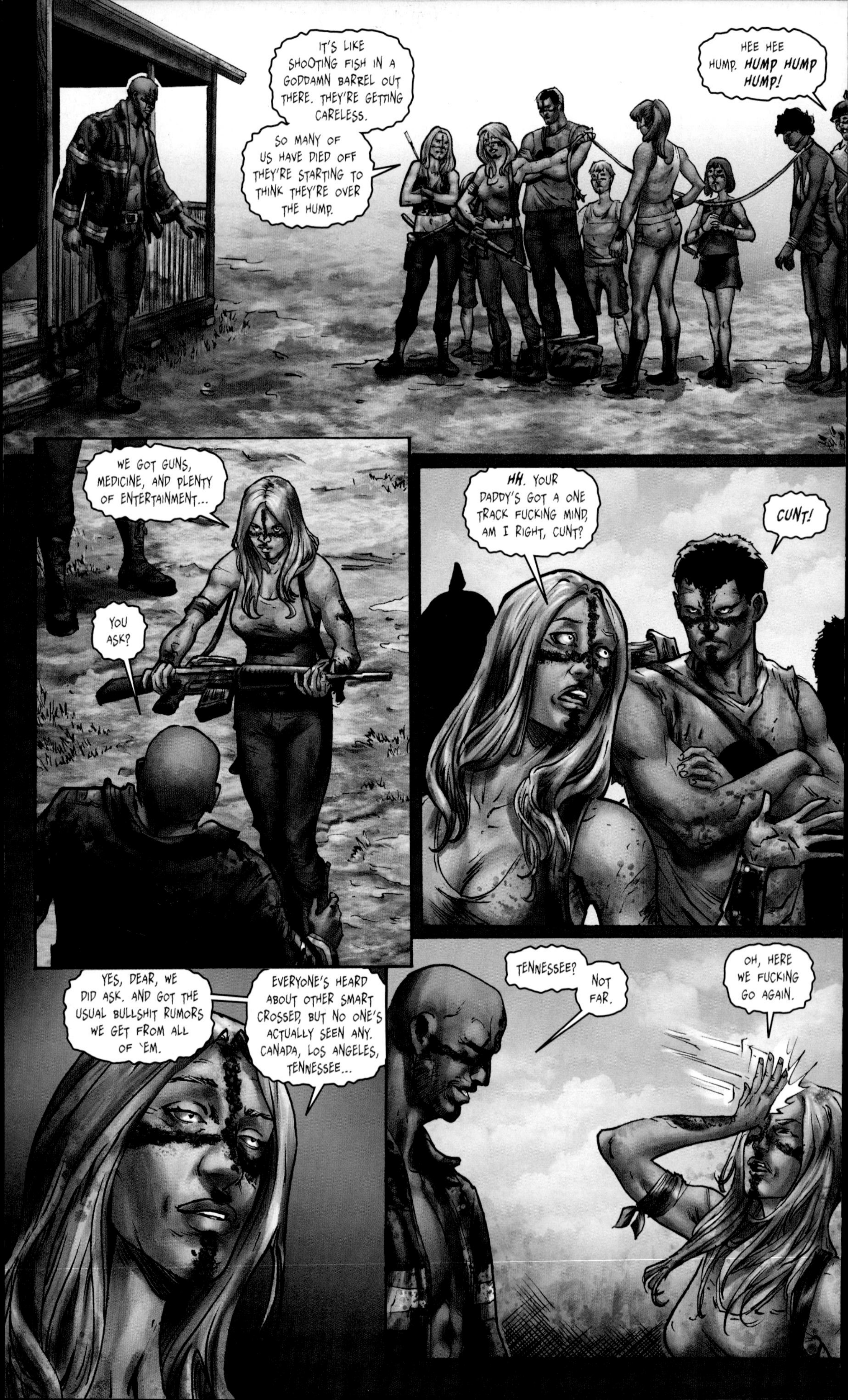
IT'S LIKE SHOOTING FISH IN A GODDAMN BARREL OUT THERE. THEY'RE GETTING CARELESS.
SO MANY OF US HAVE DIED OFF THEY'RE STARTING TO THINK THEY'RE OVER THE HUMP.
HEE HEE HUMP. HUMP HUMP HUMP!
WE GOT GUNS, MEDICINE, AND PLENTY OF ENTERTAINMENT...
YOU ASK?
HH. YOUR DADDY'S GOT A ONE TRACK FUCKING MIND, AM I RIGHT, CUNT?
CUNT!
YES, DEAR, WE DID ASK. AND GOT THE USUAL BULLSHIT RUMORS WE GET FROM ALL OF 'EM.
EVERYONE'S HEARD ABOUT OTHER SMART CROSSED, BUT NO ONE'S ACTUALLY SEEN ANY. CANADA, LOS ANGELES, TENNESSEE...
TENNESSEE?
NOT FAR.
OH, HERE WE FUCKING GO AGAIN.

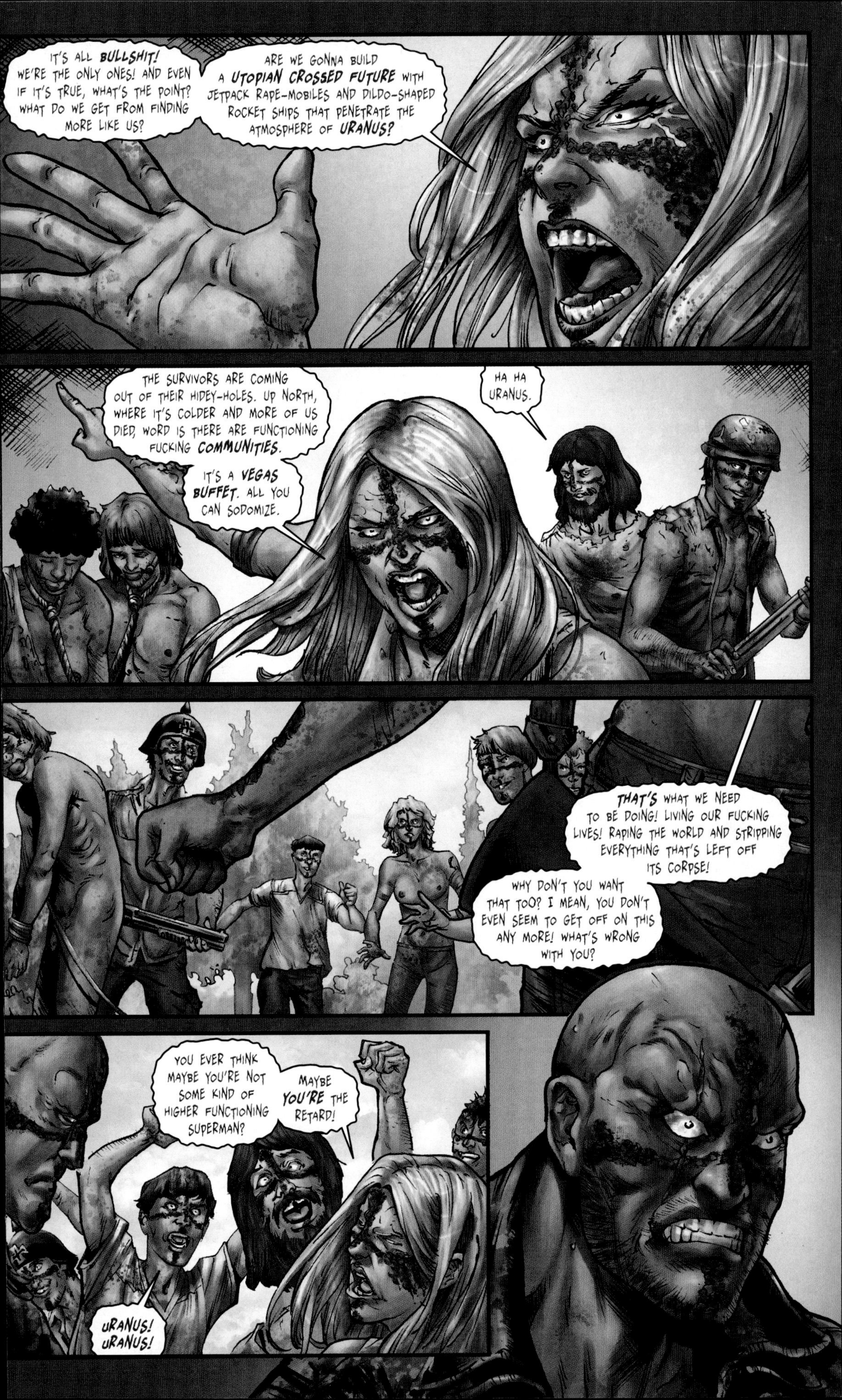
IT'S ALL BULLSHIT! WE'RE THE ONLY ONES! AND EVEN IF IT'S TRUE, WHAT'S THE POINT? WHAT DO WE GET FROM FINDING MORE LIKE US?
ARE WE GONNA BUILD A UTOPIAN CROSSED FUTURE WITH JETPACK RAPE-MOBILES AND DILDO-SHAPED ROCKET SHIPS THAT PENETRATE THE ATMOSPHERE OF URANUS?
THE SURVIVORS ARE COMING OUT OF THEIR HIDEY-HOLES. UP NORTH, WHERE IT'S COLDER AND MORE OF US DIED, WORD IS THERE ARE FUNCTIONING FUCKING COMMUNITIES.
IT'S A VEGAS BUFFET. ALL YOU CAN SODOMIZE.
HA HA URANUS.
THAT'S WHAT WE NEED TO BE DOING! LIVING OUR FUCKING LIVES! RAPING THE WORLD AND STRIPPING EVERYTHING THAT'S LEFT OFF ITS CORPSE!
WHY DON'T YOU WANT THAT TOO? I MEAN, YOU DON'T EVEN SEEM TO GET OFF ON THIS ANY MORE! WHAT'S WRONG WITH YOU?
YOU EVER THINK MAYBE YOU'RE NOT SOME KIND OF HIGHER FUNCTIONING SUPERMAN?
MAYBE YOU'RE THE RETARD!
URANUS! URANUS!

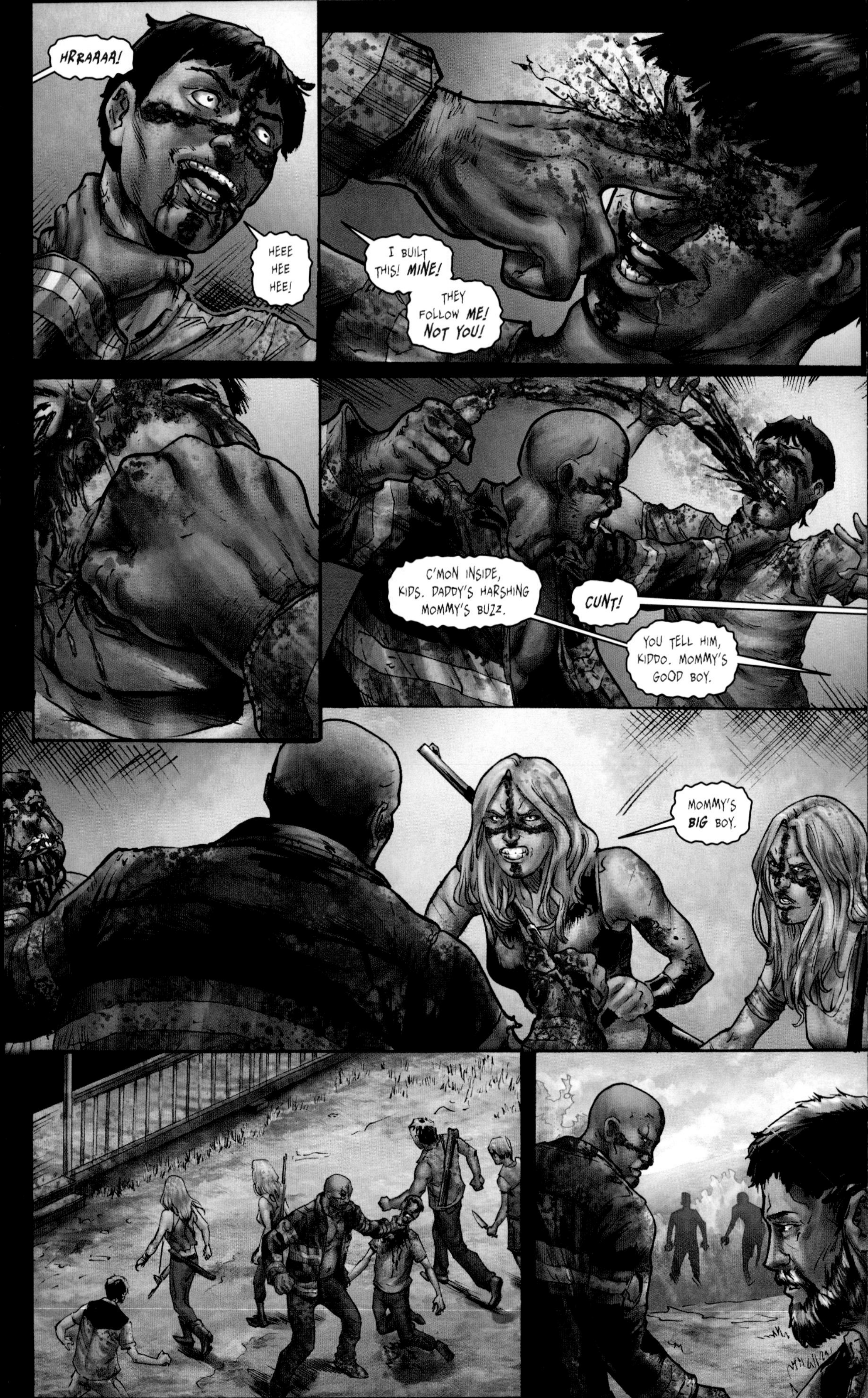
HRRAAAA!
HEEE HEE HEE!
I BUILT THIS! MINE!
THEY FOLLOW ME! NOT YOU!
C'MON INSIDE, KIDS. DADDY'S HARSHING MOMMY'S BUZZ.
CUNT!
YOU TELL HIM, KIDDO. MOMMY'S GOOD BOY.
MOMMY'S BIG BOY.

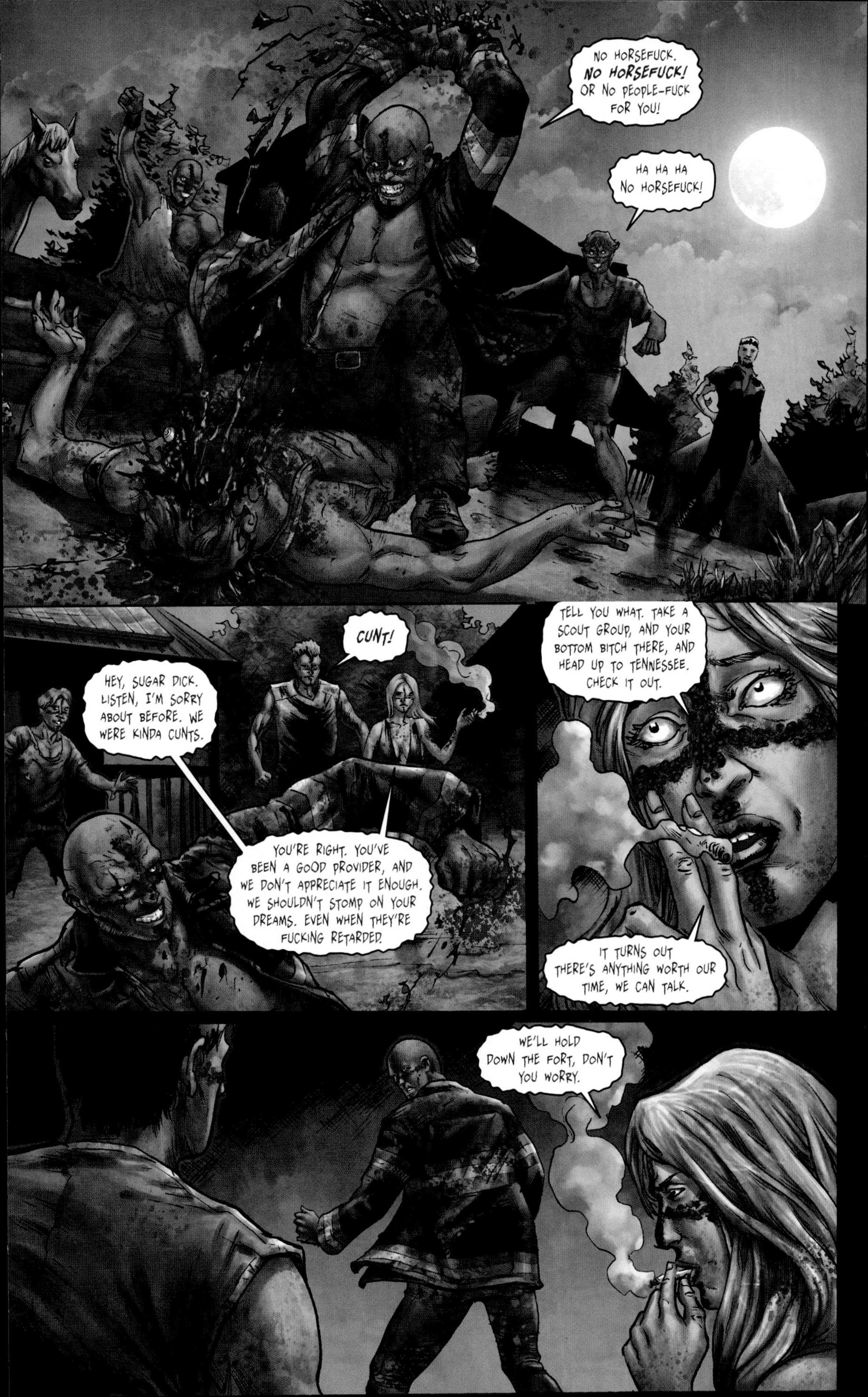
NO HORSEFUCK. NO HORSEFUCK! OR NO PEOPLE-FUCK FOR YOU!
HA HA HA NO HORSEFUCK!
HEY, SUGAR DICK. LISTEN, I'M SORRY ABOUT BEFORE. WE WERE KINDA CUNTS.
CUNT!
YOU'RE RIGHT. YOU'VE BEEN A GOOD PROVIDER, AND WE DON'T APPRECIATE IT ENOUGH. WE SHOULDN'T STOMP ON YOUR DREAMS. EVEN WHEN THEY'RE FUCKING RETARDED.
TELL YOU WHAT. TAKE A SCOUT GROUP, AND YOUR BOTTOM BITCH THERE, AND HEAD UP TO TENNESSEE. CHECK IT OUT.
IT TURNS OUT THERE'S ANYTHING WORTH OUR TIME, WE CAN TALK.
WE'LL HOLD DOWN THE FORT, DON'T YOU WORRY.

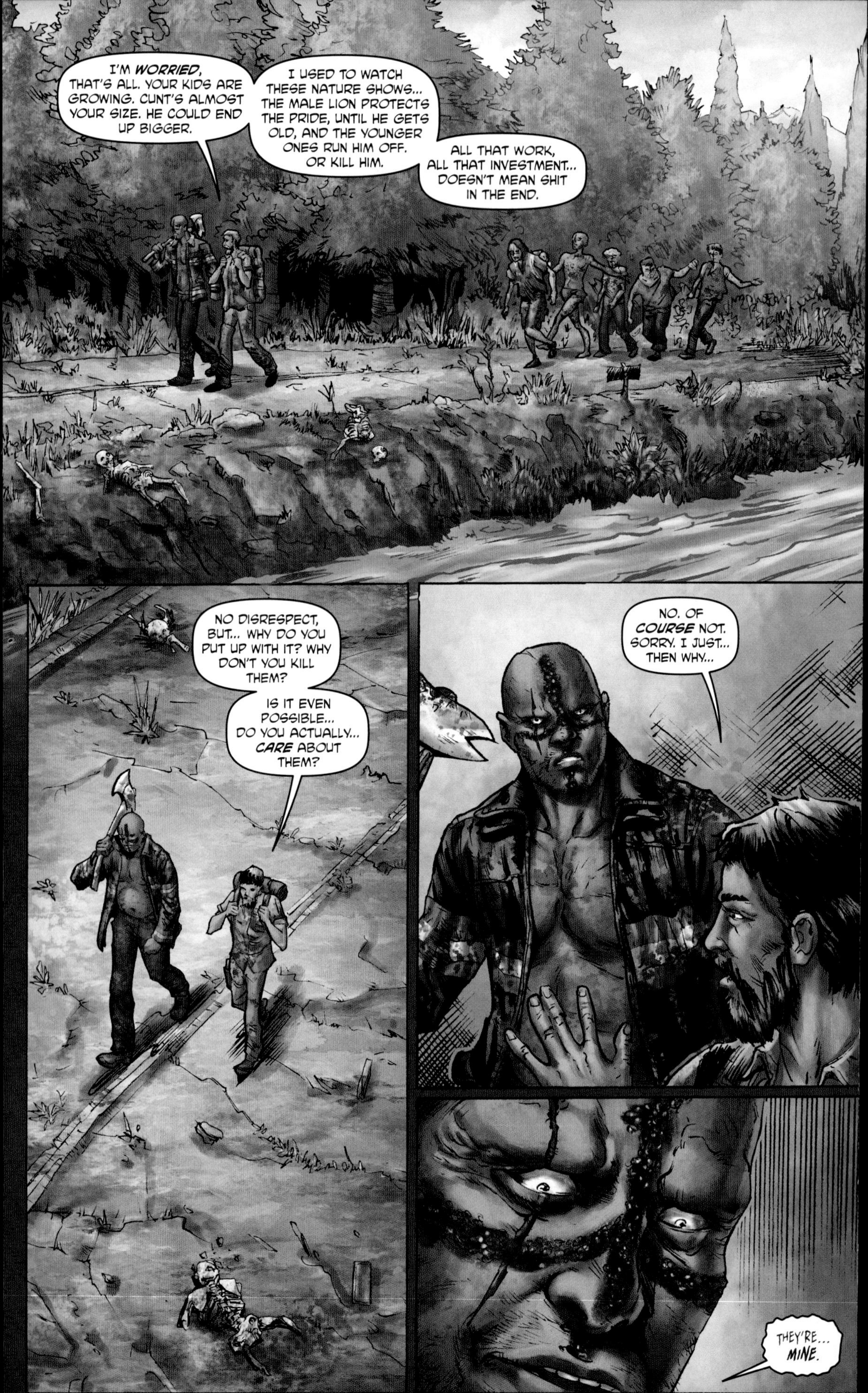
I'M WORRIED, THAT'S ALL. YOUR KIDS ARE GROWING. CUNT'S ALMOST YOUR SIZE. HE COULD END UP BIGGER.
I USED TO WATCH THESE NATURE SHOWS... THE MALE LION PROTECTS THE PRIDE, UNTIL HE GETS OLD, AND THE YOUNGER ONES RUN HIM OFF. OR KILL HIM.
ALL THAT WORK, ALL THAT INVESTMENT... DOESN'T MEAN SHIT IN THE END.
NO DISRESPECT, BUT... WHY DO YOU PUT UP WITH IT? WHY DON'T YOU KILL THEM?
IS IT EVEN POSSIBLE... DO YOU ACTUALLY... CARE ABOUT THEM?
NO. OF COURSE NOT. SORRY. I JUST... THEN WHY...
THEY'RE... MINE.

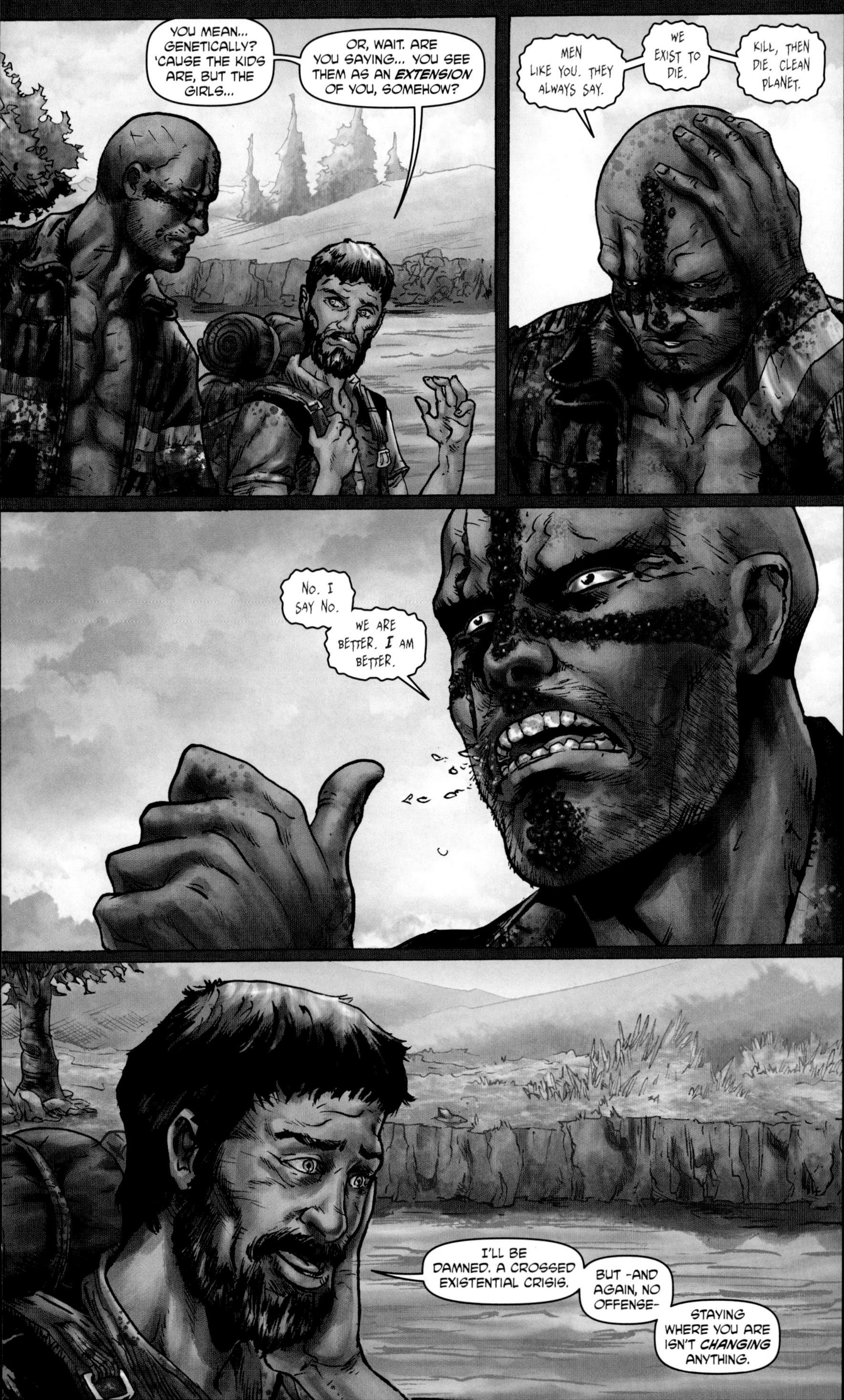
YOU MEAN... GENETICALLY? 'CAUSE THE KIDS ARE, BUT THE GIRLS...
OR, WAIT. ARE YOU SAYING... YOU SEE THEM AS AN *EXTENSION* OF YOU, SOMEHOW?
MEN LIKE YOU. THEY ALWAYS SAY.
WE EXIST TO DIE.
KILL, THEN DIE. CLEAN PLANET.
NO. I SAY NO.
WE ARE BETTER. *I* AM BETTER.
I'LL BE DAMNED. A CROSSED EXISTENTIAL CRISIS.
BUT -AND AGAIN, NO OFFENSE-
STAYING WHERE YOU ARE ISN'T *CHANGING* ANYTHING.

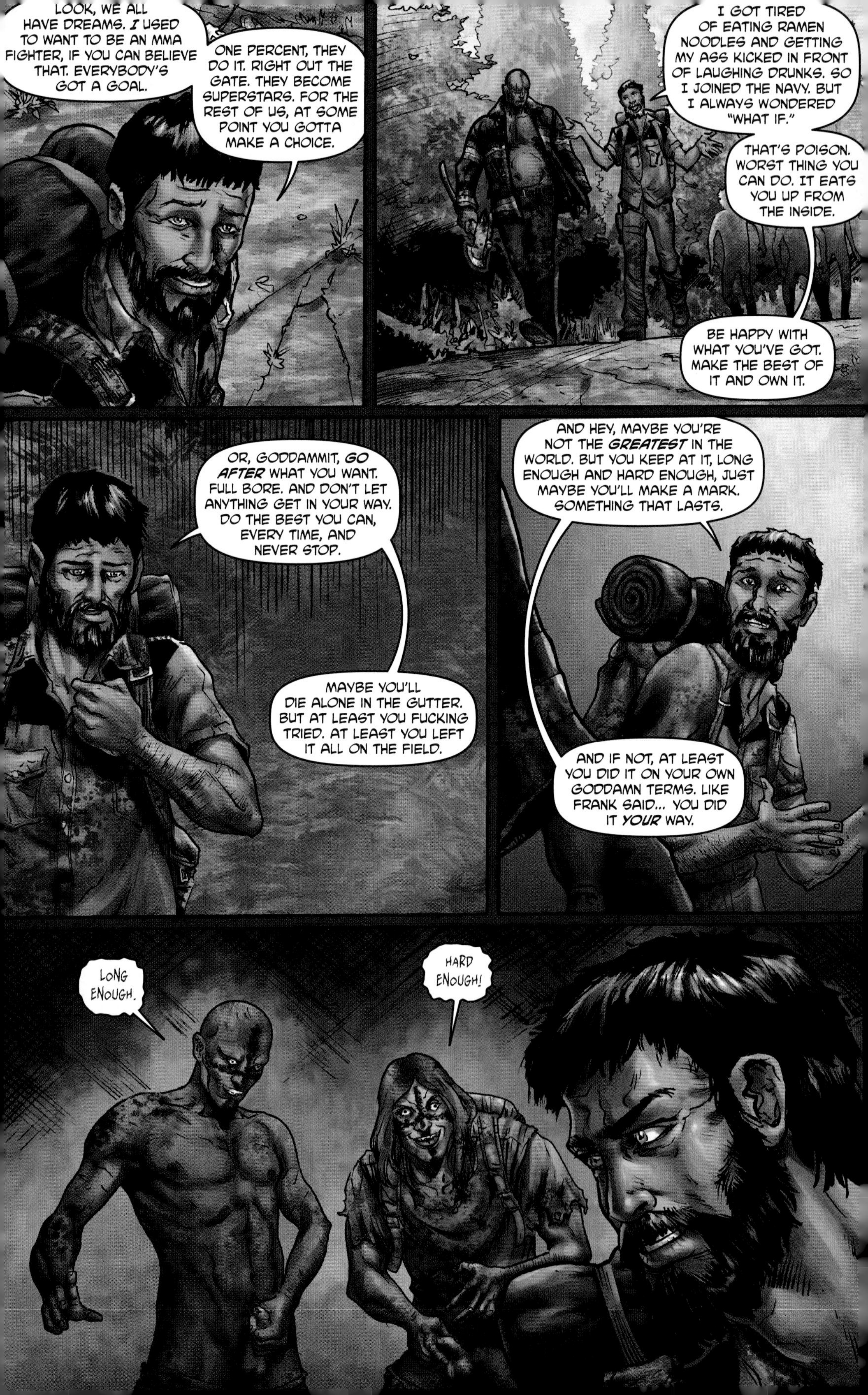
LOOK, WE ALL HAVE DREAMS. *I* USED TO WANT TO BE AN MMA FIGHTER, IF YOU CAN BELIEVE THAT. EVERYBODY'S GOT A GOAL.
ONE PERCENT, THEY DO IT. RIGHT OUT THE GATE. THEY BECOME SUPERSTARS. FOR THE REST OF US, AT SOME POINT YOU GOTTA MAKE A CHOICE.
I GOT TIRED OF EATING RAMEN NOODLES AND GETTING MY ASS KICKED IN FRONT OF LAUGHING DRUNKS. SO I JOINED THE NAVY. BUT I ALWAYS WONDERED "WHAT IF."
THAT'S POISON. WORST THING YOU CAN DO. IT EATS YOU UP FROM THE INSIDE.
BE HAPPY WITH WHAT YOU'VE GOT. MAKE THE BEST OF IT AND OWN IT.
OR, GODDAMMIT, ***GO AFTER*** WHAT YOU WANT. FULL BORE. AND DON'T LET ANYTHING GET IN YOUR WAY. DO THE BEST YOU CAN, EVERY TIME, AND NEVER STOP.
MAYBE YOU'LL DIE ALONE IN THE GUTTER. BUT AT LEAST YOU FUCKING TRIED. AT LEAST YOU LEFT IT ALL ON THE FIELD.
AND HEY, MAYBE YOU'RE NOT THE ***GREATEST*** IN THE WORLD. BUT YOU KEEP AT IT, LONG ENOUGH AND HARD ENOUGH, JUST MAYBE YOU'LL MAKE A MARK. SOMETHING THAT LASTS.
AND IF NOT, AT LEAST YOU DID IT ON YOUR OWN GODDAMN TERMS. LIKE FRANK SAID... YOU DID IT ***YOUR*** WAY.
LONG ENOUGH.
HARD ENOUGH!

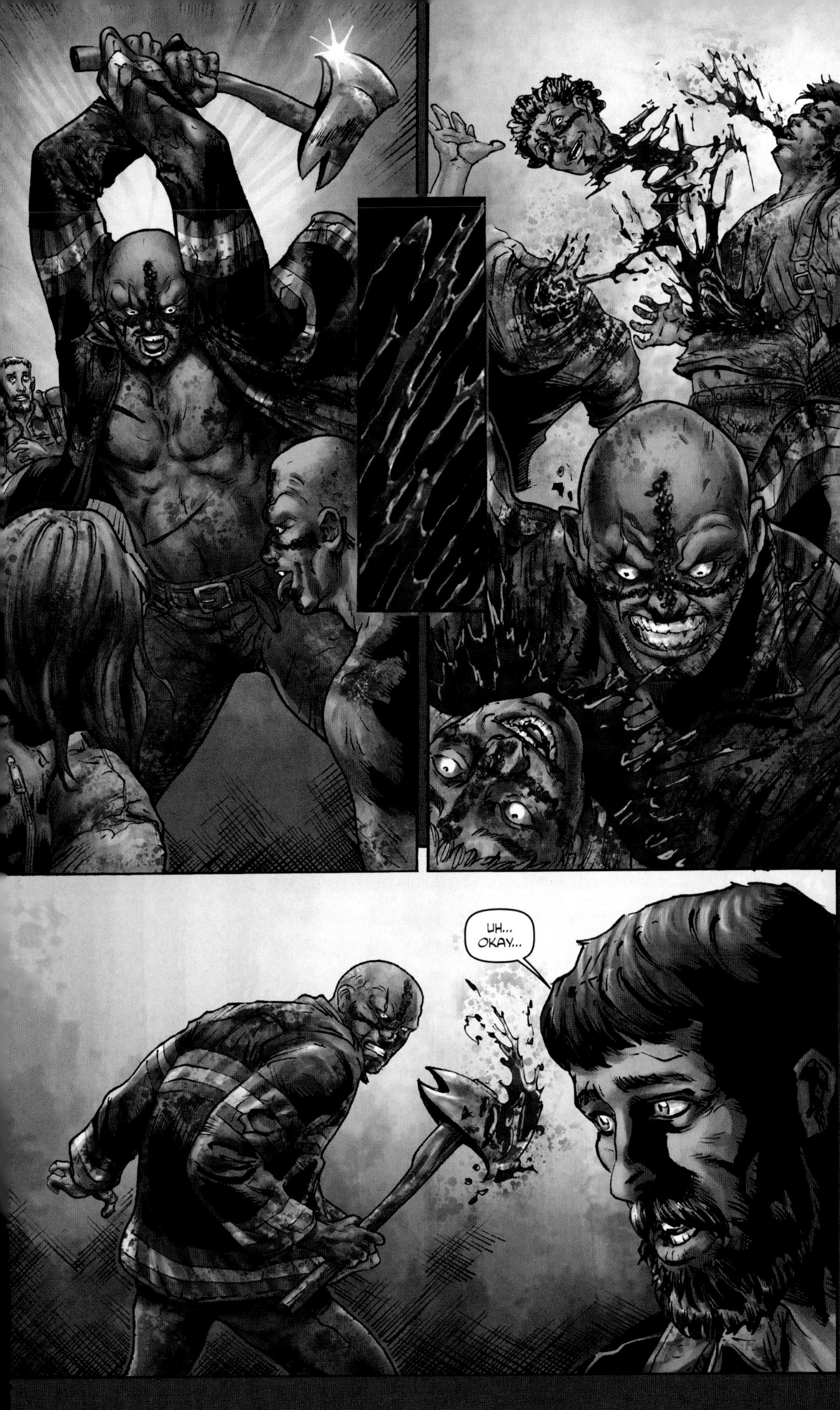
UH... OKAY...

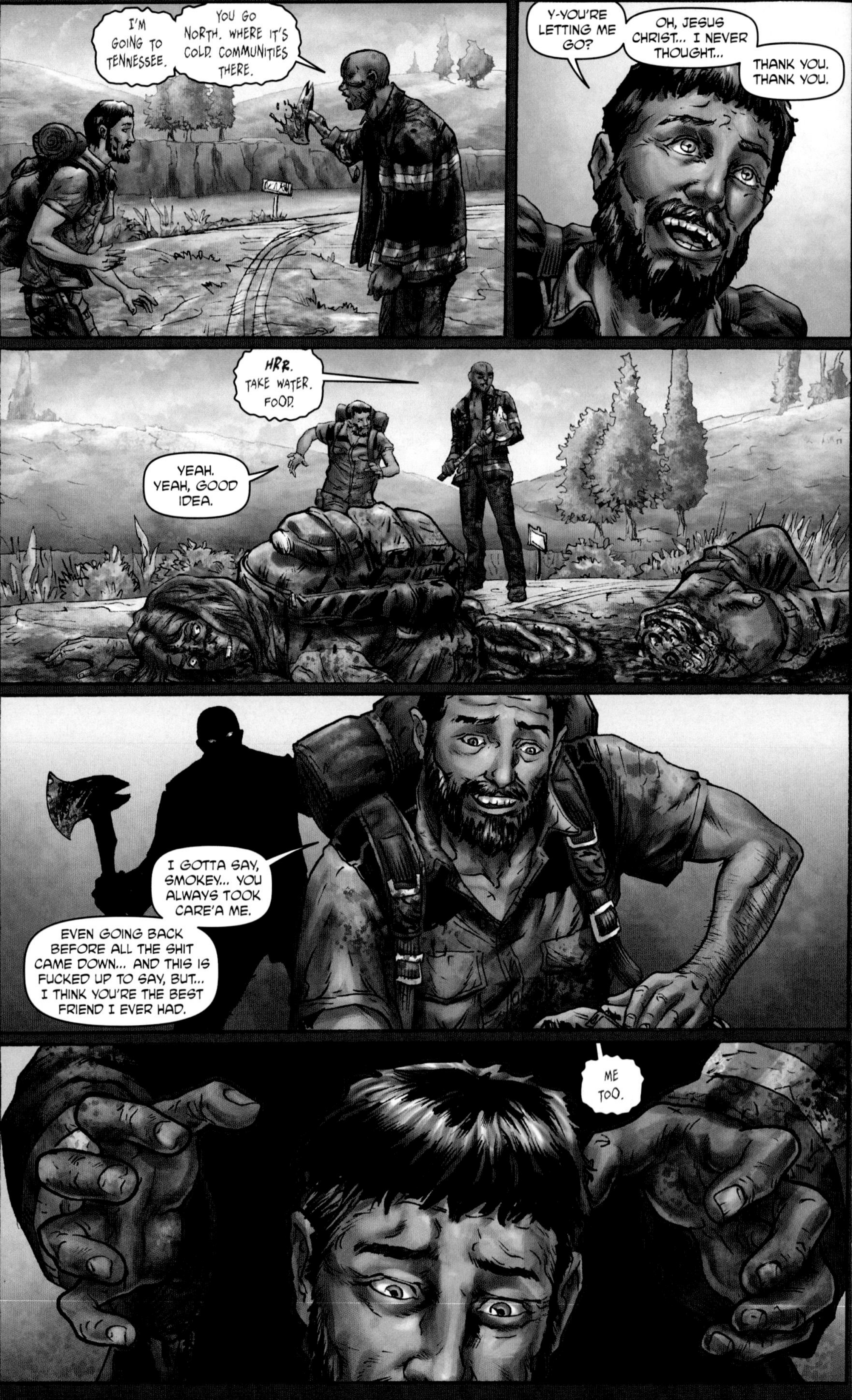
I'M GOING TO TENNESSEE.
YOU GO NORTH. WHERE IT'S COLD. COMMUNITIES THERE.
Y-YOU'RE LETTING ME GO?
OH, JESUS CHRIST... I NEVER THOUGHT...
THANK YOU. THANK YOU.
HRR. TAKE WATER. FOOD.
YEAH. YEAH, GOOD IDEA.
I GOTTA SAY, SMOKEY... YOU ALWAYS TOOK CARE'A ME.
EVEN GOING BACK BEFORE ALL THE SHIT CAME DOWN... AND THIS IS FUCKED UP TO SAY, BUT... I THINK YOU'RE THE BEST FRIEND I EVER HAD.
ME TOO.

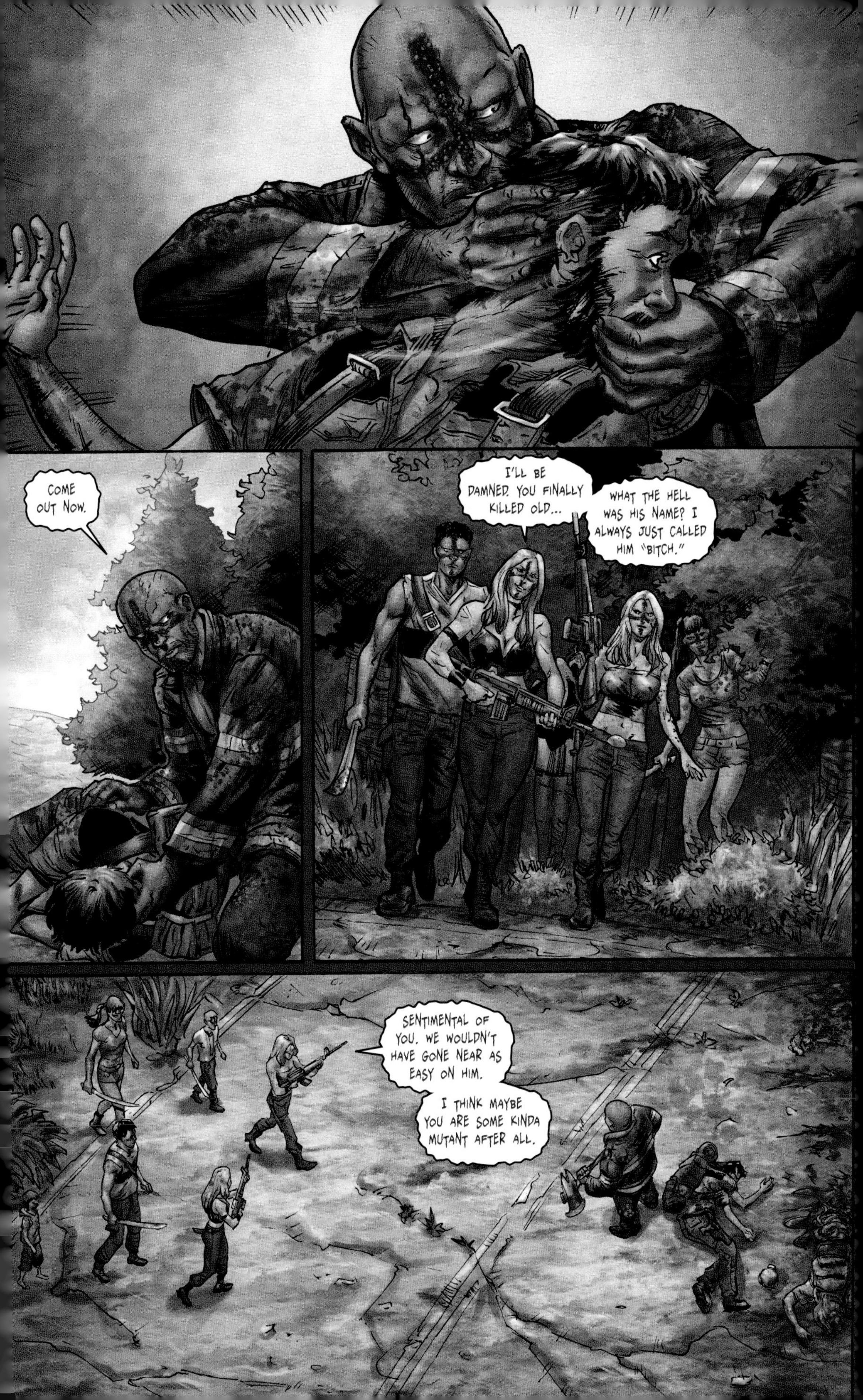
COME OUT NOW.
I'LL BE DAMNED. YOU FINALLY KILLED OLD...
WHAT THE HELL WAS HIS NAME? I ALWAYS JUST CALLED HIM "BITCH."
SENTIMENTAL OF YOU. WE WOULDN'T HAVE GONE NEAR AS EASY ON HIM.
I THINK MAYBE YOU ARE SOME KINDA MUTANT AFTER ALL.

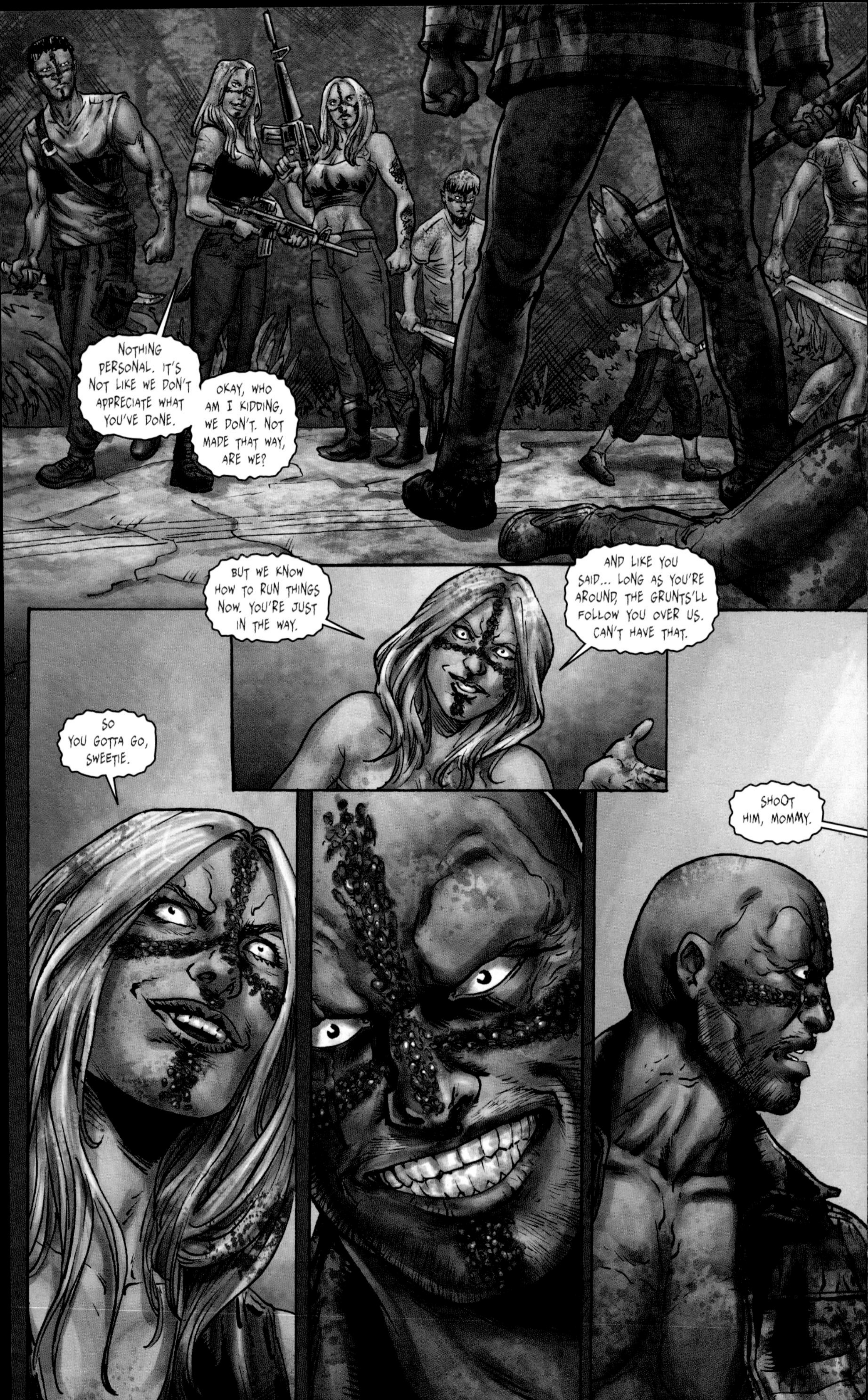
NOTHING PERSONAL. IT'S NOT LIKE WE DON'T APPRECIATE WHAT YOU'VE DONE.
OKAY, WHO AM I KIDDING, WE DON'T. NOT MADE THAT WAY, ARE WE?
BUT WE KNOW HOW TO RUN THINGS NOW. YOU'RE JUST IN THE WAY.
AND LIKE YOU SAID... LONG AS YOU'RE AROUND, THE GRUNTS'LL FOLLOW YOU OVER US. CAN'T HAVE THAT.
SO YOU GOTTA GO, SWEETIE.
SHOOT HIM, MOMMY.

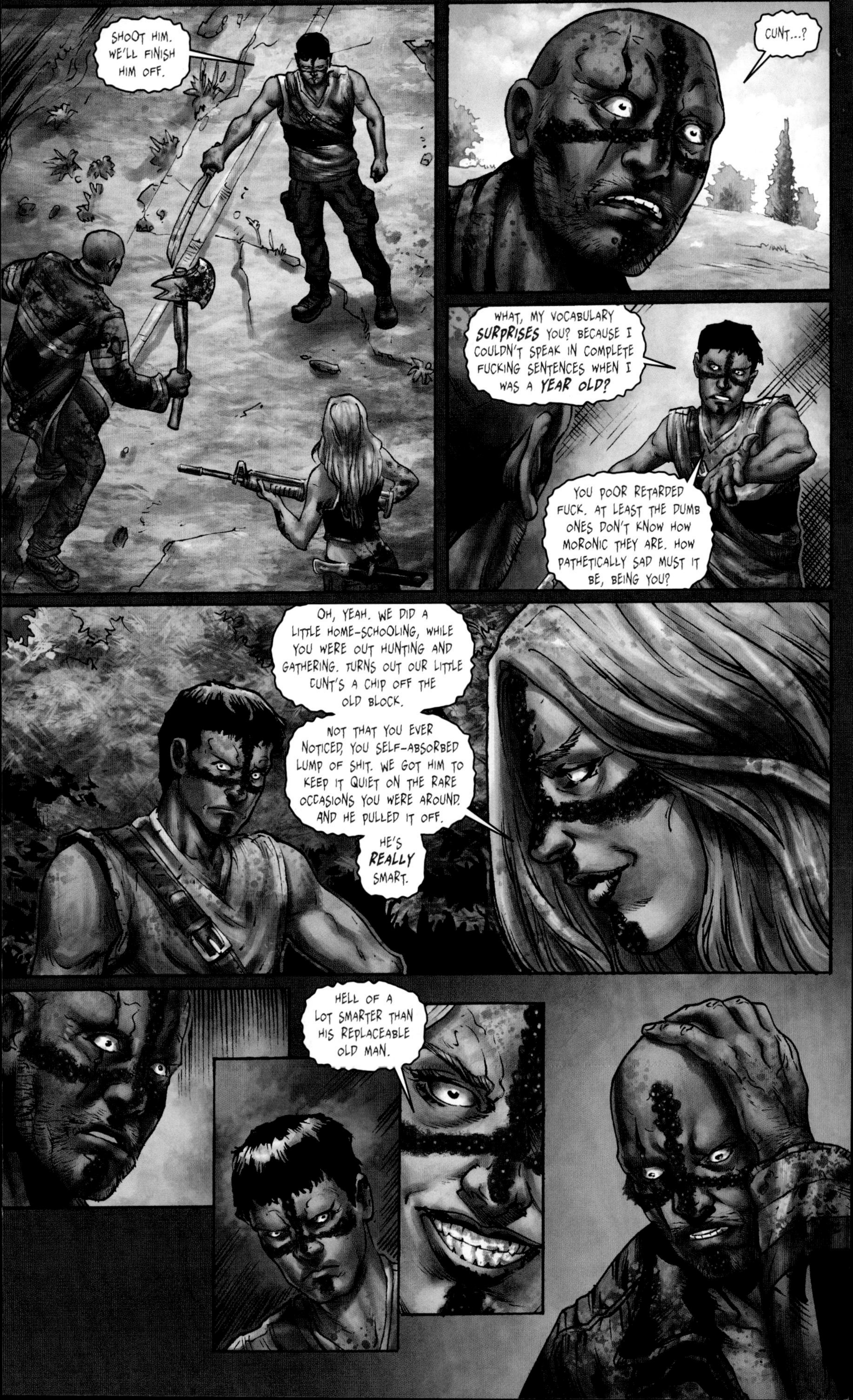
SHOOT HIM. WE'LL FINISH HIM OFF.
CUNT...?
WHAT, MY VOCABULARY SURPRISES YOU? BECAUSE I COULDN'T SPEAK IN COMPLETE FUCKING SENTENCES WHEN I WAS A YEAR OLD?
YOU POOR RETARDED FUCK. AT LEAST THE DUMB ONES DON'T KNOW HOW MORONIC THEY ARE. HOW PATHETICALLY SAD MUST IT BE, BEING YOU?
OH, YEAH. WE DID A LITTLE HOME-SCHOOLING, WHILE YOU WERE OUT HUNTING AND GATHERING. TURNS OUT OUR LITTLE CUNT'S A CHIP OFF THE OLD BLOCK.
NOT THAT YOU EVER NOTICED, YOU SELF-ABSORBED LUMP OF SHIT. WE GOT HIM TO KEEP IT QUIET ON THE RARE OCCASIONS YOU WERE AROUND. AND HE PULLED IT OFF.
HE'S REALLY SMART.
HELL OF A LOT SMARTER THAN HIS REPLACEABLE OLD MAN.

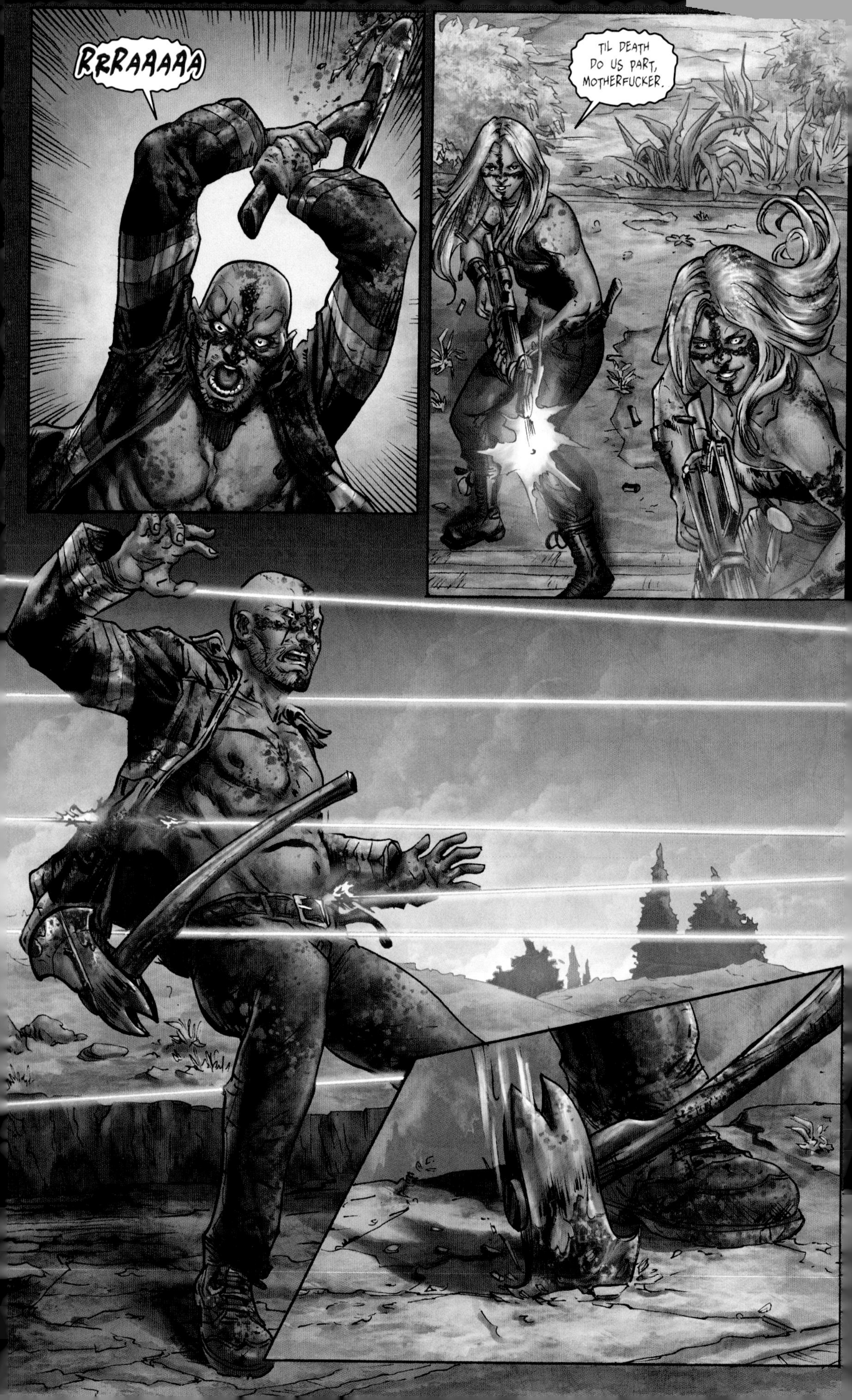
RRRAAAAA
TIL DEATH DO US PART, MOTHERFUCKER.

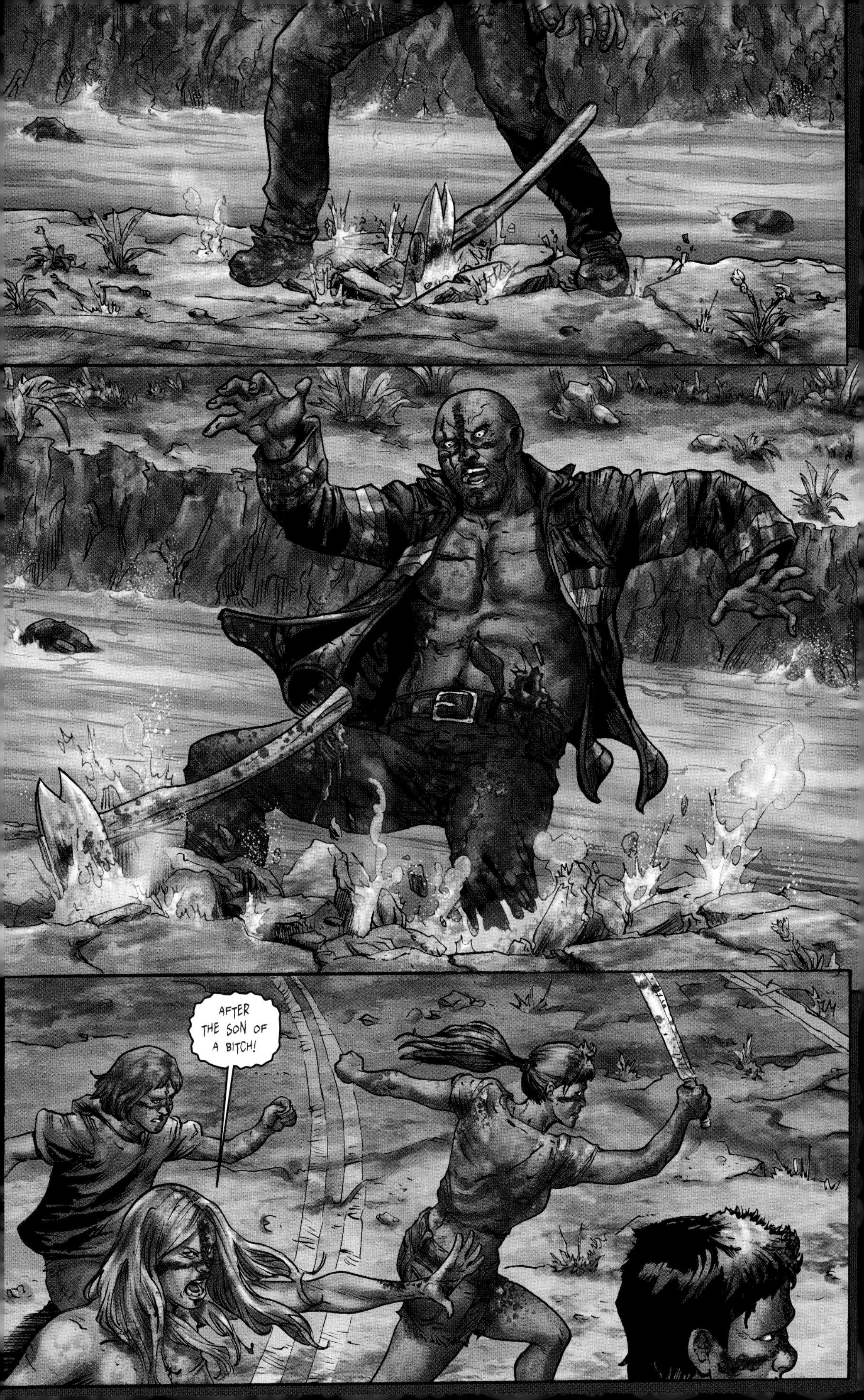
AFTER THE SON OF A BITCH!

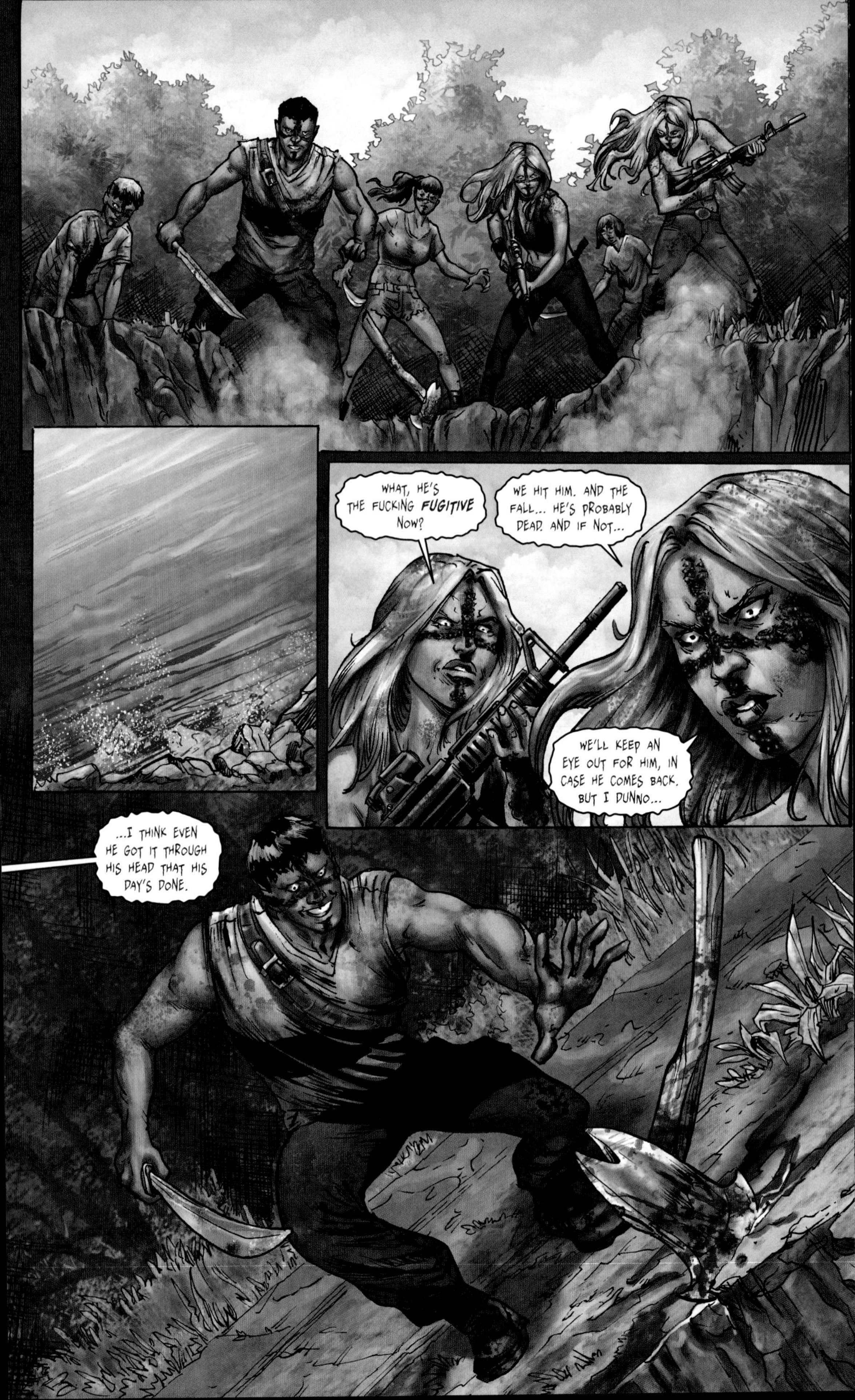
WHAT, HE'S THE FUCKING *FUGITIVE* NOW?
WE HIT HIM. AND THE FALL... HE'S PROBABLY DEAD. AND IF NOT...
WE'LL KEEP AN EYE OUT FOR HIM, IN CASE HE COMES BACK. BUT I DUNNO...
...I THINK EVEN HE GOT IT THROUGH HIS HEAD THAT HIS DAY'S DONE.

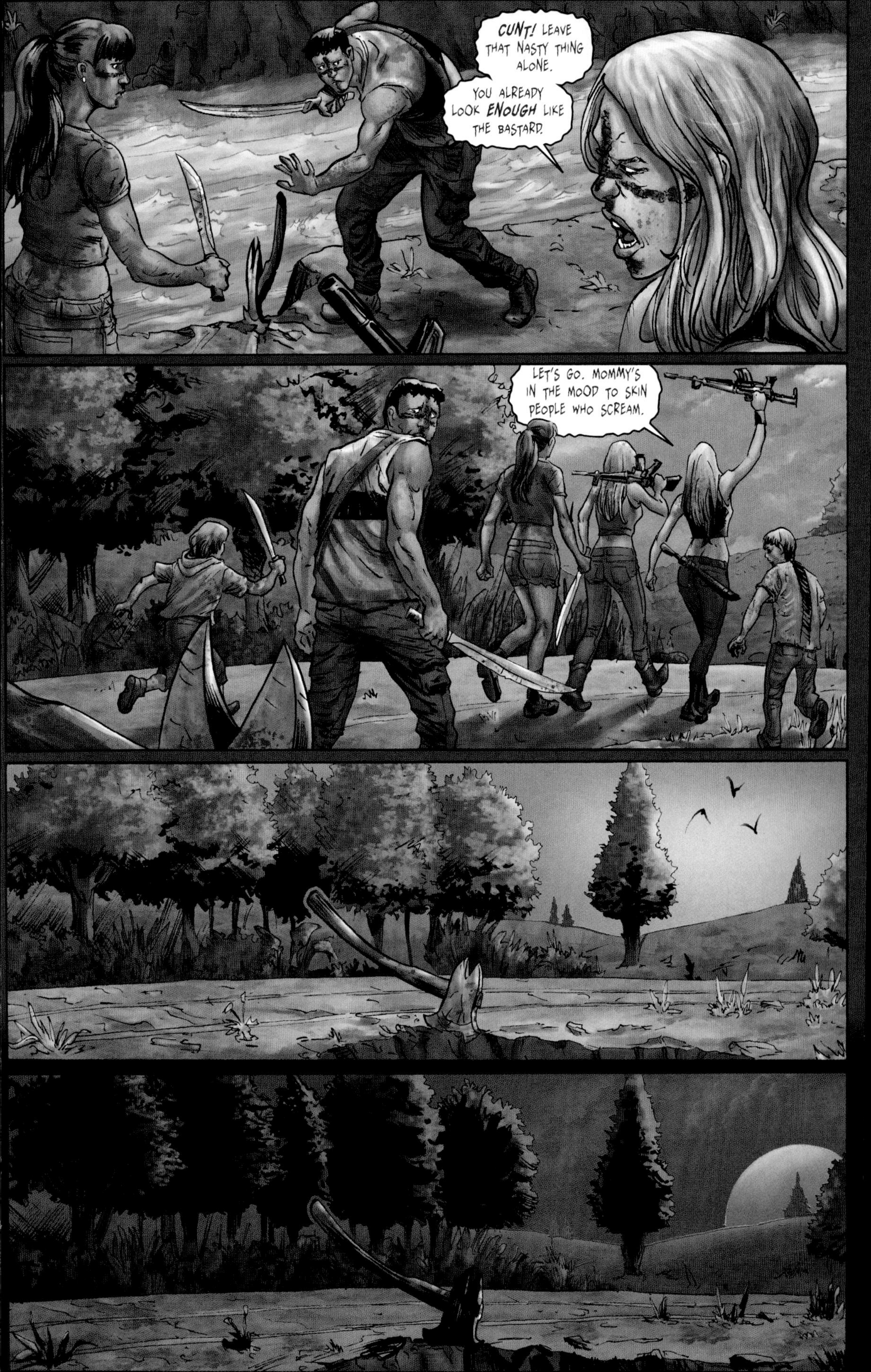
CUNT! LEAVE THAT NASTY THING ALONE.
YOU ALREADY LOOK ENOUGH LIKE THE BASTARD.
LET'S GO. MOMMY'S IN THE MOOD TO SKIN PEOPLE WHO SCREAM.

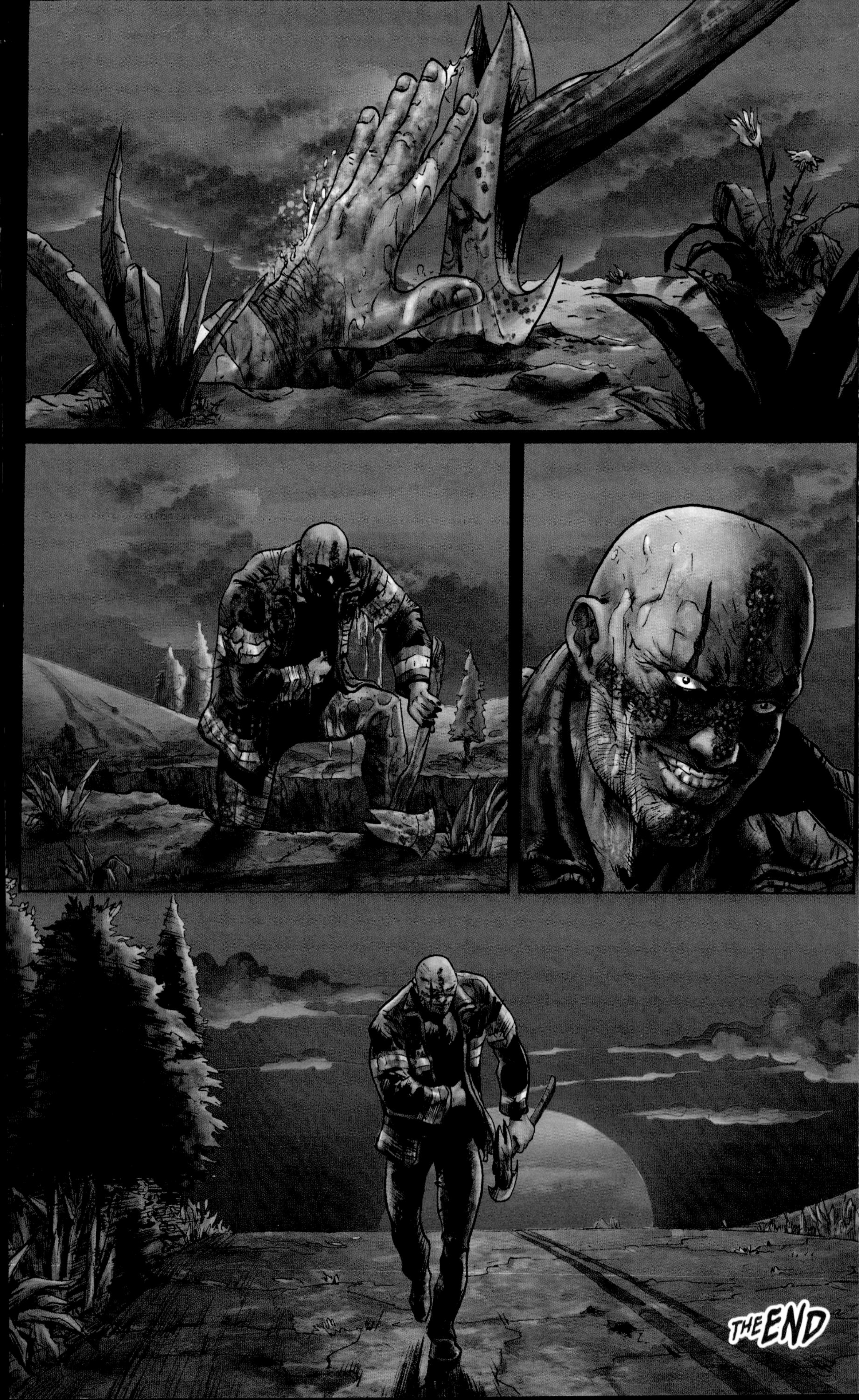
THE END

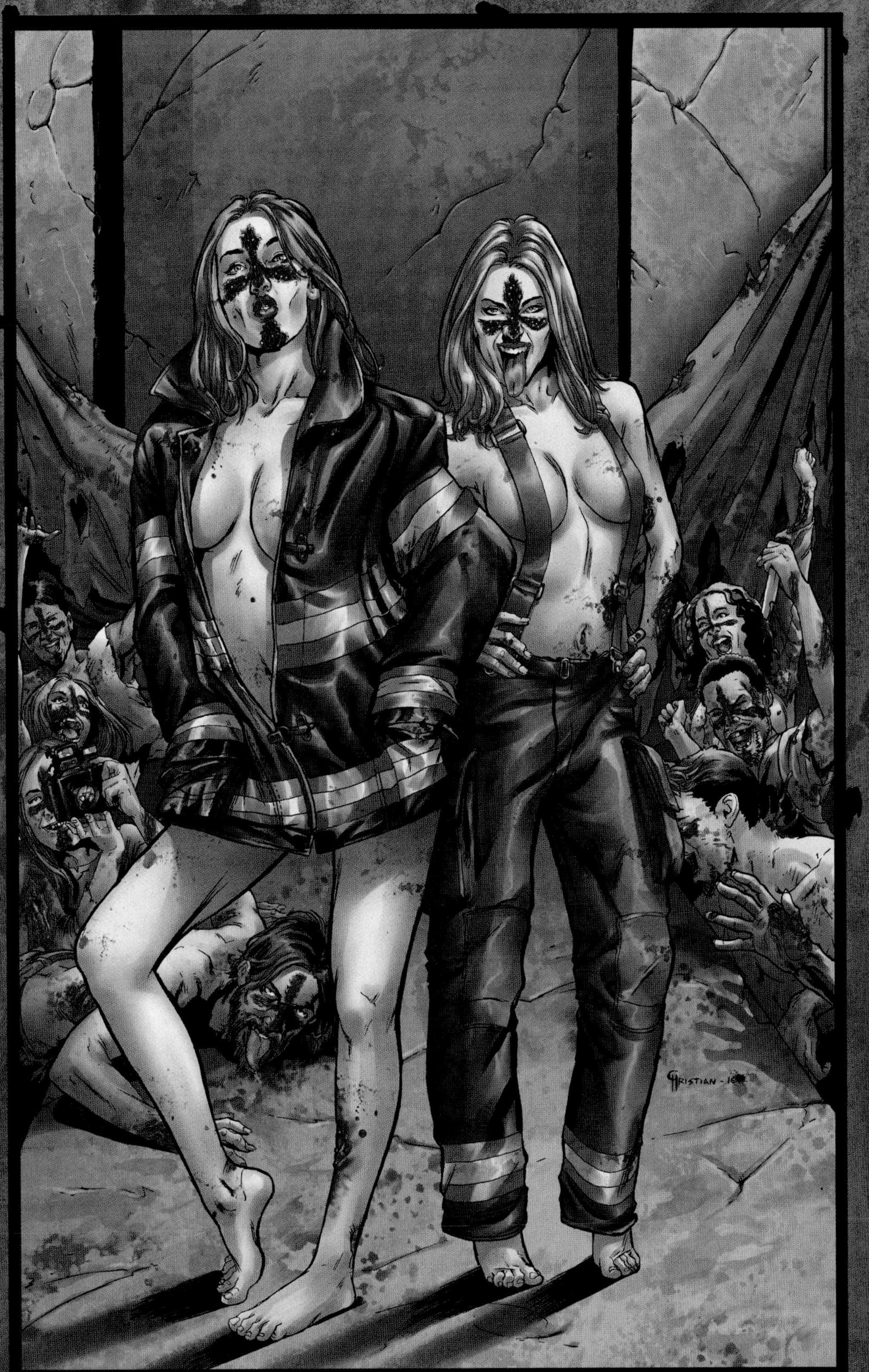

GALLERY

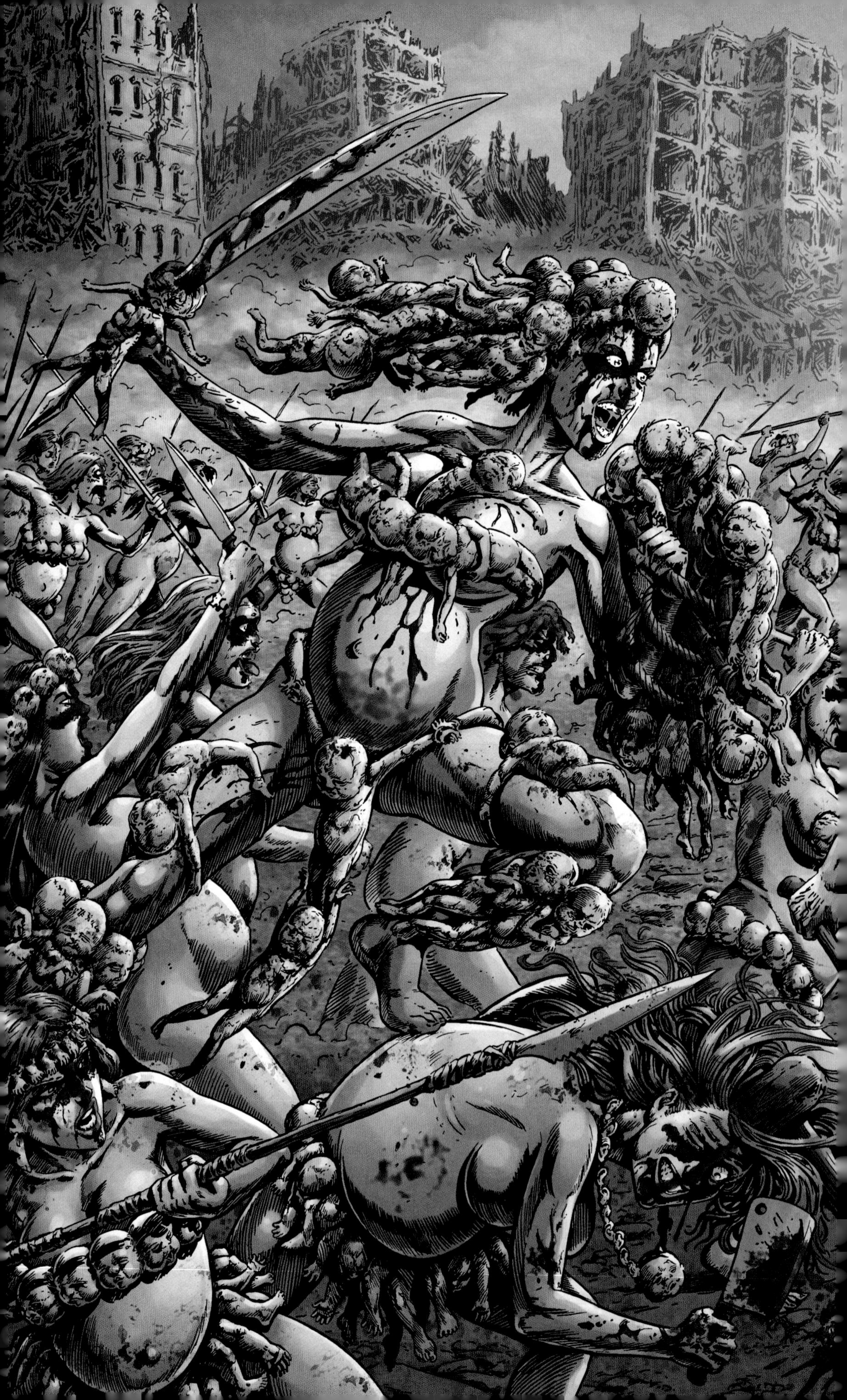

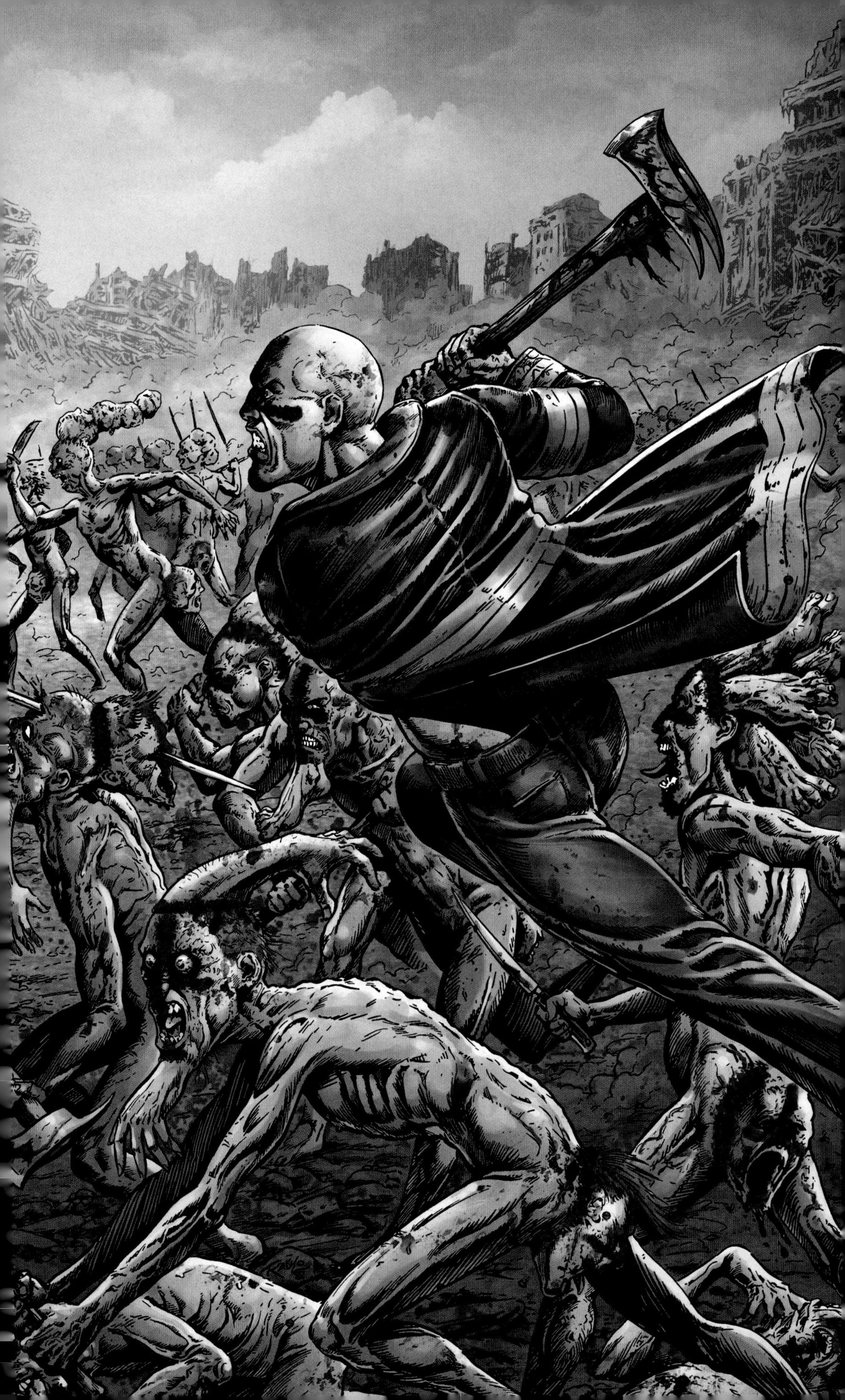

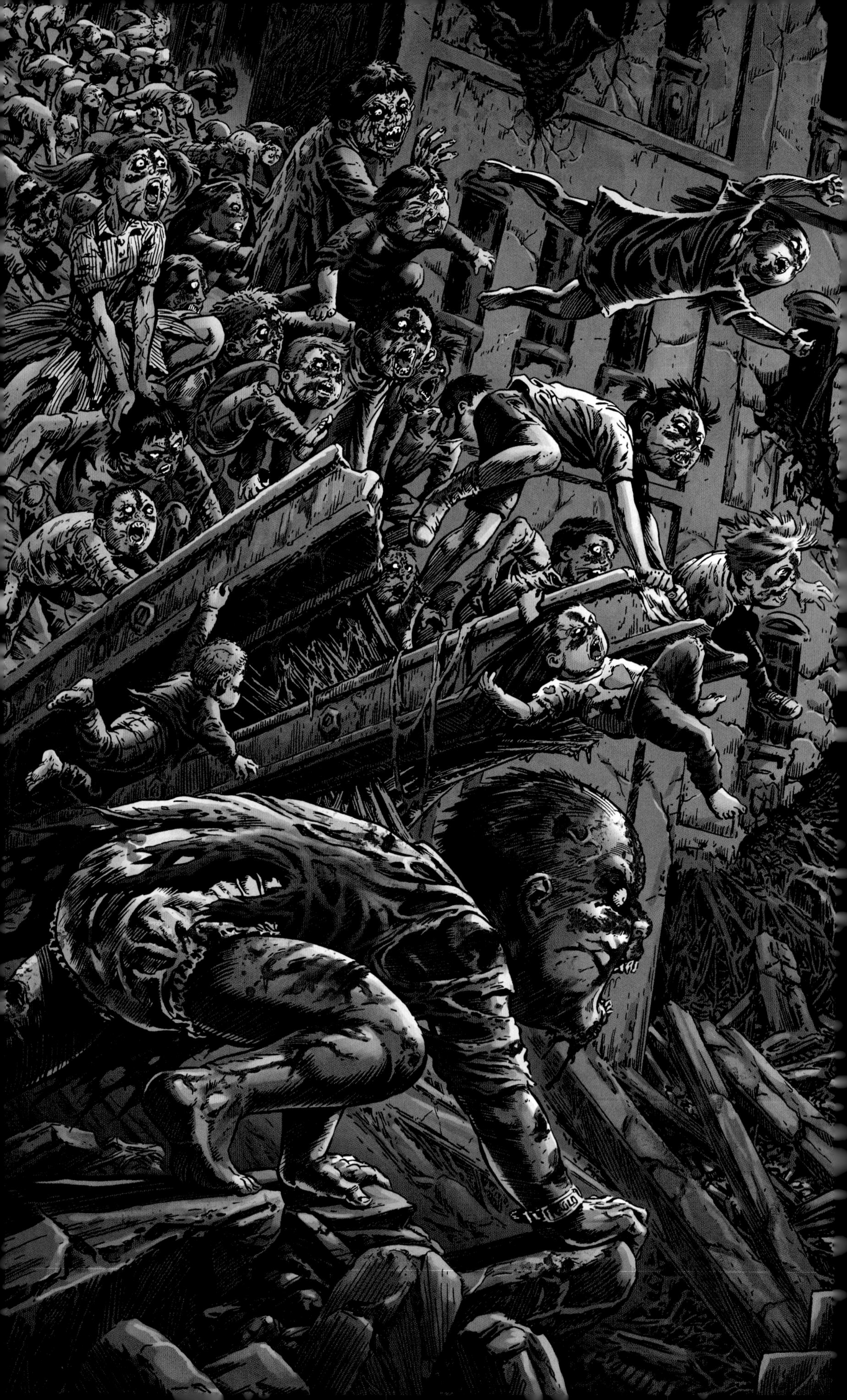

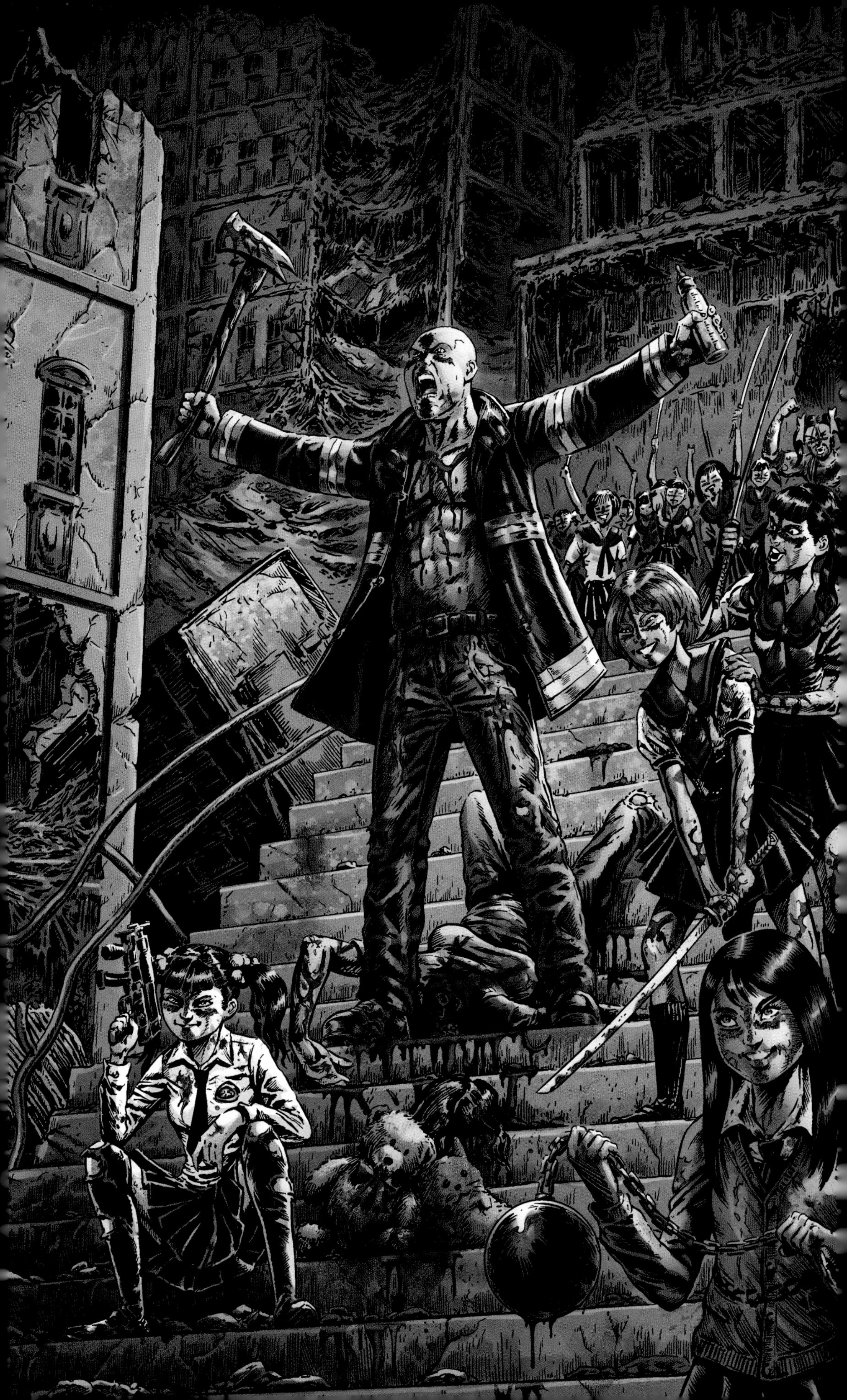

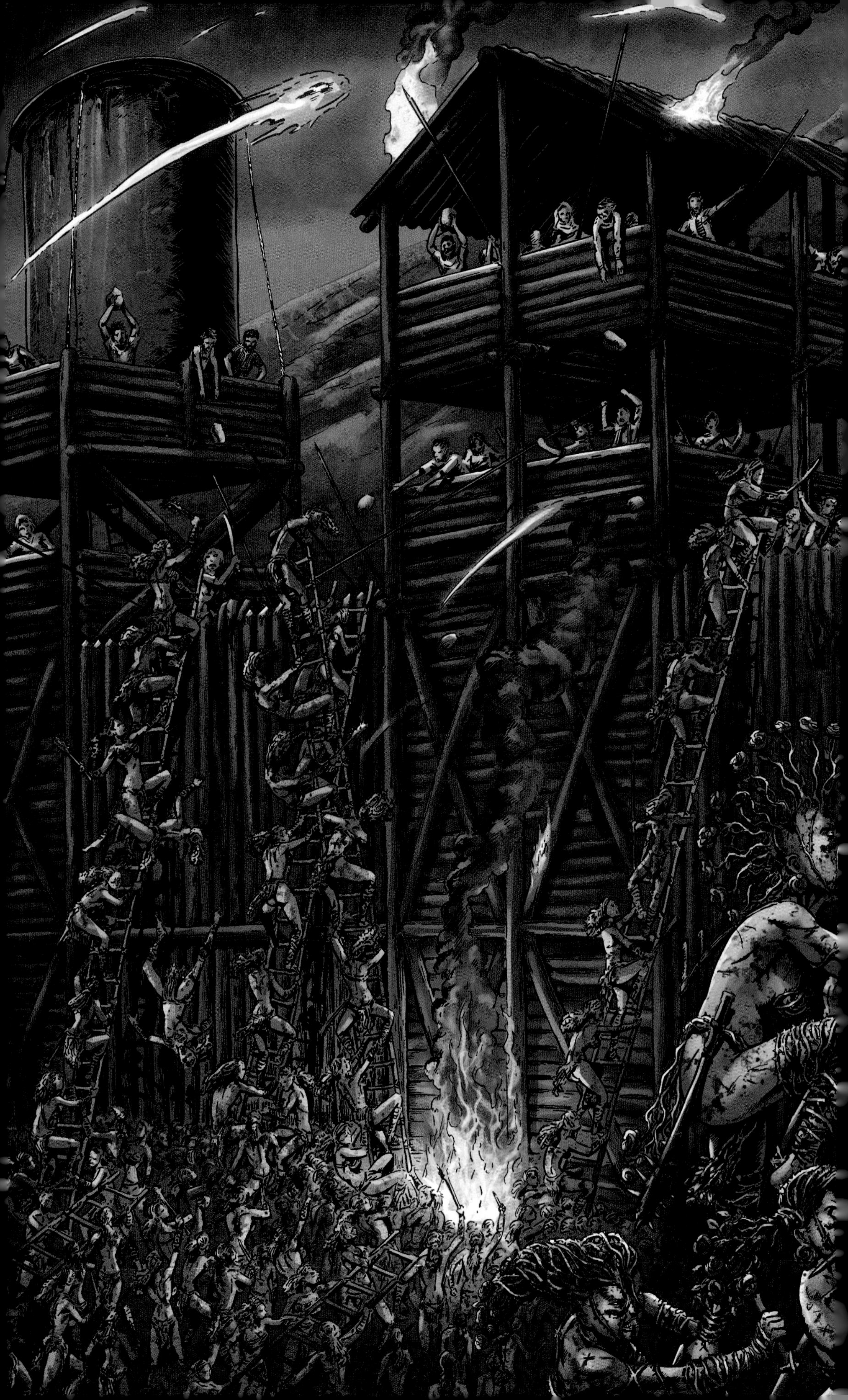

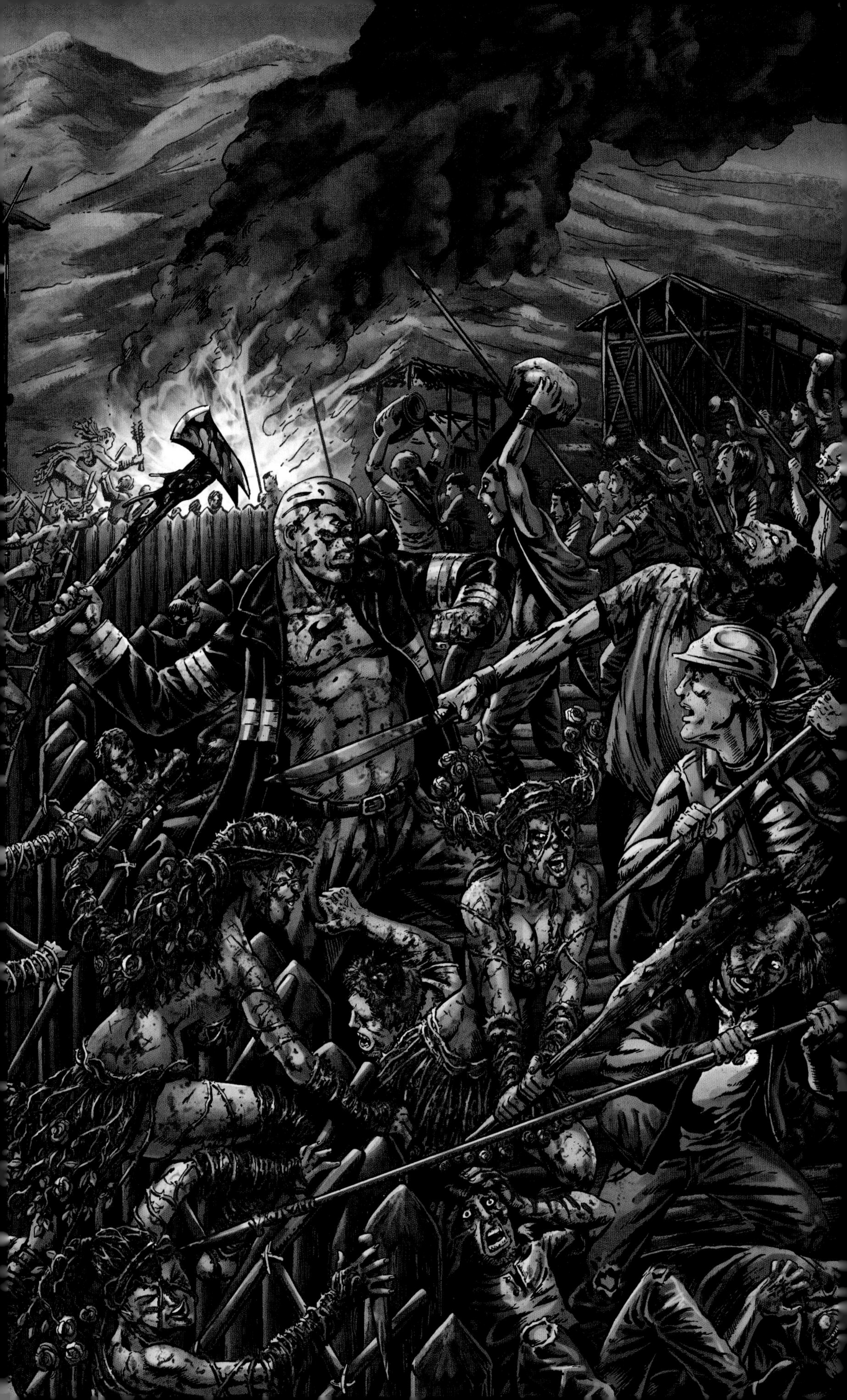

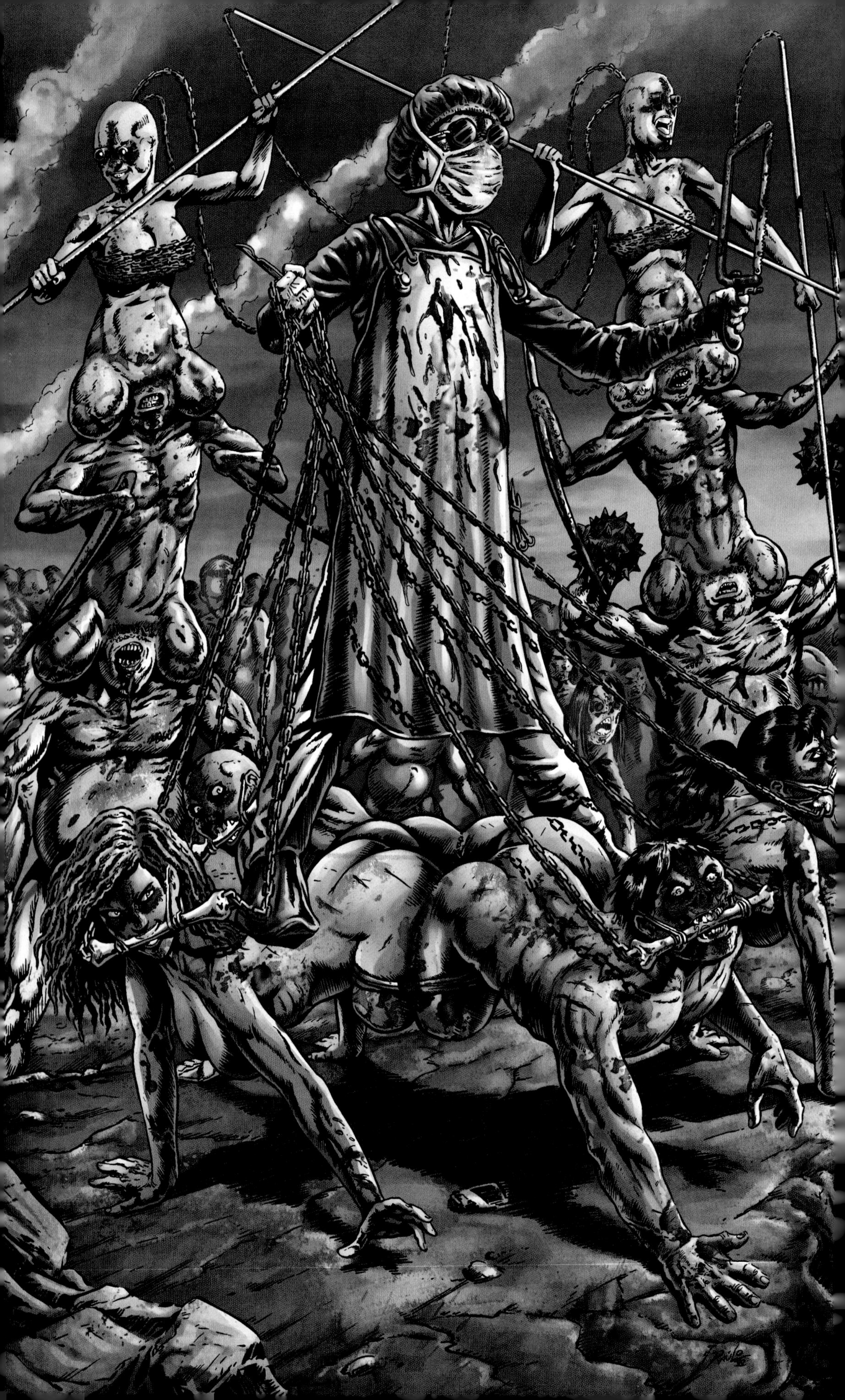

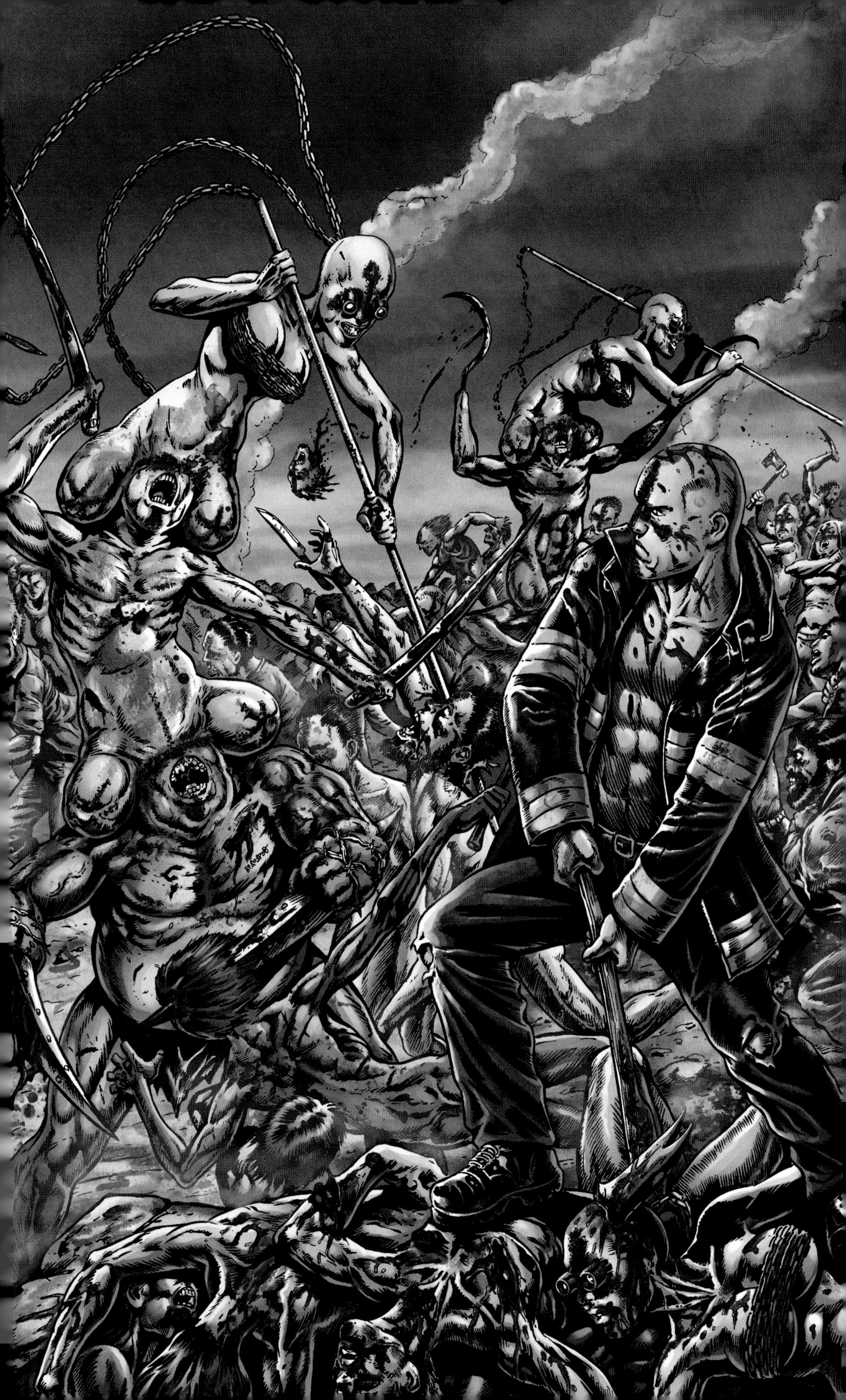

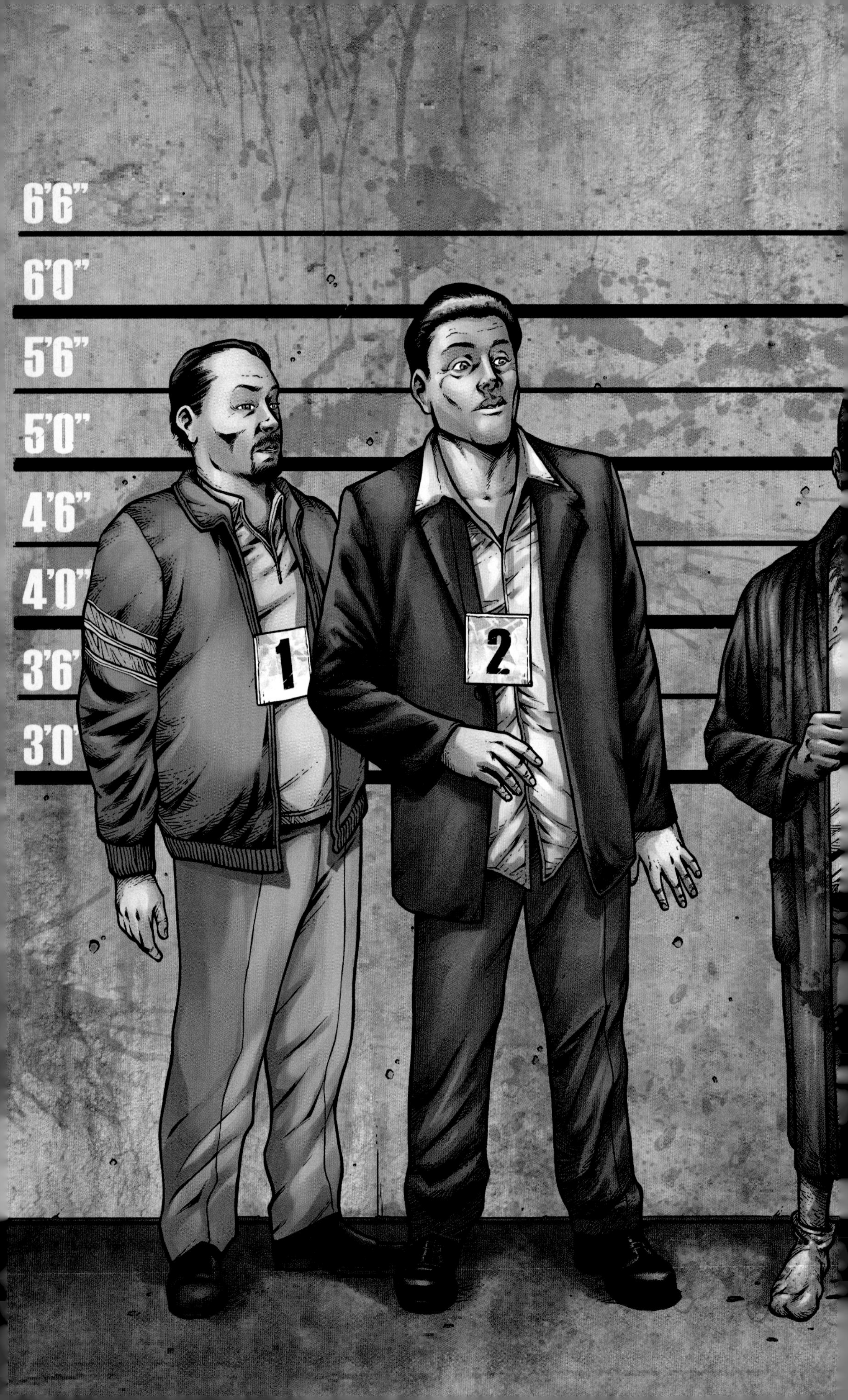
6'6"
6'0"
5'6"
5'0"
4'6"
4'0"
3'6"
3'0"
1
2

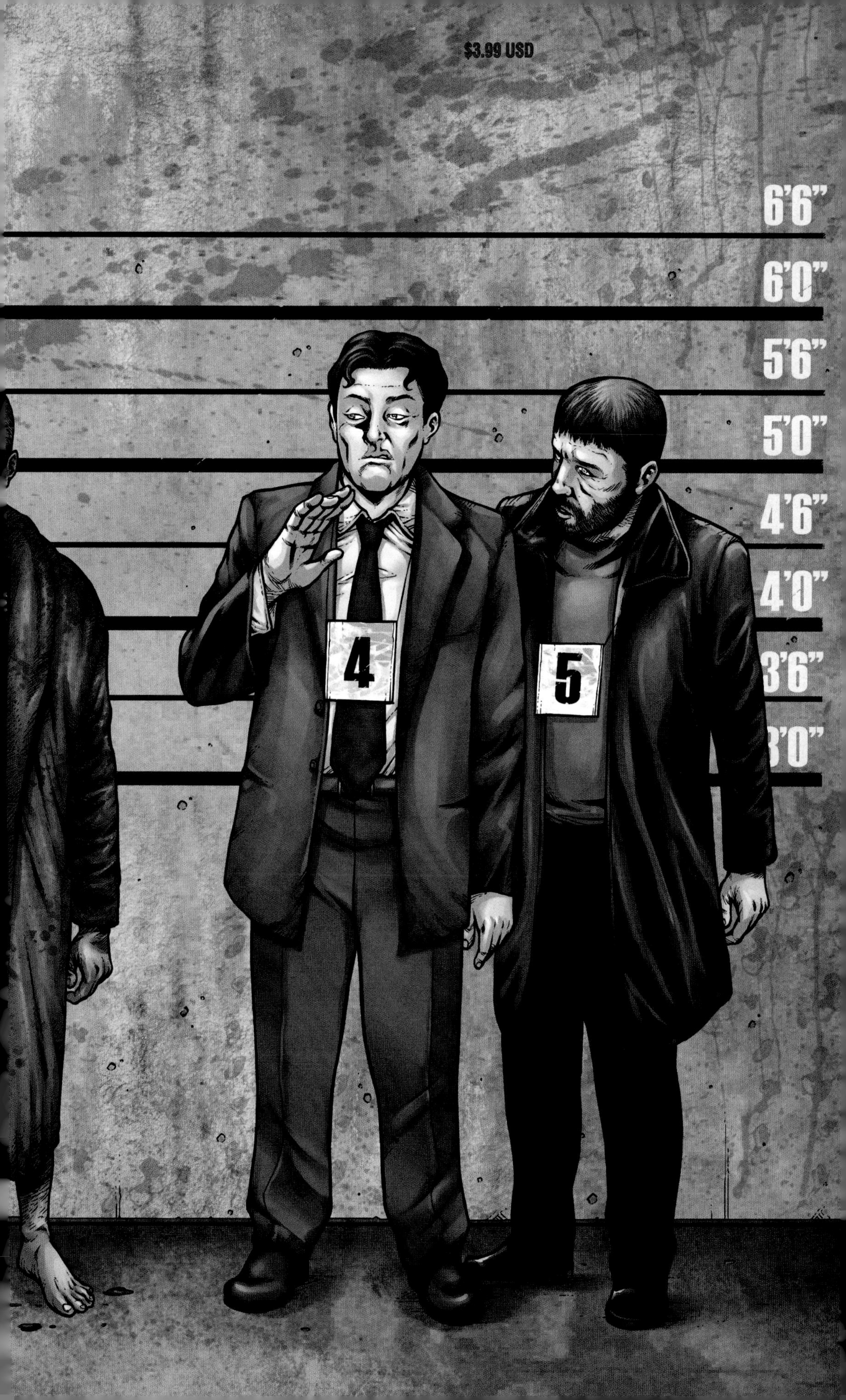
$3.99 USD
6'6"
6'0"
5'6"
5'0"
4'6"
4'0"
3'6"
3'0"
4
5

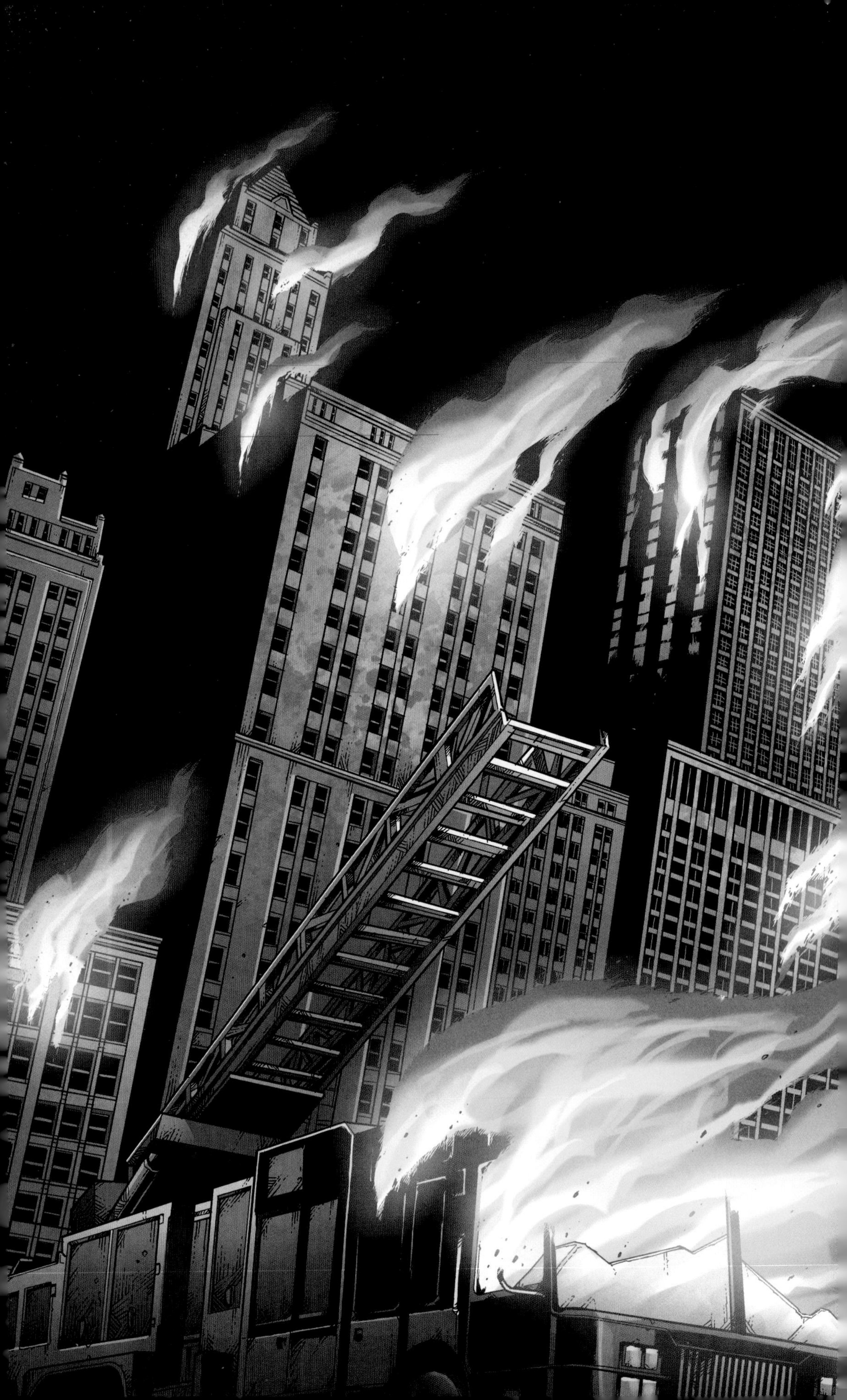

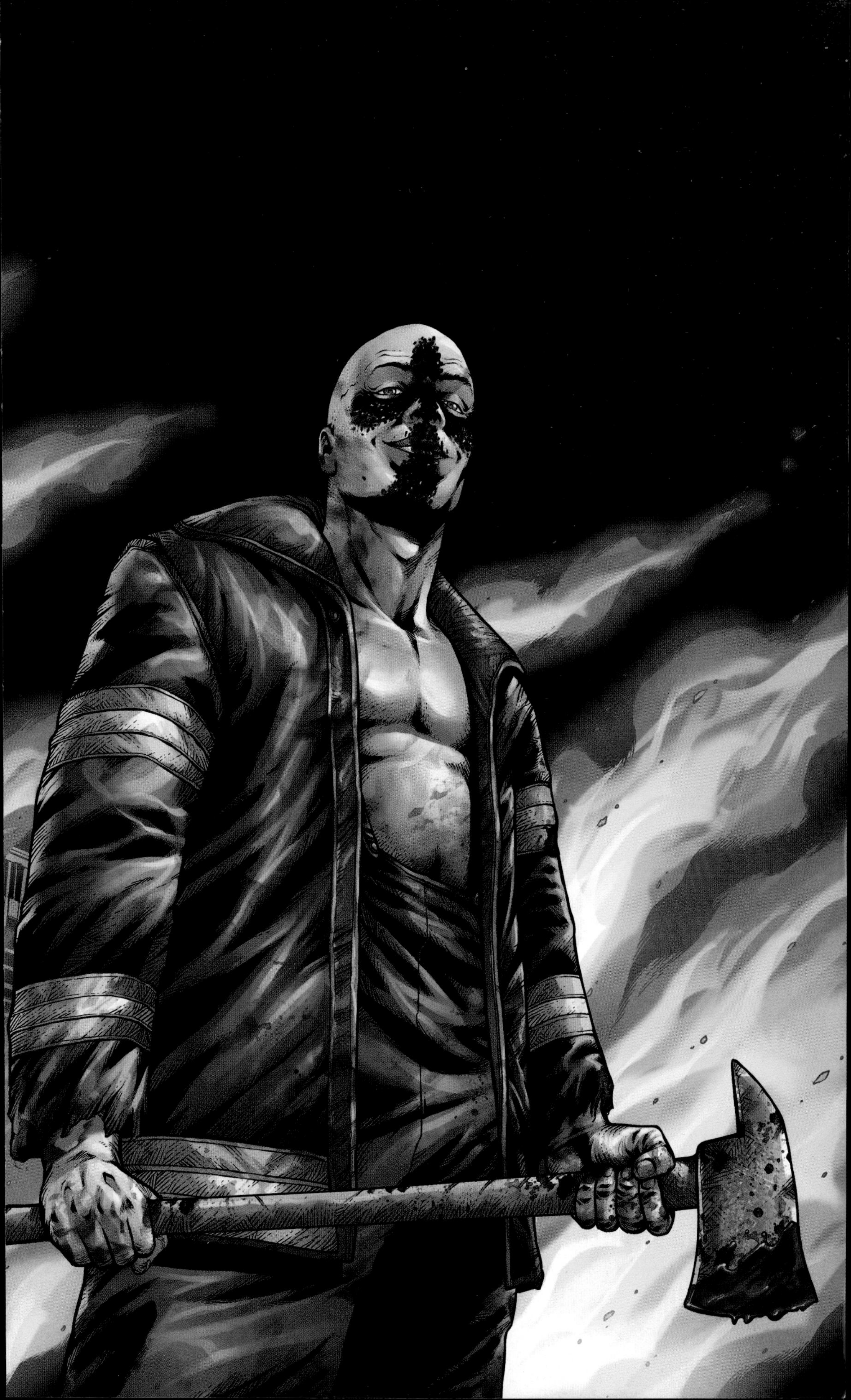

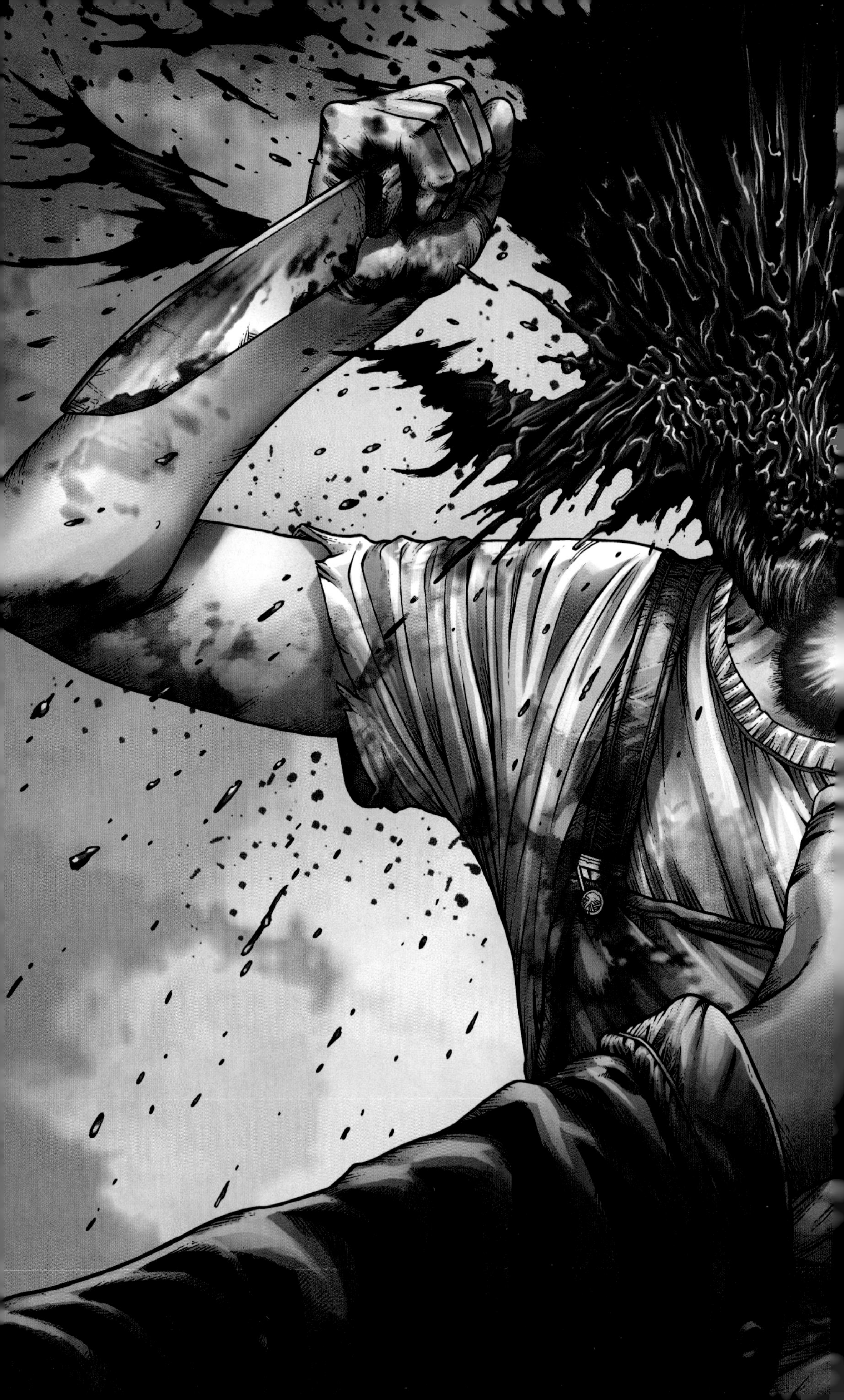

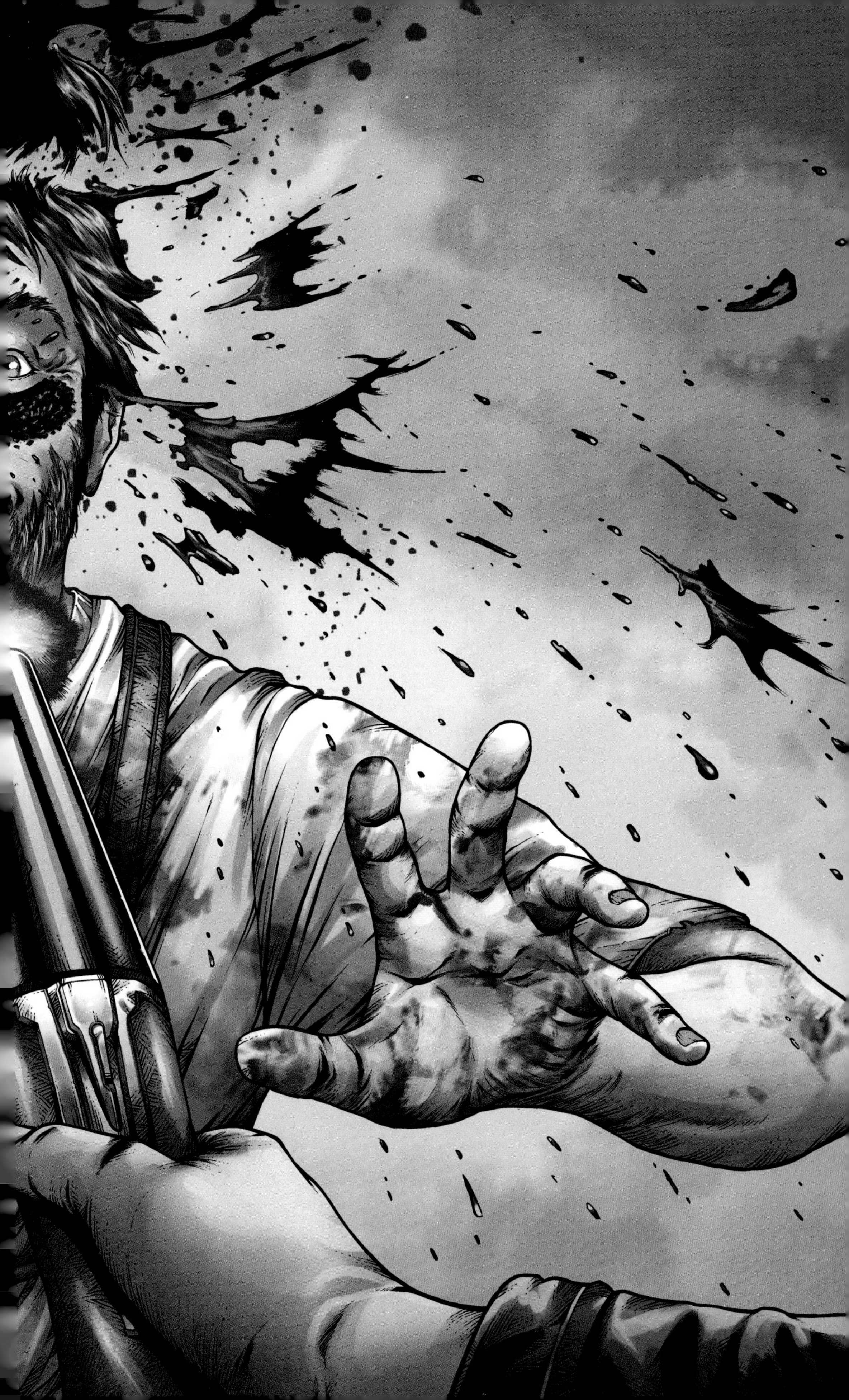

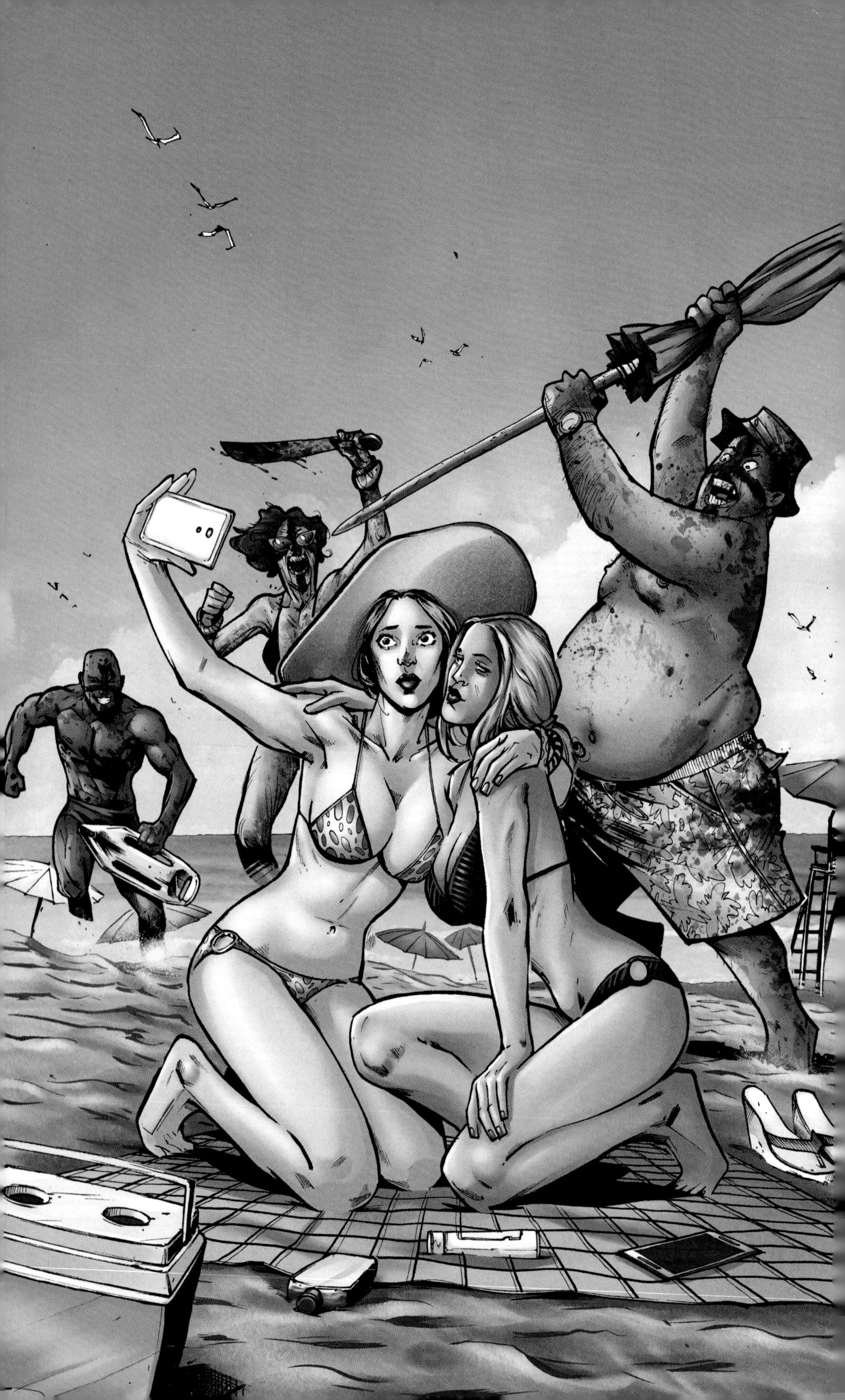